*mela*

## multi-ethnic literatures of the americas

AMRITJIT SINGH, CARLA L. PETERSON, C. LOK CHUA, SERIES EDITORS

*The MELA series aims to expand and deepen our sense of American literatures as multi-cultural and multi-lingual and works to establish a broader understanding of "America" as a complex site for the creation of national, transnational, and global narratives. Volumes in the series focus on the recovery, consolidation, and reevaluation of literary expression in the United States, Canada, and the Caribbean as shaped by the experience of race, ethnicity, national origin, region, class, gender, and language.*

# Zora Neale Hurston

# Zora Neale Hurston
## COLLECTED PLAYS

EDITED AND WITH AN INTRODUCTION BY
*Jean Lee Cole and Charles Mitchell*

RUTGERS UNIVERSITY PRESS
NEW BRUNSWICK, NEW JERSEY AND LONDON

Library of Congress Cataloging-in-Publication Data

Hurston, Zora Neale.
    Zora Neale Hurston : collected plays / edited and with an
introduction by Jean Lee Cole and Charles Mitchell.
        p. cm. — (Multi-ethnic literatures of the Americas)
    Includes bibliographical references
    ISBN 978-0-8135-4291-1 (hardcover : alk. paper) — ISBN 978-0-8135-4292-8 (pbk. : alk. paper)
    I. Cole, Jean Lee.    II. Mitchell, Charles, 1967–    III. Title.
    PS3515.U789 2008
    812'.52—dc22

                                                                                    2007033566

A British Cataloging-in-Publication record for this book is available from the British Library.

Text design by Adam B. Bohannon
Visit our Web site: http://rutgerspress.rutgers.edu
Manufactured in the United States of America

**Frontispiece: Zora Neale Hurston at a recording site in Belle Glade, Florida, 1935. Courtesy of the Library of Congress.**

# CONTENTS

# ACKNOWLEDGMENTS

Our original intentions for this project were very modest: we simply wanted to provide usable scripts for several short plays, whose typescripts were available online at the Library of Congress, for a dramatic reading performed in March 2005 at Loyola College in Baltimore, Maryland. This reading, which included the plays *Lawing and Jawing, Heaven, The House That Jack Built,* and *Railroad Camp,* was to be a feature event of the College's annual Humanities Symposium, which for that year took as its focal text Hurston's *Their Eyes Were Watching God.*

As we worked on these plays, the scope of the project grew—and grew. We enlisted the help of Shirley Basfield Dunlap, a mile down the road at Morgan State University's Theater Department; she agreed to direct the performance and provide actors from her program. When we realized how integral music was to the plays, we called on Benny Russell from the Maryland Conservatory of Music, who provided an original score. Andy Ciofalo of Loyola's Communication Department got wind of what we were doing and urged us to edit *all* of the plays available at the Library of Congress, which his department's book production course, in turn, produced as the volume *From Luababa to Polk County: Zora Neale Hurston Plays at the Library of Congress* (Apprentice House Press, 2005)—with the first copies arriving on the Loyola campus just in time for the performance. The performance itself was a rousing success, providing proof positive that Hurston's work could shine on the stage.

Having edited the majority of Hurston's theatrical works by this time, we decided to finish the job, and over the course of the next several years, located the remaining plays, discovered several believed lost, and fully annotated all of the texts. We thus have many people to thank. First, we would like to express our appreciation to our colleagues at Loyola College: Andy Ciofalo, for his steadfast belief that we *could* and *would* compile a complete edition of Hurston's plays; Kevin Atticks, the instructor of the book production class that produced *From Luababa to Polk County,* for many long (and late) hours; and Mark Osteen of the English Department, for his literary and musical prowess. We would also like to thank the College's Center for the Humanities for providing the initial funding for the March 2005 dramatic reading that got the whole snowball rolling, and the Center's administrative assistant, Patty Ingram, for her organizational finesse.

The texts themselves would not have surfaced without the efforts of Dr. Alice L. Birney of the Library of Congress, who first brought them into the public eye. Wyatt Houston Day deserves credit for his discovery of *Spears,* and gratitude for leading us to Glenn Horowitz, who helped locate a copy of the play owned by a private collector. The Western Reserve Historical Society Library and Archives provided valuable assistance in locating *The Sermon in the Valley,* as did the University of Florida Smathers Library, which located the text of *The Fiery Chariot.* At Rutgers University Press, we would like to extend our sincere appreciation for the tireless efforts of editor-in-chief Leslie Mitchner and MELA series editors Amritjit Singh, C. Lok Chua, and Carla Peterson. This edition would be much the poorer without their insightful suggestions and contributions.

And our most special thanks, of course, go to the Hurston estate, for allowing these plays to find an audience.

Jean Lee Cole
Charles Mitchell

# CHRONOLOGY

1891    Born January 7 in Notasulga, Alabama, to Lucy Potts and John Hurston, a Baptist preacher and carpenter.

1892    The family moves to Eatonville, Florida, a small black township. John Hurston takes the position of pastor of the Zion Hope Baptist Church and Macedonia Baptist Church.

1897    John Hurston elected mayor of Eatonville.

1904    After the death of her mother, Hurston sent to live with her brother in Jacksonville. For the next dozen years, lives with various family members.

1916    Joins a Northern Gilbert and Sullivan troupe as an actress's maid.

1917    Attends night school in Baltimore, eventually entering Morgan Academy.

1918    John Hurston killed in a car accident. Zora moves to Washington, D.C., to attend Howard University preparatory school.

1920    Joins the Howard Players, a dramatic club. Receives an associate degree from Howard. Joins the Zeta Beta sorority and begins to write poetry. Eugene O'Neill's *The Emperor Jones* is a hit on Broadway.

1921    Publishes first short story, "John Redding Goes to Sea," in *The Stylus,* a literary magazine at Howard University. The all-black show *Shuffle Along* causes a sensation in New York and introduces future stars Florence Mills, Paul Robeson, and Josephine Baker.

1925    Moves to Harlem. In May, wins three awards in a literary contest sponsored by *Opportunity* magazine for her short story "Spunk" and her plays *Color Struck* and *Spears*. Attends Barnard College on scholarship, majors in English, and studies anthropology under Franz Boas. Reports involvement with the Krigwa Players. Completes *Meet the Mamma* in July; the production falls through. In December, *Spears* appears in *The X-Ray: The Official Publication of Zeta Phi Beta Sorority*. Alain Locke's *The New Negro* published.

1926    Does fieldwork in Harlem for Boas using anthropometry to disprove physical theories of racial inferiority. *Color Struck* is published in *Fire!!* In November, four short stories, including "The Eatonville Anthology" and "Sweat," also published in various venues.

1927    Funded by a fellowship, Hurston travels to the South to collect folklore material. When she returns to New York, she meets Charlotte Osgood Mason, who becomes her patron and later, her employer. *The First One* is published in *Ebony and Topaz,* edited by Charles S. Johnson.

1928    Travels to Polk County, Florida, to collect folklore and spends time in turpentine camps. Receives her B.A. from Barnard. During the summer months, she visits New Orleans to research voodoo practices.

1929    In Florida, she transcribes a sermon by C. C. Lovelace that would be dramatized as *The Sermon in the Valley*. Travels to the Bahamas. Stock market crashes in October, foreshadowing the Great Depression of the 1930s.

1930    Collaborates with Langston Hughes on *The Mule-Bone* and with Porter Grainger on *Jungle Scandals*. Copyrights her version of *The Mule-Bone*, entitled *De Turkey and De Law,* and sketches written for *Jungle Scandals,* which she titles *Cold Keener*.

1931    *The Mule-Bone* production canceled by Hurston. *The Sermon in the Valley* presented by the Gilpin Players in Cleveland. Hurston contributes pieces to *Fast and Furious*, a Broadway musical review. A production of *Jungle Scandals* is canceled.

1932    *The Great Day* is presented at the John Golden Theatre on Broadway. Adds *The Fiery Chariot* to a new version called *From Sun to Sun* presented twice in two other New York venues.

1933    *All De Live Long Day* tours throughout Florida. Takes a job as a drama teacher at Bethune-Cookman College. Between August 1933 and the end of 1934, publishes four more short stories, including "The Gilded Six-Bits."

1934    "Characteristics of Negro Expression" and *Jonah's Gourd Vine* published. *The Sermon in the Valley* revived by the Gilpin Players. *Singing Steel* performed in Chicago.

1935    Works for the Works Progress Administration (WPA) in New York. *Mules and Men* is published. Copyrights *Spunk*.

1937    *Their Eyes Were Watching God* is published.

1938    Works for the Federal Writers' Project in Florida. Brings singers to the National Folk Festival in Washington, D.C. *Tell My Horse* is published.

1939    Hired to create a drama program at the North Carolina College for Negroes in Durham. Attempts to collaborate with Paul Green on *High John De Conqueror*. *Moses, Man of the Mountain* published.

1941    "Cock Robin, Beale Street" is published.

1942    Publishes "Story in Harlem Slang" and *Dust Tracks on a Road*.

1943    Publishes the story "High John de Conquer."

1944    Hired to write *Polk County* with Dorothy Waring.

1948    *Seraph on the Suwanee* published.

1949    *The Sermon in the Valley* revived in Cleveland.

1950    Takes a job as a maid in Miami while continuing to work on articles and book projects.

1956    Works as a clerk in Cocoa Beach.

1958    Employed as a substitute teacher in Fort Pierce.

1959    Mounting health problems and poverty move her to the Saint Lucie County Welfare Home.

1960    Dies of hypertensive heart disease.

1970    *Fire!!* (which includes *Color Struck*) is reissued in the anthology *Negro Periodicals in the United States* (Westport, Conn.: Negro Universities Press).

1982    *Fire!!* is reissued in an edition by Thomas H. Wirth, from the Fire!! Press.

1989    *Color Struck* and *The First One* are included in Kathy Perkins's *Black Female Playwrights: An Anthology of Plays Before 1950* (Bloomington: Indiana University Press).

1990    George C. Wolfe's *Spunk*, a musical play based on three Hurston short stories, is presented at the Public Theater in New York.

1991    *The First One* is published in *Roots of African American Drama*, edited by Leo Hamalian and James V. Hatch (Detroit, Mich.: Wayne State University Press). *Mule Bone* is published in an edition by George Houston Bass and Henry Louis Gates Jr. (New York: HarperPerennial).

1995    *Color Struck* is included in *The Portable Harlem Renaissance Reader,* edited by David Levering Lewis (New York: Penguin Books).

1996    *Fire!!* is reprinted in *Black Writers Interpret the Harlem Renaissance* (New York: Garland Publishing). *Color Struck* and *The First One* are included in *Zora Neale Hurston, Eulalie Spence, Marita Bonner, and Others: The Prize Plays and Other One-Acts Published in Periodicals*, edited by Henry Louis Gates Jr. and Jennifer Burton (New York: G. K. Hall). *The First One* is reprinted in *The Politics and Aesthetics of "New Negro" Literature*, edited by Cary D. Wintz (New York: Garland Publishing) and anthologized in *Black Theatre USA: Plays by African Americans from 1847 to Today*, edited by James V. Hatch and Ted Shine (New York: Free Press, 1996).

2001    *Color Struck* is included in *Double-Take: A Revisionist Harlem Renaissance Anthology*, edited by Venetria K. Patton and Maureen Honey (New Brunswick, N.J.: Rutgers University Press).

2002    *Polk County* produced by Arena Stage in Washington, D.C.

2004    A revised *Polk County* is performed at the McCarter Theater Center and the Berkeley Repertory Theatre.

# INTRODUCTION:
## ZORA NEALE HURSTON—A THEATRICAL LIFE

*Zora Neale Hurston: Collected Plays* marks the first time that the extant dramatic writings of Zora Neale Hurston have ever been collected in a single volume. This feat would have been impossible if not for the work of librarians at the Library of Congress. In 1997, they found over a dozen plays and sketches stored in various locations throughout their vast holdings and rescued them from obscurity by sharing them in public monthly readings. Add to this treasure trove other library holdings and pieces from several ephemeral publications and we end up with a clear picture of Hurston's theatrical output ranging from 1925 to 1944, a significant body of work that constitutes yet another facet of one of the most dynamic figures of the Harlem Renaissance. We hope this book will help to illuminate Hurston's dramatic output in the same way that Alice Walker's efforts in the 1970s brought her novels to the attention of a new generation of readers. Without production, plays are inert—incomplete blueprints for a live experience. We reproduce these works in the hope that theaters, scholars, and students today will rediscover a highly original dramatic voice.

With some notable exceptions, most critics and historians have glossed over Hurston's playwriting; her theatrical pursuits have mostly been treated as diversionary or supplementary material for understanding her novels. While the threads connecting her plays to her novels—themes, idioms, characters, plots, and settings—echo back and forth from play to story to novel and back to play again, Hurston was no theatrical dilettante. She was a serious and ambitious practitioner, and her dramatic works stand on their own merits and independently of her fiction. Even while constantly struggling with poverty, she dedicated much of her energy in the 1930s to producing plays and working to establish black theaters with little hope of financial compensation. She also maintained a passionate belief that the precious oral culture collected in her life and fieldwork found its fullest expression on the stage. As she wrote in her oft-cited essay, "Characteristics of Negro Expression" (1934), "Every phase of Negro life is highly dramatised. . . . Everything is acted out" (830). As a folklorist and ethnologist, she wanted to preserve the richness of black culture before it became diluted and disappeared, but she did not want her work to be "buried in scientific journals"—she wanted to share it with the world.[1] By depicting black culture on stage, she hoped to make it a vibrant part of American art and life.

Hurston's first formal education was a theatrical one. After a vicious argument with her stepmother, Hurston left her home in Eatonville, Florida, at the age of fourteen, taking odd jobs and moving frequently. By the time she turned twenty-four, she was broke, living in Memphis, and had little direction.

Opportunity arrived in the form of a "Miss M——," a lead in a Northern Gilbert and Sullivan troupe who offered her a job as a maid and dresser. For eighteen months, she learned the backstage workings of the trade, befriending the actors and becoming their confidante. At the same time, she continued her education by borrowing books from company members and listening to the classics of Western music. In her autobiography, *Dust Tracks on a Road,* she wrote about this time: "Everything was pleasant and exciting. If there was any more Heaven than this, I didn't want to see it" (134). Though the job ended when "Miss M——" left the stage to get married, the experience left an indelible mark on Hurston. She spent the next two decades writing plays and seeking production opportunities even though she was actively discouraged by her benefactor, Charlotte Osgood Mason, the racism of the American theater, and the economics of being a female black writer without financial resources.

Sadly, most of the attention given to Hurston's dramatic aspirations centers on her controversial and contentious collaboration with Langston Hughes from 1930 to 1931 on the play *The Mule-Bone.* The clashing of these two forceful and creative personalities marks a missed opportunity for a nascent black theater—and definitely makes good copy. However, for Hurston, it was merely a bump in the long road of her playwriting career. Because Hurston disavowed *The Mule-Bone* and because there is no way to satisfactorily disentangle each writer's contributions, we omit the play from this collection, offering *De Turkey and De Law,* the version that Hurston copyrighted as sole author in October 1930, in its place.[2] Without recounting the many twists and turns of the story, it is clear from surviving correspondence that two versions of the play—*De Turkey and De Law,* which all parties agree was Hurston's work alone, and *The Mule-Bone,* the incomplete product of the Hurston-Hughes collaboration—were submitted to the Gilpin Players on or before January 1931.[3] This influential Cleveland theater company, considered by Hughes to be "The best Little Theatre Negro group in the country,"[4] tried out New York productions and was commonly scouted by New York talent agencies. Although there is evidence that Hurston continued to revise the play as late as 1934, unless some new document is found, the copyrighted version of *De Turkey and De Law* must stand as Hurston's definitive version of the play. We encourage readers who wish to compare the two texts to examine the excellent 1991 edition of *The Mule-Bone,* issued under the slightly revised title *Mule Bone,* edited by Henry Louis Gates Jr. and George Houston Bass.

## Beginnings

Because of the disproportionate attention accorded to the Hughes episode, it has been erroneously assumed by many that Hurston's theatrical writing began with *The Mule-Bone.* In fact, it began years earlier. When *Opportunity: A Journal of Negro Life,* a National Urban League publication designed to promote African American art and literature, held a literary contest in 1925, two of her three award-winning submissions were plays: *Color Struck* won second prize in that category and *Spears* won an honorable mention.[5] At the awards banquet, Hurston met Annie Nathan Meyer, one of the founders of Barnard College, who arranged for her to attend on scholarship. Entering Barnard as its first black student, Hurston listed drama as her primary interest but was too late to sign up for a popular drama course. Undaunted, she seemed to have created her own program of study, seeing as much theater as her meager finances would allow. She particularly admired Mae West's play *Sex* (1926), which included dances faithfully appropriated from Harlem parties West attended. In this production, West, Hurston later wrote, "had much more flavor of the turpentine quarters than she did of the white bawd" ("Characteristics," 844).

But before even starting school, Hurston took up theatrical activities. In a June 5, 1925 letter, she reported that she was founding a "New Negro play company" and that Rosamond Johnson, brother of James Weldon Johnson and an established black composer and producer, was writing music for a play she had written (probably *Meet the Mamma,* copyrighted in July 1925). In addition, Flournoy Miller, one of the writers behind the hugely popular all-black musical *Shuffle Along* (1921), was supposed to hear a reading of the play. It is unknown whether or not this reading ever took place; regardless, a production never materialized.

Hurston had more near-misses during her association with the Krigwa Players, formed by W. E. B. Du Bois, then editor of *Crisis*.[6] Previously, Du Bois had created several enormous outdoor pageants, the most notable being *The Star of Ethiopia*, an episodic allegory that catalogued and celebrated the contributions of black people throughout history. Now, Du Bois turned his attention to reforming the state of black theater. Many black intellectuals agreed that theater in Harlem needed reforming. They complained that vaudeville, burlesque houses, nightclubs, and cabarets, rather than serious theater, were the main entertainments above 125th Street and that amateur performances in churches, lodges, and halls produced works of uneven quality. Eulalie Spence, a contemporary of Hurston's, lamented in *Opportunity* magazine that black playwrights "have labored like the architect who has no knowledge of geometry and the painter who must struggle to evolve the principles of perspective" (July 1928, 214). And Du Bois, along with many members of the black intellectual elite, objected that black audiences brought the same jocund and participatory behavior to serious theater as they did to variety acts, laughing at the wrong moments and talking to the performers. "Our actors," he wrote, "must be encouraged and not put on a level with mountebanks whose slightest gesture is the signal for laughter."[7] A 1925 *Messenger* editorial accused "so-called educated Negroes" of being superficial in their tastes because they preferred to "duck into a dive" rather than go to a cultural event such as the theater, proving that they were still being held in the "shackles of slavery."[8]

Du Bois believed that only "a real Negro theatre" would cultivate a proper respect for dramatic literature, on the part of either playwrights or their audience. The Krigwa Players was only one of many in the "little theatre movement" to focus on black playwrights and to present plays that, in Du Bois's words, would be

> 1. About us. That is they must have plots which reveal real Negro life as it is. 2. By us. That is they must be written by Negro authors who understand from birth and continual association just what it means to be a Negro today. 3. For us. That is, the theatre must cater primarily to Negro audiences and be supported and sustained by their entertainment and approval. 4. Near us. The theatre must be in a Negro neighborhood near the mass of ordinary Negro people.[9]

This philosophy must have greatly interested Hurston, for she put forward two plays for Du Bois to consider for production. The first was a lost play called *The Lilac Bush* that he rejected on merit. The second, entitled *The First One*, is based on an episode in the book of Genesis where Noah curses the son of Ham into servitude, a story that was historically used in the justification of slavery and commonly referred to by both African American and white writers.[10] Although Hurston put her own spin on the story, Du Bois, who believed that theater should depict the best of black society—his vaunted "Talented Tenth"—as exemplary figures for whites and role models for other blacks, objected to blackness being viewed as a curse by black characters in the play. He asked for revisions, and while Hurston seemed ready to oblige, there is no record of the play ever being performed by Du Bois's Krigwa Players or anyone else.[11]

Ultimately, Hurston's view of a "real Negro theatre" differed fundamentally from Du Bois's. Poor and from the South, unlike many of the middle-class, educated Northern blacks who participated in the Harlem Renaissance, she was always uncomfortable with those whom she called "race champions." She believed the black common man was not represented by the elitist leadership of the day. The intellectual, she wrote in an October 10, 1931 letter, wanted to "ride his misery to glory" but only as a means of finding a privileged seat at the white man's table. Instead of espousing Du Bois's notion that only the "Talented Tenth" could truly achieve black uplift, she believed that the common man (and woman) were capable of their own uplift—and in fact, that they already occupied higher ground. As Deborah G. Plant writes, "Hurston saw folk culture—her own culture—as the source of renewed Black national dignity and pride. She saw in it the foundations of African American self-affirmation and independence and the foundation of resistance to European cultural domination" (64).

In this, she initially appeared to align herself with Alain Locke's conception of "The New Negro," who rejoiced and prayed "to be delivered both from self-pity and condescension" and pursued art for art's sake ("The New Negro," 8). In the October 1926 issue of *Theater Arts Monthly*, Locke encouraged artists to jettison the stereotypes of the past and celebrate black culture, especially in the form of the folk play: "Negro drama must grow in its own soil and cultivate its own intrinsic elements; only in this way can it become truly organic, and cease being a rootless derivative" (703). Yet Locke's more anthropological view of the folk play was incompatible in some ways with Hurston's. Whereas Locke believed that the folk was valuable as an "intrinsic" and "organic" element of African American art, he also believed that it should be "cultivated" in new forms, not simply preserved for its own sake. For example, though he proclaimed the spiritual "a classic folk expression," equally important was that because of its "harmonic versatility" and "its skipped measures and interpolations it is at the very least potentially polyphonic" ("Negro Spiritual," 199). As a result, "it can therefore undergo without breaking its own boundaries, intricate and original development in directions already the line of advance in modernistic music" (ibid., 210). Evidence of the spiritual's openness to innovation could be seen, he argued, in recent works by Dvorak, Stravinsky, and Darius Milhaud that incorporated the asymmetrical rhythms and dissonances of black spirituals. In contrast, for Hurston the value of folk lay in folk itself— not in its adaptability to a modernist aesthetic. As Plant puts it,

> The Harlem Renaissance leaders looked to the folk for inspiration and artistic material, but they deracinated and 'refined' these materials, purifying them of their "barbarisms," presenting them in a manner that would reflect the 'cultured' sensibilities of the Black intelligentsia, that is, in a manner they considered acceptable and palatable to whites, while safeguarding their elitist image of the New Negro. By contrast, authentic folk life is what Hurston sought to preserve and celebrate. . . . She believed . . . in the dignity of the masses. Neither dumb nor dull, the folk could articulate their own experiences. (73)

And it was, moreover, a thing of the present, not just a cultural origin or a source of nostalgia. As Hurston wrote in 1934, "Negro folklore is not a thing of the past. It is still in the making" ("Characteristics," 836).

In an April 1928 letter to Langston Hughes, Hurston outlined her own plan for a "real Negro theatre": "I shall, or rather we shall act out the folk tales, however short, with the abrupt angularity and naiveté of the primitive 'bama Nigger." From her early experiments in adapting the Broadway musical to black themes (e.g., *Meet the Mamma*) to her own brand of vernacular slice-of-life realism (culminating in *Spunk* and *Polk County*), Hurston continued to revise her conception of a "Negro theatre" throughout her career. Although the folk material she used in her works was clearly a source of racial pride, she did not practice Du Bois's isolationist credo when it came to venues. Her efforts to present her work to both black and white audiences speak to a resistance to what many of today's playwrights of color call "self-ghettoizing."

Two pivotal experiences shaped this vision. The first came at Columbia, where she studied with renowned anthropologist Franz Boas. A cultural relativist, he dismantled the prevalent theories of racial superiority and inspired or reaffirmed Hurston's own ideas of the universality of human experience. "It seemed to me," she later wrote in *Dust Tracks on the Road*, "that the human beings I met reacted pretty much the same to the same stimuli. Different idioms, yes. Circumstances and conditions having the power to influence, yes. Inherent difference, no." Or put more simply, "black skunks are just as natural as white ones" (206). Boas also cultivated Hurston's interest in language. As a founder of modern descriptive linguistics, Boas believed that language was the key to culture. Thus, to understand a culture, one must first understand its language. As he said in an address to the American Anthropological Association in 1905:

> Would not the student of Oriental countries, who has to rely for his information on the assistance of interpreters, be considered an unsafe guide in the study of these countries? ... There are very few students who have taken the time and who have considered it necessary to familiarize themselves sufficiently with native languages to understand directly what the people whom they study speak about, what they think and what they do. There are fewer still who have deemed it worth while to record the customs and beliefs and the traditions of the people in their own words. (184–185)

Hurston, of course, had always been a natural watcher and recorder of human behavior and language. As a child, she would sit on her front porch in Eatonville, Florida, watching the parade of human activity, a "proscenium box for a born first-nighter" ("Colored Me," 152). She loved to be sent on errands so that she could hear the "men folks . . . swap stories" on the porch of Joe Clarke's store, writing, "I'd drag out my leaving as long as possible in order to hear more" (*Mules and Men*, 2). Thus, when Boas arranged a scholarship for her to take a six-month trip to the South to collect folklore, she jumped at the chance. Boas understood that a black collector had a distinct advantage over a white worker in the field, especially one with "the map of Florida on her tongue" (Hemenway, 9). The trip, however, was ultimately unsuccessful, in part because Hurston presented herself as an ethnographer rather than as one of the "folk." As she later wrote in *Dust Tracks on a Road*, "The glamor of Barnard College was still upon me. I dwelt in marble halls. I knew where the material was all right. But, I went about asking, in careful Barnardese, 'Pardon me, but do you know any folk-tales or folk-songs?' The men and women who had whole treasuries of material just seeping through their pores looked at me and shook their heads" (174–175).

## Maturity

A new alliance gave Hurston another chance to explore the hidden subcultures of the black South. In her second transformational experience, Hurston met the woman who would become her benefactor and scourge. Charlotte Osgood Mason, a Park Avenue philanthropist with a great interest in black authors, artists, and anthropology, agreed to sponsor Hurston in 1928 so that she could continue gathering folklore. The woman she would come to refer to as "Godmother" paid Hurston a monthly stipend and, in return, Hurston's finds became Mason's property. Their relationship was close and complicated. Hurston's correspondence with Mason seems to alternate between the expression of a truly loving bond and bald emotional manipulation designed to ensure Mason's financial support. At the same time, Mason's behavior shifts from great generosity to penuriousness, from praise to condescension and harshness. Some believed she was secretly racist, requiring a performance of exoticism from her charges. Others accused Hurston of performing "blackness" to keep Mason's patronage.[12] Regardless, Mason's sponsorship of Hurston would continue for at least the next five years, and the folklore Hurston collected during this time would forever change the nature of her playwriting: it moved her farther away from the standard Broadway musical and closer to her own brand of folk drama.

Sketches included in *Cold Keener* (1930) and *Fast and Furious* (1930), the plays *De Turkey and De Law* (1930) and *The Sermon in the Valley* (1931), and the different "folk concerts" she presented in 1931–1932 were the immediate products of Hurston's immersion in Florida folklore. Filled with the idioms of the railroad camp, the "jook"—which Hurston later described as the foundation of the "Negro theatre" ("Characteristics," 842)—the courtroom and the pulpit, incorporating actual Eatonville locales like Joe Clarke's storefront porch and the Macedonia Baptist Church, these works were infused with a verve and linguistic richness absent from earlier works such as the derivative *Meet the Mamma* (1925) or the often stilted *Spears* (1926) and *The First One* (1927). All of Hurston's subsequent works would further develop the form of folk drama she pioneered at this time.

These works constituted a true departure from the standard fare of the day. Even as late as the 1930s, blacks in the theater could not be viewed save through the veil of the minstrel show, a hodgepodge of musical acts and sketch comedy born of the racial prejudice that loomed large in the country's cultural consciousness. The blackface servant, as both set dressing and comic diversion, had been a feature of the American stage since the country's founding, and by the 1840s, when New York performer T. D. Rice popularized blackface performance, the practice of ethnic impersonation was accepted as a common theatrical convention. White actors (and later, black actors seeking work) painted their faces with burnt cork and exaggerated white lips, and thus adorned, populated the stage with horrific stereotypes. Among them was the ignorant and slothful Jim Crow, longing for the "carefree" days of slavery; Zip Coon, the urban figure whose dandyish clothes and high-hat manner demonstrated he had risen above his proper station; the mammy, matronly and serious; and the pickaninny, the zany, unkempt child (Topsy of *Uncle Tom's Cabin* being the most prevalent example of this type). Although these shows claimed authenticity in situation, music, and dialect, they never treated the plantation as a real place with all of its obvious moral complexities; it was the framing device to allow the singing of standard popular songs of the day—first banjo and fiddle songs and later the standard Broadway repertoire.[13]

While the minstrel show in its original form was dead by the time Hurston arrived in New York, its traditions survived in vaudeville and musical theater.[14] The 1925 theatrical season, for example, included *Topsy and Eva,* a musical version of *Uncle Tom's Cabin* in blackface, and *Lucky Sambo,* which opened with a chorus dancing the Charleston in front of Aunt Jemima's cabin. It was clear that white audiences would only accept black performers in musical comedies, and critics had strong ideas about what constituted a Negro show: namely, exuberant dancing, often incorporating some kind of jungle motif (*Spears* is an example of Hurston's stab at this genre). Even though many of the finest black performers of the age rejected these negative images, if they wanted to work professionally, they were sometimes forced to wear ragged minstrel-like costumes or appear in front of sets with painted backdrops depicting watermelon patches or plantation vistas. The theaters themselves remained segregated; black patrons had to watch from the balcony.

Even those plays that attempted to portray blacks sympathetically were problematic, to say the least. During the 1920s and 1930s, the apex of Hurston's theatrical output, shows with black themes were primarily limited to plays by white playwrights such as Eugene O'Neill (*The Emperor Jones*), Paul Green (*In Abraham's Bosom*), Marc Connelly (*The Green Pastures*), and George and Ira Gershwin (*Porgy and Bess*). Despite their forthright attempts to represent blacks seriously and realistically, racial caricature and tortured dialect remained the fare of the day. In the 1920s, only three non-musical plays by black playwrights ever made it to Broadway.[15] Even though it derived its name from the garishly lighted marquees that ran its length, the Great White Way could easily have been named for its atmosphere of ethnic exclusion.

Hurston wrote that "if we are to believe the majority of writers of Negro dialect and the burnt-cork artists, Negro speech is a weird thing, full of 'arms' and 'Ises.' Fortunately, we don't have to believe them. We may go directly to the Negro and let him speak for himself" ("Characteristics," 845–846). Her first successful attempt to show black culture from an authentically black point of view came immediately after her falling out with Hughes in 1931. After their break made the production of *The Mule-Bone* impossible, the Gilpin Players agreed to present *The Sermon in the Valley,* a dramatization of a sermon by folk preacher C. C. Lovelace that Hurston transcribed in 1929 and later included as John Pearson's final sermon in *Jonah's Gourd Vine* (1934).[16] The script produced here, never before published, is not wholly Hurston's work; Rowena Jelliffe, the co-founder of the Karamu Settlement House in Cleveland, revised Hurston's transcription to incorporate what Hurston simply described in *Jonah's Gourd Vine* as the "mighty response to the sermon all thru [*sic*] its length" (181). An unmitigated success, the show was eventually revived by the Players twice, first in 1934 and later in 1949.

In 1931, Hurston also landed her first Broadway credit with *Fast and Furious*, an all-black review. How Hurston came to be attached to this production is unknown, but she worked with a seasoned group of black musical talent, including director Forbes Robinson, composers Porter Grainger and Joe Jordan, and comedians Tim Moore and Jackie (later "Moms") Mabley. This edition contains her four contributions among the twelve sketches that made up this show: *The Courtroom* (copyrighted as *Lawing and Jawing*), *The Football Game* (copyrighted as *Forty Yards*), *The Poker Game* (copyrighted as *Poker!*), and a version of *Woofing,* which was used as a curtain-raiser. Never shy of the spotlight, Hurston also acted in the show, playing a cheerleader with Mabley in *The Football Game*.

After a trial run in August at the Boulevard Theatre in Jackson Heights, Queens, the show opened at the New Yorker Theatre on September 15, 1931. Unfortunately, it never caught on and closed after only seven performances. White critics were not kind to Hurston's first Broadway outing. *New York Times* critic Brooks Atkinson wrote of the production: "In quantity and in toothsome exuberance the minstrels give full measure," but when "the material is hackneyed, when the performers are fat and clumsy, the animalism of Negro entertainment is lumpish and unwieldy."[17] The critic at *The New York American*, no fan of black entertainment, "failed to appreciate the geniality and animal humor and vital athletics of their jumbles" and found that the show only occasionally excelled when it stopped imitating a "white folks' revue" and showed "a real frenzy of lightning-swift legs and rolling eyes."[18] Unable to find a Broadway audience, *Fast and Furious* was moved to the smaller Lafayette Theatre in Harlem in October for a limited engagement. The show was split in two—for one week the first half of the show was performed, and the next week the second was presented, retitled *Heaven and Hell*. Both runs shared the bill with a movie.[19]

In one of her most successful ventures, Hurston also tried her hand at a hybrid form that combined theater and concert. In 1932, she presented what she described to Mason in September 1931 as a "program of original Negro folklore," a "concert of the most intensely black type." As Hurston's description indicates, *The Great Day* was not strictly a theatrical work, but a performance—a "concert"—dominated by song and dance, interspersed with dramatic monologues and skits, and loosely threaded together with commentary by a sort of master of ceremonies. Perhaps because of its hybrid nature, no complete script or score of the production (or its subsequent versions) survives. As a result, we have not included it in this edition, although we do include transcriptions of the programs for this "concert," as well as two related productions, *From Sun to Sun* and *All de Live Long Day* (discussed below), in an appendix to this volume.[20]

*The Great Day* was presented January 10, 1932, at the John Golden Theatre in New York. The first act was organized around a day in the life of a railroad worker, from waking to returning to quarters and hearing a preacher's sermon. The second act took place in the evening with a scene in a jook joint, a voodoo conjure scene, and various dance numbers in the "palm woods." It is highly likely that *Railroad Camp* and *Mr. Frog*, in some version, were included in this production, as well as excerpts from other plays included in this edition, in particular, *Spunk*, which Hurston was also working on at this time. Hurston supervised all aspects of the show, renting the venue, scenery, and costumes, hiring professional actors and singers, printing programs, and even appearing as a performer. To raise money to cover costs, Hurston sold her car and radio and borrowed $530 from Mason. Porter Grainger, the composer for the ill-fated *Jungle Scandals*, arranged the music. And a *Times* description of the show suggests that Leigh Whipper, considered by many to be the finest black actor of his generation, played the master of ceremonies as well as the preacher.[21] Alain Locke, who contributed notes for the program, called the performance a "rare sample of the pure and unvarnished materials from which the stage and concert tradition has been derived; and ought to show how much more unique and powerful and spirit-compelling the genuine Negro folk-things really are."

*The Great Day* was an artistic success, receiving positive reviews in *The Evening Post* and *The Sun-Herald*. Hurston hoped that a producer would be interested in financing the show, but the vogue for black musicals that began with *Shuffle Along* in 1921 had passed, and no offer materialized. Still dedicated to the project, Hurston revised it somewhat, adding the one-act piece *The Fiery Chariot* and renaming it *From Sun to Sun*. On March 29, it was presented at the New School for Social Research and again on April 22 at the Vanderbilt Hotel, as part of a "dinner-cabaret" created by the Neighborhood Playhouse.[22] It was around this time that Mason, unhappy that her folklore "property" was being used for theatrical entertainment, barred Hurston from continuing to use what she had found while under contract. Broke, Hurston headed south to Florida but wrote in a June 8, 1932 letter that she retained her desire to establish "a real Negro theatre" separate from "overwrought members of my own race, and well-meaning but uninformed white people." She had hoped this theater could be started in Eatonville but settled for training local townspeople for another concert tour of *From Sun to Sun*. As she told a group of students at Rollins College, she was dissatisfied with the original production and needed "a cast of the Negro type rather than that of the New Yorkized Negro" to develop "a production of enduring value."[23]

In 1933, Hurston continued to rework the show. The next incarnation, *All De Live Long Day*, was presented at a number of venues throughout Florida: Eatonville, Rollins College (to a whites-only audience), the Municipal Auditorium in Orlando, Mountain Lake Club in Lake Wales, and Bethune-Cookman, a small black college in Daytona Beach. This work included a new one-act entitled *De Possum's Tail Hairs* (now lost), based on a story she included in *Mules and Men* (1935). Another version of the review, *Singing Steel*, was performed at the Chicago Women's Club Theater and the University of Chicago in 1934.

## Decline

Through professional acquaintances she made on her tours, Hurston was offered a position at Bethune-Cookman late in 1933 to create a theater program
at the college. However, in the end, she had nothing positive to say about the
experience. The tiny student body, lack of space and funds, and the meddling
of the president and faculty led her to abandon that position and seek a new
one at Fisk University. She was to study drama at Yale and return to establish
an experimental theater program at Fisk, "to create Negro drama out of the
Negro," as she wrote to James Weldon Johnson in October 1934, but her proposal was ultimately rejected.

Perhaps the most mysterious part of Hurston's theatrical career is the period
that followed her return to New York in 1935. There she was hired by the
Federal Theatre Project, a Works Progress Administration (WPA) program designed to employ theater professionals during the Depression. For six months,
she worked as a "drama coach" for the fledgling Negro Unit run by John
Houseman and based in the newly renovated Lafayette Theatre in Harlem.
There is no record of exactly what duties she performed during this time, although Houseman did call her "our most talented writer on the project."[24]
When the Unit was left with no adequate scripts after their first two productions, Hurston wrote an adaptation of the ancient Greek comedy *Lysistrata* set
in a Florida fishing village. The premise of Aristophanes' play was changed so
that the women of the village withheld sex from their husbands until they "won
their fight with the canning company for a living wage" (205). Houseman liked
the piece but found that "it scandalized both Left and Right by its saltiness," and
did not offer the "serious Negro image" that both sides wanted to promote. No
copies of the play have survived.[25] However, a play from the period that *does*
survive is *Spunk,* which was copyrighted on June 15, 1935 (obviously, the play
could have been composed some time earlier). The play was based on the story
of the same title, which, along with *Color Struck* and the story "Black Death,"
first established her as part of what she and Wallace Thurman came to call the
"Niggerati" when she was awarded second prize for the three works in the 1925
*Opportunity* contest. However, the success of the story did not translate into
success for the play, which was never produced.

Hurston left the Negro Unit after she was awarded a Guggenheim fellowship to collect folklore in Jamaica and Haiti, around the same time that director Orson Wells's notorious *Macbeth* production was marrying Shakespeare's
text to Haitian voodoo practices.[26] Unlike Wells, Hurston experienced voodoo
practices firsthand, in an earlier trip to New Orleans as well as in Jamaica and
Haiti, even subjecting herself to the harsh rigors of initiation ceremonies.
Whereas Wells used West Indian culture as set dressing, Hurston's treatment
of voodoo is far more veracious.

The year after she published her best-known work, *Their Eyes Were
Watching God* (1937), Hurston was hired for another WPA program, the

Federal Writers' Project, and was one of many assigned to create a volume entitled *The Florida Negro*, an account of black life in the state. Working from her home in Eatonville, she was paid far less than her white counterparts, but the freedom the job afforded also allowed her to work on her literary projects. During the year, she also found time to take a group of singers to the National Folk Festival in Washington, D.C., on May 6, 1938.[27] When the funding for the WPA came under fire from an increasingly conservative Congress, the program responded by staging exhibitions to gather public support. Hurston was enlisted to organize a presentation called *The Fire Dance* that presented two Bahamian and two African dances. It was performed twice in Orlando as part of the WPA's "National Exhibition of Skills" in January 1939.

As a result of her folk concert tour, Hurston was hired in 1939 to create a drama program at the North Carolina College for Negroes in Durham. Never comfortable within or adept at handling institutional bureaucracies, she was frustrated once again with the school's lack of commitment to theater. She was only given one class to teach, and her requests for a full battery of practical theater classes in all production areas fell on deaf ears. At the same time, she was thoroughly distracted by her association with Paul Green, a professor of drama at the University of North Carolina at Chapel Hill and proponent of regional folk drama. Green, a southerner who had spent his early days as a fieldhand among both poor blacks and whites, was deeply interested in problems of racial division and after hearing Hurston speak at UNC, invited her to join his playwriting seminar. There, she began to develop a play titled *High John de Conqueror*,[28] which she hoped would be produced by Green at Carolina Playmakers, the theater group associated with the university. Her efforts to collaborate with Green seemed to supplant her work at North Carolina College; not a single performance was given during her tenure at the school. She wrote to Green in January 1940: "I won't care what happens here or if nothing happens here so long as I do the bigger thing with you." At the end of six months, Hurston was more than happy to tender her resignation at Durham. Green, on the other hand, never fully committed to collaborating with her and instead, put his energies into a theatrical adaptation of Richard Wright's *Native Son*. Try as she might, lack of interest or lack of funds perpetually frustrated Hurston's theatrical ambitions.

The last significant chapter in Hurston's theatrical life occurred in 1944, when she returned to New York to work on *Polk County* for a possible Broadway run. She completed the play with what appears to be minor assistance from a white woman named Dorothy Waring. The nature of their collaboration is unclear, but when *Polk County* is read against Hurston's other plays, Waring's contribution appears to be minor. The only surviving record of their writing process describes a meeting between the two where Waring suggests that the piece take on a more "Gershwinesque feeling." Hurston's response: "You don't know what the hell you're talking about" (qtd. in Hemenway, 298). (The fact that Waring was married to *Polk County*'s potential theatrical producer, Stephen Kelen-d'Oxylion, does much, perhaps, to explain why she received credit for coauthoring the play.) Announcements were made concerning a summer opening with Hurston's friend Ethel Waters in a major role, but the necessary backers did not surface. Delays were reported by the *Times* in August, and by November, the production fell through.

Even with this final professional setback, Hurston never abandoned the theater. Friends remember her assembling another production of *The Great Day* in the 1950s with black students even as her books disappeared from public memory and she slipped further into poverty and illness. When Hurston died on January 28, 1960, in a Florida welfare home, penniless and forgotten, her papers were burned by court order. Some of them survived when a friend extinguished the fire, but we will never know how many of Hurston's plays were consumed by the blaze.

## Conclusion

In hindsight, we can see Hurston as an innovator, ahead of her time in the development of American musical theater. Hurston's later plays, which featured an easy blend of song and dialogue, ran counter to the structured scenes with abrupt Tin Pan Alley interpolations found in the white musicals of commercial Broadway. By the time she wrote *Polk County* in 1944, Broadway was still churning out dusty vaudeville and hackneyed reviews. The only notable innovation in musical theater had been *Oklahoma!* the year before, a show that boasted a new natural integration of song and story but in reality, simply alternated tableaux of authentic Western life with nostalgic Americana and stylized ballet dances. The musical world that Hurston created, with its lining songs, folk songs, blues, and spirituals, sprang from a southern culture that she experienced firsthand.

By setting most of her work in African American communities largely devoid of whites, writes biographer Valerie Boyd, Hurston "protests white oppression by stripping it of its potency, by denying its all-powerfulness in black people's lives" (305). Hurston's notorious rejection of the *Brown v. Board of Education* ruling in 1954, deplorable as it was, was nevertheless in keeping with the beliefs she held throughout her life. "It is well known that I have no sympathy nor respect for the 'tragedy of color' school of thought among us," she wrote in an editorial to a Florida newspaper. "I can see no tragedy in being too dark to be invited to a white school social affair."[29] Having experienced both black and white worlds, she saw no injustice in preserving the uniqueness of the former. Perhaps more important, she viewed invitations to "white school social affairs" as invitations to reject black culture. One wonders if Hurston was protesting what Hughes in 1926 had called "this urge within the race toward whiteness."[30]

Ultimately, Hurston embraced a radical individualism that precluded her from participating in social movements, or even recognizing the institutional forces that *Brown v. Board of Education* sought to counteract. In *Dust Tracks on a Road,* she wrote: "It would be against all nature for all the Negroes to be either at the bottom, top, or in between. It has never happened with anybody else, so why with us? . . . It is up to the individual. If you haven't got it, you can't show it. If you have got it, you can't hide it. That is one of the strongest laws God ever made."[31]

Another reason Hurston's work has been—and continues to be—so controversial is her insistence on depicting the less seemly side of African American culture. From "jooks" to brothels, turpentine camps to sawmills, "amen corners" to hoodoo huts, audiences would experience, in words made flesh, the bawdy, violent world that fascinated Hurston throughout her life. She refused to employ conventional distinctions between the laudable and the reprehensible; indeed, some of her most sympathetic characters are adulterers, killers, and thieves, and she demonstrated a consistent disdain for the educated and pious. Critics who look to Hurston's plays for racial protest literature—for what Du Bois famously described as "propaganda"—will never be won over by her comic look at black life.[32] Her plays were not meant as treatises on race relations, but rather, as racial expression *sui generis.* Like Langston Hughes, Hurston intended her works to limn and ultimately celebrate the lives of what he described as "low-down folks, the so-called common element" who "do not particularly care whether they are like white folks or anybody else" ("Negro Artist," 41). The representation of the average—perhaps even the "below-average"—was crucial, for Hughes, Hurston, and others, for the development of a "true" African American theater. As legendary actor Paul Robeson wrote in 1924: "One of the most serious drawbacks to the development of a true Negro dramatic literature" was that "we are too self-conscious, too afraid of showing all phases of our life—especially those phases which are of greatest dramatic value."

At the same time, these "phases" pose especially acute problems in the theater. Blackface minstrelsy's lampoonery of African Americans and African American cultural practices had become so entrenched by the early twentieth century, writes Theodore Kornweibel Jr., that if a black character on stage "did not carry a razor, shoot craps, believe in superstition, or do anything that they believed the typical black should do"—actions, incidentally, that abound in Hurston's plays—"white critics were confounded" (180). The desire to counteract stereotypes of black "low-down folks," to police and monitor images of African Americans, persists. In 1991, when Henry Louis Gates Jr. recommended *The Mule-Bone* to Gregory Mosher, artistic director of Lincoln Center in New York, he encountered the same worries about "what white people might think." "Why would anyone believe," Gates asks, that "there are still aspects of black culture that should be hidden because they are somehow 'embarrassing?'"

As a trained ethnologist, Hurston wanted to represent black life as she saw it being lived, warts and all. But what is perhaps clearest when one reads her work is the joy she experienced in the act of writing itself. In their introduction to

*Zora Neale Hurston: The Complete Stories* (1995), Gates and coeditor Sieglinde Lemke wrote that Hurston saw herself as "the storyteller first, the anthropologist second. She is far more interested in human motivation and the idiosyncracies of character as manifested in language-use than in what we might broadly think of as 'the nature of the Negro' or the struggle for civil rights" (xii). We believe that this anthology, which brings together the bulk of Hurston's dramatic output, will enable readers to see her as a playwright with a clear vision and voice. Her plays stand as testimonies to her racial pride and individual achievement; she lived a truly theatrical life. It is our hope that Hurston the playwright will be able to stand with Hurston the novelist, storyteller, and essayist, and finally receive the attention her efforts so richly deserve.

## Notes

1. *Zora Neale Hurston: A Life in Letters*, ed. Carla Kaplan (New York: Doubleday, 2002). Unless otherwise specified, all letters quoted are from this volume.

2. In a letter to Hughes, Carl Van Vechten, author of the controversial book *Nigger Heaven* and a good friend of both Hughes and Hurston, confirmed that he was sent the play by Hurston on November 14 and quoted the letter that accompanied it: "Langston and I started out together on the idea of the story I used to tell you about Eatonville, but being so much apart from rush of business I started all over again while in Mobile & this is the result of my work alone" (Carl Van Vechten to Langston Hughes, January 19, 1931, cited in *Remember Me to Harlem: The Letters of Langston Hughes and Carl Van Vechten, 1925–1964*, ed. Emily Bernard [New York: Alfred A. Knopf, 2001], 72). Robert Hemenway pieced together the series of events that eventually dissolved Hurston's friendship with Hughes in chapter 6 of *Zora Neale Hurston: A Literary Biography* (Urbana: University of Illinois Press, 1977).

3. The company was named for Charles Gilpin, the actor who played the role of Brutus in Eugene O'Neill's *The Emperor Jones*.

4. Hughes to Hurston, January 19, 1931, in *Mule Bone: A Comedy of Negro Life* by Langston Hughes and Zora Neale Hurston, ed. George H. Bass and Henry Louis Gates Jr. (New York: HarperPerennial, 1991), 214.

5. The judges in this category were Robert C. Benchley, Montgomery Gregory, Edith Isaacs, and Alexander Woollcott. Apparently, *Color Struck* and *The First One* were submitted again for the following year's contest. Both plays were given honorable mentions. The judges for the 1927 contest were David Belasco, Montgomery Gregory, Paul Robeson, and Stark Young.

6. This group may have been the company Hurston referred to in her June 5, 1925 letter cited in the preceding paragraph. The name Krigwa comes from the acronym CRIGWA, the Crisis Guild of Writers and Artists, an organization Du Bois founded based on the prizewinners of his *Crisis* magazine contest.

7. Qtd. in Rena Fraden, *Blueprints for a Black Federal Theatre, 1935–1939* (Cambridge: Cambridge University Press, 1994), 148.

8. Unsigned editorial (probably by Theophilus Lewis), qtd. in ibid., 150.

9. "Krigwa Players Little Negro Theatre," *The Crisis* 32 (July 1926): 134.

10. Many slaveholders from the colonial through the antebellum periods assumed blackness was part of Noah's curse and that the descendants of Ham eventually peopled Africa. See Stephen R. Haynes, *Noah's Curse: The Biblical Justification of American Slavery* (Oxford: Oxford University Press, 2002).

11. *The First One* was later recognized by Charles S. Johnson, who included it in his seminal anthology of works by Harlem Renaissance authors, *Ebony and Topaz* (1927). We use this version as our copy-text.

12. Hughes, another recipient of Osgood's "kindness" (as well as her funds), described his relationship with Mason in his autobiography *The Big Sea,* as well as basing several characters on Osgood (see "The Blues I'm Playing" and "Slave on the Block," in *The Ways of White Folks* [1934]).

13. For an in-depth analysis of minstrel practices, see the last two chapters of Nathan Huggins, *Harlem Renaissance* (New York: Oxford University Press, 1971); Dale Cockrell, *Demons of Disorder: Early Blackface Minstrels and Their World* (Cambridge: Cambridge University Press, 1997); Eric Lott, *Love and Theft: Blackface Minstrelsy and the American Working Class* (New York: Oxford University Press, 1993); William J. Mahar, *Early Blackface Minstrelsy and Antebellum American Popular Culture* (Chicago: University of Illinois Press, 1999); and James P. Byrne, "The Genesis of Whiteface in Nineteenth-Century American Popular Culture," *MELUS* 29, nos. 3–4 (Fall–Winter 2004): 133–149.

14. Community groups such as the Elks, Kiwanis, and Lions Club continued to present minstrel shows as fundraisers until the 1950s, when changing tastes and protests made them scarce.

15. The plays were Garland Anderson's *Appearances* (1925), Frank Wilson's *Meek Mose* (1928), and Wallace Thurman's *Harlem* (1929).

16. The undramatized transcription was also published as "The Sermon" in Nancy Cunard's *Negro* anthology in 1934.

17. Brooks Atkinson, "Harlem Fandango," *New York Times,* September 16, 1931, 15.

18. "'Fast and Furious': The Usual Negro Revue on an Unusually Hot Evening," *New York American,* September 17, 1931, 13.

19. At the same time she was working on *Fast and Furious,* Hurston also was tapped to write sketches for another review with Grainger called *Jungle Scandals,* no doubt a riff on the popular, all-white *George White's Scandals.* A July 23, 1931 letter to Mason suggests the piece was a month away from beginning rehearsal, but there is no evidence that the project ever got off the ground. It is likely that some sketches in the collection Hurston copyrighted as *Cold Keener* were intended for *Jungle Scandals.*

20. For facsimiles of these program notes and a photograph of actors in *The Great Day,* see Lynda Marion Hill, *Social Rituals and the Verbal Art of Zora Neale Hurston,* 17–27. Based on the titles and descriptions of the pieces included in all these programs, they appear to be closely aligned with sections of *Mules and Men* (1934) and may have provided Hurston with a way to "rehearse" the work that eventually appeared in print.

21. "Rare Negro Songs Given," *New York Times,* January 11, 1932, 29. In a telling phrase, the *New York Times* reviewer referred to this emcee as an "interlocutor," a stock character from the minstrel show tradition. Leigh Whipper is remembered for appearances in the 1929 Broadway revival of *Porgy* (play based on DuBose Heyward's 1925 novel of the same title,

which was turned into the opera *Porgy and Bess* in 1935) and the 1937 production of John Steinbeck's *Of Mice and Men*. His best-known film role was the preacher in the William Wellman western, *The Ox-Bow Incident* (1943). Whipper is believed to be the first black member of Actors Equity and founded the Negro Actors Guild. In *From Sun to Sun* and *All de Live Long Day* the master of ceremonies role was played by Hurston herself. The Library of Congress has a recording of part of one of these performances (probably *All de Live Long Day*) featuring Hurston as the master of ceremonies.

22. Hemenway discusses *The Great Day* (and its subsequent revisions) at some length in *Zora Neale Hurston: A Literary Biography,* 175–186.

23. Qtd. in Maurice J. O'Sullivan and Jack Lane, "Zora Neale Hurston at Rollins College," in *Zora in Florida*, ed. Steve Glassman and Kathryn Lee Seidel, 134.

24. *Run-Through: A Memoir by John Houseman* (New York: Simon and Schuster, 1972), 205. It is interesting to note that a play entitled *Turpentine* by J. Augustus Smith and Peter Morell, subtitled a "Folk Drama of the Florida Pine Woods," was supposed to be the first play produced by the Negro Unit and would have been floating around during Hurston's tenure. Whether or not her exposure to this melodrama later inspired *Polk County*, her own play about a turpentine camp, may never be known.

25. Another Negro Unit in Seattle produced a version of *Lysistrata* set in Ethiopia, adapted by Theodore Browne, on September 17, 1936. It presented one performance before being shut down by a WPA supervisor whose wife was offended by the play.

26. During a tour of *Macbeth*, Wells took advantage of an actor's illness to play the title character in blackface for a week.

27. A recording of this performance is available at the Library of Congress along with other songs included in her plays.

28. No drafts of this unfinished play have surfaced, but a *New York Times* column dated February 1940 reports that the Southern Regional Conference was to present "a full-length Negro play by Zora Neale Hurston" on April 6 in Chapel Hill.

29. "Court Order Can't Make Races Mix," *Orlando Sentinel*, August 11, 1955.

30. Langston Hughes, "The Negro Artist and the Racial Mountain," *Nation* 122 (June 23, 1926): 692.

31. *Dust Tracks on a Road* (HarperPerennial edition), 172. Hemenway writes that "Hurston's conservatism grew primarily from three sources: an obsessive individualism that began with the self-confidence of Eatonville and expanded to generate great self-pride, almost a kind of egotism; a long suspicion of the Communist party and collectivist government . . . ; and the social science philosophy that informed her folklore collecting" (329). See *Zora Neale Hurston: A Literary Biography*, 329–333, for more on the last point.

32. In his review of *Their Eyes Were Watching God*, Richard Wright accused Hurston of perpetuating the minstrel tradition, the technique "that makes the 'white folks' laugh."

# A NOTE ON THE TEXT

The dates attributed to the plays come from one or more of the following sources, listed in order of primacy: (1) date of production; (2) biographical sources; (3) copyright date. Readers should be aware that plays for which we only have copyright dates may have been written significantly earlier.

When possible, we have used the earliest published edition as the copy-text, as the typed manuscripts contain numerous typographical and grammatical errors that Hurston obviously would have expected to be corrected by an editor. Most of the plays, however, exist only in typescript form. In cases where more than one typescript exists, we have, when possible, used the copy submitted for copyright to the Library of Congress. We have edited the typescript plays to conform to Hurston's general usage in her published works, especially *Mules and Men* (1935), which is based on much of the same material as the plays and, as her most anthropological work, attempts to provide an accurate depiction of what she described as "a cross section of the Negro South" (*Mules and Men,* 1) and its various dialect forms. Thus, we have inserted apostrophes in contractions (e.g., "ain't," "we'se") and consistently capitalized words like "Ah" and "Ah'm," which are presented inconsistently throughout the works and even within individual plays. Apostrophes have been added to those contractions that could be confused with other words ("'cause," "'round"); short-hand expressions ("thru") have been spelled out throughout. Handwritten emendations to the typescripts have been incorporated except where noted.

We have also edited the plays to facilitate reading and stage production. Hurston did not provide cast lists for many of these plays, and even when she did, they were often incomplete. We have created complete cast lists for each play, inserting character descriptions where they exist in the original. Character names within plays have been made consistent, as have her punctuation and spelling of stage directions ("downstage center" versus "down stage [center]"). These changes have been made silently.

In several instances, we inserted lyrics for songs within the text of the plays rather than appending them to the end, as Hurston sometimes did. Stage directions are at times fragmented and therefore confusing; in these cases we have edited for clarity. And in a few instances, we have amended dialogue for sense. In these cases, changes are noted either with square brackets or with endnotes.

Our desire to present a coherent collection of Hurston's plays necessitated minor rearrangement of elements such as scene descriptions, cast lists, and typographical arrangement of stage directions so that the same elements occur in the same order in each play. For example, in some cases the "Time" and "Place" descriptions appeared before the cast list, rather than with the descriptions of "Setting" and "Action." We have placed all of these descriptions together and presented them in consistent fashion.

We encourage those interested in further study of Hurston's work to consult the original scripts, many of which are held at the Library of Congress, where page images have been made available online.

# MEET THE MAMMA (1925)

**M**eet the Mamma is perhaps most significant for the contrast it provides to Hurston's later works. In Baltimore, Hurston lived several blocks from the city's theatrical district, and opportunities to see variety entertainment were plentiful in Washington and New York. This, her first dramatic work, imitates the musical comedies, vaudeville, and reviews that dominated the stage during the 1920s.

The play's plot is paper-thin and subject to the limitations of the form of the musical review; as one of the members of the chorus states in act 2, scene 3, "that's all a musical comedy is—Chorus." Yet the piece's many diversions convey an overwhelming sense of vivacity and fun. In addition to mother-in-law and Prohibition jokes, Hurston spoofs a variety of theatrical styles, including comic opera of the Gilbert and Sullivan type, domestic melodrama, and Ibsenesque tragedy over the course of a single scene. The quick shifts in tone and style, so different from the kind of book musical performed on Broadway today, were standard practice in the 1920s.

Hurston's unapologetic, even gleeful, incorporation of black show conventions such as the jungle dance, hyper-sexualized black women, and razor-wielding roughs would not have pleased didactic critics such as Du Bois in the 1920s and may trouble present-day readers as well. Nevertheless, here we can see a foreshadowing of the musical choices she would make in her later folk dramas: a combination of blues and soulful ballads.

# Meet the Mamma
## *A Musical Play in Three Acts*

CAST:

PETER THORPE, hotel proprietor
CARRIE, his wife
EDNA FRASIER, her mother
BILL BROWN, [Pete's] friend, a lawyer
CLIFFORD HUNT, [Pete's] uncle in Africa
ESSIE, cashier
BELLHOP 1
BELLHOP 2
WAITRESS 1
WAITRESS 2
MALE DINER 1
MALE DINER 2
FEMALE DINER
ANOTHER WOMAN
BUM 1
BUM 2
WIDOW
CAPTAIN AND SEAMEN'S CHORUS
BREWERY CHORUS
BATHING BEAUTY CHORUS
GUIDE
ZIDO, an African princess
WALLA WALLA, a warrior
WARRIORS
VILLAGE DRUMMERS (male)
VILLAGE DANCERS (female)

*Time: Present.*
*Place: New York, U.S.A.; the high seas; Africa.*

ACT ONE
Scene 1. *Hotel Booker Washington, New York City.*

*Setting: One half of stage (left) is dining room, the other is a lobby (right), with desk, elevator, etc. The dining room is set with white cloths, etc. Elevator is upstage exit (center). There is a swinging door exit right and left.*

*Action: As the curtain goes up, singing and dancing can be heard, and as it ascends the chorus of waitresses and bellhops are discovered singing and dancing about the lobby and dining room. (7–9 minutes)*

ESSIE:[1] *(Looking offstage right)* Psst! Here comes the boss!

*(Everyone scurries to his or her position and pretends to be occupied. Enter Pete,[2] right, in evening clothes and cane. Walks wearily through lobby and dining room and back again, speaking to everyone in a hoarse whisper.)*

PETE: Have you seen my mother-in-law? *(Everyone answers "No.")* It won't be long now before she comes sniffing and whiffing around. I ain't been home since yesterday, and I got to have an alibi. What can I tell 'em? *(He indicates mental anguish and strolls over to bellhops' bench.)*

BELLHOP 1: Tell 'em you sat up with a sick brother Mason.

PETE: Oh no, —can't say that. I'm supposed to have been at the bedside and funeral of every Mason in New York City. There ain't supposed to be no more left.

BELLHOP 2: Tell her you went to a bone yard to meditate and see if you could make 'em get up and gallop like Man O'War.[3]

PETE: Nope, that won't do. Every time I mention bones I get the shinny in my wrist. I'm trying to fool her, boy, not tell where I was. I have been out having a yellow time.

BELLHOP 1: What kind of a time is that?

PETE: Well, I been riding in a yellow taxi with yellow girls and spending yellow money and drinking yellow whiskey. Can't none of you men *(To the audience)* help out a fellow? You fellows are the poorest bunch of liars I ever seen. I could kill that smart aleck Peter.

BELLHOP 2: What Peter?

PETE: The one that killed Ananias.[4]

I just got back from the church house
And hear what the preacher said.
It seems that a dirty look from Peter
Laid the poor old scout out dead.
They say he was killed for lying—
I can't see why that should be
That they should croak a good old scout like him
And not do a thing to me.

Now this Pete was a busy body,
Like a prohibition hound

When regular guys are having fun
He's sniffing and whiffing 'round.
He ought to've been brought to justice
And given life in jail
With only his wife for company
And never a chance for bail.

'Cause Ananias was a liar
Much needed in every club
To fix up things to tell your wife
And alibi in any rub
He could fix up a tale for the landlord
And just lie a collector to death
And explain to the wife about the sick friend
And even explain your breath.

Now, why did they kill Ananias?
I need him beside me right now
With an income tax blank before him
That baby would be a wow!
Oh, why did they kill the best liar—
That one inspired cub!
If he were alive, I'll bet you a five
He'd be a member of my club.

*(As the song ends, Edna⁵ enters right. Pete sees her.)*

PETE: *(Stage whisper)* Ambush! *(He steps backward into the open door of the elevator and is flashed upward.)*

EDNA: *(Advancing to center downstage)* Where is your boss? *(She glares about and puts ear trumpet to ear.)*

ALL: I don't know.

EDNA: Just you let me lay my eyes on him!

*(She exits left. Giggling by the chorus. Reenter Edna, left, who proceeds quickly to the elevator which is coming down.)*

EDNA: I'll go upstairs and wait for him.

*(She pauses beside the elevator, but not where she can be seen by the persons on the elevator. As it reaches the floor, the door flies open and Pete dashes out toward exit, left, as she hurries toward elevator. They collide and both sit flat on the floor with feet and legs entangled. They sit there facing and glaring at each other for two full minutes. [Pete] speaks.)*

PETE: Well, Madam, if you'll pick out what belongs to you, I'll be satisfied with what's left. *(They both arise.)*

EDNA: Where have you been? *(Puts trumpet to ear.)*

PETE: *(Pretending [to be] drunken)* Thass chuss what I been trying to fin' out.

EDNA: You poor stretched out chocolate éclair—you! Just you wait till I put my mouth on you to my daughter, you ground hog!

PETE: Listen! *(He strides angrily toward her and prepares to speak into the ear trumpet. She removes it before he can say another word and stalks majestically out, right, leaving him gesticulating wildly.)* Five hundred dollars for a new cuss word! If she could hear without that trumpet, I'd set her ears on fire! *(Enter lawyer friend, [Bill,] left.)*

BILL: Why hello, Pete, how's tricks?

PETE: *(Sadly)* Pretty low, pal—suffering from an attack of mother-in-law.

BILL: *(Laughs)* Brace up. It's the first hundred years that worries a fellow.

PETE: What can I tell my wife? I'm simply crazy about her, but her mother! Gee, I wish I'd gone home last night!

BILL: I know, old man, how you feel.

PETE: Say, how do you know? You're not married.

BILL: Oh, I had a wife once, but her husband came and took her back. I'm going to breeze over and talk to my sweet stuff. Here comes your wife.

*(He crosses to the desk and converses with Essie. Pete exits left, hurriedly. Enter Carrie,[6] right, beautifully dressed but sad.)*

CARRIE: *(To Essie)* Is my husband here?

ESSIE: No, Mrs. Pete.

CARRIE: Well, when will he be in?

ESSIE: He didn't say.

CARRIE: He hasn't been home all night and I am terribly upset. He's so mean to me.[7]

I'm blue, I'm blue, so blue,
I don't know what to do
Because my man don't stay home;
Every night he has to roam
Because I'm his, he thinks me slow
But other men don't find me so.

Everybody's man is better to me than my own
Here me cry, hear me sigh
Oh listen to me moan
He cheats me, he cheats me and stays out all night long.
When he's out, they're hanging 'round
All those long, tall, teasing browns.
Oh, I could get loving, if I'd take a chance
They'll pay the fiddler, if I'll only dance,
But my mean pappa won't bring it home
Oh—everybody's man is better to me than my own.
Oh where is my wandering boy tonight?
Go search for him where you will
Go bring him to me with all his blight
And tell him I love him still.

*(Exit Carrie right.)*

BILL: *(Crosses to center)* Say Pete, why do you put those boots on the girls?

PETE: To keep the cake-eaters from gazing at their—er—limbs.

MALE DINER 1: Say! *(Bangs fist on table. Everybody starts.)* Can't I get any service here?

*(Two waitresses hurry to him. Both speak at once.)*

WAITRESS 1 AND 2: What can we do for you?

MALE DINER 1: You can take my order for one thing.

*(They take order books and prepare to write.)*

MALE DINER 1: Crab meat cocktail.

WAITRESS 1: *(Writing)* Yes.

MALE DINER 1: Hors d'oeuvres.[8]

WAITRESS 1 AND 2: Yes.

MALE DINER 1: Russian caviar.

WAITRESS 2: Yes.

MALE DINER 1: Broiled guinea fowl.

WAITRESS 1 AND 2: Yes.

MALE DINER 1: Endive salad.

WAITRESS 1 AND 2: Yes.

MALE DINER 1: Hot apple pie, fromage de Brie—black coffee.

WAITRESS 1 AND 2: Yes, anything else?

MALE DINER 1: No, do you think you can fill that order?

WAITRESS 1 AND 2: We can fill *anything*.

MALE DINER 1: *(Drawing a pair of stockings from his coat pocket)* All right, then. Have these filled and serve with the dinner.

FEMALE DINER: Waitress, tell your boss I want to talk to him.

PETE: Yes, madam, what can I do for *you?*

FEMALE DINER: What can you *do?* You can have these teeth replaced that I broke out on those durn dum bullets you served me for biscuits. I'll sue you good and proper!

PETE: Now madam—

MALE DINER 2: *(Rising)* Say, do the cooks have to go into a trance to find out from the spirit world whether they ought to cook an order or not? Now, you just go back there and tell 'em not to break up a séance on my account. I've only been waiting an hour.

ANOTHER WOMAN: *(Limps out of elevator)* Fifty thousand dollars' damages you got to pay me for ruining my shape on that bum killinator of yours. Oh, oh! Such pains.

*(They surround Pete, who tears his hair.)*

PETE: Great gobs of gun powder! The old jinx is after *me* all right. I'll *kill* myself! Gimme a gun!

FEMALE DINER: One of those biscuits would do just as well.

BILL: *(Aside to Essie)* I've got to do something to save my pal. He'll go crazy.

*(He exits right hurriedly. Enter Carrie.)*

CARRIE: Oh, here you are, sweetheart. *(She weeps.)* Oh, you'll break my heart yet, the way you do. Where were you last night?

*([Pete] puts his arm about her, but does not speak.)*

CARRIE: *(Angrily)* You've got to answer me! *(She thrusts his arm away.)*

ALL: And us too! Yes, answer us too!

ONE OF THE BELLHOPS: *(Pushes through the crowd)* Telegram for the boss.

PETE: Here. Get out of here before I do a murder. Take it away!! It's more trouble, I'll bet. *(Exit customers running.)*

CARRIE: *(Snatches it)* It's from some woman and you're afraid to open it before me. *(He throws up his hands helplessly. She opens it and reads.)* "Luababa, West Africa. Mr. Peter Thorpe, New York City. My dear nephew: Have discovered rich diamond mine. Come at once. Millions for you. Your uncle, Clifford Hunt." *(She dances around and flings her arms about Pete's neck.)* Just think, millions! Let's start at once.

PETE: I don't care half as much about a million as I do for[9] one of your kisses— a really warm, affectionate kiss.

CARRIE: *(Kissing him)*

Well, why do you stay away from home?

PETE:

Somehow a man just loves to roam.

CARRIE:

You often leave me all alone.

PETE:

With contrite heart I do atone,
But men are creatures strong to do
The things that they will shortly rue
But such are we. *(He hugs her closely.)*

CARRIE:

I see, I see.
I love you true.

PETE:

And I love you. *(He kisses her more—even her hands.)*
If life should hold no other bliss
Than having you, I would not miss
The rest, dear sweetheart mine.

*(They remain embracing for a moment.)*

EDNA: *(Enters left)* Carrie! Are you kissing that reprobate! *(They spring apart.)*

CARRIE: Mamma, he's explained everything all right.

EDNA: Oh, yes. He can make you believe the East River is not under Brooklyn Bridge!

CARRIE: Oh, look, Mamma, he's got a telegram from his uncle in Africa. He's got diamond mines worth millions and he wants Petey dear to come. Here. *(Hands [her] the telegram.)* Read it!

EDNA: Ha, ha! I know it's the truth!

CARRIE: But, Mamma, he wouldn't want us to come if he didn't have it!

EDNA: Well, if he's got millions, he's got wives by the hundred. Do you want to take your husband to a place like that?

PETE: *(Angrily)* Now I'll be damned. *(Edna removes the ear-trumpet. He swears silently.)* By heck, I'll go get one of those trumpets and hold [it] to her head until I give her an earful!

CARRIE: *(Holding to Pete's arm)* Honey, don't you think we'd better stay here and run the hotel? I've heard that Africa is very unhealthy for Americans.

PETE: No. I'm going and you're going to leave that walking bunch of trouble and go with me.

EDNA: If you let that piece of tripe talk to me that way, you're no daughter of mine.

PETE: Oh, how I wish she wasn't.

EDNA: Take my advice, Carrie, and stay here. He treats you bad enough right where the law allows only one wife to a customer—don't go one step with him. *(She draws Carrie to her.)*

PETE: *(Snatches Carrie to him)* This is my wife.

EDNA: *(Snatches her back)* She is my child.

PETE: She'll go with me. *(Jerks her back.)*

EDNA: She'll stay with me. *(Snatches her again.)*

PETE: Let Carrie speak for herself.

CARRIE: *(Looks sadly from one to the other)* I cannot say. Give me an hour to decide.

*(She kisses first Pete then Edna then Pete again and exits by the elevator.*[10] *Pete starts to follow, but she rushes away. Pete and Edna stand glaring at each other for a full minute. Enter Bill.)*

BILL: Well, Pete, I heard of your good luck. *(Edna exits glaring.)* Can't you work me into the scheme somehow?

PETE: Sure. You know, I wouldn't want all that wealth without you to help me spend it. You and Essie get married and come along.

BILL: Sure. We've been engaged long enough now. How about it, Essie?

ESSIE: *(She comes out from behind the counter)* No indeed. Bill[11] hasn't got but one case, so I can't marry a man who can't support me in the style to which I want to get accustomed. Here, take your ring. I wouldn't go to Africa with anybody at all. I'll be in the same fix with Brown Skin Cora.

BILL: Well, all I can do is grin and bear it, Essie. But what about this Cora?

ESSIE:[12]

Brown Skin Cora, from way down Dixie way,
Came up North, but did not want to stay—
Old Man Trouble—that's how[13] she felt
Was hitting her below the belt
So she rubbed her tummy, looked at her shoes—
And wailed them low-down belly-rub blues.

I want my good old chicken and stuff
    (*Hum[med, while rubbing belly]*) Um—um—um
I know I never got enough.
    (*Hum [and belly rub]*)
Want my chicken good and brown
With lots of gravy flowing 'round and 'round.
    (*Hum [and belly rub]*)
Oh, I wish my daddy would send for me
Buy me a ticket on the F.E.C.[14]
    Oh gravy, um—(*Hum [and belly rub]*)
And the sunshine of his kiss
Is another thing I miss
That's way down south in Dixie.

Brown Skin Cora, from way down Dixie way,
Came up North, but did not want to stay.
Old Man Trouble—that's how she felt
Was landing blows below the belt
So she sighed and shook her head
And this is what she said:

I want my good old chicken and stuff
    Um—um—um
I know I never got enough
    Um—um—um
I want my chicken good and brown
With lots of gravy flowing 'round and 'round
    Um—um—um
Oh, wish my daddy would send for me
Buy me a ticket on the old I.C.[15]
For the sunshine of his kiss
Is another thing I miss.

(*She returns to desk. Enter two men, one carelessly dressed; one rather soiled. Best dressed of the two advances to Pete. He speaks.*)

BUM 1: How do, Misther Thorpe. Will you gimme a dollar? (*He reels drunkenly.*)

PETE: I know you Jim, you want to buy gin. No, I wouldn't give you a cent! I don't give my money to liquor heads.

BUM 1: *(Offended)* You refuse me a drink?

PETE: Yes, I do!!

BUM 1: *(To Bum 2)* Clarence, come here. This man won't give us no money—throw a louse on him.

*(Pete makes a rush for him; he and his companion run to exit left. Here the man turns, bows politely but shakily.)*

Iss a nice day.

*(Exeunt. Enter dowdy lady right.)*

WIDOW: Mr. Thorpe, will you assist a poor widow? *(She uses her handkerchief to her eyes.)* I know you will, you're so kind.

PETE: Anything I can do except work or lend you money.

WIDOW: Oh, it's nothing as bad as that. *(She produces a piece of paper.)* Here's a song my dear husband wrote before he died, and I want you to sing it so I can sell it and make some money. You see, all the life insurance money is spent now—

PETE: And if you can't sell this*[—] (She hands him the paper)* You'll have to go to work.

WIDOW: Yes. *(Sniffs)* It's such a beautiful thing—so touching! It was the last thing he did before he was killed. *(She begins to weep.)*

PETE: *(Patting her on the shoulder)* There, don't cry. I'll sing it for you, or die in the attempt. *(He unfolds it and reads title aloud)* "Oh, Fireman, Save my Bustle!" *(To woman)* Say, what was your husband thinking about? All right, I'll try to sing it for you. Come on boys. *(To the orchestra)* Let's help the lady out. [*(Carrie enters while Pete sings.)*]

Oh, why must love and duty call
Such distances apart
And[16] why should such a burden fall
Upon a human heart?

*(Carrie turns toward Pete.)*

My lover calls with outflung hands
The one true man who understands
My heart and has its keeping.

*(She turns to her mother.)*

But duty says go not away
Tarry with me, oh stay and play
With heart and mind a'sleeping.

(Both rush downstage to her sides and take her hands.)

PETE AND EDNA: You must decide.

(She draws her right hand away from Pete and clasps her mother's neck. Her mother holds her. They hold the picture for a moment. Pete starts away. Reenter Bill.)

PETE: (To Bill, bitterly) Let's be off then to darkest Africa—the darker the better.

BILL: (Produces papers) We can leave in an hour—we two heartbroken men.

CARRIE: (Flies to Pete and catches his arm. He shakes her off; she flings herself about his neck.) I'll go with you. (Sings)

I wish to spread my wings and try
The sea of love and romance
I do not fear a cloudy sky
For danger does but enhance.

(They embrace.)

I steer my prow to the rising sun
And sail with you till the day is done.

(They kiss again.)

I'll say good-bye to Mother.

PETE:

We two must have each other.

(First quick curtain, but up again.)

BILL: To the ship, to the ship! Away!

ALL: To Africa to stay.

(Curtain.[17])


## ACT TWO
Scene 1. *Deck of ocean liner. Captain and crew on deck.*

CAPTAIN: (Sings)

O, I am the captain of this swift greyhound
A city of floating steel
It trips and slips through the bounding waves

So strong in prow and keel
Oh the mists may wrap
And the waves may slap
But they do not worry me
For I stand by heck, on the upper deck
Of the queen of the rolling sea.

CREW:

Yes, we stand by heck, on the strong steel deck
Of the mistress of the seas
We fling our sail to the howling gale
In the very teeth of the breeze
Oh we dance and sing and do the highland fling
And let the ocean rave
Some day we'll dock her
In Davy Jones' locker[18]
And go to a sailor's grave.

*([Captain] walks to rail and gazes out to sea with glasses. Crew exit whistling refrain "Yes we stand" etc. Enter Pete, Carrie, and Bill in becoming traveling costume. They lean on the rail.)*

PETE: Bill, take it from me, you certainly are missing something by not getting a swell wife like mine. Why, we've been alone for two days and I haven't had a dull moment. Here I've been married six months and this is the first time I've had a chance to love her like I want to.

BILL: Oh, don't rub it in.

PETE: Sorry old man, that was the verse you heard, I've got to sing the chorus.

Oh, what a sweet wife I've got
Oh ain't she some good looking peach
Oh, ain't I glad I saw her before you did
And got her away from her mamma.

BILL: *(Gets down on hands and knees. Howling like a dog)* Ow-O-oo-oo . . . I just hope the S.P.C.A.[19] comes along while you are abusing me like this.

PETE: *(Laughs)* Bear with me, Bill. But remember, we are two days out from New York and my troubles and going farther every minute. Hot damn! Just think of owning diamond mines. [*(To Carrie)*] Are you happy sweetheart?

CARRIE: I'd be happy anywhere with *you,* but I do hate to leave Mamma. I'm all she's got, you know. It will be such a long time before we'll see her again.

PETE: Yes, I know, dear, but we'll try to bear up under that. Just think of our vast diamond mines—[*Aside*] over here.

*(One of crew enters and places a steamer chair on stage.*[20] *Exit left. In a moment he reenters leading someone all wrapped in a steamer rug.)*

BILL: There's someone who ain't got their sea legs on yet.

*(They all look. Pete and Carrie start.)*

CARRIE: Why—why, it's Mamma! *(She runs to embrace Edna, who drops her rug and glares at Pete.)* Mamma, how did you get on board?

EDNA: Come on early and stayed in my stateroom. Just had to come to see how you made out. This is a public boat, ain't it?

PETE: Yes, but I wish I owned it for a few minutes.

CARRIE: Now, don't you two start again. Let's do something to amuse ourselves on this long voyage.

PETE: All right. But what would be fun for me would ruin your ma.

BILL: Let's get up a poker game. Nope, I guess you ladies couldn't understand that—let's make it craps.

EDNA: *(Sneering)* This is your husband's company.

CARRIE: I have it! Let's give shows. We can all take parts.

PETE: *(Proudly)* There's brains for you! Yes, let's give shows.

EDNA: I'd just love it! Let's go in the main saloon and start right away.

ALL: Yes, let's.

*(Curtain falls on deck scene; arises immediately on grand salon.)*

[Scene 2][21]

CARRIE: Let's give grand opera first.

BILL: Do you think we can do all that high singing?

CARRIE: Sure we can. We are on the high C's.

PETE: All right, let's give opera and make it up as we go along.

CARRIE: I'll be Galli Cursey.

BILL: I'll be John Philip Souse.

EDNA: And I'll be Rosa Raza.[22]

PETE: Gee, this is gonnter be a *very* rough party. Here, Mother, you got to sing contralto, and Bill, you get gin off your mind and sing bass. That's close enough to the cellar. I'll be Caruso. That's safe. Let's all go out and come back in our new characters.

*(All exit. Quick curtain.)*

[Scene 3]

*([Curtain] goes up again; a sea-side scene, ocean background. At left a great promontory; at right a tall tree. The rock opens a door and Edna's face appears. She sings.)*

EDNA:

I am rock of the earth
Who gives the mountains birth
And trundle sloping hills
And send forth rippling rills
It is my fate to watch and wait
Till time flies back to heaven's gate.

*(Bill's face appears in the foliage.)*

BILL:

A tree, I am a tree
That stands close by the sea
I hold the strong winds in my arms
And shout and laugh in the raging storm
I murmur love songs sweet and low
As through my leaves the breezes blow.

*([Carrie] sits upright and is seen for the first time to be a part of the sea.)*

CARRIE:[23]

I spent a long time by the sea
Telling my woes, it answered me
For I was feeling blue
And the sea was lovely too
For I love you, and you're not true,
And the moon breaks the heart of the ocean too
I wept and cried
The sad sea sighed
And turned a deep, deep blue.

I know what the wild waves are saying
I know what the wild waves do

I know what the seashells are whispering
And that's why I am blue
For the moon is an errant lover
That flirts with every breeze
And kisses the chill grey mountains
And caresses the trembling trees
I call through the night for his kissing light
I am the sad blue seas.

*(Enter Pete at right, riding in a new moon boat, low over the sea. He stops and kisses Carrie prolonged as she sings chorus, and exits behind rock at left, but returns at end of chorus and sings it as a duet with her. He is stationary while he sings, then exits right. Curtain.)*

## Scene 4

*([Curtain opens on a melodrama. A] brewery [is] painted on backdrop. Action [takes place] in brewery yard. All characters in fantastic dress; the men with razors in scabbards like swords.*[24] *[Enter Pete as Count Shake N. Roll, the hero.])*

COUNT:

I am the hero, full of prunes
I'll win in spite of all.

*(He crosses and stands downstage left, arms folded. [Enter Edna as Princess Heebie Jeebie.])*

PRINCESS:

I am the bloody villainess
Who's always dark and tall.

*(She crosses also and stands a little upstage. [Enter Carrie as Lady Sweet Patootie].)*

LADY SWEET:

And I'm the little heroine
As good as gold, by heck.

*[(Enter Bill as Lord Suds.)]*

LORD SUDS:

And I'm the skulking villiyun
Who gets it in the neck.

On with the opry!

*(All exit; dim lights. Enter chorus, all laughing, singing, drinking.)*[25]

CHORUS:

> Men—and other drinkers that's feeling blue,
> Gather 'round, I got good news for you—
> I see the tear drops in your eye
> I know your throats are dusty dry.
> You yearn for suds—you miss the pail
> The glistening bar—the shining rail.
> But keep your soul bright—let nothing dim it—
> Neither rum hounds—nor twelve mile limit[26]
> The way to do it from day to day
> Is do your daily dozen with old Coué.[27]

*(Chorus)*

> Quart by quart from date to date
> It's getting better and better
> Crate by crate in every state
> It's getting wetter and wetter
> Still by still and more and more
> The stuff is coming from every shore
> A straw vote shows how the wind is blowing
> Rum must go! And we must keep it going
> Coué, Coué, Coué,
> Just say this every day.

CHORUS MAN 1: Bring on more beer.

CHORUS MAN 2: It'll cost too much, I fear.

CHORUS MAN 1: Whaddye you keer, the boss will pay. He's wed today.

CHORUS MAN 2: *(Dropping his mug)* Will wed? I thought he was gointer get married. *(Shades his eyes with his hand)* Here comes my Lord of Suds.

*(There is a blare of trumpets. Lord of Suds enters. He laughs loudly and harshly. All the people flee.)*

LORD SUDS: [*(To the tune of "[The] Downward Road is Crowded"*[28])]

> Oh, today I'm gointer get married
> Married, married
> Oh, today I'm gointer get married
> To Lady Sweet Patootie toot.

[*(Enter Princess Heebie Jeebie.)*]

PRINCESS: Psst, my Lord Suds. She walks this way with the man I love. I would see her dead. They must not see my face. I must haste away.

*(She exits right. Lord Suds taps his razor significantly and crawls into a beer barrel. He speaks.)*

LORD SUDS: Ha! Here she comes now with that cake-eater Count Shake N. Roll. I shall polish him off before her very eyes.

*(Enter Lady Sweet on the arm of Count Shake. They advance to center stage.)*

COUNT: *(Sings)*

I love but thee, no fooling, kid.

LADY SWEET:

I'll go where e'er that thou shalt hid.

COUNT: *(Sits on barrel near the one in which Lord Suds hides. Sings)*

Sit on my knee.

LADY SWEET:

No, let us flee. I mean, let's go.

COUNT:

I tell thee no.

LORD SUDS: *(Rises out of the barrel)* Ha! I have you in my power, and you shall die this hour.

COUNT: *(Stropping his razor on his boots)* I fling thy false words back among thy false teeth. Prepare to fight.

*(He tests the edge of his razor. Lord Suds does likewise. They fight a duel. Lady Sweet runs back and forth wringing her hands. Enter Princess right.)*

PRINCESS: Ha, revenge.

LADY SWEET: *(Sings)*

Oh, courage love!

PRINCESS: *(Sings)*

Sweet revenge.

*(Lord Suds receives a fatal shall[29] and falls. Princess takes the razor from his hand and cuts a few strands of hair from her head and falls dying across his form.)*

LORD SUDS: *(Rises to sitting position and sings weakly)*

I think I'm through.

PRINCESS: *(Does same)*

I think so too.

LORD SUDS: *(Repeats business)*

My blood leaks out.

PRINCESS: *(Repeats business)*

I've got the gout.

LORD SUDS: *(Repeats business)*

I am dying.

PRINCESS: *(Repeats business)*

So am I.

COUNT: *(Sings)*

I wish they'd die.

LADY SWEET: *(Sings)*

And so do I.

*(Lord Suds and Princess sit up for the last time and gaze into each other's eyes soulfully.)*

LORD SUDS AND PRINCESS: *(Sing)*

Dy-y-ing—oh—ah—

*(Ends in dying shriek. They both fall back dead. Count plants his foot on Lord's body and strikes a pose. Curtain. [Curtain rises on a] drama. Setting: A living room. Father [Bill] reads the paper; Mother [Edna] knits; [Tom, the] husband [Pete] gnaws his fingernails and watches the clock.)*

TOM: Mother, Sadie left no message for me?

MOTHER: No.

TOM: Then?

MOTHER: Yes.

TOM: I feared.

*(Enter Sadie [Carrie] with several parcels. She removes hat and coat.)*

SADIE: Well, I am here, Tom.

TOM: Yes, you are here.

SADIE: Yes, here, *here, (She flings wide her arms)* here! Shut in with this thing between us.

TOM: Then you have kept something from me.

SADIE: Yes, but how can I blame you, or even me[?]

TOM: Terrible.

SADIE: Terrible? You clod! *(She rages up and down, tearing her hair)* How calm you sit with the universe falling in shards about us.

TOM: Clod? I? *(He leaps up and bites a piece of paper from a magazine.)* The fire that has raged within me all these months! God! You call me a clod! It bites into my very flesh. *(He rushes at her to strike her. She recoils.)* That you should bring this thing upon us[—]

*([Sadie] rushes to the table and tears open a parcel and returns triumphantly with a baby dress. She shows it to him and sinks in a faint to the floor. He revives her.)*

SADIE: I—I—didn't know, Tom. Mother never told me. *(She rises and rushes at her mother.)* You! You—to keep me in ignorance that smothers out all our happiness. You! Shirking your duty to the offspring God gave you. Oh Tom. *(She reels towards him.)*

TOM: *(Standing and holding the tiny garment in a dazed manner)* It too must suffer.

MOTHER: *(Half weeping)* I never dreamed. I never knew, dear. *(She puts her arms about Sadie)* But your father is the real culprit, not I. *(She faces her husband)* Now, will you speak for the happiness of our daughter and her unborn child[?]

*(Father reads the paper for a moment; lays it down, buries his face in his hand, but remains silent. The others draw near and wait breathlessly for a sign from him. At last he motions to speak.)*

FATHER: It has come at last!

*(Sadie weeps, Mother sinks to her knees, Tom grasps a handful of hair on either side of his head and stands glaring.)*

Before I married your mother, Sadie, I was rather wild.

*(Sadie becomes hysterical; mother is crawling about on hands and knees and Tom is eating up a newspaper.)*

Yes, I was wild and, and, rather fond of the girls.

*(Tom is attacked by St. Vitus' dance; Sadie is having convulsions and Mother is weeping softly.)*

So I wore tight shoes so often that I have an ingrown toe nail! There, my secret is told at last. Do you despise me utterly, my children?

*(He looks from one to the other of the three. No one answers him. He walks bare-headed to the door slowly. The others do not move until the door closes softly. Mother rushes out after him. They reenter. Sadie puts on hat and coat and looks questioning at Tom. He appears not to see her. She picks up the garment and steals softly out by another door. Curtain. [Curtain rises on a] musical comedy. Setting: Cyclorama, Atlantic City Boardwalk. Enter Pete [Pluto Water] and Carrie [Carbona Kleaner]*[30] *in appropriate costumes, hand in hand.)*

PLUTO: *(Sings)*

> I met a little girl down by the sea
> I looked at her, she looked at me.

CARBONA:

> And soon we'll be married.

PLUTO:

> Now we first met just yesterday
> Love at sight, sure right away.

CARBONA:

> No, neither of us tarried.

BATHING BEAUTY CHORUS: *(Dancing across, singing)*

> Married, they'll soon be married.

PLUTO: Now what next?

CARBONA: Dance, of course. That's always next in a musical comedy.

*(They do a dance and end with "Black Bottom."*[31] *Reenter Chorus dancing.)*

PLUTO: Looka here, Chorus, what are you doing back here again?

FIRST CHORUS LADY: Well, that's all a musical comedy is—Chorus.

*(They dance off left. Enter Mr. and Mrs. Kleaner [Bill and Edna], arm in arm.)*

MRS. KLEANER: *(Looking roguishly at Carbona and Pluto)* Remember *(She sways on her feet)* we was young once. *(She slaps her hand to her stomach—seasick gesture.)*

MR. KLEANER: *(Clutching his stomach also)* I'm seasick too; let 'em gwan marry if they want to—I mean God bless you, my children. Say! Stop this ship from shaking! *(He starts for his stateroom, but collapses on the floor upstage.)*

PLUTO: Carbona!

*(He stretches out his arms; she falls in them weakly. She is also seasick.)*

CARBONA: Oh Pluto Water! You're so strong and clean.

*(She clutches her stomach and attempts to run off right. When she reaches Mr. Kleaner's form she tries to step over it several times but the motion of the boat carries her backward each time with one foot lifted. At last she sinks down parallel to Kleaner. Mrs. Kleaner tries to approach Pluto as the chorus stagger in holding their stomachs. They open their mouths as if singing, but no sounds come out. They collapse all over the stage. Mrs. Kleaner turns to exit right, but collapses, parallel to Carbona. A look of triumph leaps to Pluto's face. He rushes over to the glass case on the wall that contains the axe and saw and tries to open it. He finds it locked. He rushes over to the prostrate form of his mother-in-law and does a wild savage dance of triumph about her. He looks about for a weapon, but sees none. At last on the table he sees a siphon of water and gets it, sending a stream into her face. He continues to dance and soak her with the carbonated water.)*

PLUTO: Not enough water for the old girl. I ought to sink the ship while she's all spread out! *(He is still prancing. Curtain.)*

ACT THREE
Scene 1

*Scene: African jungle at night and dawn. Curtain goes up on a dim lit stage. It is night. The southern cross[32] is seen in the sky. The dense mass of the jungle comes half way downstage toward the footlights.*
    *Action: As curtain goes up, the dim figures of the party can be seen downstage right, huddled together. There is a native guide.*

VOICE OF PETE: O-o-o wee! I'm scared. Bill, every time I think about you getting me into this, I could kill you before these lions and tigers get to us. *(There is the trumpet of elephants and the head of a big bull with huge tusks appears through the foliage.)* D-d-don't be scared, Carrie. I'm here.

*(More elephants appear thrusting their heads through the trees. They withdraw shortly and the roar of a lion is heard. They all huddle closer. The lion appears left but exits upstage center.)*

VOICE OF BILL: Whew! That was a close call! This is the *longest* night I ever lived through.

VOICE OF PETE: You ain't lived through it yet. We ought to've took a taxi through this jungle.

VOICE OF BILL: Look Pete, the sky is getting lighter. Day is breaking.

*(Lights grow brighter. Birds twitter. There are the distant sounds of tom toms.)*

VOICE OF PETE: *(To guide)* Let's start right now. The sooner we get there, the better. How much farther have we to go?

GUIDE: We will arrive within an hour.

*(It is now light, but the sun has not appeared. The party hurries across stage and exits downstage left. The sky is cobalt. The jungle is a riot of color. Curtain.)*

Scene 2. *Village of Luababa.*

*There is a rhythmic beating of tom toms, the playing of some deep stringed instrument and a chant before the curtain goes up.*

*Setting: Curtain discloses a totem pole, whose grotesque head breathes fire and smoke. Elaborate religious setting. Upstage to the right is an arch decorated with masks and symbols. It is the "Door of the Sun" (eastern gate). Village is painted on the backdrop. Jungle entire left.*

*Action: [Zido,] young girls, and men are doing tribal ceremonial dance about the pole and arch—Men with gorgeously painted shields and assegais—girls carry a single red flower. All wear ceremonial masks. A number of youths play the drums. One crouches over a large flat stringed instrument that sounds cello-like. All chant as one girl [Zido] does a solo dance before the pole, then all arise and join in. Enter party, left, and stand behind shrubbery until ceremony is over. Bill starts to applaud, but is stopped by Pete.)*

PETE: Cut that out. This ain't no show! This is church to them.

BILL: Is it? I got religion right away. I'm gointer join and I'll bet nobody ever catches me back-sliding.

CARRIE: *(Impatiently)* Tell the guide to take us on to the chief. I'm dead on my feet from this jungle tramping stunt.

BILL: *(Gazing at the native girls who are going upstage toward the village.)* Looka heah, I'll bet that girl *(indicating Zido[33] who lingers behind)* is the preacher. I ought to go over and confer with the pastor.

EDNA: No, you won't either. I'm tired. Let's go on to that village. *(She points upstage.)*

BILL: Pete, I think I'll stay around here and do a little missionary work. I feel that I've been living too selfishly and these poor heathens are dying for the light. Fact is, I could give my whole life to showing them things. *(Zido departs toward village.)*

PETE: Yea bo, I feel the missionary urge myself. Now I see why so many men dedicate themselves to the mission field. *(He motions to follow girls.)*

CARRIE: *(Angrily)* Pete! *(Pulls him back)* Never mind those hunks of chocolate gelatine. I'll do all the dancing in this family.

PETE: *(Comes back and hugs her gently)* Now darling, didn't your Sunday school lessons teach you not to be selfish? While you're trying to keep a whole husband to yourself, think of all the poor unfortunate girls with no husbands at all. Don't be selfish.

EDNA: *(Pointing toward village)* Look at all those vicious looking heathens coming! Suppose they try to eat us!

PETE: Well, *you* don't need to worry. [*(To guide)*] Go on out, Friday Night, and find out what's the idea.

*(The guide meets the warriors; they talk and gesticulate for a moment.)*

BILL: Pete, I'm getting all crazy about these Africans. They're so darned cheerful.

PETE: How can you tell?

BILL: Lookit all that dark brown skin! Pure baked-in sunshine, that's all!

*(Guide returns and salutes.)*

PETE: Well, what are they going to do with us?

GUIDE: The chief says, welcome to Luababa. Advance at once. The ladies to the left to rest and bathe, the men come directly to him.

PETE: What's his name?

GUIDE: Mwa Bibo Bike! The Master of Many Spears.

PETE: *(Turning on Bill)* Thought you told me he was my uncle? Instead of getting something to eat, we'll get butchered up plain and fancy. But if he spares us for one hour, I'll fix you! You splay-footed chocolate éclair! *(To guide)* Ain't there no way we can get back to the coast before he gets us?

GUIDE: No. He has known of your coming since you left the ship. His jungle eye has watched you. His spears reach for a whole day's march of the sun. He sent me to guide you.

PETE: *(Feels Bill's head)* This is the first time I knew that hair could grow on a rock. *(To Bill)* To think I left a hotel in Harlem to get et up in Africa.

BILL: Aw shut up! I was trying to be a friend to you and get you out of trouble in New York.

PETE: Trouble? There ain't nothing in New York to hurt me. 'Course there's a few thugs and bandits and gunmen and taxi-drivers and gunwomen, but outside of that—

EDNA: Stop that jaw grinding and come on. I'm not going back in that jungle to be killed by varmints. If I must die, let me be killed decently by folks.

*(They proceed toward village. Curtain falls for a minute to indicate lapse of time till they reach the village. Drums and beating all the time.)*

Scene 3. *King's palace in village.*

*Setting: A very ornate straw hut, center stage; other houses of village on backdrop. Bright silk hangings on walls. Leopard and lion skins on walls and floor, also bright patterned mats. There is a chair of ivory elaborately carved with symbols standing within the door of the palace. A small stream runs diagonally across the stage and off left, with a rude bridge. A large drum stands near the door (right) and the stringed instrument (left).*

*Action: Arising curtain reveals six of the girls standing in the stream in the September Morn pose.*[34] *The warriors are grouped at left. They are in striking war pantomime poses. Uncle Cliff*[35] *seated in the chair with Zido seated on a pile of grass cushions beside him. A man beats upon the drum; the other instrument wails and the guide enters with Pete and Bill, who are visibly frightened. They are led directly before Uncle Cliff and the guide signals them to kneel. They do so. The girls stand erect and make a gesture of welcome.*

UNCLE CLIFF: Where do you come from?

PETE: New York City, U.S.A.

UNCLE CLIFF: Get up quick and have cushions. Did you ever hear of the city of HushPuckanny, Virginia?[36] *(He signs to the girls and boys to retire.)*

PETE: *(Pleasantly surprised)* That's my home. Pete Thorpe is my name.

UNCLE CLIFF: Not my sister Sarah's boy.

PETE: *(Boastfully)* Put it here, Uncle Cliff. I heard you was in Africa. I come hunting you.

*(He kicks Bill. Bill grimaces.)*

UNCLE CLIFF: Well, well, I'm glad to see anybody from the U.S., let alone my own nephew. What are you doing in Africa?

PETE: *(Very haughtily)* I thought I'd sell my hotel in Harlem and look around a bit. I was sorter overburdened with a business and a mother-in-law. We sold the hotel before we sailed, but we still got the mother-in-law on hand.

UNCLE CLIFF: Well boys, you've come to the right place. There ain't a mother-in-law in my kingdom.

PETE: How come?

UNCLE CLIFF: As soon as a girl gets married here, we take her mother off and feed her to the lions.

PETE: You're *some* king. Put it here. *(They shake hands.)* But how did you come to get such a *good* system?

UNCLE CLIFF: Well, you see, back in Virginia I used to love a girl and her mother just kept us apart and married her to a New York guy. Well, there wasn't anything left for me in America, so I set out wandering and finally landed in Africa with a few cents in my pocket, a gun and a dozen cartridges. I didn't know where I was going and didn't care. I beat on through the jungle for days. Just as day was breaking one morning, I arrived at this village. I heard a great shouting and wailing and came rushing up through the Door of the Sun, gun in hand. You see, I didn't know that no mortal ever steps on that holy ground. A lion had gotten into the village and killed the chief and his wife. He was in easy range, so I raised my rifle and fired. He fell dead. The natives thought I was a god, coming at sunrise through the door of the sun, and killing the lion with the "stick with the voice." I wo[uld]n't let them make a god of me. I merely told them I had been sent to be their king. They gladly crowned me and neither the people nor I have had cause to complain. This girl is the daughter of the chief the lion killed. But I have raised her as my own. She was only a few months old when the lion got her parents. She is the Princess Zido.

BILL: Gee, I'm glad she's not Pete's aunt. I think I ought to kiss her to—er—sort of make her feel at home. *(Uncle Cliff pushes him back into his seat.)*

PETE: But, King—coming back to this mother-in-law business. Have you got a real hungry lion all ready?

UNCLE CLIFF: Sure, we got one expert lion—been getting 'em for years.

PETE: Naw siree! You don't want no old tired lion in this case. You ain't seen *my* mother-in-law. What you wants is a *young,* snappy one—wild and rearing to go, and extry full of appetite.

UNCLE CLIFF: Where *is* your mother-in-law?

PETE: She['s] with my wife wherever it is you sent them to bathe and rest.

UNCLE CLIFF: *(Clapping his hands)* We'll soon fix her up. *(A huge warrior appears)* Walla Walla, take your bunch of lion catchers and go catch me a young, vicious, hungry lion and have him here in half an hour.

*(Walla Walla salaams and departs right; drums are heard offstage. A big warrior rushes up to Uncle Cliff*[37] *and gesticulates wildly, jibbering in his native tongue. Uncle Cliff listens until he has finished.)*

UNCLE CLIFF: Well, bring them all in. *(Warrior exits.)*

BILL: What did he say?

UNCLE CLIFF: There has been a killing, so I must hold the inquest at once.

> *(Enter two warriors carrying a limp body of another. They deposit it before the king. Two others bring in a man between them. All begin to gesticulate. They jabber away and shimmy in their excitement.)*

BILL: What are they saying?

UNCLE CLIFF: They tell me that Mtesa here *(He points to the prisoner)* had caught a string of fish and the other man came up and took them. Mtesa threw a spear at him—you see, Mtesa is the best spearman in Africa—bar none—and so the other fellow is dead.

BILL: Well, what's your verdict?

UNCLE CLIFF: Death from natural causes. As good a spearman as Mtesa is, it's natural for a man to die if he aims at him. Case dismissed.

PETE: Say, Uncle King, do you mind us looking over your harem while we're waiting for the lion?

UNCLE CLIFF: I have none. Never have been married. If I can't have what I want, I won't have what I can get. But I'll have Zido and the girls to dance the "Birth of Love" for you.

> *(He claps his hands and the girls enter, followed by the male musicians. They take their places. Enter Carrie and her mother.)*

PETE: *(Whispers to Uncle Cliff)* Here comes my mother-in-law.

UNCLE CLIFF: She won't be your mother-in-law much longer.

> *(There is a lion's roar offstage. Uncle Cliff rises and places seats for the ladies. Bill and Carrie are on the left of the king; as Edna approaches to sit she stares at Uncle Cliff and he at her.)*

UNCLE CLIFF: Edna! My old sweetheart.

EDNA: Cliff!

UNCLE CLIFF: How did you find me?

EDNA: Following my daughter and her husband. I didn't know you were here, but—er—I'm mighty glad.

PETE: *(Aside)* That poor lion won't get no dinner right away. I can see that.

*(Edna moves to sit on the cushions.)*

Uncle Cliff: Wait, sit in this chair, Edna. I'm sorry it's no better.

EDNA: But that's your throne. You are a king.

UNCLE CLIFF: And you are a queen, if I got anything to say.

BILL: King, you ain't forgetting about the dance you promised us.

UNCLE CLIFF: *(To Zido)* "The Birth of Love," Zido.

*(The music begins and the chorus dances first, then Zido takes center stage. Bill and Pete indicate they are captivated by the dancers. Bill seems carried away by Zido.)*

BILL: *(Reaching into his vest pocket and producing a wedding ring)* I'm gointer lasso that shimmy and domesticate it. She's *mine!*

UNCLE CLIFF: Hey, wait awhile! You don't make love to a jungle girl like that. What you need to win her is a "love stick."

BILL: What is a love stick?

UNCLE CLIFF: I'll show you. *(He speaks to one of his warriors.)* He'll bring one in a minute. You'll have to learn to make "jungle love." *(The warrior returns with two or three clubs about the size of a baseball bat.)* This is the *great* love maker. *(He hands one to Bill.)*

BILL: *(Puzzled)* Say, King, what's the idea?

UNCLE CLIFF: *(With a wise wink)* My men tell me one love stick is worth a hundred compliments.

BILL: *(Enlightened)* I get you, King. Just leave me alone with the princess for a few minutes.

*(Uncle Cliff rises to go. He offers his arm to Edna and Carrie.)*

UNCLE CLIFF: Come Edna, I want you to see our diamond mines and select some stones for yourself and friends.

PETE: *(Astonished)* Real diamonds, Uncle Cliff?

UNCLE CLIFF: Sure. Come on and make your own selections.

PETE: *(Hurrying after party)* Lead on, not soon, but now if not quicker.

*(The party exits left; only Bill and Zido are left on stage. Bill practices several swings with the club, flexes the muscles of his arms, limbers up generally. Then with club in hand [he] approaches Zido who is picking flowers all the while. A warrior enters left with a club in his right hand. He is car-*

*rying a limp girl under the left arm. He exits right. Zido's back is still turned. Bill lifts his club to strike. Zido turns smiling sweetly and offers him a flower. He drops [the] club. He seizes her hand with the flower, kisses it. He leads her over to the throne. She sits on it. He kneels at her feet and pantomimes a proposal. She accepts. They kiss fervently. She breaks away and attempts to run offstage across the bridge.)*

BILL: *(Striking a commanding pose)* Zido! Come back here and finish kissing me! A half-kissed man is a mad man. *(He overtakes her. She yields coquettishly. He catches both of her hands in one of his and holds them behind her. Pulls her backward halfway to the ground, giving her a prolonged kiss.)* Boys, this is love! [*(Sings)*]

The fly's ankles, the eel's hips
Ain't got nothing on my baby's lips.

*(There is the sound of men's voices laughing offstage left and Pete and Uncle Cliff enter left. Pete is carrying a large bag which he drops on the floor as soon as he enters, and mops his head with handkerchief.)*

PETE: *(To Bill)* Man, we're rich! *(Points to the bag.)* All that's diamonds.

BILL: *(To Pete)* I found one too while you were gone. *(He and Zido look coyly at each other.)*

UNCLE CLIFF: I could see it coming, so I brought you this. *(He hands Bill a large stone)* That's for her engagement ring. I know you want to do things in United States style.

BILL: Thanks, King. I'm gointer marry her up so bad she'll never get over it long as she lives. *(He looks offstage left.)* But where are the women?

UNCLE CLIFF: They selected some little trinkets from my treasure room and went to try them on. *(Looks offstage left.)* Here they are now.

*(Enter Carrie and Edna.[38] They have taken off their American clothes and Edna wears a bandeau, a breechcloth, anklets, and headdress, all of diamonds. The wristlets are of ostrich. A high ostrich headdress rises from the diamond circlet about her head. Carrie wears no headdress of ostrich, but she has a similar outfit entirely of topaz. She advances to center stage.)*

PETE: *(In admiration)* Hot damn! I sure married my cupful when I roped this baby. *(He advances and hugs her.)* When I get back to Harlem, I'm gointer buy that old hotel for her to keep her shoes and stockings in.

BILL: *(In amazement)* Looka here, man, what's coming! *(All look to left at Edna.)*

PETE: Meet the mamma! My mother-in-law sure has been hiding something all these years. *(He rushes up to her.)* Mamma, give your boy a kiss! *(He snatches a kiss quickly and looks down at her legs)* I always knew there was something swell about you, but I couldn't find out what it was.

CARRIE: *(Pulls him away)* Don't be foolish!

PETE: Foolish? I'm sensible now.

BILL: *(To Zido)* Why—er—don't *you* wear diamond pants too, honey?

*(Edna laughs and pinches his cheek.)*

ZIDO: *(Making grimace)* Hurt too bad. Can't sit down.

PETE: Now let's set out for the coast and America.

BILL AND EDNA: The good old United States.

UNCLE CLIFF: You all speak so happily of America. You're going back. You'll leave me twice as sad and lonely when you leave as when you came. *(He looks significantly at Edna.)*

PETE: *(Pulling Carrie)* Come on, folks; let's get packed.

*(All exit except Edna and Uncle Cliff.)*

EDNA: *(To Uncle Cliff)* Aren't you coming too?

UNCLE CLIFF: Why should I leave?

EDNA: *(Coyly)* I thought maybe you had not forgotten me entirely.

UNCLE CLIFF: *(Warmly)* I haven't. I have thought of you every day for all these years. See that little bridge? I built it with my own hands. And while I was doing it, I thought a lot about you—and me.

EDNA: *(Eagerly)* Why?

UNCLE CLIFF:[39]

Life is but a walk o'er a bridge
With the river of life beneath
With years full of trouble
And moments of bliss
According to friends we meet.

Bright dreams quickly fading
Youth's days quickly gone
Soon fled to the nevermore
A stumble in shadow
A step in the dark
And then, love, the other shore.

*(Chorus)*
If you with me will walk o'er the bridge

I'll care not how years may go
We'll care not for clouds
We'll laugh at the rain
Nor mind how the river flows
We'll just clasp hands and wander along
Singing love's old sweet song
When summer's gone
And we cross the ridge
With skies no longer blue
I'll not be sad
I'll just be glad
I've walked o'er the bridge with you.

*(They do a second chorus as a duet, standing up on the center of the bridge. At the end the others enter, all dressed as they came. Uncle Cliff turns to them happily.)*

UNCLE CLIFF: Well, folks, Edna has consented to be the queen. Being now her boss, I command her to go and cover the royal shape. From now on, that diamond suit can be worn only before the royal eyes.

*(They laugh. She exits quickly. He comes down from the bridge and joins the others center stage.)*

UNCLE CLIFF: Say folks, who's gointer run my kingdom when I'm back in America?

BILL: So you're going?

UNCLE CLIFF: I ain't gointer stay.

PETE: Say, turn it over to Walla Walla. He's a noble lion-tamer. But say, tell him to let up on the mother-in-laws. They ain't so bad after all. I've got a peachy one since I know her better.

*(Reenter Edna dressed for travel. She puts Uncle Cliff's pith hat on his head and takes his arm.)*

UNCLE CLIFF: The bearers will take our baggage to the coast for us—and back to God's country—the U.S.A.! *(He takes Edna's hands and gazes lovingly at her)* I know we won't be sorry, will we?

*(Hand in hand they start over the bridge slowly. They sing in duet the chorus of "Over the Bridge" and the others fall in line. First Pete and Carrie, then Bill and Zido. They sing to curtain. It goes up again for a minute and natives are dancing farewell to them boisterously.)*

CURTAIN

# COLOR STRUCK (1926)

**C**olor Struck, along with the following play, *Spears,* constitute Hurston's calling card to the Harlem theater world. The two plays, along with the short stories "Spunk" and "Black Death," all won prizes in the first *Opportunity* literary contest organized by Charles S. Johnson in 1925. Judged by a panel of white and black writers, including Fannie Hurst, Eugene O'Neill, Alain Locke, and James Weldon Johnson, Hurston literally stole the show: she not only won the second place award in drama for *Color Struck,* but also took second place in fiction for "Spunk" as well as honorable mentions for *Spears* and "Black Death." The four works taken together show that even at this early point in her career, Hurston was experimenting with different ways to represent the black experience: *Color Struck* is a "social problem" play examining the pervasiveness of "colorism" in African American society, while *Spears,* set in an imaginary African kingdom, indulges in the primitivism that was all the rage at the time. "The Black Death" and "Spunk," in turn, are set in Eatonville; neither functions as "propaganda" in the Du Boisian sense, but foreshadow instead Hurston's turn toward the folk in the late 1920s and 1930s.

Although never produced, *Color Struck* has received critical attention because of its treatment of the theme of "colorism"—the tendency within the black population to privilege those of lighter skin color. To be "color struck," in the context of the play, means to accept the premise that light skin equals desirability in sexual and economic terms, a complete internalization of white racial values. The play begins in 1900 in a Florida Jim Crow railway car where couples are traveling to a regional cakewalk dance competition. The cakewalk originated in the antebellum south as a mockery by plantation slaves of their masters' formal ballroom dance, but it later came to be appreciated it for its own sake. A combination of stiff elegance and a rambunctious, prideful strut, the dance spurred interest that led to competitions where the winners took home a cake, at first a mean cornbread cake on the plantation and after the Civil War, a highly decorated pastry. By the turn of the century, the cakewalk had become widely imitated by whites and was absorbed into minstrel shows as a closing number. But it was also appropriated by black artists who celebrated it in musicals such as *Clorindy, or The Origin of the Cakewalk* in 1898, the *Creole Show* in 1899, and in the black-only ballroom setting represented in *Color Struck.*

The play opens in a Jim Crow railway car; however, there are no complaints of segregation or inequality, only jocularity and a proud sense of community. This harmony is broken with the entrance of Emmaline (called Emma) and her boyfriend John, whom she accuses of being interested in "yellow" or "half-white girls." Despite John's sincere dedication and commitment, it is clear that Emma loathes her own dark skin to the point that she refuses to dance when they reach the venue, denying her own performance of self and the symbolic celebration of their union. When the play jumps twenty years ahead, Emma's poor sense of self has manifested itself in economic terms. Poor and abandoned with a sick mulatto child by her white lover (who never appears), she hates herself even more with John's reappearance.

Although *Color Struck* can arguably be a mirror reflecting our own color prejudices, the play is more than a morality tale against racial self-hatred or a plea against self-segregation. Possessive and destructive love (exemplified by Emma's line "jealous love is the only kind I got") was a recurring theme throughout Hurston's career. From her early short story "Under the Bridge" to *Seraph on the Suwanee*, Hurston was interested in how the human heart finds ways to seed its own destruction. The tragic ending of Hurston's play asks us questions about the color of our own failings and how we visit them on our loved ones.

# Color Struck
## *A Play in Four Scenes*

CAST:

JOHN TURNER, a light brown-skinned man
EMMALINE BEAZELY,[1] a black woman
EFFIE, a mulatto girl
DINKY
ADA
WESLEY, a boy who plays an accordion
JOE CLARKE
OLD MAN LIZZIMORE
LOU LILLIAN, Emma's daughter, a very white girl
RAILWAY CONDUCTOR
DOCTOR
MAN 1
MAN 2
MAN 3
ST. AUGUSTINE MAN
SEVERAL WHO PLAY MOUTH ORGANS, GUITARS, BANJOS
DANCERS, PASSENGERS, etc.

*Time: Twenty years ago and present.*
*Place: A Southern city.*

### Scene 1

*Setting: Early night. The inside of a "Jim Crow"[2] railway coach. The car is parallel to the footlights. The seats on the downstage side of the coach are omitted. There are the luggage racks above the seats. The windows are all open. There[3] are exits in each end of the car—right and left.*

*Action: Before the curtain goes up there is the sound of a locomotive whistle and a stopping engine, loud laughter, many people speaking at once, good-natured shrieks, strumming of stringed instruments, etc. The ascending curtain discovers a happy lot of Negroes boarding the train dressed in the gaudy, tawdry best of 1900. They are mostly in couples—each couple bearing a covered-over market basket which the men hastily deposit in the racks as they scramble for seats. There is a little friendly pushing and shoving. One pair just miss a seat three times, much to the enjoyment of the crowd. Many "plug" silk hats are in evidence, also sun-flowers in button holes. The women are showily dressed in the manner of the time, and quite conscious*

35

*of their finery. A few seats remain unoccupied. Enter Effie left, above, with a basket.*

DINKY: (*Standing, lifting his "plug" in a grand manner*) Howdy do, Miss Effie, you'se lookin' jes' lak a rose. (*Effie blushes and is confused. She looks up and down for a seat.*) Fack is, if you wuzn't walkin' 'long, Ah'd think you *wuz* a rose— (*He looks timidly behind her and the others laugh.*) Looka here, where's Sam at?

EFFIE: (*Tossing her head haughtily*) I don't know an' I don't keer.

DINKY: (*Visibly relieved*) Then lemme scorch you to a seat. (*He takes her basket and leads her to a seat [in the] center of the car, puts the basket in the rack and seats himself beside her with his hat at a rakish angle. Sliding his arm along the back of the seat*) How come Sam ain't heah—y'all on a bust?

EFFIE: (*Angrily*) A man dat don't buy me nothin' tuh put in *mah* basket, ain't goin' wid *me* tuh no cake walk. (*The hand on the seat touches her shoulder and she thrusts it away.*) Take yo' arms from 'round me, Dinky! Gwan hug yo' Ada!

DINKY: (*In mock indignation*) Do you think I'd look at Ada when Ah got a chance tuh be wid you? Ah always wuz sweet on you, but you let old Mullet-head Sam cut me out.

MAN 1: (*With head out of the window*) Just look at de darkies coming! (*With head inside coach*) Hey, Dinky! Heah come Ada wid a great big basket.

(*Dinky jumps up from beside Effie and rushes to exit right. In a moment they reenter and take a seat near entrance. Everyone in coach laughs. [Ada] turns and calls back to Effie.*)

ADA: Where's Sam, Effie?

EFFIE: Lord knows, Ada.

ADA: Lawd a mussy! Who you gointer walk de cake wid?

EFFIE: Nobody, Ah reckon. John and Emma gointer win it nohow. They's the bestest cake-walkers in dis state.

ADA: You'se better than Emma any day in de week. Cose Sam cain't walk lak[4] John. (*She stands up and scans the coach.*) Looka heah, ain't John an' Emma going? They ain't on heah!

(*The locomotive bell begins to ring.*)

EFFIE: Mah Gawd, s'pose dey got left!

MAN 1: (*With head out of window*) Heah they come, nip and tuck—whoo-ee! They'se gonna make it! (*He waves excitedly.*) Come on Jawn! (*Everybody crowds the windows, encouraging them by gesture and calls. As the whistle blows twice, and the train begins to move, they enter panting and laughing at left. The only seat left is the one directly in front of Effie.*)

DINKY: (*Standing*) Don't y'all skeer us no mo' lak dat! There couldn't be no cake walk 'thout y'all. Dem shad-mouf[5] St. Augustine coons would win dat cake and we would have tuh kill 'em all bodaciously.

JOHN: It was Emmaline nearly made us get left. She says I wuz smiling at Effie on the street car and she had to get off and wait for another one.

EMMA: (*Removing the hatpins from her hat, turns furiously upon him*) You wuz grinning at her and she wuz grinning back jes' lak a ole chessy cat!

JOHN: (*Positively*) I wuzn't.

EMMA: (*About to place her hat in rack*) You wuz. I seen you looking jes' lak a possum.

JOHN: I wuzn't. I never gits a chance tuh smile at nobody—you won't let me.

EMMA: Jes' the same every time you sees a yaller face, you *takes* a chance. (*They sit down in peeved silence for a minute.*)

DINKY: Ada, les' we all sample de basket. I bet you got huckleberry pie.

ADA: No I ain't, I got peach an' tater pies, but we ain't gonna tetch a thing tell we gits tuh de hall.

DINKY: (*Mock alarm*) Naw, don't do dat! It's all right tuh save the fried chicken, but pies is *always* et on trains.

ADA: Aw shet up! (*He struggles with her for a kiss. She slaps him but finally yields.*)

JOHN: (*Looking behind him*). Hellow, Effie, where's Sam?

EFFIE: 'Deed, I don't know.

JOHN: Y'all on a bust?

EMMA: None ah yo' bizness, you got enough tuh mind yo' own self. Turn 'round!

(*She puts up a pouting mouth and he snatches a kiss. She laughs just as he kisses her again and there is a resounding smack which causes the crowd to laugh. And cries of "Oh you kid!" "Salty dog!" Enter conductor, left, calling tickets cheerfully and laughing at the general merriment.*)

RAILWAY CONDUCTOR: I hope somebody from Jacksonville wins this cake.

JOHN: You live in the "Big Jack"?

RAILWAY CONDUCTOR: Sure do. And I wanta taste a piece of that cake on the way back tonight.

JOHN: Jes' rest easy—them Augustiners ain't gonna smell it. (*Turns to Emma.*) Is they, baby?

EMMA: Not if Ah kin help it.

(*Somebody with a guitar sings: "Ho Babe, Mah Honey 'Tain't No Lie." The conductor takes up tickets, passes on and exits right.*)

WESLEY: Look heah, you cake walkers—y'all oughter git up and limber up yo' joints. I heard them folks over to St. Augustine been oiling up wid goose-grease, and over to Ocala they been rubbing down in snake oil.

WOMAN'S VOICE: You better shut up, Wesley, you just joined de church last month. Somebody's going to tell the pastor on you.

WESLEY: Tell it, tell it, take it up and smell it. Come on out, you John and Emma and Effie, and limber up.

JOHN: Naw, we don't wanta do our walking steps—nobody won't wanta see them when we step out at the hall. But we kin do something else just to warm ourselves up.

(*Wesley begins to play "Goo Goo Eyes" on his accordion, the other instruments come in one by one and John and Emma step into the aisle and "parade" up and down the aisle—Emma holding up her skirt, showing the lace on her petticoats. They two-step back to their seat amid much applause.*)

WESLEY: Come on out, Effie! Sam ain't heah so you got to hold up his side too. Step on out.

(*There is a murmur of applause as she steps into the aisle. Wesley strikes up "I'm Gointer Live Anyhow Till I Die." It is played quite spiritedly as Effie swings into the pas-me-la[6]—*)

WESLEY: (*In ecstasy*) Hot stuff I reckon! Hot stuff I reckon!

(*The musicians are stamping. Great enthusiasm. Some clap time with hands and feet. She hurls herself into a modified Hoochy Koochy,[7] and finishes up with an ecstatic yell. There is a babble of talk and laughter and exultation.*)

JOHN: (*Applauding loudly*) If dat Effie can't step nobody can.

EMMA: Course you'd say so 'cause it's her. Everything she do is pretty to you.

JOHN: (*Caressing her*) Now don't say that, honey. Dancing is dancing no matter who is doing it. But nobody can hold a candle to you in nothing.

(*Some men are heard tuning up—getting pitch to sing. Four of them crowd together in one seat and begin the chorus of "Daisies Won't Tell." John and Emma grow quite affectionate.*)

JOHN: (*Kisses her*) Emma, what makes you always picking a fuss with me over some yaller girl? What makes you so jealous, nohow? I don't do nothing.

*(She clings to him, but he turns slightly away. The train whistle blows, there is a slackening of speed. Passengers begin to take down baskets from their racks.)*

EMMA: John! John, don't you want me to love you, honey?

JOHN: (*Turns and kisses her slowly*) Yes, I want you to love me, you know I do. But I don't like to be accused o' ever' light colored girl in the world. It hurts my feeling. I don't want to be jealous like you are.

*(Enter at right conductor, crying "St. Augustine, St. Augustine." He exits left. The crowd has congregated at the two exits, pushing good-naturedly and joking. All except John and Emma. They are still seated with their arms about each other.)*

EMMA: (*Sadly*) Then you don't want my love, John, 'cause I can't help mahself from being jealous. I loves you so hard, John, and jealous love is the only kind I got.

*(John kisses her very feelingly.)*

Just for myself alone is the only way I knows how to love.

*(They are standing in the aisle with their arms about each other as the curtain falls.)*

## Scene 2

*Setting: A weather-board hall.*[8] *A large room with the joists bare. The place has been divided by a curtain of sheets stretched on*[9] *a rope across from left to right. From behind the curtain there are occasional sounds of laughter, a note or two on a stringed instrument or accordion. General stir. That is the dance hall. The front is the ante-room where the refreshments are being served. A "plank" seat runs all around the hall, along the walls. The lights are kerosene lamps with reflectors. They are fixed to the wall. The lunch-baskets are under the seat. There is a table on either side upstage with a woman behind each. At one, ice cream is sold, at the other, roasted peanuts and large red-and-white sticks of peppermint candy.*

*People come in by twos and threes, laughing, joking, horse-plays, gauchely flowered dresses, small waists, bulging hips and busts, hats worn far back on the head, etc. People from Ocala greet others from Palatka, Jacksonville, St. Augustine, etc. Some find seats in the ante-room, others pass on into the main hall. Enter the Jacksonville delegation, laughing, pushing proudly.*

DINKY: Here we is, folks—here we *is*. Gointer take dat cake on back tuh Jacksonville where it belongs.

ST. AUGUSTINE MAN: Gwan! Whut wid you mullet-head Jacksonville coons know whut to do wid a cake? It's gointer stay right here in Augustine where de *good* cake walkers grow.

DINKY: 'Tain't no walkers never walked till John and Emmaline prance out—you mighty come a tootin'.

(*Great laughing and joshing as more people come in. John and Emma are encouraged, urged on to win.*)

EMMA: Let's we git a seat, John, and set down.

JOHN: Sho will—nice one right over there.

(*They push over to wall seat, place basket underneath, and sit. Newcomers shake hands with them and urge them on to win.*
  *Enter Joe Clarke and a small group. He is a rotund, expansive man with a liberal watch chain and charm.*)

DINKY: (*Slapping Clarke on the back*) If you don't go 'way from here! Lawdy, if it ain't Joe.

CLARKE: (*Jovially*) Ah thought you had done forgot us people in Eatonville since you been living up here in Jacksonville.

DINKY: Course Ah ain't. (*Turning.*) Looka heah folks! Joe Clarke oughta be made chairman uh dis meetin—Ah mean Past Great-Grand Master of Ceremonies, him being the onliest mayor of de onliest colored town in de state.

GENERAL CHORUS: Yeah, let him be—thass fine, *etc.*

DINKY: (*Setting his hat at a new angle and throwing out his chest*) And *Ah'll* scorch him to de platform. Ahem!

(*Sprinkling of laughter as Joe Clarke is escorted into the next room by Dinky.*
  *The musicians are arriving one by one during this time. A guitar, accordion, mouth organ, banjo, etc. Soon there is a rapping for order heard inside and the voice of Joe Clarke.*)

CLARKE: Git yo' partners one an' all for de gran' march! Git yo' partners, gentmens!

MAN 2: (*Drawing basket from under bench*) Let's we all eat first.

(*John and Emma go buy ice cream. They coquettishly eat from each other's spoons. Old Man Lizzimore crosses to Effie and removes his hat and bows with a great flourish.*)

LIZZIMORE: Sam ain't here t'night, is he, Effie.

EFFIE: (*Embarrassed*) Naw suh, he ain't.

LIZZIMORE: Well, you like chicken? (*Extends arm to her.*) Take a wing! (*He struts her up to the table amid the laughter of the house. He wears no collar.*)

JOHN: (*Squeezes Emma's hand*) You certainly is a ever loving mamma—when you ain't mad.

EMMA: (*Smiles sheepishly*) You oughtn't to make me mad then.

JOHN: Ah don't make you! You makes yo'self mad, den blame it on me. Ah keep on tellin' you Ah don't love nobody but you. Ah knows heaps uh half-white girls Ah could git ef Ah wanted to. But (*He squeezes her hand again*) Ah jus' wants *you!* You know what they say! De darker de berry, de sweeter de taste!

EMMA: (*Pretending to pout*) Oh, you tries to run over me an' keep it under de cover, but Ah won't let yuh. (*Both laugh.*) Les' we eat our basket!

JOHN: All right. (*He pulls the basket out and she removes the table cloth. They set the basket on their knees and begin to eat fried chicken.*)

MALE VOICE: Les' everybody eat—motion's done carried. (*Everybody begins to open baskets. All have fried chicken. Very good humor prevails. Delicacies are swapped from one basket to the other. John and Emma offer the man next [to] them some supper. He takes a chicken leg. Effie crosses to John and Emma with two pieces of pie on a plate.*)

EFFIE: Y'll have a piece uh mah blueberry pie—it's mighty nice! (*She proffers it with a timid smile to Emma who freezes up instantly.*)

EMMA: Naw! We don't want no pie. We got coconut layer-cake.

JOHN: Ah—Ah think Ah'd choose a piece uh pie, Effie. (*He takes it.*) Will you set down an' have a snack wid us? (*He slides over to make room.*)

EFFIE: (*Nervously*) Ah, naw, Ah got to run on back to mah basket, but Ah thought maybe y'all mout' want tuh taste mah pie. (*She turns to go.*)

JOHN: Thank you, Effie. It's mighty good, too.

(*He eats it. Effie crosses to her seat. Emma glares at her for a minute, then turns disgustedly away from the basket. John catches her shoulder and faces her around.*)

JOHN: (*Pleadingly*) Honey, be nice. Don't act lak dat!

EMMA: (*Jerking free*) Naw, you done ruint mah appetite now, carryin' on wid dat punkin-colored old gal.

JOHN: Whut kin Ah do? If you had a acted polite Ah wouldn't a had nothin' to say.

EMMA: Naw, youse jus' hog-wile ovah her 'cause she's half-white! No matter whut Ah say, you keep carryin' on wid her. Act polite? Naw, Ah ain't gonna be deceitful an' bust mah gizzard fuh nobody! Let her keep her dirty ole pie ovah there where she is!

JOHN: (*Looking around to see if they are overheard*) Sh-sh! Honey, you mustn't talk so loud.

EMMA: (*Louder*) Ah—Ah ain't gonna bite mah tongue! If she don't like it she can lump it. Mah back is broad—(*John tries to cover her mouth with his hand.*) She calls herself a big cigar, but *I* kin smoke her!

(*The people are laughing and talking for the most part and pay no attention. Effie is laughing and talking to those around her and does not hear the tirade. The eating is over and everyone is going behind the curtain. John and Emma put away their basket like the others, and sit glum. Voice of master of ceremonies [Joe Clarke] can be heard from beyond curtain announcing the pas-me-la contest. The contestants, mostly girls, take the floor. There is no music except the clapping of hands and the shouts of "Parse-me-lah" in time with the hand-clapping. At the end [Clarke] announces winner. Shadows seen on curtain.*)

CLARKE: Mathilda Clarke is winner—if she will step forward she will receive a beautiful wool[10] fascinator. (*The girl goes up and receives it with great hand-clapping and good humor.*) And now since the roosters is crowin' foah midnight, an' most of us got to git up an' go to work tomorrow, the Great Cake Walk will begin. Ah wants de floor cleared, 'cause de representatives of de several cities will be announced an' we wants 'em to take de floor as their names is called. Den we wants 'em to do a gran' promenade roun' de hall. An' they will then commence to walk fuh de biggest cake ever baked in dis state. Ten dozen eggs—ten pounds of flour—ten pounds of butter, and so on and so forth. Now then—(*He strikes a pose*) for St. Augustine—Miss Lucy Taylor, Mr. Ned Coles.

(*They step out amid applause and stand before stage.*)

For Daytona—Miss Janie Bradley, Enoch Nixon.

(*Same business.*)

For Ocala—Miss Docia Boger, Mr. Oscar Clarke.

(*Same business.*)

For Palatka—Miss Maggie Lemmons, Mr. Senator Lewis.

(*Same business.*)

And for Jacksonville, the most popular walkers in de state—Miss Emmaline Beazeley, Mr. John Turner.

*(Tremendous applause. John rises and offers his arm grandiloquently to Emma.)*

EMMA: *(Pleadingly, and clutching his coat)* John, let's we all don't go in there with all them. Let's we all go on home.

JOHN: *(Amazed)* Why, Emma?

EMMA: 'Cause, 'cause all them girls is going to [be] pulling and hauling on you, and—

JOHN: *(Impatiently)* Shucks! Come on. Don't you hear the people clapping for us and calling our names? Come on!

*(He tries to pull her up—she tries to drag him back.)*

Come on, Emma! 'Tain't no sense in your acting like this. The band is playing for us. Hear 'em? *(He moves feet in a dance step.)*

EMMA: Naw, John, Ah'm skeered. I loves you—I—

*(He tries to break away from her. She is holding on fiercely.)*

JOHN: I got to go! I been practicing almost a year—I—we done come all the way down here. I can walk the cake, Emma—we got to—I got to go in! *(He looks into her face and sees her tremendous fear.)* What you skeered about?

EMMA: *(Hopefully)* You won't go in[11]—You'll come on go home with me all by ourselves. Come on John. I can't, I just can't go in there and see all them girls—Effie hanging after you—

JOHN: I got to go in—*(He removes her hand from his coat)*—whether you come with me or not.

EMMA: Oh—them yaller wrenches! How I hate 'em! They gets everything they wants—

CLARKE: [*(From inside)*] We are waiting for the couple from Jacksonville— Jacksonville! Where is the couple from—

*(Wesley parts the curtain and looks out.)*

WESLEY: Here they is out here spooning! You all can't even hear your names called. Come on John and Emma.

JOHN: Coming. *(He dashes inside. Wesley stands looking at Emma in surprise.)*

WESLEY: What's the matter, Emma? You and John spatting again? *(He goes back inside.)*

EMMA: *(Calmly bitter)* He went and left me. If we is spatting we done had our last one. *(She stands and clenches her fists.)* Ah, mah God! He's in there with her—Oh, them half whites, they gets everything, they gets every-thing everybody else wants! The men, the jobs—everything! The whole world is got a sign on it. Wanted: Light colored. Us blacks was made for cobble stones. (*She muffles a cry and sinks limp upon the seat.*)

CLARKE: [(*From inside*)] Miss Effie Jones will walk for Jacksonville with Mr. John Turner in place of Miss Emmaline Beazeley.

Scene 3

*[The] dance hall, decorated with palmetto leaves and Spanish moss—a flag or two. Orchestra consists of guitar, mandolin, banjo, accordion, church organ and drum.*

*Emma springs to her feet and flings the curtains wide open. She stands staring at the gay scene for a moment defiantly then creeps over to a seat along the wall and shrinks into the Spanish moss, motionless.*[12]

CLARKE: (*On platform*) Couples take yo' places! When de music starts, gentle-men parade yo' ladies once 'round de hall, den de walk begins.

(*The music begins. Four men come out from behind the platform bearing a huge chocolate cake. The couples are "prancing" in their tracks. The men lead off the procession with the cake—the contestants make a grand slam around the hall.*)

Couples to de floor! Stan' back, ladies an' gentlemen—give 'em plenty room.

(*Music changes to "Way Down in Georgia." Orchestra sings. Effie takes the arm that John offers her and they parade to the other end of the hall. She takes her place. John goes back upstage to the platform, takes off his silk hat in a graceful sweep as he bows deeply to Effie. She lifts her skirts and curt-sies to the floor. Both smile broadly. They advance toward each other, meet midway, then, arm in arm, begin to "strut." John falters as he faces her, but recovers promptly and is perfection in his style. Fervor of spectators grows until all we are taking part in some way—either hand-clapping or singing the words. [After seven to nine minutes,] they have reached frenzy. Quick curtain. It stays down a few seconds to indicate ending of contest and goes up again on John and Effie being declared winners by [the] judges.*)

CLARKE: (*On platform, with John and Effie on the floor before him*) By unani-mous decision de cake goes to de couple from Jacksonville!

(*Great enthusiasm. The cake is set down in the center of the floor and the winning couple parade around it arm and arm. John and Effie circle the cake happily and triumphantly. The other contestants, and then the entire assembly, fall in behind and circle the cake, singing and clapping. The fes-*

*tivities continue. The Jacksonville quartet step upon the platform and sing a verse and chorus of "Daisies Won't Tell." Cries of "Hurrah for Jacksonville! Glory for the big town," "Hurrah for Big Jack.")*

MAN 3: (*Seeing Emma*) You're from Jacksonville, ain't you? (*He whirls her around and around.*) Ain't you happy? Whoopee!

*(He releases her and she drops upon a seat. She buries her face in the moss.*
*Quartet begins on chorus again. People are departing, laughing, humming, with quartet cheering, John, the cake, and Effie being borne away in triumph.)*

## Scene 4

*Time: Present. The interior of a one-room shack in an alley. There is a small window in the rear wall upstage left. There is an enlarged crayon*[13] *drawing of a man and woman—man sitting cross-legged, woman standing with her head on his shoulder. A center table, red cover, a low, cheap rocker, two straight chairs, a small kitchen stove at left with a wood-box beside it, a water-bucket on a stand close by. A hand towel and a wash basin. A shelf of dishes above this. There is an ordinary oil lamp on the center table but it is not lighted when the curtain goes up. Some light enters through the window and falls on the woman [Emma] seated in the low rocker. The door is center right. A cheap bed is against the upstage wall. Someone [Lou Lillian] is on the bed but is lying so that [her] back is toward the audience.*
*Action: As the curtain rises, [Emma] is seen rocking to and fro in the low rocker. A dead silence except for the sound of the rocker and an occasional groan from the bed. Once a faint voice says, "Water," and the woman in the rocker arises and carries the tin dipper to the bed.*

EMMA: No mo' right away—Doctor says not too much. (*Returns dipper to pail.—Pause.*) You got right much fever—I better go git the doctor agin.

*(There comes a knocking at the door and she stands still for a moment, listening. It comes again and she goes to [the] door but does not open it.)*

Who's that?

JOHN: (*[From] outside*) Does Emma Beazely live here?

EMMA: Yeah—(*pause*)—who is it?

JOHN: It's me—John Turner.

EMMA: (*Puts hands eagerly on the fastening*) John? did you say John Turner?

JOHN: Yes, Emma, it's me.

*(The door is opened and [he] steps inside.)*

EMMA: John! Your hand. (*She feels for it and touches it.*) John, flesh and blood.

JOHN: (*Laughing awkwardly*) It's me all right, old girl. Just as bright as a basket of chips. Make a light quick so I can see how you look. I'm crazy to see you. Twenty years is a long time to wait, Emma.

EMMA: (*Nervously*) Oh, let's we all just sit in the dark awhile. (*Apologetically*) I wasn't expecting nobody and my house ain't picked up. Sit down. (*She draws up the chair [for John]. She sits in rocker.*)

JOHN: Just to think! Emma! Me and Emma sitting down side by each. Know how I found you?

EMMA: (*Dully*). Naw. How?

JOHN: (*Brightly*). Soon's I got in town I hunted up Wesley and he told me how to find you. That's who I come to see, you!

EMMA: Where you been all these years, up north somewheres? Nobody 'round here could find out where you got to.

JOHN: Yes, up north. Philadelphia.

EMMA: Married yet?

JOHN: Oh yes, seventeen years ago. But my wife is dead now and so I came as soon as it was decent to find *you*. I wants to marry you. I couldn't die happy if I didn't. Couldn't get over you—couldn't forget. Forget me, Emma?

EMMA: Naw, John. How could I?

JOHN: (*Leans over impulsively to catch her hand*) Oh, Emma, I love you so much. Strike a light honey so I can see you—see if you changed much. You was such a handsome girl!

EMMA: We don't exactly need no light, do we, John, tuh jus' set an' talk?

JOHN: Yes, we do, honey. Gwan, make a light. Ah wanna see you.

(*There is a silence.*)

EMMA: Bet you' wife wuz some high-yaller dickty-doo.

JOHN: Naw she wasn't neither. She was jus' as much like you as Ah could get her. Make a light an' Ah'll show you her pictcher. Shucks, ah gotta look at mah old sweetheart. (*He strikes a match and holds it up between their faces and they look intently at each other over it until it burns out.*) You ain't changed none atall, Emma, jus' as pretty as a speckled pup yet.

EMMA: (*Lighter*) Go 'long, John! (*Short pause*) 'Member how you useter bring me magnolias?

JOHN: Do I? Gee, you was sweet! 'Member how Ah useter pull mah necktie loose so you could tie it back for me? Emma, Ah can't see to mah soul how we lived all this time, 'way from one another. 'Member how you useter make out mah ears had done run down and you useter screw 'em up agin for me? (*They laugh.*)

EMMA: Yeah, Ah useter think you wuz gointer be mah husban' then—but you let dat ole—

JOHN: Ah ain't gonna let you alibi on me lak dat. Light dat lamp! You cain't look me in de eye and say no such. (*He strikes another match and lights the lamp.*) 'Course, Ah don't wanta look too bossy, but Ah b'lieve you got to marry me tuh git rid of me. That is, if you ain't married.

EMMA: Naw, Ah ain't. (*She turns the lamp down.*)

JOHN: (*Looking about the room*) Not so good, Emma. But wait till you see dat little place in Philly! Got a little "Rolls-Rough,"[14] too—gointer teach you to drive it, too.

EMMA: Ah been havin' a hard time, John, an' Ah lost you—oh, ain't nothin' been right for me! Ah ain't never been happy.

(*John takes both of her hands in his.*)

JOHN: You gointer be happy now, Emma. 'Cause Ah'm gointer make you. Gee whiz! Ah ain't but forty-two and you ain't forty yet—we got plenty time. (*There is a groan from the bed.*) Gee, what's that?

EMMA: (*Ill at ease*) Thass mah chile. She's sick. Reckon Ah bettah see 'bout her.

JOHN: You got a chile? Gee, that great! Ah always wanted one, but didn't have no luck. Now we kin start off with a family. Girl or boy?

EMMA: (*Slowly*) A girl. Comin' tuh see me agin soon, John?

JOHN: Comin' agin? Ah ain't gone yet! We ain't talked, you ain't kissed me an' nothin', and you ain't showed me our girl. (*Another groan, more prolonged.*) She must be pretty sick—let's see.

(*He turns in his chair and Emma rushes over to the bed and covers the girl securely, tucking her long hair under the covers, too—before he arises. He goes over to the bed and looks down into her face. She is mulatto. Turns to Emma teasingly.*)

Talkin' 'bout *me* liking high-yallers—*yo'* husband musta been pretty near white.

EMMA: (*Slowly*) Ah never wuz married, John.

JOHN: It's all right, Emma. (*Kisses her warmly.*) Everything is going to be O.K. (*Turning back to the bed.*) Our child looks pretty sick, but she's pretty. (*Feels her forehead and cheek.*) Think she oughter have a doctor.

EMMA: Ah done had one. 'Course Ah cain't git no specialist an' nothin' lak dat. (*She looks about the room and his gaze follows hers.*) Ah ain't got a whole lot lak you. Nobody don't git rich in no white-folks' kitchen, nor in de washtub. You know Ah ain't no school-teacher an' nothing' lak dat.

(*John puts his arm about her.*)

JOHN: It's all right, Emma. But our daughter is bad off—run out an' git a doctor—she needs one. Ah'd go if Ah knowed where to find one—you kin git one the quickest—hurry, Emma.

EMMA: (*Looks from John to her daughter and back again.*) She'll be all right, Ah reckon, for a while. John, you love me—you really want me sho' nuff?

JOHN: Sure Ah do—think Ah'd come all de way down here for nothin'? Ah wants to marry agin.

EMMA: Soon, John?

JOHN: Real soon.

EMMA: Ah wuz jus' thinkin', mah folks is away now on a little trip—be home day after tomorrow—we could git married tomorrow.

JOHN: All right. Now run on after the doctor—we must look after our girl. Gee, she's got a full suit of hair! Glad you didn't let her chop it off.

(*Looks away from bed and sees Emma standing still.*)

JOHN: Emma, run on after the doctor, honey.

(*She goes to the bed and again tucks the long braids of hair in, which are again pouring over the side of the bed by the feverish tossing of the girl.*)

What's our daughter's name?

EMMA: Lou Lillian. (*She returns to the rocker uneasily and sits rocking jerkily. He returns to his seat and turns up the light.*)

JOHN: Gee, we're going to be happy—we gointer make up for all them twenty years. (*Another groan.*) Emma, git up an' gwan git dat doctor. You done forgot Ah'm de boss uh dis family now—gwan, while Ah'm here to watch her whilst you're gone. Ah got to git back to mah stoppin'-place after a while.

EMMA: You go git one, John.

JOHN: Whilst Ah'm blunderin' 'round tryin' to find one, she'll be gettin' worse. She sounds pretty bad—(*Takes out his wallet and hands her a bill*)—get a taxi if necessary. Hurry!

EMMA: (*Does not take the money, but tucks her arms and hair in again, and gives the girl a drink.*) Reckon Ah better go git a doctor. Don't want nothin' to happen to *her*. After you left, Ah useter have such a hurtin' in heah (*Touches bosom*) till she come an' eased it some.

JOHN: Here, take some money and get a good doctor. There must be some good colored ones around here now.

EMMA: (*Scornfully*) I wouldn't let one of 'em tend my cat if I had one! But let's we don't start a fuss.

(*John caresses her again. When he raises his head he notices the picture on the wall and crosses over to it with her—his arm still about her.*)

JOHN: Why, that's you and me!

EMMA: Yes, I never could part with that. You coming tomorrow morning, John, and we're gointer get married, ain't we? Then we can talk over everything.

JOHN: Sure, but I ain't gone yet. I don't see how come we can't make all our arrangements now.

(*Groans from bed and feeble movement.*)

Good lord, Emma, go get that doctor!

(*Emma stares at the girl and the bed and seizes a hat from a nail on the wall. She prepares to go but looks from John to bed and back again. She fumbles about the table and lowers the lamp. Goes to door and opens it. John offers the wallet. She refuses it.*)

EMMA: Doctor right around the corner. Guess I'll leave the door open so she can get some air. She won't need nothing while I'm gone, John.

(*She crosses and tucks the girl in securely and rushes out, looking backward and pushing the door wide open as she exits. John sits in the chair beside the table. Looks about him—shakes his head. The girl on the bed groans, "water," "so hot." John looks about him excitedly. Gives her a drink. Feels her forehead. Takes a clean handkerchief from his pocket and wets it and places it upon her forehead. She raises her hand to the cool object. Enter Emma running. When she sees John at the bed she is full of fury. She rushes over and jerks his shoulder around. They face each other.*)

I knowed it! (*She strikes him.*) A half white skin.

(*She rushes at him again. John staggers back and catches her hands.*)

JOHN: Emma!

EMMA: (*Struggles to free her hands*) Let me go so I can kill you. Come sneaking in here like a pole cat!

JOHN: (*Slowly, after a long pause*) So this is the woman I've been wearing over my heart like a rose for twenty years! She so despises her own skin that she can't believe any one else could love it!

(*Emma writhes to free herself.*)

Twenty years! Twenty years of adoration, of hunger, of worship!

(*On the verge of tears he crosses to door and exits quietly, closing the door after him.*
*Emma remains standing, looking dully about as if she is half asleep. There comes a knocking at the door. She rushes to open it. It is the doctor. White. She does not step aside so that he can enter.*)

DOCTOR: Well, shall I come in?

EMMA: (*Stepping aside and laughing a little*) That's right, doctor, come in.

(*Doctor crosses to bed with professional air. Looks at the girl, feels the pulse and draws up the sheet over the face. He turns to her.*)

DOCTOR: Why didn't you come sooner? I told you to let me know of the least change in her condition.

EMMA: (*Flatly*) I did come—I went for the doctor.

DOCTOR: Yes, but you waited. An hour more or less is mighty important sometimes. Why didn't you come?

EMMA: (*Passes hand over her face*) Couldn't see.

DOCTOR: (*Looks at her curiously, then sympathetically takes out a small box of pills, and hands them to her.*) Here, you're worn out. Take one of these every hour and try to get some sleep.

(*He departs. She puts the pill-box on the table, takes up the low rocking chair and places it by the head of the bed. She seats herself and rocks monotonously and stares out of the door. A dry sob now and then. The wind from the open door blows out the lamp and she is seen by the little light from the window rocking in an even, monotonous gait, and sobbing.*)

[CURTAIN]

# SPEARS (1926)

$S$ *pears,* a short two-act play, won an honorable mention in the first *Opportunity* literary contest organized by Charles S. Johnson in 1925, and was later published in *X-Ray,* the magazine of the Zeta Phi Beta sorority, in December 1926. It was never produced.

The play is notable for the contrast it provides with *Color Struck,* in terms of its setting, themes, and rendering of dialogue. Setting the play in an imaginary African kingdom, Hurston exploits the then-faddish interest in "primitive" cultures and peoples that foreshadowed, to a certain degree, her eventual relationship with Charlotte Osgood Mason, a champion of primitivism who believed that American society could be rejuvenated through contact with African American (and African) culture. While Langston Hughes wrote wryly, in his 1926 essay "The Negro Artist and the Racial Mountain," of "the tom-tom of revolt" felt by blacks "against weariness in a white world, a world of subway trains, and work, work, work; the tom-tom of joy and laughter, and pain swallowed in a smile," Hurston, seemingly without irony, sets her characters dancing to the tom-tom beat of "darkest Africa." Obviously, Hurston's representation of Africa comes out of her own imaginings rather than any lived experience, and the wild costumes and dances described in the play were certainly based in fantasy rather than the ethnographical approach that would characterize her later work (she did not begin her studies with Franz Boas until 1926).

One wonders, then, how the play was awarded a prize in the *Opportunity* contest. Certainly it was not due to a paucity of submissions—Johnson received over seven hundred. The answer, perhaps, lies in the underlying message of the play: that loyalty to one's community can overcome poverty and privation. Despite the stilted and stereotypically mannered "African" idioms employed by the characters, and the intrusion of exotic displays such as the rain dance at the end of act 1 and the battle scene in act 2, this message comes through clearly. Nevertheless, the play panders to the voyeuristic interests of the "Nordics," as Hughes described them in his 1940 autobiography *The Big Sea,* who came to Harlem nightclubs in the 1920s to watch blacks "like amusing animals in a zoo." Both *Meet the Mamma* and *Spears* demonstrate Hurston's willingness to cater to the popular; it was only after her exposure to Boas's ideas and, more important, the fieldwork she undertook in the South in 1928–1929, that she found a different course as a writer.

# Spears
## *A Play in Two Acts*

CAST:

    ULEDI, A Lualaba[1] warrior

    MONANGA WA BIBAU BIKI, King of Lualaba

    ZAIDI,[2] Daughter of Monanga

    BOMBAY, old Councilor to king

    TIPO TIPO, servant of king

    WAGANGA, medicine man

    MONOKO MWA NKOI, Chief of [the] Wahehe

    VENT VOGEL, his servant

    A WITCH WOMAN of Lualaba

    1ST WARRIOR

    2ND WARRIOR

    WIFE OF BOMBAY

    WOMEN, WARRIORS on either side

MONANGA WA BIBAU BIKI is dressed in a lion's skin with a circlet of vulture feathers about his head. Anklet of lion's teeth about his ankle.

ULEDI and all of the warriors are bare to the waist except for a small skin below the loins that hangs down behind, except that Uledi wears a tuft of lion's tail about his neck.

MONOKO MWA NKOI wears a leopard's skin with the circle of claws suspended from his neck.

TIPO [TIPO] and VENT VOGEL wear loin cloths only.

[WAGANGA] the medicine man and [the] WITCH WOMAN are gorgeously dressed in bone jewelry with their bodies painted. Rings in noses and ears.

ZAIDI wears monkey-fur bands about wrists and several bone and copper wire bracelets on her arms. Some above elbow. She wears numerous necklaces, bands of ostrich about her ankles. A loin cloth of monkey-fur held in front by a miniature shield. A circlet of white ostrich about her head.

*Time: Present.*
*Place: Africa.*

## ACT 1

*Setting: The courtyard before the temple of Monanga. In the background is the wattled walls of the house. There is one narrow door in each wall. The roof is flat. A tusk or two of ivory is on the roof with other trophies of the chase. A bunch or two of dried tobacco can be seen. Trees about and behind it. At left there are numerous trees through which an avenue opens into the Court. A totem pole stands in center court. Two drums, a large and small one near wall of house.*

*The action: As the curtain goes up several warriors are discovered stretched upon the earth of the courtyard in positions of fatigue. An air of dejection hangs over all. One warrior is making spear heads. Another raises himself upon his elbows and regards him scornfully.*

1st WARRIOR: Fool. Why do you waste your little strength in useless work? Why do you want a spear head with no game?

2nd WARRIOR: Oh, I shall go down to the Gombe to spear fish. Perhaps I shall have luck. (*He nods to the totem pole.*)

1st WARRIOR: You shall not have luck. I was at the river only this morning and found nothing but the tracks of the rhinoceros—the water in the river is low.

2nd WARRIOR: If only the rain would come! Then would come the grass again and the elephants—good hunting.

1st WARRIOR: And full stomachs. (*Rubs his stomach.*) Oh, such hunger pains! (*He leans on his elbow and looks about.*) But where is Uledi? I have not seen the fire devourer today.

2nd WARRIOR: Who knows? He made new spear heads yesterday. Perhaps he hunts or fishes, or raids the store-houses of other tribes. He has fed on lion's heart.

(*He rises and exits still examining the spear he has made. The other man lies prone again. A drum is heard faintly in the distance and he raises his head again and stares off stage right.*)

1st WARRIOR: Here comes the slayer of lions, the eater of fire now. (*Enter Uledi through door in village wall, right.*) You walk well fed. Have you found good hunting?

ULEDI: Yes, there is always good hunting for the brave. The lion never starves.

1st WARRIOR: (*Eagerly*) Where? Meat! Tell me quickly, Uledi. Where did you find food?

ULEDI: (*Squats upon the ground.*) Why should I tell you? You would not dare touch it. (*He laughs scornfully—the drums can be heard again, louder this time as if nearer.*) Does Monanga Wa hold council today?

1ST WARRIOR: I heard Mtesa say that Tipo said that Bombay said he would.

(*Several men enter and squat about the court. Those who are lying about squat. Some smoke and exchange a word or two. Enter from avenue Tipo Tipo carrying a huge umbrella over Monanga Wa. The king is stately but a little haggard from hunger and affairs of state. He is followed by Bombay who carries a stool. The procession proceeds upstage left, passing behind the totem pole. Bombay places the stool and the king seats himself. Tipo plants the umbrella in the ground so that it shelters him [the king] and squats at the king's feet. Bombay squats facing the warriors. All this is done quickly. All of the warriors except Uledi rush forward with outstretched arms. Tipo and Bombay press them back.*)

ALL: Monanga Wa, we are hungry. Our bones show in our skins. We shall die— we are hungry.

MONANGA WA: The Wahehe must not hear of our [*line of text missing*] says he has found a way to feed us. He is old and very wise. (*Bombay nods arrogantly.*) We could go to the North to hunt but grass is scarce there also and the beasts are gone. If we go to the South, our enemies, the Wahehe, will make war. But Bombay will save us he says. (*Bombay bows grandiloquently and rises.*)

BOMBAY: Monanga Wa bibau Biki has spoken well. I am very wise. I shall save the Lualaba with my wisdom which is greater than all his spears.

ULEDI: Rather starve than be smothered in your boasts. Tell us your plans and we shall see your wisdom.

BOMBAY: We will sell our young women to the Wahehe for good. We shall not miss them. There are too many women and always will be.

ULEDI: Bombay is an old man. (*Winks.*)

A WARRIOR: But not very wise. (*There is a general stir of disapproval.*)

BOMBAY: Is the counsel of an old man cast away? We should sell our women that we may live.

WARRIOR: What for?

MONANGA WA: The Wahehe must not hear of our weakened condition. (*The door opens and Zaidi enters followed by a number of women old and young. She steps timidly toward the king.*) What are you women doing in the council?

ZAIDI: We are hungry, father—we want food. There was only a handful of grain in our house yesterday and now that is eaten. We shall starve.

MONANGA WA: (*Raising his hand*) Shut up! Must I hear of women's stomachs before my warriors are fed? (*Zaidi shrinks as if she fears a blow. The other women turn to run back into the house. Uledi rises and approaches the girl.*)

ULEDI: Wait, Zaidi, I have meat and grain for you. Wait here. I shall not be long. (*Exit Uledi right. Zaidi and the women come downstage left, and squat huddled together timidly.*)

BOMBAY: Does my great wisdom prevail over the words of hot-mouthed youths? (*Reenter Uledi bearing a long strip of dried meat, a small measure of grain and a small pumpkin. The men look hungrily at the food; some stand. He gives the food to the girl who takes it readily—Bombay's mouth falls open in amazement. Zaidi tears off a bit of flesh and thrusts it into her mouth, and gives a piece to each woman, who eats. Uledi squats beside her.*)

ULEDI: There shall be more for you Zaidi when that is gone.

BOMBAY: (*Snapping his fingers in scorn*) Does my wisdom—

CHORUS OF MEN: Oh shut up! (*They follow each morsel of meat from the girl's hand to her mouth with their eyes and make the motion of swallowing when she does. Bombay alternates between licking his chops hungrily and dancing up and down to attract attention to himself. He seats himself on the ground and places his short sword to his breast.*)

BOMBAY: Since the Lualaba no longer need my wisdom I shall die. (*Several warriors rush to stop him and four women leave the group about Zaidi and rush screaming to him.*)

WIFE OF BOMBAY: Our master must not even scratch his honorable skin. (*She snatches the knife from his hand.*) May water never swallow him, may spears never bite him! (*The other three wives fuss about his person wailing and exclaiming. Bombay reconciles himself to living and the women return to their places about Zaidi.*)

MONANGA WA: Bombay, my people still hunger. (*Significantly.*)

BOMBAY: (*Frightened*) But, Master, the young men will not listen to my wisdom.

ULEDI: No, his wisdom is very bad.

MONANGA WA: If the young women go, there will be no children and the tribe will die.

A WARRIOR: The women of the Lualaba have never been sold to our enemies. Let us keep them.

ULEDI: Yes, if we must die, let us die with our[3] women.

ZAIDI: Bombay is cruel. (*All the women gather about Uledi and glare at Bombay.*)

BOMBAY: (*Exasperated, leaps up and runs across stage toward avenue exit.*) If an old man's wisdom is ignored he must fling himself into the river.

(*He pauses expecting someone to stop him. The men laugh and talk. He looks toward the women but they seem not to hear. He sits upon the ground and puts his knife again to his breast, but his wives are flirting with Uledi and pay no attention to him. He exits down the avenue tearing his top-knot in chagrin. There is a shout of laughter, then Uledi arises and approaches Monanga Wa.*)

ULEDI: O, Father of the Lualaba, O slayer of many lions, O Mighty Spear Wielder, hear your servant who would give his life for you.

MONANGA WA: Let the brave Uledi speak.

ULEDI: Our god Mulunga loves us, for the Lualaba is the mightiest nation between the seas—the sun sleeps at one side and arises on the other. From the east to the west our countries stretch so far the sun just rides swiftly to cross it in one day. You are king over many chiefs. Then let our medicine man make rain for us at once and if Mulunga does not send it when the sun goes into his hut tomorrow, he will send *me* to bring food for all the tribe. As soon as the rain falls, grass will spring up, the elephants will return and we shall feast again. The Gombe will be full with water and fish will come again. We shall be fat and fear nothing. (*Uledi backs to his place. The king is visibly pleased, the warriors beat upon their shields with pleasure.*)

MONANGA WA: Tipo Tipo, go summon Waganga and the witch woman. (*Tipo exits right, running. They enter almost immediately.*) Waganga, make medicine for rain at once. Do you think you are kept fat for nothing? My warriors are hungry.

(*Waganga pours water from a gourd into the mouth of the head carved upon the totem pole and shouts three times. The witch woman removes a white chicken (rooster) from a basket and ties one of its legs to the totem pole at the ground. Waganga goes from Warrior to Warrior, King first, and touches their lips with his finger tips—a low wail is heard from the witch woman that is taken up by the entire company. The drums begin softly and increase. The woman kneels and wails in a high monotone. Waganga does his wild dance about the pole. The chicken flutters in fright. The entire company rises and dances about the pole led by Waganga. The drums beat furiously; the dancing grows wilder, more abandoned and they assume*

*various gestures of pleading and supplication to the totem pole. This con-*
*tinues for nine minutes.*
*Quick curtain. Curtain need not be used here at all.)*

ACT 2

*Scene: Same as Act 1.*
*Time: Immediately after the ceremonial dance. Late afternoon, sun*
*fading.*
*Action: As curtain goes up everyone is about to leave the court. The witch*
*woman is seen departing (right) with her chicken. The 2nd Warrior (who*
*had announced his intention of spearing fish in the river) dashes in and*
*falls breathless in the center of the stage; all gather about him. The king*
*crowds up to him.*

2ND WARRIOR: Monanga Wa, (*Breathing hard*) the Wahehe!

ALL: (*Consternation*) The Wahehe?

2ND WARRIOR: Yes, master. I went to the river to spear fish, but the water of the
Gombe is lean. Many Wahehe had crossed. I saw their tracks on the
stones, and I saw three impi hiding in the brush. I flew with vulture wings
to bring the news. (*There is a commotion offstage right, and Bombay with
an arrow stuck through his top-knot comes dashing up the avenue and
grasps the king's knees displaying great fright.*)

BOMBAY: Master! Master! Save me. I went down to the river to end my life and
the impi of the Wahehe all but killed me. (*Monanga Wa withdraws the
arrow and examines it.*)

MONANGA WA: The Wahehe have heard of our famine or the leopard would
not dare walk in the lion's tracks. (*Drums are heard approaching up the
avenue.*)

ULEDI: But master, the lion is still alive and he is most terrible when hungry.
Here comes an enemy. (*He seizes his spear and is about to hurl it but the
king restrains him. Enter Vent Vogel. He carries a vessel full of grain and as
the men make way for him, marches up before Monanga who stands, spear
in hand. Vent Vogel makes obeisance, but haughtily.*)

VENT VOGEL: Monoko Mwa Nkoi, my master, says that you have offended him
and he is very angry.

MONANGA WA: Why should I fear your master's anger?

(*Vent Vogel stoops and pours out the grain upon the ground and glances
about to see the effect of his action upon the Lualaba.*)

VENT VOGEL: The warriors of my master are like the grains of corn. Think of
his terrible anger.

MONANGA WA: The spears of Lualaba are as the hairs on his skin. (*He throws his lion skin upon the ground before Vent Vogel.*) And they have all been fed upon lion hearts.

VENT VOGEL: Your impi are very lean. The Wahehe are fat and strong. Your men have invaded our country and stolen our meat and grain and killed three warriors. My master demands a hundred bullocks, fifty goats and fifty women for wives and the daughter of Monanga for himself. He waits not far away—he is Mouth of a Leopard, whatever his jaws catch they never let go. (*He stands very erect with his arms folded across his breast, and looks arrogantly about him. Consternation is written on the faces of most of the people. Uledi breaks from the crowd of young men upstage right and rushes downstage center, where the king and Vent Vogel stand facing each other. He draws his short sword and seizing Vent by the top-knot, chops it off with one stroke and stuffs it into his [Vent Vogel's] mouth.*)

ULEDI: You are meat for dogs. Do you dare to speak to Master of Many Spears as if he were no more than your lying, boasting, Mouth of a Leopard? I killed your warriors and took your meat and grain. Go tell your master to come and I shall deal with him likewise. (*Vent Vogel makes a gesture toward his knife but quickly changes his mind and makes a bow to Monanga and backs quickly down the avenue and away.*)

MONANGA WA: War. (*His whole being expresses despair. He leans upon his spear with his shield resting upon the ground.*) War, war, and famine! The Lualaba shall perish.

BOMBAY: Our people shall not perish if you listen to my words of wisdom. Uledi has brought all this upon us. I saw him with the meat. Do everything that Mouth of a Leopard says and he will not make war. Then send the hot mouthed Uledi, the trouble maker, bound to Monoko that he may do with him what he wills.

MONANGA WA: Seize him and bind him. I will not send him to Monoko, our enemy, but he shall die.

(*Uledi is bound. Zaidi rushes forward and kisses the ground at Monanga's feet, kisses his feet and speaks while kneeling.*)

ZAIDI: Will my father permit his slave to speak?

MONANGA WA: Yes, child, but quickly. Women were not made to counsel men but to serve them.

ZAIDI: We women have no minds at all. We know nothing—what we saw yesterday is today forgotten. Each day the sun takes our thoughts with him into his hut and does not bring them back to us again. But my father is wise and remembers all things. Each day is something remembered. If he will look into his mind perhaps he will see many things there about Uledi; how he saved the life of Zaidi on Lake Tanganyika; how he fought with the Soko and brought home many slaves; how he led the impi to the Gombe and would not let the Wahehe pass; how he received the lion on the point of his spear when everyone else had fled; how he is first to hear your voice always. If Uledi has done wrong let me be killed in his place, for who will lead the impi when he is dead? The Wahehe will come and make us slaves if he be dead. Your slave has spoken. (*She kisses her father's hands and puts her forehead to the earth.*)

MONANGA WA: Get up, Zaidi. You have spoken well. He shall not die, neither will I kill my daughter. (*The warriors begin to caper with joy, one cuts the cords that bind Uledi.*)

ULEDI: (*He prostrates himself first and places the king's foot upon his head— then rises to speak:*) O Master, do nothing to please Monoko Mwa Nkoi. He is our enemy and only a chief, while you are king of many chiefs. He has crossed into our country so let us fight! (*A shout from the impi who brandish spears, shields and knives.*)

BOMBAY: But our men are hungry—they cannot march.

ULEDI: The more reason to fight now. We will not have to march for he has marched to us. If we win, their meat and grain and cattle and wines shall all be ours. The Wahehe shall be our slaves. If we lose we shall die and have no need for food and women. Mouth of a Leopard sends empty boasts, but our spears shall speak for us. Master of Many Spears, have your Warriors ever fled?

(*The warriors catch fire from Uledi and begin sharpening spears and knives and arrows.*)

MONANGA WA: (*Brandishing his spear.*) Uledi is the son of a lion. His words make my spear tremble with joy. We shall fight! (*There is commotion off-stage right and a bloody spear is hurled into the court. It imbeds itself in the earth and silence falls on the people.*)

MONANGA WA: A declaration of war. (*Enter Monoko at the head of a band of Wahehe warriors. The Lualaba all withdraw upstage right about Monanga. Uledi steps forward to meet Monoko.*)

ULEDI: Does the Chief of the Wahehe wish to talk palaver with the King of Lualaba?

MONOKO: (*Haughtily*) You are not he.

ULEDI: But the King of Lualaba talks palaver only with kings.

MONOKO: (*Very angry*) Then tell your speechless King that the Mouth of a Leopard waits by the rise, the Leopard shall return, and whatever he takes Gombe for his pay. If he does not send it by moon rise, the Leopard shall return, and whatever he takes hold of he never lets go.[4] Who knows? Tomorrow I might be King of Kings, and Monanga—nothing.

ULEDI: (*Sarcastically*) Very true, who knows? The Mulunga works mysteriously.

MONOKO: (*Significantly*) Remember, I wait! (*He walks toward avenue exit.*)

ULEDI: You will not wait long, and you shall receive full measure.

MONOKO: Ah ha! I see you fear: and you are wise. My anger is terrible. (*Exit. He is hissed by the entire assembly. Monanga steps forward, shakes his spear after Monoko.*)

MONANGA WA: (*Exceedingly angry*) Oh you shall be paid!

BOMBAY: (*Running hastily up to king*) Master, Master! Beware. It is best to do as Monoko says. Our warriors are very hungry.

(*Monanga slaps Bombay to the ground and strikes his shield with his spear.*)

MONANGA WA: Waganga!

(*The medicine man makes a flying leap to the center of the stage before the King.*)

War!

(*The warriors begin to grow excited. Waganga puts fire into the mouth of the totem pole.*)

Ah, Uledi, my spear trembles with joy. I have spent my life behind this great tooth—it has bitten all my enemies down.

ULEDI: You have made the Lualaba mighty—I shall fight to keep them so.

MONANGA WA: And be king after me. You must drag the leopard skin from Monoko's shoulders. The Wahehe must pay us tribute.

(*Waganga is going from one warrior to the other striking them lightly upon the chest with a bone. Each stands erect and presents his breast proudly. All weapons are upon the ground. After each warrior is struck he picks up his weapon and takes his place in rank. Soon all the men and women are separated by this process, the men near the pole. One of the warriors drags forth a large flat instrument covered with rhinoceros hide and plays a mournful three tone air with a small hammer and the flat of his hand. The drums beat monotonously. All the men surround the totem pole in a circle and present arms to it, then begin a slow rhythmic step about the pole; the tempo in-*)

creases and they dance wildly. Women with huge leaves before them represent forest. [They make an] attack gesture as all bear down gracefully toward the footlight, shields held in defense, spears couchant and finish with
a great south.[5] Uledi leads offstage by avenue and all follow. Monanga exits
last and only the women are left. The drums continue to beat offstage in two
directions. The women crowd about the totem pole in ritualistic dance.
Zaidi holds up her hand, and all pause.)

ZAIDI: Hear the drums? Their voices will summon our men for ten days'
march to sweep the enemy away. But if they fail—

(She covers her eyes with her hand. Enter Uledi—Zaidi leaves the women
and meets him.)

ULEDI: Do I see tears in your eyes?

ZAIDI: I don't want Monoko to take me away. I don't want to go into his house
of wives—ugh!

ULEDI: (Tenderly) Only when I am dead shall he touch you. The battle will be
very hard. Many of our men are too weak to answer. But if I live—

ZAIDI: Yes, you must live.

ULEDI: I hurry away. Stay here till I return if— (He backs to exit.)

ZAIDI: (Following him quickly) You must live. I wait here. (He exits—she continues to look behind him for a moment then runs back to join the women.
They dance—the drums grow louder and the women show fright.)

WOMAN: Our hungry men can never stand against the Wahehe—

ZAIDI: What, those cowards? They dared not attack us until we were weakened
by hunger. But our men are sons of the lion. They slay the enemy even in
dying. (She stoops and picks up a broken spear shaft.) Look! With a blow
like this (She gestures) my father, the Master of Many Spears, slays three
at a time, and Uledi, he dashes in among the enemy giving death! Death!!
Death!!! (She gestures with every "death").

(The drums grow louder; shouts and cries and sounds of struggle are heard
offstage. The women show intense fright, some beneath the totem, others
run wildly about.)

WOMAN: The Wahehe! Let us run and hide ourselves. (Some start offstage
right.) The enemy is there. (The entire company except Zaidi runs left but
they stop in fright.) There is fighting here.

(At last they exit up stage center in a body. Zaidi begging them all the while
to remain with her. They brush her aside and rush off. Alone she timidly approaches the totem pole and squats there supplicating. The din offstage

*increases. She covers her head with her arms. The struggle reaches the avenue entrance and she looks offstage and becomes terrified.)*

ZAIDI: *(Screams)* Mouth of a Leopard!

*(She bows her head upon the earth and covers it with her arms in dread expectation. The sound of furious fighting at the entrance continues for a full minute—glimpses of Monoko and Uledi struggling fiercely. Then Uledi enters, breathing heavily, with the leopard skin of Monoko in his hand and his spear and shield in the other. He looks tenderly at the terrified girl and walks slowly across stage to her. She shudders at the footsteps but does not raise her head.)*

ULEDI: Zaidi!

*(He stands almost directly over her. She raises her head timidly; sees first the leopard skin, and trembles. Uledi kneels also and calls her name again. She looks up this time into his face and starts happily. He spreads the skin upon the ground, and taking her hand, leads her upon it. They stand there and Monanga enters with three captive Wahehe prisoners. There is cheering offstage.*

*Thunder and lightning—1st curtain. It goes up and discovers a hard rain pouring down.)*

CURTAIN

# THE FIRST ONE (1927)

This play retells the biblical story of Ham, which was frequently used by slaveowners in the antebellum period to explain the origin of the black race as a people destined to servitude. In Genesis 9, Noah, with his sons Ham, Shem, and Japheth, and their respective wives, escape the great flood. One night Noah becomes drunk; Ham sees him in his nakedness and tells his brothers. Shem and Japheth cover him, averting their eyes, and when Noah awakens, he curses Ham's son Canaan, saying that he would be a "servant of servants. . . unto his brethren." After Emancipation, African American divines offered a counter-interpretation of the Ham story. Noting that the descendants of Ham came to rule over the lands of Egypt and Ethiopia, they argued that blacks were not servants, but descended from royalty; while acknowledging Noah's curse, they also pointed to Psalm 68:31, which declared, "Princes shall come out of Egypt; Ethiopia shall soon stretch out her hands unto God."

Hurston's version of the story emphasizes the salvation of Ham through the love of Eve (Ham's wife is not actually named in the Bible). In conflating the story of Ham with that of Adam and Eve, Hurston appears to suggest that the "land of Canaan" is equivalent to a new Garden of Eden, a land "where the sun shines forever," a land, as described in Genesis, where they could be naked without shame. While Eve initially weeps at Ham's blackness, he remains her "beloved"; the kisses she bestows upon him in love are the antithesis of the repulsion expressed by Shem, Noah, and his wife. Eve and Ham leave the white world of Noah for one of sunshine, love, and music, and Ham predicts that the whites, while retaining their white skins, will be consumed by their "flocks, and fields and vineyards, to covet, to sweat, to die and know no peace."

According to biographer Valerie Boyd, W. E. B. Du Bois considered *The First One* for his Little Negro Theatre in 1926, but a production never materialized. However, it was published in Charles S. Johnson's 1927 anthology *Ebony and Topaz*, and reprinted numerous times in the late 1980s and 1990s.

# The First One
## *A Play in One Act*

CAST:
  Noah
  Mrs. Noah
  Their Sons:
    Shem
    Japheth
    Ham
  Eve, Ham's wife
  Mrs. Shem
  Mrs. Japheth
  The children of Shem, Japheth, and Ham and their wives (six or seven)

*Time: Three years after the flood.*
*Place: Valley of Ararat.*

> *Setting: Morning in the Valley of Ararat. The Mountain is in the near dis-*
> *tance. Its lower slopes grassy with grazing herds. The very blue sky beyond*
> *that. These together form the background. On the left downstage is a brown*
> *tent. A few shrubs are scattered here and there over the stage indicating the*
> *temporary camp. A rude altar is built center stage. A shepherd's crook, a goat*
> *skin water bottle, a staff and other evidences of nomadic life lie about the*
> *entrance to the tent. To the right stretches a plain clad with bright flowers.*
> *Several sheep or goat skins are spread about on the ground upon which the*
> *people kneel or sit whenever necessary.*
>
> > *Action: Curtain rises on an empty stage. It is dawn. A great stillness, but*
> > *immediately Noah enters from the tent and ties back the flap. He is clad in*
> > *[a] loose fitting dingy robe tied about the waist with a strip of goat hide.*
> > *Stooped shoulders, flowing beard. He gazes about him. His gaze takes in the*
> > *entire stage.*

NOAH: (*Fervently*) Thou hast restored the Earth, Jehovah, it is good. (*Turns to the tent.*) My sons! Come, deck the altar for the sacrifices to Jehovah. It is the third year of our coming to this valley to give [a] thanks offering to Jehovah that He spared us.

*(Enter Japheth bearing a haunch of meat and Shem with another. The wife of Noah and those of Shem and Japheth follow laying on sheaves of grain*

*and fruit [dates and figs]. They are all middle-aged and clad in dingy garments.)*

NOAH: And where is Ham—son of my old age? Why does he not come with his wife and son to the sacrifice?

MRS. NOAH: He arose before the light and went. (*She shades her eyes with one hand and points toward the plain with the other.*) His wife, as ever, went with him.

SHEM: (*Impatiently*) This is the third year that we have come here to this valley to commemorate our delivery from the flood. Ham knows the sacrifice is made always at sunrise. See! (*He points to the rising sun.*) He should be here.

NOAH: (*Lifts his hand in a gesture of reproval*) We shall wait. The sweet singer, the child of my loins after old age had come upon me is warm to my heart—let us wait.

(*There is offstage, right, the twanging of a rude stringed instrument and laughter. Ham, his wife and son come dancing on downstage right. He is in his early twenties. He is dressed in a very white goat skin with a wreath of shiny green leaves about his head. He has the rude instrument in his hands and strikes it. His wife [Eve] is clad in a short blue garment with a girdle of shells. She has a wreath of scarlet flowers about her head. She has black hair, is small, young and lithe. She wears anklets and wristlets of the same red flowers. Their son, about three years old, wears nothing but a broad band of leaves and flowers about his middle. They caper and prance to the altar. Ham's wife and son bear flowers. A bird is perched on Ham's shoulder.*)

NOAH: (*Extends his arms in greeting*) My son, thou art late. But the sunlight comes with thee.

(*Ham gives bird to Mrs. Noah, then embraces Noah.*)

HAM: (*Rests his head for a moment on Noah's shoulder*) We arose early and went out on the plain to make ready for the burnt offering before Jehovah.

MRS. SHEM: (*Tersely*) But you bring nothing.

HAM: See thou! We bring flowers and music to offer up. I shall dance before Jehovah and sing joyfully upon the harp that I made of the thews of rams. (*He proudly displays the instrument and strums once or twice.*)

MRS. SHEM: (*Clapping her hands to her ears*) Oh, Peace! Have we not enough of thy bawling and prancing all during the year? Shem and Japheth work always in the fields and vineyards, while you do naught but tend the flock and sing!

MRS. JAPHETH: (*Looks contemptuously at both Ham and Noah*) Still, thou art beloved of thy father . . . he gives thee all his vineyards for thy singing, but Japheth must work hard for his fields.

MRS. SHEM: And Shem—

NOAH: (angrily) Peace! Peace! Are lust and strife *again* loose upon the Earth? Jehovah might have destroyed us all. Am I not lord of the world? May I not bestow where I will? Besides, the world is great. Did I not give food and plenty to the thousands upon thousands that the water licked up? Surely there is abundance for us and our seed forever. Peace! Let us to the sacrifice.

(*Noah goes to the heaped up altar. Ham exits to the tent hurriedly and returns with a torch and hands it to Noah who applies it to the altar. He kneels at the altar and the others kneel in a semi-circle behind him at a little distance. Noah makes certain ritualistic gestures and chants:*)

Oh mighty Jehovah, who created the Heaven and the firmaments thereof, the Sun and Moon, the stars, the Earth and all else besides—

OTHERS:

I am here
I am here, O, Jehovah
I am here
This is Thy kingdom, and I am here.

(*A deep silence for a moment.*)

NOAH: Jehovah, who saw evil in the hearts of men, who opened upon them the windows of Heaven and loosed the rain upon them—And the fountains of the great deep were broken up—

OTHERS:

I am here
I am here, O, Jehovah
I am here
This is Thy kingdom, and I am here.

NOAH: Jehovah, who dried up the floods and drove the waters of the sea again to the deeps—who met Noah in the Vale of Ararat and made covenant with Noah, His servant, that no more would He smite the Earth—And seed time and harvest, cold and heat, summer and winter, day and night shall not cease forever, and set His rainbow as a sign.

NOAH AND OTHERS:

We are here O Jehovah
We are here

We are here
This is Thy kingdom
And we are here.

*(Noah arises, makes obeisance to the smoking altar, then turns and blesses the others.)*

NOAH: Noah alone, whom the Lord found worthy; Noah whom He made lord of the Earth, blesses you and your seed forever.

*(At a gesture from him all arise. The women take the meat from the altar and carry it into the tent.)*

Eat, drink and make a joyful noise before Him. For He destroyed the Earth, but spared us.

*(Women reenter with bits of roast meat—all take some and eat. All are seated on the skins.)*

MRS. NOAH: *(Feelingly)* Yes, three years ago, all was water, water, water! The deeps howled as one beast to another. *(She shudders.)* In my sleep, even now, I am in that ark again being borne here, there on the great bosom.

EVE: *(Wide-eyed)* And the dead! Floating, floating all about us—We were one little speck of life in a world of death! *(The bone slips from her hand.)* And there, close beside the ark, close with her face upturned as if begging for shelter—my *mother!* *(She weeps, Ham comforts her.)*

MRS. SHEM: *(Eating vigorously)* She would not repent. Thou art as thy mother was—a seeker after beauty of raiment and laughter. God is just. She would not repent.

EVE: But the unrepentant are no less loved. And why must Jehovah hate beauty?

NOAH: Speak no more of the waters. Oh, the strength of the waters! The voices and the death of it! Let us have the juice of the grape to make us forget. Where once was death in this valley there is now life abundant of beast and herbs. *(He waves towards the scenery.)* Jehovah meets us here. Dance! Be glad! Bring wine! Ham, smite thy harp of ram's thews and sing!

*(Mrs. Noah gathers all the children and exits to the tent. Shem, Japheth, their wives and children eat vigorously. Eve[1] exits, left. Ham plays on his harp and capers about singing. Eve reenters with [a] goat skin of wine and a bone cup. She crosses to where Noah reclines on a large skin. She kneels and offers it to him. He takes the cup—she pours for him. Ham sings—)*

HAM:

I am as a young ram in the spring
Or a young male goat.

The hills are beneath my feet
And the young grass.
Love rises in me like the flood
And ewes gather round me for food.

*(His wife joins in the dancing. Noah cries, "Pour," and Eve hurries to fill his cup again. Ham joins others on the skins. The others have horns suspended from their girdles. Eve fills them all. Noah cries "pour" again and she returns to him. She turns to fill the others' cups.)*

NOAH: *(Rising drunkenly)* Pour again, Eve, and Ham, sing on and dance and drink—drown out the waters of the flood if you can. *(His tongue grows thick. Eve fills his cup again. He reels drunkenly toward the door, slopping the liquor out of the cup as he walks.)* Drink wine, forget water—it means death, *death!* And bodies floating, face up!

*(He stares horrified about himself and creeps stealthily into the tent, but sprawls just inside the door so that his feet are visible. There is silence for a moment, the others are still eating. They snatch tid-bits from each other.)*

JAPHETH: *(Shoves his wife)* Fruit and herbs, woman! *(He thrusts her impatiently forward with his foot. She exits left.)*

SHEM: *(To his wife)* More wine!

MRS. SHEM: *(Irritated)* See you not that there is plenty still in the bottle?

*(He seizes it and pours. Ham snatches it away and pours. Shem tries to get it back but Ham prevents him. Reenter Mrs. Japheth with figs and apples. Everybody grabs. Ham and Shem grab for the same one, Ham gets it.)*

MRS. SHEM: *(Significantly)* Thus he seizes all else that he desires. Noah would make him lord of the Earth because he sings and capers. *(Ham is laughing drunkenly and pelting Mrs. Shem with fruit skins and withered flowers that litter the ground. This infuriates her.)*

NOAH: *(Calls from inside the tent)* Eve, wine, quickly! I'm sinking down in the water! Come drown the water with wine.

*(Eve exits to him with the bottle. Ham arises drunkenly and starts toward the tent door.)*

HAM: *(Thickly)* I go to pull our father out of the water, or to drown with him in it. *(Ham is trying to sing and dance.)*

I am as a young goat in the sp-sp-sp—

*(He exits to the tent laughing. Shem and Japheth sprawl out in the skins. The wives are showing signs of surfeit. Ham is heard laughing raucously inside the tent. He reenters still laughing.)*

HAM: (*In the tent door*) Our father has stripped himself, showing all his wrinkles. Ha! Ha! He's as no young goat in the spring. Ha! Ha! (*Still laughing, he reels over to the altar and sinks down behind it still laughing.*) The old ram, Ha! Ha! Ha! He has had no spring for years! Ha! Ha! (*He subsides into slumber. Mrs. Shem looks about her exultantly.*)

MRS. SHEM: Ha! The young goat has fallen into a pit! (*She shakes her husband.*) Shem! Shem! Rise up and become owner of Noah's vineyards as well as his flocks! (*Shem kicks weakly at her.*) Shem! Fool! Arise! Thou art thy father's first born. (*She pulls him protesting to his feet.*) Do stand up and regain thy birthright from (*She points to the altar*) that dancer who plays on his harp of ram thews, and decks his brow with bay leaves. Come!

SHEM: (*Brightens*) How?

MRS. SHEM: Did he not go into the tent and come away laughing at thy father's nakedness? Oh (*She beats her breast*) that I should live to see a father so mocked and shamed by his son to whom he has given all his vineyards! (*She seizes a large skin from the ground.*) Take this and cover him and tell him of the wickedness of thy brother.

MRS. JAPHETH: (*Arising takes hold of the skin also*) No, my husband shall also help to cover Noah, our father. Did I not also hear? Think your Shem and his seed shall possess both flocks and vineyard while Japheth and his seed have only the fields? (*She arouses Japheth, he stands.*)

SHEM: He shall share—

MRS. SHEM: (*Impatiently*) Then go in (*The women release the skin to the men*) quickly, lest he wake sober, then will he not believe one word against Ham who needs only to smile to please him.

(*The men lay the skin across their shoulders and back over to the tent and cover Noah. They motion to leave him.*)

MRS. SHEM: Go back, fools, and wake him. You have done but half.

(*They turn and enter the tent and both shake Noah. He sits up and rubs his eyes. Mrs. Shem and Mrs. Japheth commence to weep ostentatiously.*)

NOAH: (*Peevishly*) Why do you disturb me, and why do the women weep? I thought all sorrow was washed away by the flood. (*He is about to lie down again but the men hold him up.*)

SHEM: Hear, father, thy age has been scoffed, and thy nakedness made a thing of shame here in the midst of the feasting where all might know—thou, the lord of all under Heaven, hast been mocked.

MRS. SHEM: And we weep in shame, that thou our father should have thy nakedness uncovered before us.

NOAH: (*Struggling drunkenly to his feet*) Who, *who* has done this thing?

MRS. SHEM: (*Timidly crosses and kneels before Noah*) We fear to tell thee, lord, lest thy love for the doer of this iniquity should be so much greater than the shame, that thou should slay us for telling thee.

NOAH: (*Swaying drunkenly*) Say it, woman, shall the lord of the Earth be mocked? Shall his nakedness be uncovered and he be shamed before his family?

SHEM: Shall the one who has done this thing hold part of thy goods after thee? How wilt thou deal with them? Thou hast been wickedly shamed.

NOAH: No, he shall have no part in my goods—his goods shall be parceled out among the others.

MRS. SHEM: Thou art wise, father, thou art just!

NOAH: He shall be accursed. His skin shall be black! Black as the nights, when the waters brooded over the Earth!

(*Enter Mrs. Noah from tent, pauses by Noah.*)

MRS. NOAH: (*Catches him by the arm*) Cease! Whom dost thou curse?

NOAH: (*Shaking his arm free. The others also look awed and terrified and also move to stop him. All rush to him. Mrs. Noah attempts to stop his mouth with her hand. He shakes his head to free his lips and goes [on] in a drunken fury*) Black! He and his seed forever. He shall serve his brothers and they shall rule over him—Ah—Ah— (*He sinks again to the ground. There is a loud burst of drunken laughter from behind the altar.*)

HAM: Ha! Ha! I am a young ram—Ha! Ha!

MRS. NOAH: (*To Mrs. Shem*) Whom cursed Noah?

MRS. SHEM: Ham—Ham mocked his age. Ham uncovered his nakedness, and Noah grew wrathful and cursed him. Black! He could not mean *black*. It is enough that he should lose his vineyards. (*There is absolute silence for a while. Then realization comes to all. Mrs. Noah rushes in the tent to her husband, shaking him violently.*)

MRS. NOAH: (*Voice from out of the tent*) Noah! Arise! Thou are no lord of the Earth, but a drunkard. Thou hast cursed my son. Oh water, Shem! Japheth! Cold water to drive out the wine. Noah! (*She sobs.*) Thou must awake and unsay thy curse. Thou must! (*She is sobbing and rousing him. Shem and Japheth seize a skin bottle from the ground by the skin² door and dash off right. Mrs. Noah wails and the other women join in. They beat their breasts. Enter Eve through the tent. She looks puzzled.*)

EVE: Why do you wail? Are all not happy today?

MRS. NOAH: (*Pityingly*) Come, Eve. Thou art but a child, a heavy load awaits thee.

(*Eve turns and squats beside her mother-in-law.*)

EVE: (*Caressing Mrs. Noah*) Perhaps the wine is too new. Why do you shake our father?

MRS. NOAH: Not the wine of grapes, but the wine of sorrow bestirs me thus. Turn thy comely face to the wall, Eve. Noah has cursed thy husband and his seed forever to be black, and to serve his brothers and they shall rule over him.

(*Reenter the men with the water bottle, running. Mrs. Noah seizes it and pours it in his [Noah's] face. He stirs.*)

See, I must awaken him that he may unspeak the curse before it is too late.

EVE: But Noah is drunk—surely Jehovah hears not a drunken curse. Noah would not curse Ham if he knew. Jehovah knows Noah loves Ham more than all. (*She rushes upon Noah and shakes him violently.*) Oh, awake thou (*She shrieks*) and uncurse thy curse.

(*All are trying to rouse Noah. He sits, opens his eyes wide and looks about him. Mrs. Noah caresses him.*)

MRS. NOAH: Awake, my lord, and unsay thy curse.

NOAH: I am awake, but I know of no curse. Whom did I curse?

MRS. NOAH AND EVE: Ham, lord of the Earth. (*He rises quickly to his feet and looks bewildered about.*)

JAPHETH: (*Falls at his feet*) Our father, and lord of all under Heaven, you cursed away his vineyards, but we do not desire them. You cursed him to be black—he and his seed forever, and that his seed shall be our servants forever, but we desire not their service. Unsay it all.

NOAH: (*Rushes downstage to the footlights, center. He beats his breast and bows his head to the ground.*) Oh, that I had come alive out of my mother's loins! Why did not the waters of the flood bear me back to the deeps! Oh Ham, my son!

EVE: (*Rushing down to him*) Unspeak the curse! Unspeak the curse!

NOAH: (*In prayerful attitude*) Jehovah, by our covenant in this valley, record not my curses on my beloved Ham. Show me once again the sign of covenant—the rainbow over the Vale of Ararat.

SHEM: (*Strikes his wife*) It was thou, covetous woman, that has brought this upon us.

MRS. SHEM: (*Weeping*) Yes, I wanted the vineyards for thee, Shem, because at night as thou slept on my breast I heard thee sob for them. I heard thee murmur "Vineyards" in thy dreams.

NOAH: Shem's wife is but a woman.

MRS. NOAH: How rash thou art, to curse unknowing in thy cups the son of thy loins.

NOAH: Did not Jehovah repent after He had destroyed the world? Did He not make all flesh? Their evils as well as their good? Why did He not with His flood of waters wash out the evil from men's hearts, and spare the creatures He had made, or else destroy us all, *all?* For in sparing one, He has preserved all the wickedness that He creates abundantly, but punishes terribly. No, He destroyed them because vile as they were it was His handiwork, and it shamed and reproached Him night and day. He could not bear to look upon the thing He had done, so He destroyed them.

MRS. NOAH: Thou canst not question.

NOAH: (*Weeping*) Where is my son?

SHEM: (*Pointing*) Asleep behind the altar.

NOAH: If Jehovah keeps not the covenant this time, if He spare not my weakness, then I pray that Ham's heart remains asleep forever.

MRS. SHEM: (*Beseeching*) O lord of the Earth, let his punishment be mine. We coveted his vineyards, but the curse is too awful for him. He is drunk like you—save him, Father Noah.

NOAH: (*Exultantly*) Ah, the rainbow! The promise! Jehovah will meet me! He will set His sign in the Heavens! Shem hold thou my right hand and Japheth bear up my left arm.

(*Noah approaches the altar and kneels. The two men raise his hands aloft.*)

Our Jehovah who carried us into the ark—

SHEM AND JAPHETH: Victory, O Jehovah! The sign.

OTHERS: (*Beating their breasts*) This is Thy kingdom and we are here.

NOAH: Who saved us from the Man of the Waters.

SHEM AND JAPHETH: Victory, O Jehovah! The sign.

OTHERS: We belong to Thee, Jehovah, we belong to Thee.

*(There is a sudden, loud raucous laugh from behind the altar. Ham sings brokenly, "I am a young ram in the spring.")*

NOAH: *(Hopefully)* Look! Look! To the mountain—do ye see colors appear?

MRS. NOAH: None but what our hearts paint for us—ah, false hope.

NOAH: Does the sign appear? I seem to see a faint color just above the mountain.

*(Another laugh from Ham.)*

EVE: None, none yet. *(Beats her breast violently, speaks rapidly.)* Jehovah, we belong to *Thee*, we belong to *Thee*.

MRS. NOAH AND EVE: Great Jehovah! Hear us. We are here in Thy valley. We who belong to Thee!

*(Ham slowly rises. He stands and walks around the altar to join the others, and they see that he is black. They shrink back terrified. He is laughing happily. Eve approaches him timidly as he advances around the end of the altar. She touches his hand, then his face. She begins kissing him.)*

HAM: Why do you all pray and weep?

EVE: Look at thy hands, thy feet. Thou art cursed black by thy father. *(She exits weeping left.)*

HAM: *(Gazing horrified at his hands)* Black! *(He appears stupefied. All shrink away from him as if they fear his touch. He approaches each in turn. He is amazed. He lays his hand upon Shem.)*

SHEM: *(Shrinking)* Away! Touch me not!

HAM: *(Approaches his mother. She does not repel him, but averts her face.)* Why does my mother turn away?

MRS. NOAH: So that my baby may not see the flood that hath broken the windows of my soul and loosed the fountains of my heart.

*(There is a great clamor offstage and Eve reenters left with her boy in her arms, weeping, and all the other children in pursuit jeering and pelting him with things. The child is also black. Ham looks at his child and falls at Noah's feet.)*

HAM: *(Beseeching in agony)* Why, Noah, my father and lord of the Earth, why?

NOAH: *(Sternly)* Arise, Ham. Thou art black. Arise and go out from among us that we may see thy face no more, lest by lingering the curse of thy blackness come upon all my seed forever.

*(Ham grasps his father's knees. Noah repels him sternly, pointing away right. Eve steps up to Ham and raises him with her hand. She displays both anger and scorn.)*

EVE: Ham, my husband, Noah is right. Let us go before you awake and learn to despise your father and your God. Come away, Ham, beloved, come with me, where thou canst never see these faces again, where never thy soft eyes can harden by looking too oft upon the fruit of their error, where never thy happy voice can learn to weep. Come with me to where the sun shines forever, to the end of the Earth, beloved, the sunlight of all my years.

*(She kisses his mouth and forehead. She crosses to door of tent and picks up a water bottle. Ham looks dazedly about him. His eyes light on the harp and he smilingly picks it up and takes his place beside Eve.)*

HAM: (*Lightly cynical to all*) Oh, remain with your flocks and fields and vineyards, to covet, to sweat, to die and know no peace. I go to the sun. (*He exits right across the plain with his wife and child trudging beside him. After he is offstage comes the strumming of the harp and Ham's voice happily singing: "I am as a young ram in the spring." It grows fainter and fainter until it is heard no more. The sun is low in the west. Noah sits looking tragically stern. All are ghastly calm. Mrs. Noah kneels upon the altar facing the mountain and she sobs continually.*)

[MRS. NOAH:]

We belong to Thee, O Jehovah
We belong to Thee.

*(She keeps repeating this to a slow curtain.)*

CURTAIN

# COLD KEENER (1930)

*Cold Keener* was copyrighted in October 1930, just months before the failure of *Fast and Furious* and during the period when Hurston was writing sketches for the eventually aborted *Jungle Scandals*. The sketches collected here almost certainly comprise the material she had written for *Jungle Scandals*. Whether Hurston was to be the sole author of *Jungle Scandals* is unknown; however, this collection certainly contains enough material for a full evening. Part fantasy, part slice-of-life, the sketches amount to a celebration of a black culture filled with music, ribald humor, and an unapologetic impulse to profane the sacred.

The play's title remains a mystery. The term may refer to a motley assortment of things, or it may employ the word *keener* as being a shrewd person or even a card sharp (these meanings of the word are now obsolete). As mysterious as the title is its organizational structure—or lack thereof. In her introduction to the online collection of *Zora Neale Hurston Plays at the Library of Congress,* Alice Birney at the Library of Congress speculates that the play "illustrates Hurston's concept of 'primitive angularity' in dramatic structure: the parts are linked only by their differences."

The first play, *Filling Station*, centers on a battle of words between a Ford owner and a Chevrolet owner who encounter each other at a gas station located on the Alabama-Georgia state line. Arguing over the behavior of white folks from their respective home states and the quality of their respective automobiles, it ends with an empty and comical threat of violence. *Cock Robin* takes its cue from the English nursery rhyme "Who Shot Cock Robin?" but intimates that the title character's death is a result of his activities as the local lothario. Hurston published another version of this story as "Cock Robin Beale Street" in July 1941, which includes the locations of the Grease Spot, Shimmy Shack, and a pool room also represented in the play. It is unclear whether Hurston intended for the characters in the play to be dressed as animals, but the short story suggests that they could easily be personifications of animals without any elaborate costumes.

*Heaven* centers on Jim, a victim of the disastrous Johnstown flood of 1889, which killed over 2,200 people and was until that point the worst natural disaster in American history. Arriving in heaven, Jim finds the afterlife filled with white and black angels who play guitars and harmonize songs. Although told to hold off on any high flying, he is determined to try his wings and "fly all over heben." A comic crash shows he has flown too fast too soon—but a satisfied Jim will make no apology for trying. In *Mr. Frog,* a Florida swamp is the setting for an abstract dance between a tree and the four winds that leads to the singing of the folk song "Frog Went a-Courting." *Lenox Avenue,* in turn, is set in one of Harlem's hallmark locations. A center for illegal drugs, the area was described by Wallace Thurman as "a defeated dung heap flung out to cover the subway underneath" (Thurman, *Collected Writings,* 33). Others, in contrast, remembered the warmth they felt when they emerged from the train to find nothing but black faces. Claude McKay wrote that "it was a rare sensation again to be just one black among many," while Langston Hughes remembered that he wanted to shake the hands of all he saw after making the journey.[1] Hurston includes a variety of characters, from gay and lesbian passersby to street preachers to quarrelling couples, all under the belligerent eye of a beat cop.

Hurston returns to a southern setting for *The House That Jack Built,* where a lascivious schoolteacher bullies his students until they overwhelm him with song. In *Bahamas*, two Harlemites travel to the Bahamas to join the Emperor Jones, who is traveling to Africa to expel the European powers with his "conquering black legions." The character echoes Eugene O'Neill's 1920 expressionistic play, *The Emperor Jones,* where Brutus Jones, a Pullman car attendant, travels to a Caribbean island, seizes political control, and proclaims himself emperor until he is destroyed by the violent phantoms of his past. But as Barbara Speisman notes, in Hurston's play, the character is a satirical take on Marcus Garvey, the Jamaican nationalist who spearheaded the back-to-Africa movement. (The play also invites comparison with Thurman's very different take on Garvey in *Jeremiah the Magnificent* [1933].) Despite Hurston's ironic treatment of Jones, the final moments of joyous singing as the ship sails shifts the focus away from the ultimate failure of Garvey's enterprise to the celebration of a community joined in spirit and purpose. This sensibility is shared by the last two sketches, *Railroad Camp*, essentially a "lining song" sung by a gang of railroad workers, and *Jook*, a scene in a rural night club. These plotless plays exemplify Hurston's belief that the characters and dialogue she reproduced from her fieldwork as an anthropologist needed no further dramatization.

The "jook joint" had a special significance for Hurston, who may have been exposed to them in Nashville as a girl, long before her research brought her to the rough-and-tumble work camps of Florida. In "The Characteristics of Negro Expression," she characterizes the jook as the cradle of black artistic practice:

> Musically speaking, the Jook is the most important place in America. For in its smelly, shoddy confines has been born the secular music known as the blues, and on blues as been founded jazz. . . . The Negro dances circulated over the world were also conceived inside the Jooks. They too make the round of Jooks and public works before going into the outside world. (842)

Songs from this play can be found in the section "In the Jook" in her folklore concerts *The Great Day* and *From Sun to Sun,* which were produced in 1932. However, the programs suggest that the dialogue of the play was not included. *Jook* could be more accurately described as a precursor to the sawmill camp section of *Mules and Men* (1934) and Hurston's last play, *Polk County* (1945).

# Cold Keener
## *A Review*

## *Filling Station*

CAST:
PROPRIETOR
FORD DRIVER
CHEVROLET DRIVER
GIRL

*Time: Present.*
*Place: A point on the Alabama-Georgia state line.*

Setting: *A filling station upstage center. It stretches nearly across the stage. The road passes before and through it. There is a line down the center of the stage from the center of the filling station to the footlights that says on the left side, "Alabama State Line," and on the right, "Georgia State Line." The name of the station is "The State Line Filling Station." There are two gas pumps equal distance from the center of the station, so that the door of the house appears between them.*

Action: *When the curtain goes up, a fat Negro is r[e]ared back in a chair beside the door of the station asleep and snoring. There is an inner tube lying beside him that has fallen out of his hand as he slept. It is a bright afternoon. There is the sound of a car approaching from the Alabama side and a Model T Ford rattles up to the pump on the upstage side of the pumps and stops at the one nearest to the left entrance. He stops his car with a jerk. The Proprietor is still asleep. The Ford driver blows his horn vigorously and wakes him. He picks up the tube beside him and arises with it in his hand, stretching and yawning.*

PROPRIETOR: *(Sleepily)* How many?

FORD DRIVER: Two.

PROPRIETOR: Two what?

FORD DRIVER: Two pints.

*(The Proprietor gets a quart cup out and measures the gas and wrings the hose to be sure to get it all, then he pours it in the tank.)*

FORD DRIVER: You better look at my water and air, too.

*(He has a very expensive and ornate cap on the radiator, but otherwise the car is most dilapidated. As the Proprietor pours the water into the radiator, the driver gets out of the car and stands off from it looking it over)*

FORD DRIVER: Say, Jimpson, they tells me you got a new mechanic 'round here that's just too tight.

PROPRIETOR: That's right. He kin do more wid 'em than the man that made 'em.

FORD DRIVER: Well, looka here. My car kinda needs overhauling and maybe a little paint. Look her over and tell me just what you could make her look like a brand new car for.

*(Proprietor lifts the hood and looks. Walks around and studies the car from all angles. Then stops at the front and examines the radiator cap.)*

PROPRIETOR: Well, I tell you. You see it's like this. This car needs a whole heap of things done to it. But being as you'se a friend of mine—tell you what I'll do. I'll just jack that radiator cap up and run a brand new Ford under it for four hundred and ninety-five dollars.

FORD DRIVER: *(Indignantly)* Whut de hen-fire you think I'm gointuh let you rob me outa my car. That's a *good* car.

*(A car enters from the Alabama side with a good-looking girl in it alone. She stops on the downstage side of the pumps, but somewhat ahead of the Ford. The Proprietor rushes over to the left side of her car.)*

PROPRIETOR: *(Pleasantly)* Yes, ma'am!

GIRL: I had a flat down the road and I changed it, but it's not fixed. Do you vulcanize?[2]

PROPRIETOR: We do everything but the buzzard lope³—and that's gone outa style. (*He takes the tire off the back and goes inside, and comes right out again with it.*) Do you want it on the wheel or on the spare?

(*Girl alights and goes [a]round to back of car.*)

GIRL: On the spare, I guess.

(*The Proprietor tries to put it on. Ford Driver tries to help. They get in each other's way.*)

PROPRIETOR: (*Peeved*) Man, let go of this thing.

FORD DRIVER: (*Peeved*) Don't you see I'm helpin' you?

PROPRIETOR: (*Angry*) Leggo! I can't utilize my self for you!

(*Ford Driver lets go so suddenly that the tire falls to the ground. The girl grabs it before either of them and lifts it on the rack and gives it a good kick and the tire goes into place perfectly. She gets into the car, hands the proprietor a dollar and drives off.*)

PROPRIETOR: (*Admiringly*) That's a tight little piece of pig-meat! Damned if I don't believe I'll go to Georgia!

FORD DRIVER: She ain't no pig-meat. That's a married 'oman.

PROPRIETOR: You know her?

FORD DRIVER: Nope, never seen her before.

PROPRIETOR: Well, how can you tell she's married?

FORD DRIVER: Didn't you see that kick? A woman that can kick like that done had some man to practice on.

(*Enter from Georgia side a man driving a Chevrolet—old and battered. He stops on the downstage side of the right hand pump.*)

PROPRIETOR: (*Advancing to the car*) What's yours?

CHEVROLET DRIVER: Make it a gallon—goin' way over in Alabama. (*He alights and strolls towards the center of the stage where the Ford Driver is already standing.*) 'Lo stranger, how's Alabama?

FORD DRIVER: Just fine—couldn't be no better. How's you Georgy folks starvin'?

CHEVROLET DRIVER: Starvin'? Who ever heard tell of anybody starvin' in Georgy—people so fat in Georgy till I speck Gabriel gointuh have to knock us in de head on Judgment Day so we kin go 'long wid de rest.

FORD DRIVER: He might have to knock some of them Georgy crackers in de head, but you niggers will be all ready and waitin' for de trumpet.

CHEVROLET DRIVER: How come?

FORD DRIVER: *(Snickering)* 'Cause dem crackers y'all got over there sho is hard on zigaboos.

CHEVROLET DRIVER: *(Peeved)* Lemme tell *you* something, coon. We got *nice* white folks in Georgy! But them Alabama red-necks is too mean to give God a honest prayer without snatchin' back amen!

FORD DRIVER: Who mean? I know you ain't talking 'bout them white folks in *my* state. Alabama is de best state in de world. If you can't git along there, you can't get along nowhere. But in Georgy they hates niggers so bad till one day they lynched a black mule for kickin' a white one.

CHEVROLET DRIVER: Well, in Alabama a black horse run away with a white woman, and they lynched the horse, and burnt the buggy and hung the harness.

FORD DRIVER: Well, in Georgy they don't 'low y'all to call a white female mule Maud.

CHEVROLET DRIVER: What they call her then?

FORD DRIVER: Miss Maud—and you know it durn well, too.

CHEVROLET DRIVER: Well, they tell me y'all can't go into a store and ask for a can of Prince Albert tobacco—not wid dat white man on it—you got to ask for Cap'n Albert.

FORD DRIVER: Well, they tell me they don't 'low y'all niggers to laugh on de streets in Georgy. They got laughin' barrels on certain corners for niggers, and when you gets tickled you got to hold it till you can make it to one of them barrels and stick yo' head in. Then you can cut loose. Laughin' any old place just ain't allowed.

CHEVROLET DRIVER: Well, over in Alabama, if they tell a funny joke in the theatre, y'all ain't allowed to laugh till the white folks git through. Then a white man way down front turns 'round and look way up in the peanut gallery and say, "All right, niggers, y'all kin laugh now." Then y'all just "kah, kah!"

FORD DRIVER: That's all right. They don't 'low y'all to ride no faster than ten miles an hour. If you ride any faster—you liable to get in front of some white folks.

CHEVROLET DRIVER: Well they don't 'low y'all to ride nothin' but Fords so you can't pass nobody.

FORD DRIVER: Now, what's de matter wid a Ford?

CHEVROLET DRIVER: What you askin' me for? I ain't no dictionary.

FORD DRIVER: Naw, you ain't nuthin'—do, you wouldn't be drivin' dat ole money rattler you drivin'.

CHEVROLET DRIVER: You can't talk about no Chevvie now. They got everything that a good car need. Speed! Oh, boy!

FORD DRIVER: Yeah, 'bout eight miles a week.

CHEVROLET DRIVER: Still, every time I look back I see a Ford—way behind.

FORD DRIVER: And every time I look in front I see a Chevvie—in my way. On every highway, at every turn, on every hill, on every side road, you see a Ford hitting it up.

CHEVROLET DRIVER: And a Chevvie passing it.

FORD DRIVER: Dat's a lie and otherwise you ain't really seen a Ford run yet. Now I was going down to Miami and I had dat old car doing seventy-eight, man.

CHEVROLET DRIVER: I went dat same road and had mine doing ninety.

FORD DRIVER: I mean I was doin' seventy-eight on the curves, otherwise I was doing a hundred and fifty.

CHEVROLET DRIVER: That was draggin' along. I was doin' two hundred and wasn't pushin' her. Fact is, I was in second.

FORD DRIVER: Man, I was doin' one hundred fifty in first. By the time I got as far south as Jacksonville, I was really running. Man, I come down that Florida Number Four[4] going faster than the word of God! I was doing three hundred in second.

CHEVROLET DRIVER: You ain't lying—you sho was doing dat, 'cause I remember passing you just before we got to Daytona Beach—I knowed I had done seen you somewhere. I'm a Chevvie-shovin' fool.

FORD DRIVER: You'se a Chevvie-shovin' liar, 'cause I wasn't on Number Four, I was on Number Two, and I passed everything on de road.

CHEVROLET DRIVER: Aw, yeah, you was on Number Four. I seen you. I was goin' four hundred miles an hour when I passed you and I thought you was having tire trouble. I didn't know you was moving.

FORD DRIVER: You'se a seven-sided liar. I passed you before you got to St. Augustine, and I was airing out at eight hundred miles an hour.

CHEVROLET DRIVER: And I come by you so fast till my wind said "wham!"

FORD DRIVER: *(Picking up a wrench)* Halt! Don't you drive dat damn Chevvie another inch—do, I'll comb yo' head wid dis wrench and part it slap in de middle! Put her in neutral!

CHEVROLET DRIVER: Aw, man, don't be so evil! You know I got de best car.

FORD DRIVER: I don't know no such a thing. You'se just a great big old Georgy something-ain't-so. . . . And look who buys 'em! *(Sings)*

I got a Ford, you got a Ford . . .

CHEVROLET DRIVER: *(Sings)*

Everybody who couldn't get a Chevvie got a Ford . . .[5]

FORD DRIVER: Know what, man? De angels in heben ain't flew a lick since de new Ford come out.

CHEVROLET DRIVER: How come?

FORD DRIVER: 'Cause de minute God seen them new Fords, he called up Detroit long distance and told Ford, "Send up ten thousand brand new Fords for my angels to get around in." And, man, them angels is giving Jerusalem Street and Amen Avenue an acre of fits. . . . Anyhow, nobody can't beat Ford at nothin' he start. Know what he said to John D. Rockefeller?

CHEVROLET DRIVER: Naw, what was it?

FORD DRIVER: Well, they was sittin' around woofing[6] one day 'bout how much money they had. So John D. told Henry, says, "I'm the richest man in the world! I got enough money to build a solid gold highway clear 'round the world." Know what Ford told him? "Go 'head and build it, and if I like it, I'll buy it and put one of my tin lizzies on it."

CHEVROLET DRIVER: Know what they're going to have on the new Chevvies?

FORD DRIVER: A lot of debt.

CHEVROLET DRIVER: Nope. They're going to have a piano attached to the steering wheel and a radio in the ceiling.

FORD DRIVER: Ford is goingter put twin beds on each running board and a bath over the spare tire.

CHEVROLET DRIVER: And General Motors is going to put a horn in the back so you can tell the road hogs what you think of them after you pass.

FORD DRIVER: The Ford is going to be so you won't have to tell 'em. It will know what you're thinking and tell 'em itself. . . . Tell you how fast a Ford is—a gang of hants[7] passed my house while I was sittin' on de porch. My car was parked out front. Well, them hants was going at de rate of ten miles a minute. My old man been dead 'bout three years and I seen him wid these other hants and I wanted to ast him something he forgot to tell us before he died, so I jumped in dat Ford and run dem hants down and overtook 'em. Yessuh! Dat Ford is a hant catcher.

CHEVROLET DRIVER: They's too slow for my line of work. Me, I had done put in a order for a car when I seen dat hant convention comin' down de road 'bout two thousand miles a hour. So I run to de Chevvie factory and I says, "Got my car ready?" Mr. Sloan[8] tole me no, but he was working on it. I says hurry up, I got to make it to a hant convention before they assemble, and they's on de way right now. Mr. Sloan molded me a motor and put it together and equipped her, and I throwed in some gas and oil and led dat hant parade into Diddy-Wah-Diddy.[9]

CHEVROLET DRIVER: That's right! Stand there with your mouth lookin' like a hole in the ground and lie like the cross ties from New York to Key West.

FORD DRIVER: Dat ain't no lie—dat's de truth, man—and the gearshift and everything is going to be solid silver.

CHEVROLET DRIVER: The new Chevvies will be solid gold with diamond wheels.

FORD DRIVER: And the new Fords will have a lawyer in the tool box—as soon as you have a collision, the lawyer will spring right out and begin to collect damages.

CHEVROLET DRIVER: You mean the garbage man will start to collecting junk—otherwise the new Chevvies can't have no collision.

FORD DRIVER: How come?

CHEVROLET DRIVER: Because—they're built against it. They got two sets of wheels. One set is put on crossways and they fit up under the housing. On a straight road, when you see somebody about to hit you, you just press a button and the non-collision wheels will hit the ground and run the car right off sideways. And on a curve it's got low compression springs so it can just squat level with the ground and run right under any car that's too far to the left.

FORD DRIVER: *(Menacing)* Git dat damn Chevvie up off dat ground and outa them woods!

CHEVROLET DRIVER: *(Seizing a jack handle)* Come on and make me. I dare you to move! Fool with me and three years from now, you'll be a three year old hant!

PROPRIETOR: *(Coming out of door)* Boys, boys, don't get too tonic, now.

FORD DRIVER: Tell dat crazy guy something. I'll lam him wid lightning! (*Glares a while.*) Nohow, no Ford don't have to go squattin' 'round no curve— 'cause the new Ford's got wings and they flies 'round all curves and over bad places in the road.

CHEVROLET DRIVER: (*Looks angry for a moment, then laughs*) You way late wid dis flyin' business, big boy. De Chevrolet *been* flyin'—dat's whut Lindbergh flew to Paris in—a Chevvie.

FORD DRIVER: (*Rushes at Chevrolet Driver*) Pull dat damn Chevvie down out de air! Put it on de ground before I send you to hell! (*The Proprietor has a hard time restraining him.*) Stop dat lyin' on Lindbergh and de ocean before I lam you so hard till I'll kill de governor of Georgy.

PROPRIETOR: (*Separating them*) Aw, y'all cut it out! Cut it out before I gets mad, too. (*They back off from one another.*) And gimme my tools, too. (*They lay down their weapons.*)

FORD DRIVER: You low-down Chevvie-shover.

CHEVROLET DRIVER: You dirty Ford-owner!

(*They feint at each other and both climb hurriedly into their cars.*)

FORD DRIVER: I'm going home and get my .38 Special—and you better not be here when I get back. (*He starts his motor.*)

CHEVROLET DRIVER: (*Starts his motor*) Yes, and I'm going to get my .44 Burner and you better not be gone.

(*They simultaneously back off, glaring at each other. Curtain.*)

# Cock Robin

CAST:
  Cock Robin
  Owl
  Sparrow
  Crow
  Jaybird
  Beetle
  Mrs. Blackbird
  Sister Buzzard
  Mrs. Crow
  Fly
  Mrs. Fish
  Mrs. Beetle
  Bull
  Other Animals: Wrens, Owls, Fish, Crows,
     Blackbirds, Beetles, Jaybirds

*Time: Present.*
*Place: Any city.*

> *Scene: A city street in colored town.*
>
> *Setting: Straight across the stage, upstage, are (1) a cheap restaurant with a crude sign on which is written "The Grease Spot"; (2) a cheap pool hall called "The Eight Rock";[10] [and] (3) a dingy rooming house, "The Shimmy Shack." All have practical doors and windows. All are two-story buildings with numerous small-paned windows. There is a generous sidewalk and the rest of the stage is street.*
>
> *Action: At the rise there are characteristic noises from each of the places.*

Voice from the Grease Spot: Adam and Eve on a raft—wreck 'em! Clean up de kitchen for one! Let one come gruntin', one come switchin', snatch one from de rear![11]

Voice from the Eight Rock: Now, I'm going to show you some of Blue Baby's stuff . . .

Another voice: Aw, shut up! You trying to show yo' grandma how to milk ducks—shoot! (*A crack of balls.*)

*([In the] Shimmy Shack, somebody [is] playing blues on the piano. There is a sudden turmoil in the Shack and three shots are heard. The door flies open and Cock Robin staggers out with three arrows sticking in him and falls dead on his back on the sidewalk. All the windows fly up and heads are thrust out. Crowds pour out of the doors. Sparrow[12] is looking out of the second-story window of the Shack.)*

JAYBIRD: *(Standing over Cock Robin)* It's Cock Robin!

BEETLE: *(Gazing down on him)* Dat's him all right, and murdered in de first degree.

OWL: Who! Who! Who kilt Cock Robin?

MRS. BLACKBIRD: I just knowed something bad was going to happen—I dreamed last night the air was *full* of feathers.

BEETLE: I don't know who kilt him—but I do know he was due for a first class killin'. He give these married men more aid and assistance than de ice man.

SISTER BUZZARD: *(Belligerently)* I don't keer who kilt him. . . . But nobody better not cast no slams at my hotel. *(Points to Shack)* They bet' not say my shack ain't respectable and they bet' not tell me my eye is black.

OWL: *(Officiously)* Hey, Sister Buzzard, let's squat dat rabbit and jump another one. What we wants to know is—who kilt Cock Robin?

SPARROW: *(Has a bow and quiver of arrows, coming out of Shack to center stage. Very belligerently)* I, the sparrow, with my bow and arrow, and I kilt Cock Robin—who wants to know?

OWL: *(Warily)* 'Course we don't keer nothin' 'bout you killin' him, Brother Sparrow, we wants to know how come.

SPARROW: Well, I'll tell you. When me and my wife first started to nestin' she never laid nothin' but plain white eggs. But since Cock Robin been hanging 'round our place—every time I go out on a worm hunt, when I come back, she'll done laid another blue egg.

JAYBIRD: *(Begins to pick feathers violently)* Now, you done got me to scratchin' where I don't itch—come to think of it, I done seen two or three blue eggs in *my* nest.

CROW: *(Glaring at his wife)* You been complaining 'bout my singing ever since this guy *(Points at Cock Robin)* has been 'round here. 'Nother thing—I ain't never brought home nothin' but worms, and I been seeing a powerful lot of grasshoppers' bones around lately.

MRS. CROW: *(Crying and trembling)* Oo-oo, you done got me so nervous—I got de haystacks. *(She flutters and an egg falls to the floor.)*

CHORUS OF VOICES: She's lain a egg! And it's blue—robin egg blue.

JAYBIRD: Dere now! De mule done kicked Rucker!

OWL: Let's get dis killin' straight. Brother Sparrow say he kilt him for just causes . . .

CROW: And I don't blame him—when they get so they kin lay mo' eggs in my nest than I kin—they's got to be some changes made.

OWL: Who saw him die?

FLY: I, said the fly, with my little eye. I saw Cock Robin die.

OWL: Tell us 'bout it, Brother Fly.

FLY: I was in de Grease Spot when Mrs. Sparrow and Cock Robin passed, and I heard him say something was on fire—I don't know what—and he says to Mrs. Sparrow, "Come on up in the Shimmy Shack and let's put it out" and she says "All right." So they went on up—and the next thing I know, Bull Sparrow was killin' him.

OWL: Who caught his blood?

MRS. FISH: I did, Brother Owl—in my little dish. *(Wiping a tear)* He had such a lovely voice. *(A general skeptical titter runs around.)*

OWL: Since y'all done voted me in as chairman of dis committee—we better make some arrangement 'bout funeralizin' him. Who'll make his shroud?

MRS. BEETLE: I, Mrs. Beetle, with my thread and needle—I'll make Cock Robin's shroud.

OWL: Now, since I got a spade and shovel, I'll dig his grave. Now who'll bear his pall?

WRENS: We, said the wren[s], both the cock and the hen—we'll bear Cock Robin's pall.

OWL: Now, who'll mourn his love?

*(All of the females present come rushing up to the Owl. All the characters come down out of the building and crowd up close.)*

VOICE: Me, Brother Owl, I'll mourn his love! I really can mourn, too. (*They push and jostle each other.*)

OWL: Hear! Hear! Let's have some order. Don't need but one chief mourner. I'm going to put this thing to a vote and give the job to Sister Dove—she's had more experience in mournin' than anybody else, so she'll mourn Cock Robin's love. Now, who'll toll the bell?

BULL: I'll toll dat bell, Brother Owl.

CROW: How come I can't toll it[?] I ain't been 'signed to no duty yet.

BULL: I said I was going to toll that bell, and that's all there is to it. I can pull and it takes pull to toll bells. *(To Owl)* Just put my name down as bell-toller.

OWL: Now, we got things ready, what hall is we goin' funeralize him from?

CROW: He was a Great Grand Exalted Ruler of the High-Roostin' Crows[13]— we oughter conduct de funeral.

BEETLE: He was a Prime and Supreme Butler of the Noble Muckty Beetle Bugs—turn over de 'rangements to us.

JAYBIRD: I know so well, we're going to have something to say over Cock Robin when he was Superior Subordinate Exalted Contaminator in the Personal Parading Jay Birds.

OWLS: We, Order of Night-Stepping Owls, better take over this whole thing to keep peace. He was a member in good standing.

FISH: We certainly going to put a word in, 'cause he was a Bottom Ruler in the Order of the Never Been Caught Fishes.

BLACKBIRDS: Everybody knows de Ever Blooming Blackbirds really puts 'em away. A heap of you folks that's whooping for dis funeral don't know what to do wid one when you gits it.

OWL: Dat's a good idea! Every one of you lodges parade yo' material and de best one gits de funeral. *(Great cheers and hubbub)* Now, you crows got first chance.

*(Everyone exits but the Owl and the Bull. The Owl takes a high chair and sits in front of the Eight Rock to review the parade. Enter the Crows with a band.)*

CROW: *(Salutes Owl)* We're going to put Cock Robin in a bronze casket wid ten carriages and strut like this.

*(The band strikes up, the chief crow is the drum major, and they do a hot strut across the stage. Enter the Beetles. [They] salute Owl.)*

BEETLES: We'll put Cock Robin in a copper casket wid fifteen carriages and romp like this.

*(They do their stuff and take places beside the Crows. Enter the Jaybirds and same business.)*

JAYBIRD: Mr. Chairman, we'll put him in a silver casket wid twenty carriages and spread our junk like so.

*(They join Crows and Beetles. Enter Fish—same business.)*

FISH: We'll put him in a crystal casket and have thirty carriages. *(They begin to prance.)* We're gointer strut our stuff, we're gointer strut our stuff, Good Lawd! We're gointer spread our mess.

*(Enter Blackbirds—same business.)*

BLACKBIRDS: We'll put him in a solid gold casket wid fifty carriages, and we'll do the Palmer House and strut like Stavin' Cheney.[14]

OWL: I don't know who to 'cide on.

BULL: I don't keer who gits de funeral. I'm going to march in front.

OWL: How come, Brother Bull? You don't belong to none of these lodges.

BULL: I know it, but, Brother Owl, you know very well that Bull goes in front of everything.

OWL: Dat's de truth . . . Now, which one of you lodges think you kin do de best job?

ALL: Us! We! Me! Leave de Crows have him! . . . Give him to de Blackbirds . . . De Beetles is the only ones! . . . Let de Fishes funeralize him! . . . [*Etc., etc.*]

OWL: *(After rapping for order)* Well, whoever pays de bills can have de body. Who gointer pay de bills?

*(There is profound silence for a moment, then Brother Crow speaks up.)*

CROW: Well, brothers and sisters, since we'se all here at one time, you know Sister Speckled Hen is having a grand barbecue and fish fry down on Front Street and Beale[15]—why not let's have one grand consolidated, amalgamated fraternal parade down to her place and enjoy the consequences?

ALL: Yes, yes! Let's go!

*(They begin to organize. The Bull sets his hat at a reckless angle, seizes an elaborate baton and begins to line up the lodges. Then he places himself at the head. The Owl brings up the rear.)*

BULL: We're all set! *(To orchestra)* Turn it on, professor, and let the bad luck happen! *(They strut off.)*

# Heaven[16]

CAST:
  JIM
  ST. PETER
  ST. JOHN
  CHARLES KNOWLES
  OLD MAN
  FIRST ANGEL
  SECOND ANGEL
  THIRD ANGEL
  FOURTH ANGEL
  FIRST BLACK ANGEL
  SECOND BLACK ANGEL

*Setting: Heaven, showing the Tree of Life and the intersection of Hallelujah Avenue and Amen Street. The pearly gates stretch across the stage like a curtain. There is a peep-hole in the door. A flight of golden stairs ascends from the orchestra pit in midstage. Just inside the gates, John has a jeweled pulpit that holds the record books.*

*Action: At the rise the gates are closed, but a listless drone of "Holy" can be heard and the sound of crowns being cast and retrieved.[17] There comes a sound of a mouth organ being played in a blues mood way down the golden stair. Enter by the stairs a sour-faced man, [who is] neatly dressed and knocks at the gate. The peep-hole flies open and St. Peter peeps out and looks doubtfully at the candidate.*

ST. PETER: Well, who is it?

KNOWLES: One Charles Knowles.

ST. PETER: What do you want?

KNOWLES: I want to enter.

ST. PETER: You don't look just right to me. What good have you ever done?

KNOWLES: *(Thinks a moment)* Well, one time I met a little girl and she was crying because she had lost her money so I gave her three cents.[18]

ST. PETER: *(Over his shoulder)* Look on the books there, John, and see if it's there.

ST. JOHN: *(After a short pause)* Yes, it's here.

ST. PETER: Well, what else did you ever do?

KNOWLES: One time I met a little boy crying because he had lost his money and I gave him two cents.

ST. PETER: (*Over his shoulder*) See if that's there, John.

ST. JOHN: (*After a pause*) Yes, it's here.

ST. PETER: Is that all you ever gave away?

KNOWLES: Yes.

ST. JOHN: (*After a pause*) Well, Peter, you gointer let him in?

ST. PETER: No. Give him his nickel and let him gwan somewhere else.

*(He hands the man a nickle and slams shut the peep-hole. The man turns slowly and descends the stairs. The music of the mouth organ is much nearer now. St. Peter opens the peep-hole and looks out with pleased interest as a Negro with a torn hat and the general appearance of a roustabout ascends the stairs and stops before the gate. A dead silence falls. He wipes off his mouth organ and puts it in his pocket. He takes his hat in his hand and faces St. Peter timidly.)*

ST. PETER: (*Amiably*) What's your name?

JIM: Jim—thass whut they call me—Jim.

ST. PETER: (*Opening the gates*) Well come in, Jim. We're mighty glad to see you. *(Jim steps timidly in.)* Where did you come from, Jim?

JIM: (*Gazing awed upon the magnificence*) From Johnstown. Didn't you hear 'bout de great flood?

*(Enter four angels walking two and two. One couple enters left, one couple enters right, and [they] meet at the tree.)*

FIRST AND SECOND ANGELS: Ooo ooh! Y'all ain't seen no water!

ST. PETER: That's all right about the water. We all seen it. Just go with John and get fixed up. Everybody will be nice to you. *(To John)* Take him and dress him up.

*(John takes Jim's arm and starts off right.)*

JIM: Man, dat water was ten foot deep! You ain't never seen no water lessen you seen de Johnstown flood!

*(They exit right. Angels pass and repass, all gorgeously clad. Reenter John with Jim elaborately gowned. John leads him to a seat, places a golden harp beside him and goes back to his post.)*

JIM: Man, dat was some water! *(Feels his pockets as if hunting for something, looks worried for a moment.)* Oh, John, where's my harp?

ST. JOHN: There it is, right on the seat beside you.

JIM: *(Picks up the golden harp and looks it over.)* This here ain't *my* harp. Where's de one I been playin' all de time?

ST. JOHN: Oh, that's in your robe pocket.

*(Jim feels and pulls it out and wipes it off and blows a chord or two. All the angels look interested.)*

JIM: As I was sayin', I ain't never seen it rain lak it rained in Johnstown.

*(He commences to blow and all the angels tune in with him and heaven is full of harmony. Two huge black angels fly out from the back of heaven and seat themselves beside Jim. Both of them play guitars. John keeps time with his foot. Peter jingles his keys. This keeps up till an old patriarch with a long beard and crooked staff enters at left and proceeds slowly to the Tree of Life. There he pauses, looks pensively about. Jim notices him and stops the music and approaches him.)*

JIM: Hello, old folks, how long you been here?

OLD MAN: Oh, a long time.

JIM: I just got here from de Johnstown flood. Man, dat was some water! Chickens floatin', folks floatin', horses floatin', houses floatin'! Man, dat was water.

OLD MAN: *(Starting away in disgust)* Aw, shucks, you ain't seen no water.

*(He exits right. Jim looks hurt and puzzled for a moment then calls out to Peter.)*

JIM: Say, Peter, thought you said everybody here was nice and sociable. See how dat ole man treated me when I tryin' to show him manners and politeness by tellin' him 'bout de flood?

PETER: You can't tell that man 'bout no flood—that's Noah.

*(Jim sits down, crushed.)*

FIRST BLACK ANGEL: That's all right, Jim, you'll know better next time. Come on, let's play some more.

JIM: Never mind, I wants to fly some.[19]

SECOND BLACK ANGEL: You can't fly till they tell you.

JIM: Oh yes, I kin, too. They *my* wings, ain't they? Y'all just lak colored folks— let 'em be 'round de place awhile and they tries to boss de job. (*He gets up and starts off upstage center.*)

FIRST BLACK ANGEL: Now, where you goin'?

JIM: I'm goin' to climb up on some high tower of elevation and fly all over heben.

SECOND BLACK ANGEL: You better wait. You gointer break up somethin' and they'll sho take yo' wings off and Lawd knows when you'll git any more.

JIM: Aw, y'all just jealous—done got too old on de job. I'm goin' try my wings.

(*He exits. The other angels shake their heads sadly and turn again to music. There is a series of tremendous crashes and John and Peter rush offstage upstage center and return with Jim very mussed up. They lead him solemnly to the same seat and snatch off his wings and seat him, frowning disapprovingly upon him all the while. They return to their posts. Jim sits quiet for a moment then picks up the golden harp.*)

FIRST BLACK ANGEL: Unh hunh, I told you you was gointer git yo'self into all kinds of trouble flyin' so fast!

JIM: Aw, I don't keer.

SECOND BLACK ANGEL: Yeah, and now you ain't got no mo' wings neither.

JIM: (*Makin' ready to strike his harp*) I don't keer. I was a flyin' fool when I had 'em. (*Starts to play and sing. Quick curtain.*)

# Mr. Frog

CAST:
  FROG ON TOADSTOOL
  MR. FROG
  MISS MOUSIE
  OLD UNCLE RAT
  REVEREND BUZZARD
  FROG CHORUS
  MR. BEE
  MRS. SNAKE
  MR. BUG
  MR. TICK
  DR. FLY
  TORTOISE
  CHORUS OF BIRDS, BEETLES, AND FLIES
  DANCERS: PINE TREE, SOUTH WIND, WEST WIND, EAST WIND,
        NORTH WIND

*Time: When animals talked.*
*Place: A Florida swamp.*

> *Setting: All action is seen from actors' viewpoint. Full stage. Water is seen through the cypress and magnolia and pine trees. Spanish moss hangs from the trees. There is a large hollow log at left near the entrance. A long-leaf pine is downstage center. A huge toadstool is near footlights at extreme right. The lake in the back glints through all this. The pine tree is a girl dancer. Several birdnests are seen in the tree tops. One large tree near center downstage has a large hollow.*
>
> *[Action:] At the rise, the sun is setting. The tree is motionless. With the music it begins to sway slightly, but increases its motion all the time. Enter downstage left the South Wind, [who] dances with the tree for about a minute. Enter West Wind upstage right and both dance with tree. Enter East Wind upstage left, [who] joins the dance, then the North Wind downstage right. The tempo increases with the entrance of each wind. The tree is influenced by each. When all four winds are on, there is a violent wind dance for a minute till the sun finally sets and the winds take their places at their entrances and sink to the ground and remain there.*
>
> *In the darkness hundreds of fireflies swarm over the scene. The scene is lighted from the ground to indicate marsh gas (Jack O' Lantern).[20] There is silence for about thirty seconds, then enter a big frog upstage center [who]*

*leaps to the toadstool downstage right and sits there for a moment staring about him. The voice of an alligator booms from the water. An owl hoots, a chorus of frogs, birds, beetles, flies, a snake, all enter from different points and take places among the trees and bushes. A huge buzzard takes his seat on the hollow log. There is a working door in the log. The frog chorus is down near the footlights in irregular formation. They croak a few seconds.*

FROG ON TOADSTOOL: *(Sings)*

Mister Frog went courtin' he did ride.

FROG CHORUS: *(Jumping up and down rhythmically)*

Unh hunh, unh hunh.

*(Enter Mr. Frog downstage right riding a tortoise, dressed in green satin or velvet, white vest, sword, spurs and boots.)*

FROG ON TOADSTOOL: *(Sings)*

Mr. Frog went courtin' he did ride, sword and pistol by his side.

FROG CHORUS:

Unh hunh, unh hunh.

FROG ON TOADSTOOL:

He rode right up to Miss Mousie's door.

FROG CHORUS:

Unh hunh, unh hunh.

FROG ON TOADSTOOL:

Rode right up to Miss Mousie's door where he'd often been before.

CHORUS: *(All birds and everything join frog chorus)*

Unh hunh, unh hunh.

*(Tortoise reaches hollow log and [Mr. Frog] knocks on the door. It opens shyly and Miss Mousie creeps out, behaving coyly.)*

FROG ON TOADSTOOL: *(Singing)*

And he took Miss Mousie on his knee.

CHORUS:

Unh hunh, unh hunh.

MR. FROG:

Oh, I took Miss Mousie on my knee, said Miss Mousie won't you marry me? *(Suits the action to the song.)*

CHORUS:

Unh hunh, unh hunh.[21]

MISS MOUSIE: *(Coyly)*

Not without my pa's consent.

CHORUS:

Unh hunh, unh hunh.

MISS MOUSIE:

Not without my pa's consent, would I marry the president.

CHORUS:

Unh hunh, unh hunh.

*(Enter Old Uncle Rat from the log, very jovial. He bursts into a big laugh and everybody joins with him for a half minute. He beams happily on all.)*

FROG ON TOADSTOOL:

Old Uncle Rat, he laughed and cried.

CHORUS:

Unh hunh, unh hunh.

FROG ON TOADSTOOL:

Old Uncle Rat he laughed and cried.

CHORUS:

Unh hunh, unh hunh.

FROG ON TOADSTOOL:

Old Uncle Rat he laughed and cried, to see his daughter be a bride.

CHORUS:

Unh hunh, unh hunh.

MR. FROG:

Where, oh where will the wedding be?

CHORUS:

Unh hunh, unh hunh.

MR. FROG:

Where, oh where will the wedding be?

OLD UNCLE RAT:

Down in de holler of de ol' oak tree.

CHORUS:

Unh hunh, unh hunh.

*(Bride and groom retire into log. The guests begin to approach the tree slowly.)*

MR. FROG:

What, oh what will the supper be?

CHORUS:

Unh hunh, unh hunh.

MR. FROG:

What, oh what will the supper be?

OLD UNCLE RAT:

Good fat meat and de black eye pea.

CHORUS:

Unh hunh, unh hunh, unh hunh, unh hunh, unh hunh, unh hunh.

FROG ON TOADSTOOL:

And the first come in was Mister Bee.

CHORUS:

Unh hunh, unh hunh.

*(Enter Mr. Bee with a guitar.)*

FROG ON TOADSTOOL:

The first come in was Mister Bee, wid his fiddle on his knee.

CHORUS:

Unh hunh, unh hunh.

*(Enter bridal couple [who] proceed to the hollow oak and take their places. Reverend Buzzard performs the ceremony.)*

REVEREND BUZZARD: *(To groom)*

Do you take Miss Mousie to be your wife?

CHORUS:

Unh hunh, unh hunh.

*(Bride and groom nod assent in time to the music.)*

MR. FROG:

Yes, I take this woman to be my wife, to love her and kiss her for all my life.

CHORUS:

Unh hunh, unh hunh.

*(Old Uncle Rat tries to cry. Reverend Buzzard kisses the bride. They step away from the altar and seat themselves. General noise of congratulation in various ways—according to the species.)*

FROG ON TOADSTOOL:

And the nex' come in was Mrs. Snake.

CHORUS:

Unh hunh, unh hunh.

FROG ON TOADSTOOL:

And the next come in was Mrs. Snake, pass all around dat wedding cake.

CHORUS:

Unh hunh, unh hunh.

*(She is passing the cake, decorated with fireflies. Everybody takes a piece.)*

FROG ON TOADSTOOL:

And the next come in was Mr. Bug.

CHORUS:

Unh hunh, unh hunh.

FROG ON TOADSTOOL:

And de next come in was Mr. Bug, passed all around dat whiskey jug.

CHORUS:

Unh hunh, unh hunh.

FROG ON TOADSTOOL:

And the next come in was Mr. Tick.

CHORUS:

Unh hunh, unh hunh.

*(Enter Mr. Tick [who] starts gobbling everything in sight.)*

FROG ON TOADSTOOL:

And de next come in was Mr. Tick, et so much till it made him sick.

CHORUS:

Unh hunh, unh hunh.

*(Mr. Tick is flat on his back in the center of the wedding party.)*

FROG ON TOADSTOOL:

And then they sent for Doctor Fly.

CHORUS:

Unh hunh, unh hunh.

*(Enter Dr. Fly.)*

FROG ON TOADSTOOL:

And then they sent for Doctor Fly, said Mr. Tick, you sho will die.

CHORUS:

Unh hunh, unh hunh.

*(Mr. Tick is dragged out by his hind legs into the bushes out of sight. The groom loads his wife on the tortoise and they start off right. Everybody throws rice, etc., behind them.)*

FROG ON TOADSTOOL:

And that was the last of the wedding day.

CHORUS:

Unh hunh, unh hunh.

FROG ON TOADSTOOL:

And that was the last of the wedding day, and that is all I have to say.

CHORUS:

Unh hunh, unh hunh.

*(The bride and the groom exit to a slow curtain and leave the chorus dancing and singing, "unh hunh, unh hunh, unh hunh, unh hunh.")*

# Lenox Avenue

CAST:
OFFICER
YOUNG MAN
MAN 1
WOMAN 1
PREACHER
PREACHER'S FOLLOWERS, a man and two women
GIRL
MAN 2
MAN 3
MAN 4
MAN 5
LOIS
VARIOUS STREET PEOPLE

*Time: Present.*
*Place: New York City.*

 *Scene: Lenox Avenue at 135th Street.*
  *Setting: Backdrop showing intersection and houses. The autos are on a scenic band[22] and keep whizzing past.*
  *Action: When the curtain rises (children's game insert)[23] there is a traffic officer at the intersection. A very effeminate young man enters left with a large cretonne sewing bag on his wrist. Officer glares at him a moment, then yells at him.*

OFFICER: Come here.

YOUNG MAN: *(Looks all about himself)* Are you speaking to me?

OFFICER: Who else but you? Make it snappy! *(Young man approaches center of intersection where Officer is standing.)* What you got in that bag?

YOUNG MAN: My knitting.

OFFICER: *(Scornfully)* Oh yeah? And where are you going with your knitting?

YOUNG MAN: To the army.

OFFICER: *(Surprised)* To the army? Say! What are *you* going to the army for?

YOUNG MAN: Oh well, the boys must have their socks, you know. *(Waves a fluffy goodbye.)* Toodle-oo, old cabbage, I must try to get the boys out of the trenches before Christmas.

*(He exits right. Officer glares after him. Enter right, a man and woman nearing middle age. They are angry. He is walking a little ahead of her and pauses to talk back at her.)*

MAN 1: Aw, go bag yo' head, woman! You ain't got nothin' to do wid me. It's none of yo' business where I been.

WOMAN 1: *(Catching up to him)* I'm yo' wife, ain't I? I reckon I got something to say 'bout you bugabooing 'round town all night.

MAN 1: Aw, naw you ain't. God gives every man a lovable chance, and if he don't take it—that's his hard luck. But I'm telling you straight, the world ain't gointer owe *me* nothin' but a hole in de ground when I die.

*(She glares at him, arms akimbo. He starts to walk.)*

WOMAN 1: You big old evil mule you! You so evil till one drop of yo' spit would poison all the fish in the ocean. Hold on, I ain't through wid you yet!

MAN 1: You might as well be through. I'm through wid you. I got a brand new costume that you don't fit. I'm playin' a brand new game and you ain't it. Bye-bye, mama, you can't snore in my ear no more.

WOMAN 1: *(Slurringly)* Don't put dat lie out, papa. You ain't near through wid me!

MAN 1: Woman, I'm just too through. You gimme the close up cramps every time I look at you.

WOMAN 1: *(Snapping her fingers)* Brother, don't hang dat nasty wash out in my back yard. You ain't through wid me and I know it.

MAN 1: Aw yeah. I don't keer if I never see you no more. That would be soon aplenty.

WOMAN 1: *(Gets right up in his face)* You might as well stop dat wringing and twisting, 'cause I know you want me some 'gin *(again)*, 'cause I'm a damn sweet woman and you know it.

MAN 1: *(He looks her in the eye for a moment, then grabs her by the arm and faces her about.)* Aw, come on and let's go home, woman. I hates to hear folks fussin' on the streets.

*(They exit right. Enter a street preacher with two sisters and a brother. The preacher has a pair of cymbals and a bag. The sisters carry tambourines. The brother has a soap box. He places the box on the curb and the quartet*

*sings a song, "Wouldn't Mind Dying if Dying Was All." After this the preacher mounts the box and speaks. A crowd collects.)*

PREACHER: You folks ain't right. You needs to be born agin. Now I see some of y'all askin', "How kin a man enter de second time into his mother's esophagus and be born agin . . ."

VOICE FROM THE EDGE OF THE CROWD: What kind of a woman is that!

PREACHER: And moreover, you don't pray enough. You get down on yo' knees and mumble something and jump in yo' beds. Why can't you pray in de bed? You know some of y'all does everything in de bed but praise de Lawd. *(To the brother)* Let's sing "Brothers Get Yo' Peckers Ready, Let's Peck on de Rock."

*(The cymbals and tambourines start. The officer runs over.)*

OFFICER: Hey! Get de hell outa here, blocking the street!

*(They all exit right followed by the crowd. Only two men remain on the curb. Enter left a very slender girl in a form fitting, long dress. It is quite tight about the buttocks. They eye her till she almost reaches the right exit.)*

MAN 2: Man, if these new styles keep on the way they're going, we'll find out that the snake's got hips.

*(She keeps right on off right. Enter right two women. One is small and doll-like and the other is tall and masculine. They stroll across, arm in arm. At center they pause and whisper a moment, then stroll on across stage to exit at left. The two men glare behind them, then look at each other.)*

MAN 3: Well, Bo, I still got this consolation—ain't nobody but a man and the Holy Ghost been the father of a family yet.

*(Enter a man at left with a folded newspaper under his arm. He stands on the corner for a moment, then starts walking rapidly across Lenox Avenue. When he reaches the center, the officer stops him.)*

OFFICER: Where you going in such a hurry—trying to get run over?

MAN 4: No, sir.

OFFICER: Well, then, where you think you going?

MAN 4: To Brooklyn.

OFFICER: Oh yeah? Have you learned the trade? What do you know about going to Brooklyn?

MAN 4: Oh, I know a lot about it.

OFFICER: Got your papers on you?

MAN 4: *(Embarrassed)* I didn't get my diploma. You see, my father died and I had to leave school at eighteen, but I've been taking evening courses at Columbia University. You know, my father was an ambitious man, but life was hard so he never did find out how to get to Brooklyn, but he had high hopes for me. And on his death-bed he made me promise I'd carry on. So I've attended what lectures I could afford, read everything I could find, talked with taxi drivers and police officers—so today I felt I knew enough to try it, in spite of the fact that I didn't have my papers. *(He wrings his hands and looks exalted and wistful.)*

OFFICER: Spell compresstibility.

MAN 4: C-O-M . . . uh, er . . . P-E-R . . . er, oh I don't think I can spell that.

OFFICER: So you trying to bootleg to Brooklyn, eh? I ought to run you in! The nerve of some of you guys! And can't even spell compresstibility. That's what's the matter with the subway and the L—a whole lot of you amateurs trying to use 'em. Get on back uptown before I hang a charge on you. Beat it!

*(The fellow turns to run off left and the cop stands akimbo glaring after him. Enter right a good-looking girl walking briskly with a suitcase, followed by a man.)*

MAN 5: Lois! Wait there a minute, baby.

LOIS: *(Sourly)* From now on, my name's lost so far as you're concerned. And otherwise, I don't want you following me around.

MAN 5: Can't a man follow his wife?

LOIS: He sho kin, but there ought to be a law against it. I done told you I don't want you no more, so give yo' shoe-leather a break.

MAN 5: Don't talk like that, baby. *(Reaches in his pocket and takes out a bill.)* Here, take this money and have us a good supper when I get home from work.

LOIS: When you get home tonight, brother, I'll be spreading my junk in another town.

MAN 5: Who with?

LOIS: You wouldn't know, but, baby, I'm going to throw him some waves the ocean ain't never seen.

MAN 5: *(Angrily)* Yeah, and you stand up here and tell me that just one more time and I'm going to beat you if they have a lawsuit in West Hell.

LOIS: You better not hit me, nigger.

MAN 5: I'll hit you just as sure as Jesus rode a jackass.

*(She starts to walk off. He catches her arm.)*

LOIS: Turn go of me, fool! I dare you to hit me! If you stick your rusty foot in *my* face you going to jail.

MAN 5: How come I'm going to jail?

LOIS: 'Cause there's a cop right there on the corner and I'm going to holler like a pretty white woman! *(Quick curtain.)*

# [The] House That Jack Built

CAST:
  De Otis Blunt
  Teacher
  Nellie
  Walter
  Girl 1
  Girl 2
  Boy 1
  Boy 2
  Boy 3
  Other students

*Time: Present.*
*Place: Deep South.*

> *Scene: Old-fashioned schoolhouse.*
> *Setting: A platform at left. Two practical windows in backdrop with a wall blackboard in between them. Two rows of benches.*
> *Action: At the rise the pupils are all seated and attentive. The teacher is an aging man. They are large children and the girls are pretty. Everyone is neat and tidy but De Otis. He is seated in the last row next to the blackboard. One good-looking boy [Walter] is sitting by a pretty girl [Nellie] and flirting.*

TEACHER: Remember this is Friday afternoon. As soon as we finish this lesson we'll go into the recitation exercise. *(To [Walter and Nellie])* Pay attention to the lesson. *(There is a general buzz over the room. He raps for order.)* Who's doing all this talking? *(Fixes his eye on De Otis)* Come out here, De Otis. I'll teach you how to keep on talkin' when I say quit.

DE OTIS: Aw, it twant me talkin'.

TEACHER: *(Angrily)* Come out here, sir!

DE OTIS: *(Sulkily rises)* Everybody is talkin' *but* me!

TEACHER: Come on out here, De Otis.

> *(De Otis reaches the platform and gets a couple of licks and starts on back. Several of the pupils make faces at him and he makes faces back. His back*

*is towards the platform, but the teacher can see the faces the others are making.)*

TEACHER: *(To De Otis)* What are you makin' faces at these girls for? Come on back, De Otis.

DE OTIS: Aw, they makin' faces at me!

TEACHER: Come on back, De Otis.

*(He goes angrily back to the desk and gets two more licks.)*

Now see can't you behave yourself.

*(De Otis resumes his seat. [Nellie] holds up her hand.)*

TEACHER: *(Flirtatiously)* What is it, Nellie?

NELLIE: May I be excused please?

TEACHER: Yes, dear, you may go. *([Walter] lifts his hand.)* Well, what do *you* want?

WALTER: May I be excused?

TEACHER: No!

*(Girl 1, sitting on front seat, puts her foot on top of the desk. Teacher raises the rule to reprimand her, but his curiosity gets the better of him and he sits staring up under her clothes. The school titters. He catches himself and frowns. He glares down at De Otis.)*

Come out here, De Otis.

DE OTIS: Aw, you just pickin' on me 'cause I ain't got no clothes. I ain't doin' nothin'.

*(He goes up to the desk. While the teacher is thrashing him [Walter] sneaks out. De Otis returns to his seat and then the teacher misses the boy and looks frantic.)*

TEACHER: Where's Walter?

GIRL 1: He excused himself.

TEACHER: *(Slams his ruler down in fury two or three times and knocks his roll book off the desk.)* Come out here, De Otis! Come on and fetch it to me! Don't make me have to come down there after it!

*(De Otis pouts on up to the desk and gets a couple of licks in the hand and returns to his seat.)*

TEACHER: *(To Boy 1)* Go tell Nellie and Walter to come here and don't come back here telling me you can't find 'em. *(The boy exits.)* Now we'll finish this spelling lesson and go on to the recitations. Anybody don't know a speech today will get a good whipping and be kept after school.

*(Enter Walter, Nellie and [Boy 1 who] take their seats. To Walter)*

Go to the board.

*(Walter goes.)*

Spell "mouse."

*(Walter writes it correctly.)*

Now spell "cat."

*(Walter writes "pussy." Teacher gets very angry.)*

I didn't ask you what kind of a cat! Where is your mind anyhow? *(Very wild)* Come out here De Otis!

DE OTIS: Aw, what I got to do wid it?

TEACHER: Come out here, De Otis!

*(He comes grumbling and gets a licking.)*

TEACHER: Now, we'll have the regular Friday afternoon exercise. Begin at the front seats and go back. *(He glances at Walter to begin.)*

WALTER: *(Comes to the platform and bows stiffly)* When I was a lil boy the girls all call me cousin—now I'm a big man, I love 'em by the dozen. *(He bows and resumes his seat.)*

NELLIE: *(Holds out her skirt and bows.)*

Raccoon up de 'simmon tree
Possum on de ground
Raccoon shake de 'simmons down
Possum pass 'em 'round.

BOY 2: *(Comes up dancing and bows.)*

Little boy, little boy, who made yo' britches?
Mama did de cuttin' and papa did de stitches.

*(He finishes with a "break" and takes his seat.)*

GIRL 2: *(Frightened stiff—she sings-songs it rapid fire.)*

I come from haunts of coot and hern
I make a sudden sally
And sparkle out among the fern
To bicker down the valley.
I slip, I slide, I gloom, I glance

Among my skinning swallows
I make the fretted sunbeams dance
Above my shimmering shallows.

*(She vainly tries to remember more, but after two or three false starts and much head and leg scratching, she retires weeping. All the rest say "I didn't learn none" or "I forgot mine," or "Some one[24] done said mine" till one boy in the next to the last seat.)*

BOY 3:

Little fishes in de brook
Willie ketch 'um wid a hook
Mama fry 'em in de pan
Papa eat 'em like a man.

TEACHER: It's your time, De Otis. Come on out.

DE OTIS: Somebody done said mine.

TEACHER: Well, you better say somebody else's or get a real good killin' and stay after school.

DE OTIS: *(Scratches his head, legs, back—then stands up.)* I believe I know one, sir.

TEACHER: You better had of found one. Come on up here.

*([De Otis] ascends the platform but does not bow. He puts one hand on his hip.)[25]*

DE OTIS:

Oh, this is the house that Jack built.

Oh, this is the malt that lay in de house that Jack built.

This is the rat that ate the malt that lay in the house that Jack built.

Oh-ah-h—this is the cat that killed the rat that ate the malt that lay in the house that Jack built.

Oh! This is the dog that worried the cat that killed the rat that ate the malt that lay in the house that Jack built.

*(By this time he is walking back and forth across the platform and gesturing, and the others are keeping time with their feet. Even the teacher has joined in.)*

This is the cow with the crumpled horn that tossed the dog that worried the cat that killed the rat that ate the malt that lay in the house that Jack built.

*(All have left their seats and are dancing in chorus.)*

A-ah—this is the maiden all forlorn that milked the cow with the crumpled horn that tossed the dog that worried the cat that killed the rat that ate the malt that lay in the house that Jack built.

Oh, this is the man all tattered and torn that kissed the maiden all forlorn that milked the cow with the crumpled horn that tossed the dog that worried the cat that killed the rat that ate the malt that lay in the house that Jack built.

A-a-ah—this is the priest all shaven and shorn that married the man all tattered and torn that kissed the maiden all forlorn that milked the cow with the crumpled horn that tossed the dog that worried the cat that killed the rat that ate the malt that lay in the house that Jack built.

Ah, this is the cock that crowed in the morn that woke the priest all shaven and shorn that married the man all tattered and torn that kissed the maiden all forlorn that milked the cow with the crumpled horn that tossed the dog that worried the cat that killed the rat that ate the malt that lay in the house that Jack built.

Oh, this is the fox that lived under the thorn that stole the cock that crowed in the morn that woke the priest all shaven and shorn that married the man all tattered and torn that kissed the maiden all forlorn that milked the cow with the crumpled horn that tossed the dog that worried the cat that killed the rat that ate the malt that lay in the house that Jack built.

Ah—this is Jack with his hound and horn that caught the fox that lived under the thorn that stole the cock that crowed in the morn that woke the priest all shaven and shorn that married the man all tattered and torn that kissed the maiden all forlorn that milked the cow with the crumpled horn that tossed the dog that worried the cat that killed the rat that ate the malt that lay in the house that Jack built.

Ah—this is the horse of the beautiful form that carried Jack with his hound and horn that caught the fox that lived under the thorn that stole the cock that crowed in the morn that woke the priest all shaven and shorn that married the man all tattered and torn that kissed the maiden all forlorn that milked the cow with the crumpled horn that tossed the dog that worried the cat that killed the rat that ate the malt that lay in the house that Jack built.

Ah—this is the groom that every[26] morn curried the horse of the beautiful form that carried Jack with his hound and horn that caught the fox that lived under the thorn that stole the cock that crowed in the morn that woke the priest all shaven and shorn that married the man all tattered and torn that kissed the maiden all forlorn that milked the cow with the crumpled horn that tossed the dog that worried the cat that killed the rat that ate the malt that lay in the house that Jack built.

Ah—this is Sir John Barley Corn that owned the horse of the beautiful form that carried Jack with his hound and horn that caught the fox that lived under the thorn that stole the cock that crowed in the morn that woke the priest all shaven and shorn that married the man all tattered and torn that kissed the maiden all forlorn that milked the cow with the crumpled horn that tossed the dog that worried the cat that killed the rat that ate the malt that lay in the house that Jack built.

*(De Otis dances till he shudders down to the floor and lies there shivering in rhythm.)*

# *Bahamas*

CAST:
  GOOD BLACK
  JOE WILEY
  EMPEROR JONES
  MAN
  SEAMEN'S CHORUS
  DRUMMERS
  DANCERS

*Time: Present.*
*Place: Harlem.*

> *Scene: Seventh Avenue at 135th Street. Just a street scene on backdrop.*
>   *[Action:] All action from actors' right and left. At the rise, several persons are passing up and down avenue. One man [Good Black] is standing by himself as if waiting for someone. It is in broad daylight. A man stops and speaks to him.*[27]

MAN: Hello, Good Black, how you get 'em?

GOOD BLACK: Got the town by the tail, man. How they treating you?

MAN: Man, I got this town so skeered of me till the buildings lean backwards when I go down the streets. (*Looks Good Black over thoughtfully.*) But you look kinda pentecostal to me, brother. What's the matter?

GOOD BLACK: (*Looking at his watch*) Joe Wiley told me to meet him here at one o'clock and here it is after two. I hates to wait on anybody—even myself.

MAN: (*Looks off right*) Here he comes now. See you later.

> (*He exits right. Enter Joe Wiley with a cablegram in his hand.*)

JOE: (*Very jovial*) I bet you done run a hot! (*Good Black sulks.*) Whew! I can smell the smoke! (*Good Black laughs in spite of himself.*)

GOOD BLACK: Nigger buddy,[28] where you been all dis time? Got me tied out here croppin' grass like a mule.

JOE: (*Extends cablegram to Good Black who takes it and reads it.*) I got that just as I started to leave home. Ain't that grand?

111

GOOD BLACK: *(Reading aloud)* I am about to sail from the Bahamas for Africa, but I would like to see you again before I go. I am sending my flag-ship, the *Bellamina,* to bring you and your friends out. Signed: The Emperor Jones. *(Slaps Joe on the back)* Say, that's all to the mustard! Let's go.

JOE: *(Shakes hands and puts the cable in his pocket)* That's copasetty,[29] man, just thirty-eight and two. I'm already packed.

GOOD BLACK: When will the boat be here?

JOE: Arrives tonight, sails for Nassau tomorrow.

GOOD BLACK: *(Making an exaggerated motion of tip-toeing[30] away)* Excuse me while I take a creep! I'm going to shake hands with the Emperor Jones. *(Starts towards right exit.)*

JOE: *(Seizes his arm and joins him)* Come, if you're coming, let's go if you're going.

*(They tip their hats to the audience and exit joyfully. The curtain descends for a moment. A ship's siren can be heard and the sounds of anchor and chains, etc. Shouts of greeting, etc. The curtain arises on the ship warping into Prince George's Wharf. The crew is singing "Ceasar Riley."[31] In the Bahamas. Joe and Good Black are standing on the deck as the boat comes in. The Emperor Jones in all his glory is standing on the wharf surrounded by a group of his nobles and ladies. He is making a speech.)*

EMPEROR JONES: To Africa! When I get there with my conquering black legions I am not going to ask Great Britain what they are doing there. I'm just going to say, "Get out!" *(Applause.)* I'm not going to ask France "What are *you* doing here?" I'm going to say, "Get out!" I'm not going to ask Belgium "What are *you* doing here?" I'm going to say "Get out!" *(Great applause.)* Ninety days from now I shall have an ambassador at the Court of St. James. *(Applause.)* Ninety days from now I shall have an ambassador at the Court of Paris. *(Applause.)* Ninety days from now I shall have an ambassador at the Court of St. Petersburg. *(Hurrah!)* Ninety days from now I shall have an ambassador at the Court of Moscow. *(Applause.) And* ninety days from now, I shall have a Black House, side by side with the White House in Washington. *(Great storm of applause.)* Board the fleet, let us sail for Africa and freedom!

*(The seamen on the wharf sing a salute to the ship as she comes in.)*[32]

SEAMEN'S CHORUS:

Bellamina, Bellamina, Bellamina in the harbor,
Bellamina, Bellamina, Bellamina in the harbor.
Put Bellamina on de dock
Paint Bellamina bottom black.

Oh the Maisie, oh the Maisie, oh the Maisie set me crazy
Oh the Maisie, oh the Maisie, oh the Maisie set me crazy
Put Bellamina on de dock
Paint Bellamina, black, black, black.[33]

*(As the song ends, Joe and Good Black descend the gangplank and are ceremoniously received by Emperor Jones.)*

EMPEROR JONES: My old friend—Joe Wiley!

JOE: Your High and Mighty Majesty. *(Turns to Good Black)* And this is my friend, Mr. Good Black, who wanted to come along.

EMPEROR: Mighty glad to see you, Mr. Good Black. *(To Joe)* I thought you might have brought some ladies along.

JOE: Sorry. The ones I could have got to come would have been in my way *(He looks meaningly at the ladies)* after I got here.

EMPEROR: I guess it's just as well you didn't. You know the American girls are the snappiest lot on earth but you have ruined 'em by giving 'em too much rope. Now they are a whole woman and half a man. But let me introduce you to the court. *(He stands between the two and grows very rigid. The court circles about him in review, as each passes and bows very low, he bawls out)* Mr. Joe Wiley, Mr. Good Black, meet the Duke of Egypt, Lady Carrie Hawkins, Sir Willie, Jenkins, K. C. O. C.—Knight Commander of the Sublime Order of the Congo[—]Sir Lemuel Nixon, General of the Black Legions and Duke of Guinea, Sir Jasper Blunt, Earl of Uganda, Lady Mittie Harris, Countess of the Nile.

*(They all go back to their places singing "Don't You Hurry, Worry with Me" and pee vee voo.[34] Music of drums and cowbells are heard approaching.)*

JOE: What's that?[35]

*(Parade passes in review.)*

EMPEROR: The John Canoe parade in your honor.[36]

GOOD BLACK: Gee, that's swell—can I get in it or is it just private?

EMPEROR: Save it for tonight. This is going to be tight like so, boy! When night comes, we are holding a fire-dance.[37] To celebrate your coming and my departure for Africa with my conquering black legions. *(Drums are heard at a distance as the lights continue to fade. It is dark almost at once.)* Hear those drums! Let's go to the fire-dance.

*(Drums grow louder to a quick curtain. It goes up on a clearing in a tropic wood. It is lighted by a large bonfire to one side. Drummers near the fire. They are dancing when the curtain goes up. They are singing"* "T-i-o,

*T-i-o, mama say T-i-o, mama say T-i-o." They sing one verse before the Emperor and his party arrive. Enter Emperor followed by party. He is very informal. He is joyfully hailed by the dancers.)*

EMPEROR: *(To drummers)* Heat up dat drum, boy, and knock me something!

DRUMMER: *(Holding drum over fire and tunes it)* That's it right now. *(When he gets it right he plays a flourish, dances a step, plays flourish again and cries.)* Gimbay!

*(All the dancers begin to get excited. Everybody gets in the circle and begins to clap as the drums begin to play.)*

EMPEROR: *(Gets into the ring to dance[, with three others. Sings])*

Wish I had a nickel
Wish I had a dime
Wish I had a pretty girl
To love me all the time.

Down de road baby—

Wish I had a needle
Fine as I could sew
I'd sew my baby to my side
And down the road I'd go.

*(Refrain)* Down the road, baby—

*(The drums flourish and change [to new rhythm. Four dancers enter ring].)*

Bimini gal is a hell of a trouble
Never get licking till you go down to Bimini
Eh, lemme go down to Bimini
Never get a licking till you go down to Bimini.

*(Drums flourish and change rhythm. Three dancers enter ring.)*

Mama, I saw a sailboat
A-sailing in the harbor
I saw a yaller boy aboard it
And I took him to be my lover.

It's killing mama, etc.

*[(Drums flourish and change rhythm.)]*

Went to Key West to buy me a dress
How you going to make it ripple tail
How you going to shake it, shake it, shake it.

*(Song [changes.])*

Lime, oh lime juice and all
Lime, oh lime, 'Dessa hold your back
'Dessa hold your back,
Odessa, Odessa, Odessa.

*[(Drums flourish and change rhythm. One dancer enters ring.)]*

Mother may I go to school?
Yes, my darling, you may go
You may put on a ribbon bow.
Why you wheel Miss Curry so?
Wheel Miss Curry buck her so
Wheel Miss Curry, wheel Miss Curry, wheel Miss Curry, *etc.*

Mama, Mama, the old gray cat, she get so fat
She will not run at the old she-rat
Children lose de fine tooth comb
And head run away wid de lice
Oh, something in de hand more than common
Something in de hand more than common.

*[(Drums flourish and change rhythm.)]*

Mama lay! de drum bust!
Mama lay! de drum bust!
Oh, when I do so, do so
Oh, when I do so, do so
Oh, when I do so, do so
De drum bust!

*(Quick curtain. When it goes up again the Emperor is in front leading the crowd.)*

EMPEROR: To the ships. Let us sail for Africa!

*(Song: "Hoist Up de John B. Sail." [Then, sung] offstage:)*

Bellamina, Bellamina, Bellamina in the harbor
Bellamina, Bellamina, Bellamina in the harbor
Put Bellamina on the dock
Paint Bellamina bottom black.

# Railroad Camp

CAST:
 Cap'n
 Crew Man 1
 Crew Man 2
 Crew Man 3
 Crew Man 4
 Crew Man 5
 Water Boy

*Time: Present.*
*Place: Railroad track in Florida.*

> *Setting: Palmettos, oak trees hung with Spanish moss on the backdrop. In the foreground a length of railroad track on an embankment. A hand car stands at right end of track.*
>
> *Action: Ten men are spiking rails with sledge hammers. The boss is squatting up the line and signaling corrections. The water boy has a pail and dipper and stands in the middle of the track and leads the singing. At the rise they are singing.*[38]

[CREW:]

> Dat ol' (*wham*) black gal (*wham*)
> She keep on grumblin' (*wham*)
> New pair shoes (*wham*), new pair shoes (*wham*)
> I'm goin' (*wham*) buy her (*wham*)
> Shoes and stockings (*wham*), slippers too (*wham*) slippers too (*wham*).
> I'm goin' (*wham*) buy her
> Draws and dresses (*wham*) shimmy too (*wham*) shimmy too (*wham*).

CAP'N: Line it!

> *(They drop hammers and grab lining bars and sing:)*

> When I go and come agin'
> You won't know me from Nappy Chin.

CREW: Boys, can't you line it, boys can't you shake it![39]

> *(The Cap'n hollers "whoop!" The crew moves to another length.)*

CAP'N: Jonah head!

CREW: *(Sings)*

> Cap'n keep a hollerin' 'bout Jonah head
> Dis linin' bar 'bout to kill me dead.
> Boys, can't you line it, boys, can't you shake it.

CAP'N: Whoop! Center head!

CREW:

> Me and my gal goin' 'cross de field
> Heard 31 when it left Mobile
> Boys, can't you line it, boys, can't you shake it.

CAP'N: Center back!

CREW:

> Me and my partner and two, three more
> Standin' on de corner seein' de 'gator roar
> Boys, can't you line it, boys, can't you shake it.

CAP'N: Whoop!

CREW:

> Hear a mighty rumblin' 'round de river bend
> Must be de Southern crossin' de L and N.[40]
> Boys, can't you line it, boys, can't you shake it.

CAP'N: Whoop!

CREW:

> Wake up in de mornin' hear de ding dong ring
> Look on de table see de same old thing.
> Boys, can't you line it, boys, can't you shake it.

CAP'N: Center head!

CREW:

> Tip at de White House, tip at de gate
> I got a gal got a Cadillac "8"[41]
> Boys, can't you line it, boys, can't you shake it.

CAP'N: Center back!

CREW:

> Line it, boys, and don't get lost
> Ain't no heben for de section boss.
> Boys, can't you line it, boys, can't you shake it.

Cap'n: Hammer gang!

*(Men drop lining bars and get hammers.)*

Crew:

Mr. Dugan (*wham*) on de L and N (*wham*)
Got de pay car (*wham*) on de rear end (*wham*)

Cap'n: Whip steel!

Crew:

Mr. Davenport (*wham*) got de new store (*wham*)
Behind de depot (*wham*) whyncher pick 'em
Set 'em over (*wham*)

Cap'n: Whip it hot!

Crew:

I got a woman she's pretty but she's too bull dozin'[42]
I got a woman she's pretty but she's too bull dozin'
She won't live long, Lord, Lord, she won't live long.

I got a woman, she's got money 'cumulated
I got a woman, she's got money 'cumulated
In de bank, Lord, Lord, in de bank.

Big fat woman shakes like jelly all over
Big fat woman shakes like jelly all over
When she walk, Lord, Lord, when she walk.

Every pay day de wimmen all call me daddy
Every pay day de wimmen all call me daddy
I wonder why, Lord, Lord, I wonder why.

Bad Lazarus set on de commissary counter
Bad Lazarus set on de commissary counter
And walked away, Lord, Lord, and walked away.

High sheriff told de deppity, see can you find Bad Laz'rus
High sheriff told de deppity, see can you find Bad Laz'rus
Dead or live, Lord, Lord, dead or live.

Deppity ast de sheriff where in de world can I find him
Deppity ast de sheriff where in de world can I find him
I don't know, Lord, Lord, I don't know.

And they found him way up in between two mountains
And they found him way up in between two mountains
With head hung down, Lord, Lord, with head hung down.

And they blowed him, blowed him with a great big number
And they blowed him, blowed him with a great big number
A forty-five, Lord, Lord, a forty-five.

Laz'rus cried out, turn me over on my wounded
Laz'rus cried out, turn me over on my wounded
My wounded side, Lord, Lord, my wounded side.

And they drug him, drug Bad Laz'rus to his shanty
And they drug him, drug Bad Laz'rus to his shanty
On his wounded side, Lord, Lord, his wounded side.

Laz'rus cried out, bring me a cool drink of water
Laz'rus cried out, bring me a cool drink of water
I'm burning down, Lord, Lord, I'm burning down.

I got a wife and two or three chillun on de mountain
I got a wife and two or three chillun on de mountain
Cryin' for bread, Lord, Lord, cryin' for bread.

Laz'rus daddy went running to de field and crying
Laz'rus daddy went running to de field and crying
Whoa, har, gee Lord, Lord, whoa, har, gee.

Laz'rus mother come running and crying
Laz'rus mother come running and crying
Done kilt my son, Lord, Lord, done kilt my son.

I can stand right here and look 'way over in Alabama
Stand right here and look 'way over in Alabama
It look so far, Lord, Lord, it look so far.

When I get back to Georgy southern Alabama
When I get back to Georgy southern Alabama
Be long farewell, Lord, Lord, be long farewell.

CREW MAN 1: Water boy!

*(Boy carries him water, he lifts the dipper and drinks and squirts some from his mouth on the ground.)*

CREW MAN 1: Say, nigger buddy,[43] dis water is hotter'n two boxes of matches—
go git some fresh water!

WATER BOY: I'm Mr. Pickhandle Slim, when you get time—lousy wid bucks!
Got money's mama and grandma's change.

CREW MAN 1: Aw, boy, go 'head on get some cool water before I be all over you
just like gravy over rice—you must smell yo'self.

REST OF CREW: Aw yeah, he's gettin' too mannish. Go 'head and get us a cool
    drink.

*(Boy exits left.)*

CAP'N: Line it!

*(The crew exchange hammers for bars. Water boy returns. The crew take
their places and sing.)*

CREW:

    When I get in Illinois,
    I'm going to spread de news about de Florida boys.
        Shove it over! Hey, hey, can't you line it

*(Shaking rail and grunt at the end)*

        Can't you move it.

    Me and my buddy and two, three more
    Going to ramshack Georgy everywhere we go.
        Shove it over! Hey, hey, can't you line it
        Can't you move it.

    Tell you what de hobo told de bum
    Get any cornbread save me some.
        Shove it over! Hey, hey, can't you line it
        Can't you move it.

    Cap'n got a burner I'd like to have
    A thirty-two twenty wid a shiny barrel.
        Shove it over! Hey, hey, can't you line it
        Can't you move it.

    Cap'n got a special he try to play bad
    But I'm going to take it if he makes me mad.
        Shove it over! Hey, hey, can't you line it
        Can't you move it.

    Here come a woman walkin' 'cross de field
    Mouth exhaustin' like an automobile
        Shove it over! Hey, hey, can't you line it
        Can't you move it.

    Wake up, Cap'n, and light yo' lamp
    Highway robbers is in yo' camp.
        Shove it over! Hey, hey, can't you move it
        Can't you line it.

Come on, honey, let's go to bed
Get a lil baby and name him Red.
    Shove it over! Hey, hey, can't you move it
    Can't you line it.

If lil Sissy was a gal of mine
She shouldn't do nothin' but starch and iron.
    Shove it over! Hey, hey, can't you move it
    Can't you line it.

Whut's de matter wid de Cap'n he must be cross
It's done five-thirty and he won't knock off.
    Shove it over! Hey, hey, can't you move it
    Can't you line it.

*(A whistle blows in the distance and the Cap'n signals that work is over. The men hurriedly pile the tools on the hand car and climb on, and four of them get to the handles.)*

CREW MAN 2: Come on let's go! I got a belly like Eatin' Flukus today.

CREW MAN 3: Who was dis Eatin' Flukus?

CREW MAN 2: He et up camp meetin', backed off Association and drank Jordan dry.

REST OF CREW: That's me right now, let's go!

*(They begin to work the handles and one of the crew sings:)*

CREW MAN 4:

Oh Lulu, oh gal, want to see you so bad.

CREW MAN 5: Blow it like an elephant and do it like an airedale. *(He breaks out with another song)*[44]

Gointer see my long-haired babe,
Gointer see my long-haired babe,
Lord, I'm going 'cross de water
To see my long-haired babe.

Whut you reckon Mr. Treadwell said to Mr. Goff
Lord, I b'lieve I'll go South
And pay they poor boys off.

*(Slow curtain as this is sung.)*

Lord, I ast dat woman
To lemme be her kid.
And she looked at me

And begin to smile
Said I b'lieve I'll try you
For my kid awhile.

*(Last two lines ought to be sung after curtain is down.)*

# *Jook*

CAST:
  NUNKIE
  STACK-OF-DOLLARS
  BUNK
  BLACK-BOY
  SACK-DADDY
  BIG-SWEET
  PLANCHITA
  JAMES PRESLEY[45]
  ELLA WARD[46]
  DRAWS-LEG
  BLUE-FRONT
  MUTTSY[47]

*Time: Present.*
*Place: A sawmill jook house.*

> *Scene: Interior of main room in the jook. There is a dilapidated piano in one corner. A small rough table against the wall in the upstage corner. There are a few chairs scattered around against the wall.*
>
> *Action: When the curtain goes up, Nunkie is at the piano playing and singing. There are three couples on the floor slow-dragging and joining in with the singing in spots.*

NUNKIE: *(Singing)*[48]

> Babe, I'm lonesome, I'm the lonesomest man in your town.
> Got experience of women—small town turnt me down.
>
> Aw, I wants to tell you people whut de Florida East Coast done for me.
> Took my regular—come and got my used-to-be.
>
> Say, look here sweet baby, you sho don't know my mind,
> When you see me laughing, laughing just to keep from crying.
>
> If you ever been down you know just how I feel.
> I been down so long, down don't worry me.
>
> Says, storm is rising, wind begin to blow
> My house done blowed down, I ain't got no place to go.

Roll me wid yo' stomach, feed me wid yo' tongue
Do it a long time baby till de sunshine come.

I'd rather be in Tampa, wid de whippoorwill
Than to be 'round here, baby, with a hundred dollar bill.

I'd rather see my coffin rolling in my door,
Than my baby to tell me she don't want me no more.

I'm sittin' here lookin' a thousand miles away,
I'm going to pack up my suitcase and make my get-away.

Says, my heart struck sorrow, tears come rolling down,
Says, it seem like, baby, I'm got to leave this town.

If anybody ast you, baby, who composed this song,
Tell 'em Little Johnny Barton, he been here and gone.

*(Enter Draws-Leg at left and gets to the center of the floor. He joins in the song and turns about half-dancing.)*

DRAWS-LEG: Here! Gimme a woman. I can't do all this by myself. *(To one of the men)* Say there Bunk, lend me Planchita for a hot minute, do, I won't git well.

*(He pulls the girl away from the other man who laughs it off. He and Planchita begin to dance fancy. Bunk walks towards the right exit and looks offstage. Nunkie begins to play very fast and the dancers laugh and keep up with the music as long as they can. When Draws-Leg and Planchita laughingly give up like the rest, Nunkie stops playing and turns from the piano laughing.)*

BUNK: *(Looking into the room off right)* Hey, Black-Boy, how you doing it?

BLACK-BOY: *(Off stage)* Come on in here and find out.

BUNK: Aw, naw! Y'all ain't goingter hem me up in there! Come on out here so when I wins yo' money, I got a running chance.

*(General laughter and the noise of scraping chairs. Enter Black-Boy, Stack-of-Dollars, Blue-Front and Muttsy. They stroll straight for the table and begin to place chairs.)*

STACK: Now, Bunk, you been bugabooing 'round here; come here and lemme see if you know anything about skinning.

*(All the men but Nunkie gather about the table. Nunkie plays softly and sings in a whisper along with him. The game begins with Black-Boy dealing.)*

BUNK: *(Pointing to his card)* See dat deuce? It's going to carry de whole deck down.

STACK: I don't bleeve it.

BLUE-FRONT: I bet you a fat man I'll be here last.

BUNK: A dollar I knows de best one!

STACK: A stack of dollars you don't. Deal!

BLACK-BOY: (*Sings*)[49]

> Let de deal go down, boys.
> When yo' card gets lucky, oh partner,
> You oughter be in a rollin' game.
> Let de deal go down, boys,
> Let de deal go down.

> Lost all my money, oh partner
> In the rollin' game.
> Let de deal go down, boys,
> Let de deal go down.

BUNK: (*Threatening*) I see you peepin' them card, Black-Boy!

BLACK-BOY: (*Laughing*) Aw, I ain't tryin' to carry no cub[50]—y'all too wise for dat.

BUNK: I don't mind you winnin' my money, but if you try to beat me out of it, if God send me a pistol, I'll send him a man.

STACK: (*To Bunk*) You know he ain't gointer try nothin' funny in here. He know us ain't no fools. They kilt Fat Sam shootin' at Big Boy so all de fools in de world is done dead. Let de deal go down.

ALL: (*As they play cards*)

> I'm going back to de 'bama, where
> They don't want no change.
> Let de deal go down, boys,
> Let de deal go down.

> No mo' rollin' partner,
> Till de man pay off.
> Let de deal go down, boys,
> Let de deal go down.

STACK: Hey, hey! There you go, Blue-Front. You done fell.

ALL: (*As two more cards are dealt off the deck*)

> Ain't had no trouble, partner,
> Till I stop by here.
> Let de deal go down, boys,
> Let de deal go down.

STACK: Dat's yo' cup Sack-Daddy! Here come Bunk! *(Laughs triumphantly)* This must be de fall of de year. Now it me and Black-Boy. So good a man, so good a man!

ALL: *(As three cards fall)*

> When I get in de 'bama, partner,
> Won't be troubled wid you.
> Let de deal go down, boys,
> Let de deal go down.
> Let de deal go down, boys,
> Let de deal go down.

STACK: *(Jumps to his feet in triumph)* I'm de best! *(Rakes in the pot.)* I'm too hard for you boys. Who wants to skin me? Who wants me, any, some or none?

SACK-DADDY: I hear you cacklin', I know yo' nest ain't far. Shuffle 'em, Black-Boy and less go.

BIG-SWEET: *(Crosses to the table and lays her hand on the cards)* Don't skin no more, Sack-Daddy. Read de deck for me.

SACK-DADDY: I ain't goin' to read nothing till you tell me who you shacked up wid. A man is liable to get shot lessen he know something.

BIG-SWEET: Aw, stop woofin' and read dem cards.

SACK-DADDY: All right, Big-Sweet. *(He takes up the cards and walks to the center of the stage. As he calls off a card he lets it fall to the floor.)*

> Ace means the first time that I met you
> Deuce means there was nobody there but us two
> Trey means the third party, Charlie was his name
> Four spot means the fourth time you tried that same old game
> Five spot means five years you played me for a clown
> Six spot means six feet of earth when the deal goes down
> Now I'm holding the seven for each day in the week
> Eight spot means eight hours that you sheba'ed with your sheik
> Nine spot means nine hours that I work hard every day
> Ten spot means tenth of every month I brought you home my pay
> The jack is Three-card Charlie who played me for a goat
> The queen, that's you pretty mama, also trying to cut my throat
> The king stands for sweet papa Sack-Daddy and he's going to wear the crown
> So be careful y'all ain't flat-footed when de deal goes down.

PLANCHITA: Now you done gimme de blues. Play something, Nunkie.

NUNKIE: You always holler play, but you don't never put out nothin'.

PLANCHITA: ([*Arms*] *akimbo*) Who, me? I ain't putting out nothin' but old folks' eyes, and I ain't doin' that till they dead. I'm like de cemetery, I'm takin' in but never no put out.

*(Nunkie starts to play. All start to dance.)*[51]

ALL:

See you when yo' troubles get like mine.
See you when yo' troubles get like mine.
See you when yo' troubles get like mine.

Wonder will he answer if I write.
See you when yo' troubles get like mine.
See you when yo' troubles get like mine.

All of my Sunday clothes in pawn.
See you when yo' troubles get like mine.
See you when yo' troubles get like mine.

Comin' a time when a woman won't need no man.
See you when yo' troubles get like mine.
See you when yo' troubles get like mine.

Don't you hear that East Coast when she blow?
See you when yo' troubles get like mine.
See you when yo' troubles get like mine.

Blow like she never blowed before.
See you when yo' troubles get like mine.
See you when yo' troubles get like mine.

Make me down a pallet on de floor.
See you when yo' troubles get like mine.
See you when yo' troubles get like mine.

Laid in jail my back turned to de wall.
See you when yo' troubles get like mine.
See you when yo' troubles get like mine.

Going down de long lonesome road.
See you when yo' troubles get like mine.
See you when yo' troubles get like mine.

BIG-SWEET: *(Leans up against the piano and all but weeps.)* God I wish I knowed where I could slip up on a drunk! *(Sound of a guitar is heard off-stage left. She jumps [up] with pleasure.)* God I b'lieve that's James Presley. *(Rushes [a]cross to left exit.)* Dat James! Come on in here and play me something.

*(Enter James Presley with a guitar 'round his neck. Everybody greets him. They get him a seat and a drink. He tunes up.)*

JAMES: *(To Nunkie)* You fram behind me.

NUNKIE: All right, less go. Somebody git me another drink. *(It is brought.)*

JAMES and NUNKIE:

Cold rainy day, some old cold rainy day
I'll be back some old cold rainy day.

All I want is my railroad fare,
[Take me back where I was born.][52]

Old Smoky Joe, Lord, he died on the road
Saying I'll be home some day.

Cold rainy day, some old cold rainy day,
I'll be back some old cold rainy day.

Oh, de rocks may be my pillow, Lord,
De sand may be my bed
I'll be back some old cold rainy day.

*([While the musicians play] the others sing and dance. The men yell out in exuberance as they dance slowly and sensuously.)*

BLACK BOY: Oh, wha[t] evil have I done! Roll yo' hips—don't roll yo' eyes.

SACK-DADDY: Turn it on and let de bad luck happen—Shake yo' hips, mama.

STACK: Ten dollars for a whoop, six bits for a squall! If you can't shimmy, shake yo' head.

BUNK: I hear you cacklin', mama, I know yo' nest ain't far. Don't you vip another vop till [I] get in there.

*(As the dance comes to a close, the musicians drift on into "John Henry"[53] and Ella Ward grabs a guitar out of the corner beside the piano, walks to the center of the stage and puts one foot up on the chair and begins to sing the verses to a slow curtain.)*

ELLA:

John Henry driving on de right-hand side.
Steam drill driving on de left,
Says 'fore I let yo' steam drill beat me down
I'll hammer my fool self to death.
I'll hammer my fool self to death.

Captain ast John Henry
What is dat storm I hear?
He said Cap'n dat ain't no storm,
Nothin' but my hammer in de air,
Nothin' but my hammer in de air.

John Henry had a lil baby
Holdin' him in his right hand,
Says, lil baby don't you cry
You'll never be a steel drivin' man,
You'll never be a steel drivin' man.[54]

John Henry told his Cap'n,
Bury me under de sills of de floor,
So when they get to playin' good old Georgy skin,
Bet 'em fifty to a dollar more,
Bet 'em fifty to a dollar more.

John Henry had a lil woman,
De dress she wore was red.
Says I'm goin' down de track and she never looked back.
I'm goin' where John Henry fell dead,
I'm goin' where John Henry fell dead.

Who gointer shoe yo' pretty lil feet
Who gointer glove yo' hand,
Who gointer kiss yo' rosy cheek,
Who gointer be yo' man,
Who gointer be yo' man[?]

My father's goin' to shoe my pretty lil feet,
My brother's goin' to glove my hand,
My sister's goin' to kiss my rosy cheek,
John Henry gointer be my man,
John Henry gointer be my man.

Says, where did you get yo' pretty lil dress,
De shoes you wear so fine?
I got my shoes from a railroad man,
My dress from a man in de mines,
My dress from a man in de mines.

[CURTAIN]

# DE TURKEY AND DE LAW (1930)

D e *Turkey and De Law* is essentially a dramatization of Hurston's short story, "The Bone of Contention" (unpublished during Hurston's lifetime), which centers on an altercation between Dave Carter, "the local Nimrod," and Jim Weston, the town bully. In the story, Dave shoots a turkey, which Jim then claims as his own. As they struggle over the carcass, Jim hits Dave with the hock-bone of a mule and knocks him unconscious. A few days later, a makeshift trial for assault degenerates into a battle between the Methodist and Baptist congregations of the town and a comical debate over whether a mule bone can be considered a weapon. The play follows this plot but adds the motivation that the men hope to use the turkey to gain the affections of Daisy, the town flirt, a character borrowed from another Hurston work, "The Eatonville Anthology" (1926).

On the surface, the play is simply a comedy centered on a silly confrontation and a love triangle. It is better understood and enjoyed, however, as a loving portrayal of Eatonville's various characters and life in the town, expressed through games, doing "the dozens," card-playing, and singing. The scenes in act 1 taking place at Joe Clarke's storefront could be seen as a dramatization of the following passage from "The Eatonville Anthology":

> The *town* was collected at the store-post office as is customary on Saturday nights. The *town* has had its bath and with its week's pay in pocket fares forth to be merry. The men tell stories and treat the ladies to soda-water, peanuts and peppermint candy. (67–68)

The emphasis on "the *town*" encapsulates the collection of anecdotes that make up "The Eatonville Anthology": the work is a portrait of a community. Likewise, the play, given the thin narrative thread that holds it together, functions better as a collection of anecdotes and sketches, ranging from the "Chick-ma-chick" game played by the town's children at the outset of the play, to the insults hurled from one congregation to the other during the courtroom scene of act 2. The play's lack of focus and awkward pacing makes it a flawed piece of drama, but it remains, nevertheless, a good-natured account of small-town life and the absurd behavior of lovers everywhere.

*De Turkey and De Law,* as several scholars have noted, very closely resembles a play Hurston co-wrote with Langston Hughes titled *The Mule-Bone* (1930–1931), which was reissued in 1991 in a volume titled *Mule Bone* edited by Henry Louis Gates Jr. and George Houston Bass. The genesis of the play, therefore, demands clarification. Here is a brief synopsis of how one play became two. In February 1930, Hurston was sent by Charlotte Osgood Mason to Westfield, New Jersey, to assemble and shape her folklore material into a book, only a few doors away from Langston Hughes, who at the time was also a Mason protégé. Through sheer proximity, the longstanding friendship between the two blossomed into a secret project: a Negro folk comedy devoid of the grotesqueries of minstrelsy. In a January 1931 letter to Arthur Spingarn, Hughes wrote, "I would do the construction, plot, whatever characterization I could, and guide the dialog. Miss Hurston was to put in the authentic Florida color, give the dialog a true Southern flavor, and insert many excellent turns of phrase and 'wise-cracks' which she had in her mind and among her collections." They worked from April to May, finishing acts 1 and 2 before Hurston left Westfield in June.

The eventual falling-out over the play centered on the role of Louise Thompson, who was briefly married to Wallace Thurman in 1928 and worked as a secretary for Mason. (Thompson later had a long career as a labor activist.) She took dictation from the two writers, but since there was no money to pay her for these extra duties, Hughes offered her a financial stake in future royalties and the position of business manager for a future Broadway production, compensation that Hurston found unwarranted. Unaware that Hurston perceived the offer as a conspiracy to wrest control of the play away from her, Hughes assumed that Hurston would continue to work on act 2 while traveling in the South. However, Hurston instead finished the play herself and copyrighted it under the title *De Turkey and the Law* in October 1930. Hughes claims that they were to meet in New York in November and continue work on the play, but Hurston missed appointments and seemed determined to avoid collaborating. In the same month, Hurston sent a copy of the script to Carl Van Vechten, a white writer and patron of African American artists. In a November 1930 letter to Van Vechten, she stated her version of Hughes's role in the development of the script: "Langston and I started out together on the idea of the story I used to tell you about in Eatonville, but being so much apart from rush of business, I started all over again while in Mobile and this is the result of my work alone." Unbeknownst to Hurston, Van Vechten then sent the script to an employee of Samuel French, a theatrical rights and publication company, who sent the script to Rowena Jelliffe and the Gilpin Players in Cleveland, who were eager to produce the play.

According to Hughes, two different scripts, one of them *De Turkey and De Law* and the other, the result of their earlier work, found their way to Cleveland by early 1931, and a production was slated for February.[1] Both authors traveled to the Midwestern city to reestablish their collaboration, though they never succeeded in actually working together. When Hurston discovered that Thompson had visited Cleveland (on an unrelated matter, as it turns out) and seen Hughes, it inflamed the differences between the two authors and in early February, Hurston cancelled the performance before any revisions were made to either script.

After the collapse of the project, both plays languished for decades. *De Turkey and De Law* was effectively forgotten, and *Mule Bone* was not produced until 1991, when it was presented by Lincoln Center in New York using George Houston Bass and Henry Louis Gates Jr.'s *Mule Bone* edition. Based on a draft labeled "Cleveland, 1931," Bass and Gates's script was probably a version of the play containing acts 1 and 3 co-written by Hurston and Hughes in Westfield, New Jersey, and act 2 written by Hurston when she was in the South.

A side-by-side comparison between *De Turkey and De Law* and the Bass and Gates edition of *Mule Bone* shows the following differences and similarities. Act 1 of *De Turkey and De Law* appears to be largely Hurston's work, and constitutes her attempt to excise Hughes's contributions and return the play to the spirit of "The Bone of Contention," which was centered on a fight over a turkey rather than a fight over a girl. Act 2 appears to be Hurston's alone, although Hughes claims to have played a significant role in con-structing the plot and adding situations. Act 3, however, is almost identical to the Cleveland text, casting doubt on Hurston's position that *De Turkey and De Law* was, in Hurston's words, "the result of my work alone."

Due to inconsistencies and gaps in the "testimony" of both Hurston and Hughes, we may never know precisely how the two writers worked together or what went so terribly wrong with the *Mule-Bone* project. We reproduce the October 1930 script copyrighted by Hurston because it was the text she claimed as her own, and also because it helps shed light on the work of two important writers as well as the nature of collaboration itself.

# De Turkey and De Law
## *A Comedy in Three Acts*
## *With Langston Hughes*

CAST:[2]

JIM WESTON, a young man and the town bully (a Methodist)
DAVE CARTER, the town's best hunter and fisherman (Baptist)
DAISY BLUNT, the town vamp
MRS. BLUNT, her mother
JOE CLARKE, the Mayor, Postmaster, storekeeper (Baptist)
MATTIE CLARKE, Joe's wife
WALTER THOMAS, a villager (Methodist)
HOYT THOMAS, Walter's wife
TOD HAMBO, a villager (Baptist)
MRS. HAMBO
JOE LINDSAY, a villager (Baptist)
MRS. LINDSAY
LIGE MOSELEY, a villager (Methodist)
LUM BAILEY,[3] the Marshall
MRS. BAILEY
REVEREND SIMMS (Methodist)
REVEREND SINGLETARY (Baptist)
LULU, a villager
JENNY, a villager
BOOTSIE, a young woman
TEETS, a young woman
BIG 'OMAN, a young woman
LUCY TAYLOR, a villager (Methodist)
IDA JONES, a villager
DELLA LEWIS, a villager (Baptist)
SHANK NIXON, a villager (Methodist)
MRS. NIXON
MRS. McDUFFY, a villager
MRS. ANDERSON, a villager
ESSIE, a young girl
ESSIE'S LITTLE SISTER
JOHN WESLEY TAYLOR, a young boy
MARY ELLA, a young Baptist girl

WILLIE, a young Methodist boy
OTHER VILLAGERS, CHILDREN, DOGS

### ACT ONE

*Setting: A Negro village in Florida in our own time. All action from view-point of an actor facing the audience.*

*Place: Joe Clarke's store porch in the village. A frame building with a false front. A low porch with two steps up. Door in center of porch. A window on each side of the door. A bench on each side of the porch. Ax handles, hoes and shovels, etc. are displayed leaning against the wall. Exits right and left. Street is unpaved. Grass and weeds growing all over.*

*Time: It is late afternoon on a Saturday in summer. Before the curtain rises the voices of children are heard, boisterous at play. Shouts and laughter.*

JOHN WESLEY TAYLOR: [*(Offstage)*] Naw, I don't want to play wringing no dish rag! We gointer play chick mah chick mah craney crow.[4]

ESSIE: [*(Offstage)*] Yeah, less play dat, and I'm gointer to be de hen.

JOHN WESLEY TAYLOR: And I'm gointer be de hawk. Lemme git myself a stick to mark wid.

*(The curtain rises slowly. As it goes up the game is being organized. The boy who is the hawk [John Wesley Taylor] is squatting center stage in the street before the store with a short twig in his hand. The largest girl [Essie] is lining up the other children behind her.)*

ESSIE: *(Looking back over her flock)* Y'all ketch holt of one 'nother's clothes so de hawk can't git yuh. *(They do.)* Y'all straight now?

CHILDREN: Yeah.

*(The march around the hawk commences.)*

ESSIE AND CHICKS:

>    Chick mah chick mah craney crow
>    Went to de well to wash my toe
>    When I come back my chick was gone.
>    What time ole witch?

JOHN WESLEY TAYLOR: *(Making a tally on the ground)* One!

ESSIE AND CHICKS:

>    Chick mah chick [mah craney crow
>    Went to de well to wash my toe
>    When I come back my chick was gone.
>    What time ole witch?]

*(While this is going on Walter Thomas from the store door eating peanuts from a bag appears and seats himself on the porch beside the steps.)*

JOHN WESLEY TAYLOR: *(Scoring again)* Two!

*(Enter a little girl right. She trots up to the [Essie].)*

ESSIE'S LITTLE SISTER: *(Officiously)* Titter, mama say if you don't come on wid dat soap she gointer wear you out.

ESSIE AND CHICKS:

> Chick mah chick [mah craney crow
> Went to de well to wash my toe
> When I come back my chick was gone.
> What time ole witch?]

*(While this is being sung, enter Joe Lindsay [who] seats himself on right bench. He lights his pipe. The little girl stands by the fence rubbing her leg with her foot.)*

JOHN WESLEY TAYLOR: *(Scoring)* Three!

LITTLE SISTER: *(Insistent)* Titter, titter! Mama say to tell you to come on home wid dat soap and rake up dat yard. I bet she gointer beat you good.

ESSIE: *(Angrily)* Aw naw, mama ain't sent you after me, nothin' of de kind! Gwan home and leave me alone.

LITTLE SISTER: You better come on! I'm gointer tell mama how 'omanish you actin' 'cause you in front of dese boys.

ESSIE: *(Makes a threatenin' gesture)* Aw, don't be so fast and showin' off in company. Ack lak you ain't got no sense!

LITTLE SISTER: *(Starts to cry)* Dat's all right. I'm going home and tell mama you down here playing wid boys and she sho gointer whup you good, too. I'm gointer tell her you called me a fool too, now. *(She walks off, wiping her eyes and nose with the back of her hand.)* Yeah, I'm goin' tell her! Jus' showin' off in front of ole John Wesley Taylor. I'm going to tell her too, now.

ESSIE: *(Flounces her skirt)* Tell her! Tell her! Turn her up and smell her! *(Game resumes.)*

> Chick mah chick [mah craney crow
> Went to de well to wash my toe
> When I come back my chick was gone.
> What time ole witch?]

JOHN WESLEY TAYLOR: Four! *(He rises and imitates a hawk flying and trying to catch a chicken. Calling in a high voice.)* Chickie!!

ESSIE: *(Flapping her wings to protect her young)* My chickens 'sleep.

JOHN WESLEY TAYLOR: Chickie!!

ESSIE: My chickens 'sleep.

JOHN WESLEY TAYLOR: I shall have a chick.

ESSIE: You shan't have a chick.

JOHN WESLEY TAYLOR: I'm going home. *(Flies off.)*

ESSIE: There's de road.

JOHN WESLEY TAYLOR: I'm comin' back.

*(During this dialog [John Wesley Taylor] is feinting and darting in his efforts to catch a chicken and the chickens are dancing defensively.)*

ESSIE: Don't keer if you do.

JOHN WESLEY TAYLOR: My pot's a-boiling.

ESSIE: Let it boil.

JOHN WESLEY TAYLOR: My guts a-growling.

ESSIE: Let 'em growl.

JOHN WESLEY TAYLOR: I must have a chick.

ESSIE: You shan't have nairn.

JOHN WESLEY TAYLOR: My mama's sick.

ESSIE: Let her die.

JOHN WESLEY TAYLOR: Chickie!!

ESSIE: My chickens 'sleep!

*(Hawk [John Wesley Taylor] darts quickly around the hen [Essie] and grabs a chicken and leads him off and places the captive on his knees at the store porch. After a brief bit of dancing he catches another, then a third who is a chubby little boy. The little boy begins to cry.)*

LITTLE BOY: I ain't gointer play 'cause you hurt me.

JOHN WESLEY TAYLOR: Aw, naw, I didn't hurt you.

LITTLE BOY: Yeah you did too. You pecked me right here. *(Points to top of his head)*

JOHN WESLEY TAYLOR: Well if you so touchous you got to cry every time any-body look at you, you can't play wid us.

LITTLE BOY: *(Smothering sobs)* I ain't cryin'.

*(He is placed with the other captives. [John Wesley Taylor] returns to game.)*

JOHN WESLEY TAYLOR: Chickie.

ESSIE: My chickens 'sleep!

VOICE FROM A DISTANCE: Titter! You Titter!!!

ESSIE: Yassum.

VOICE: If you don't come here wid dat soap you better!

ESSIE: *(Shakes herself poutingly, half sobs)* Soon's I git grown I'm gointer run away. Everytime a person gits to havin' fun, it's "come here, Titter and rake de yard." She don't never make Bubber do nothin'. *(She exits into the store.)*

JOHN WESLEY TAYLOR: Now we ain't got no hen.

ALL THE GIRLS: *(In a clamor)* I'll be de mama hen! Lemme be it!

*(Enter Hambo left [who] stands looking at the children.)*

HAMBO: Can't dese young uns keep up a powerful racket, Joe?

LINDSAY: They sho kin. They kin git round so vig'rous when they whoopin' and hollerin' and rompin' and racin, but just put 'em to work now and you kin count dead lice fallin' off of 'em.

*(Enter Essie⁵ from the store with the soap. Hambo pulls out a plug of tobacco from his hip pocket and bites a chunk from it.)*

HAMBO: De way dese chillun is dese days is—Eat? Yes! Squall and holler? Yes! Kick out shoes? Yes! Work? No!!

LINDSAY: You sho is tellin' de truth. Now look at dese! I'll bet every one of 'em's mammies sent 'em to de store an' they out here frolickin'. If one of 'em was mine, I'd whup 'em till they couldn't set down. *(To the children)* Shet up dat racket and gwan home!

*(The children pay no attention and the game gets hotter.)*

VOICE: *(offstage)* You Tit-ter!! You Tit-ter!!

WALTER: Titter, don't you hear yo' ma callin' you?

ESSIE: Yassuh, I mean, naw suh.

LINDSAY: How come you can't answer, then? Lawd knows de folks just ruins chilluns dese deys. Deys skeered tuh whup 'em right. Den before they gits twenty de gals done come up wid somethin' in dey arms an' de boys on de chain gang. If you don't whup 'em, they'll whip you.

HAMBO: Dat sho is whut de Lawd loves. When I wuz a boy they *raised* chillen then. Now they lets 'em do as they please. There ain't no real chastising no more. They takes a lil tee-ninchy switch and tickles 'em. No wonder de world is in sich uh mess.

VOICE OFFSTAGE: You Tit-ter!! Aw Titter!!

ESSIE: *(Stops to listen)* Yassum!

VOICE OFFSTAGE: If you don't come here, you better!

ESSIE: Yassum! *(To her playmates)* Aw shucks! I got to go home.

*(She exits right, walking sullenly. The game has stopped.)*

LINDSAY: *(Pointing at Essie)* You see dat gal shakin' herself at her mammy? De sassy lil binch[6] needs her guts stomped out. *(To Essie)* Run! I'm comin' on down there an' tell yo' ma how 'omanish you is, shakin' yo'self at grown folks.

*(Essie walks slower and shakes her skirt contemptuously. Lindsay jumps to his feet as if to pursue her.)*

You must smell yo'self!

*(Essie exits.)*

Now de rest of you Haitians scatter 'way from in front dis store. Dis ain't no place for chillen, nohow. *(Gesture of shooing)* Gwan! Thin out! Every time a grown person open they mouf y'all right dere to gaze down they throat. Git!

*(The children exit sullenly right. In the silence that follows the cracking of Walter's peanut shells can be heard very plainly.)*

HAMBO: Walter, God a'mighty! You better quit eatin' them ground peas de way you do. You gointer die wid de colic.

LINDSAY: Aw, 'tain't gointer hurt him. I don't b'lieve uh cord uh wood would lay heavy on Walter's belly. He kin eat mo' peaders than Brazzle's mule.

WALTER: *(Laughing)* Aw naw, don't throw me in wid dat mule. He could eat up camp-meetin', back off Association and drink Jordan dry.

LINDSAY: And still stay so po' till he wuzn't nothin' atall but a mule frame. *(Enter Lige Moseley right.)* 'Tain't never been no mule in de world lak dat ole yaller mule since Jonah went to Joppy.

*(Lige seats himself on the floor on the other side of the steps. Pulls out a bone toothpick and begins to pick his teeth.)*

LIGE: Y'all still talking bout Brazzle's ole useter-be mule?

HAMBO: Yeah. 'Member dat time Brazzle hitched him to de plow and took him to Eshleman's new ground?

LIGE: And he laid down before he'd plow a lick. Sho I do! But who ever seen him work? All you ever did see was him and Brazzle fightin' up and down de furrows. *(All laugh.)* He was so mean he would even try to kick you if you went in his stall to carry him some corn.

WALTER: Nothin' but pure concentrated meanness stuffed into uh mule hide. Thass de reason he wouldn't git fat—just too mean.

LIGE: Sho was skinny now. You could use his ribs for a washboard and hang de clothes up on his hips to dry. *(All laugh.)*

HAMBO: Lige, you kin lie lak cross ties from Jacksonville to Key West. But layin' all sides to jokes, when they told me dat mule was dead, uh just took and knocked off from work to see him drug out lak all de rest of de folks, and folkses, dat mule wuz too contrary to lay down on his side and die. He laid on his raw-boney back wid his foots stickin' straight up in de air lak he wuz fightin' something.

LINDSAY: He wuz—bet he fought ole death lak a natural man. Ah seen his bones yistiddy, out dere on de edge of de cypress swamp. De buzzards done picked 'em clean and de elements done bleached 'em.

LIGE: Everybody went to dat draggin' out. Even Joe Clarke shet up his store dat mornin' and went. *(Turns his head and calls into the store)* Didn't you, Mr. Clarke?

CLARKE: *[(Offstage)]* Didn't I whut? *(Enters and stands in door.)*

LIGE: Shet up yo' store and go to de draggin' out of Brazzle's ole mule.

CLARKE: I God, yeah. It was worth it. *(Sees Hambo.)* I didn't know you was out here. Lemme beat you uh game of checkers.

HAMBO: Lissen at de ole tush hawg! Well, go git de board, and lemme beat you a pair of games befo' de mail gits in.

CLARKE: *(To others)* Beat old me! *(To Hambo)* Come on here, youse my fish. *(Calls into store)* Mattie, bring me dat checker-board and de checkers! *(To men on porch)* You got to talk to wimmen-folks lak dat—tell 'em every lil thing—do, she'd come rackin' out here wid de board by itself.

*(Enter Mrs. Clarke with homemade checkerboard and coffee can containing the much-used checkers. Clarke sits on a keg and faces Hambo. They put the board on their knees and pour out the checkers.)*

HAMBO: You want black or red?

CLARKE: Oh, I don't keer which—I'm gointer beat you anyhow. You take de black.

*(They arrange them. The others get near to look on. Hambo sits looking at the board without moving.)*

HAMBO: Who's first move?

CLARKE: Black folks always go to work first. Move!

*(Hambo moves and the game[7] proceeds with the spectators very interested. Enter Lum Bailey right and joins the spectators. A woman enters left with a market basket and goes on in[to] the store. The checkers click on the board. A girl, about twelve, enters right and goes into the store and comes out with a stick of peppermint candy.)*

WALTER: Naw you don't Hambo!—Don't you go in dere! Dat's a trap—
   *(Pointing)* Come right here and you got him.

LIGE: *(Pointing)* Back dat man up, Hambo, do, he'll git et up.

*(There is the noise of the checkers for a half minute then a general shout of triumph.)*

SPECTATORS: You got him now, Hambo! Clarke, he's sho got you.

CLARKE: *(Chagrined)* Aw, he ain't done nothing! Jes' watch me.

HAMBO: *(Jeering)* Yeah, gwan move! Ha! Ha! Go 'head and move.

SPECTATORS: Aw, he got you, Bro' Mayor—might as well give up. He got you in de Louisville Loop.

CLARKE: Give up what? He can't beat me! *(Peeved)* De rest of y'all git from over me, whoopin' and hollerin'! I God, a man can't hear his ears.

*(The men fall back revealing the players clearly.)*

HAMBO: Aw, neb' mind 'bout them, Joe, go 'head and move. You ain't got but one move to make nohow—go 'head on and take it.

CLARKE: *(Moving a checker)* Aw, here.

HAMBO: *(Triumphant)* Now! Watch me boys whut Ah'm gonna do to him. Ah'm gonna laff in notes, while Ah work on him.

*(He lifts a checker high in the air preparatory to the jump, laughing to the scale and counting each checker he jumps out loud.)*

Do, sol, fa, me, la! One! *(Jumps a checker)* La, sol, fa, me, do! Two! *(Jumps another)* Do, re, fa, me, do! Three! Me, re, la, so, fa! Four!

*(The crowd is roaring with laughter.)*

Sol, fa, me, la, sol, do! Five! Ha! Ha! Boys I got de ole tush hawg! I got him in de go-long. *(He slaps his leg and accidentally knocks the board off his knee and spills the checkers.)*

CLARKE: Too bad you done dat, Hambo, 'cause Ah was gointer beat you at dat. *(He rises and starts towards the door of the store as the crowd roars in laughter.)*

HAMBO: You mean you was gointer beat me to de door, not a game of checkers. Ah done run de ole coon in his hole.

LIGE: Well, Hambo, you done got to be so hard at checkers, come on less see whut you can do wid de cards. *(He pulls out a soiled deck from his coat pocket and moves toward the bench at the left of the porch.)* You take Lum and me and Walter will wear you out.

HAMBO: You know I don't play no cards.

LUM: We ain't playin' for no money, just a lil Florida flip.

HAMBO: Y'all can't play no Florida flip. 'Fore Ah joined de church there wasn't a man in de state could beat me wid de cards. But Ah'm a deacon now, in Macedonia Baptist—Ah don't bother wid de cards no mo'.

*(He and Joe Lindsay go inside store.)*

LIGE: Well, come on Lum. Walter, git yo'self a partner.

WALTER: *(Looking about)* 'Tain't nobody to git. *(Looks off right)* Here come Dave Carter.

LIGE: You can't do nothin' wid him dese days. He useter choose a game of cards when he wasn't out huntin', but now when he ain't out huntin' varmints he's huntin' Daisy Blunt.

*(Enter Dave right with a shot-gun slung over his shoulder.)*

WALTER: Come on, fish, lemme bend a five-up over yo' head. You looks just like my meat.

DAVE: Ah'm on mah way to kill me a turkey gobbler, but if you and Lum thinks y'all's tush hawgs Ah'll stop long enough to take you down a button-hole lower. *(He sets his gun down and finds a seat and draws it up to the card table.)*

WALTER: Naw, Dave, we ain't going to fool wid no button-holes—we gointer tear off de whole piece dat de button-holes is in. *(They all get set.)* All right boys, turn it on and let de bad luck happen.

LIGE: *(Probing the deck)* My deal.

WALTER: Watch yo'self Dave, don't get to worryin' 'bout Daisy and let 'em ketch yo' jack.

LUM: *(Winking)* What you reckon he gointer be worryin' 'bout Daisy for? Dat's Jim's gal.

DAVE: Air Lawd, a heap sees but a few knows. Deal de cards man—you shuf-flin' a mighty lot.

WALTER: Sho is—must be tryin' to carry de cut to us.

LIGE: Aw, we ain't gonna cheat you, we gonna beat you. *(He slams down the cards for Dave to cut.)* Wanna cut 'em?

DAVE: Nope. 'Tain't no use cuttin' a rabbit out when you kin twist him out. Deal 'em!

*(Lige deals and turns up the Jack of spades.)*

WALTER: Yee-ee! Did you snatch dat Jack?

LIGE: Man, you know I ain't snatched no Jack. Whut you doin'?

WALTER: I'm beggin!

LIGE: Go ahead and tell 'em I sent you.

WALTER: Play just like Ah'm in New York, partner. *(Scratches his head)* We oughter try to ketch dat Jack.

LIGE: Stick out yo' hand an' you'll draw back a nub.

WALTER: Whut you want me to play for you, partner?

DAVE: Play me a baby diamond.

*(Walter plays, then Lum, then Dave.)*

LUM: *(Triumphant)* Looka pardner, they doin' all dat woofin' on uh queen—sendin' women to do uh man's work. Watch me stomp her wid mah king.

*(He slams his card down and collects the trick.)*

Now come on under dis ace!

*(They all play and he collects the trick.)*

Now whut you want me to play for you, pardner?

LIGE: How many times you seen de deck?

LUM: Twice.

LIGE: Pull off wid yo' king.

*(Lum plays the king of spades. All the others play.)*

> Look at ole low pardner. Ah knowed Ah wuz gointer ketch him! Come right back at 'em.

LUM: *(Stands up and slams down the ace)* Pack up, pardner. Ah'm playin' mah knots, now all play now. Ho! Ho! Dere goes de queen! De Jack's a gentleman! *(Lige takes the Jack and sticks it up on his forehead in braggadocio.)* Here comes de ten spot, pardner, Ah'm dumpin' to yuh!

LIGE: *(As he plays the Jack)* Everybody git up off it and dump. High, low, Jack, game and gone from de first four.

WALTER: Gimme dem cards! Y'all carried de cub to us dat time. *(Riffles the cards elaborately)* But de deal is in de high, tall house now. Dis is Booker T. Washington spreading his mess. *(Offers cards to Lige)* Cut?

LIGE: Yeah, cut 'em and shoot 'em. I'd cut behind mah ma.

*(He cuts and Walter deals.)*

WALTER: Well, whut sayin'?

LUM: I'm beggin'.

WALTER: Get up off yo' knees. Youse dat one.

LIGE: Walter, you sho stacked dese cards.

WALTER: Aw, stop cryin' and play, man. Youse too old to be hollerin' titty-mama.

LUM: Dis ain't no hand, dis is a foot. What you want me to play for you partner?

LIGE: Play yo' own hand, partner—I ain't nobody. Lead yo' bosses.

*(He leads the ace of clubs. Play goes round to dealer and Walter takes the card off the deck and slams it down.)*

WALTER: Get up, ol' deuce of diamonds and gallop off wid yo' load. Pardner, how many times you seen de deck?

DAVE: Two times—

*(They make signals.)*

WALTER: Watch dis ol' queen. Less go! *(He begins to sing—Dave joins in.)*

When yo' card gits lucky, oh pardner,
You oughter be in a rollin' game.[8]

Ha! Ha! Wash day and no soap! *(He sticks the Jack upon his forehead. He stands up and sings again.)*

Ah'm goin' to de 'bama, Lawd.
Pardner don't want no change.

*(He collects that trick and plays again. Dave also stands.)*

DAVE: Here come de man from de White House—ol' king of diamonds. *(Sings, all join.)*

Ah'm goin' back to de 'bama, Lawd.
Pardner won't be worried wid you.

*(He collects the trick.)*

Never had no trouble, Lord pardner,
Till I stopped by here.

*(They all stand hilariously [and] slam down their cards.)*

WALTER: Aw, we'se just too hard for you boys—we eats our dinner at de black-smith shop. Y'all can't bully dis game. *(He solemnly reaches over and takes Dave's hand.)*

DAVE: *(To Walter)* Mr. Hoover, you sho is a noble president.[9] We done stuck dese shad-moufs full of cobs. They skeered to play us any mo'.

LIGE: Who skeered? Y'all jus' playin' ketch up nohow. Git back down and lemme wrap uh five-up 'round yo' neck.

DAVE: *(Looking off right)* Squat dat rabbit an' less jump another one. Here come Daisy.

WALTER: Aw Lord, you ain't no mo' good now. But Ah don't blame you, Dave, she looks warm.

*(Enter Daisy right with a scarlet hibiscus over each ear and smiling broadly.)*

LIGE: *(Jumps down and takes Daisy by the arm)* Come on up here, Daisy, and ease Dave's pain. He's so crazy 'bout you his heart 'bout to burn a hole in his shirt.

*(She steps up on the porch.)*

DAVE: *(Bashfully)* Aw, y'all gwan. Ah kin talk.

DAISY: *(Arms akimbo, impudently)* Oh kin you? *(She gets up close to Dave.)*

DAVE: *(Pleased)* You better git 'way from me 'fore Jim come 'long.

DAISY: *(Coquettishly)* Ain't you man enough to cover de ground you stand on?

DAVE: Oh, Ah can back my crap! Don't worry 'bout me. Where you headed for?

DAISY: *(Audaciously)* Where *you* goin'?

DAVE: Out by de cypress swamp to kill us uh turkey. It's uh great big ole gobbler—been alurrin' me fer six months. Ah'm gointer git him today for you, and yo' mama gointer cook him.

DAISY: Ah sho would love the ham of [a] turkey.

DAVE: *(Patting his gun barrel)* Well me an' ole Hannah sho gointer git you one. Look here, Daisy, will you choose uh bag of ground peas?

DAISY: I jus' love goobers.

DAVE: *(Sticking out his right elbow)* You lak chicken?

DAISY: Yeah.

DAVE: Take uh wing.

 *(She locks arms with him and they strut inside the store.)*

LIGE: Ah b'lieve dat fool is got some gumption. Jim Weston better watch out.

WALTER: Oh I ain't never figgered Dave was no fool. He's uh bottom fish. Jim talks all de time but Dave will run him uh hot—here he come now. *(Looks off left. All look the same way.)*

LUM: Lawd, don't he look mean? *(He chuckles.)* Ah bet he know Daisy's here wid Dave. Ah wouldn't take nothin' for dis.

 *(Enter Jim Weston left with a guitar looking very glum. He stops beside the step for a moment. Takes off his hat and fans with it.)*

JIM: Howdy do, folks.

ALL: Howdy do, Jim.

JIM: Don't do all they say. *(He sees the gun leaning against the rail.)* Who gun dat? *(Points at the gun.)*

LIGE: You know so well whose gun dat is. Ah jus' heard him say he's goin' out to git his gal uh ham of a turkey gobbler out 'round de cypress swamp. He's inside now treatin' her to peaders and candy. *(He winks at the others and they wink back.)*

WALTER: *(Turns and calls into the store)* Say, Dave! Don't try to keep Daisy in dere all day. Her feller out here waitin' to scorch her home.

DAVE: *(From inside store)* Let him come git her if she want him.

LIGE: Umph! Dere now, de mule done kicked Rucker! *(Calls inside to Dave)* I hear you crowin', rooster. I know yo' nest ain't far.

HAMBO: *(From inside store)* Yeah, dis rooster must know something—he's gittin' plenty grit in his craw.

*(General laughter. There is a gay burst of laughter from inside the store. In a moment Dave enters from the store with Daisy on his left arm. With his right he is stuffing shells into his pocket. The air is tense. Lindsay, Hambo and Joe Clarke all enter behind the couple.)*

DAVE: *(Releases Daisy and steps to the edge of the porch right in front of Jim and looks up at the sky)* Well, sun's getting low—better git on out to de swamp and git dat gobbler. *(He turns and picks up the gun and breaks it.[10])*

JIM: *(Sullenly)* 'Lo Daisy.

DAISY: *(Brightly)* Hello Jimmy. *(She is eating peanuts.)* Ain't Dave smart? He's gonna kill me uh turkey an' Ah kin eat all Ah wants.

JIM: He ain't de onliest person kin shoot 'round here.

LIGE: Yeah, but he's best marksman just de same. 'Tain't no use talkin' Jim. You can't buck Dave in de woods. But you got de world beat wid uh git-fiddle. Yessuh, Dave is uh sworn marksman but you kin really beat de box. Less have uh tune.

JIM: Oh, I ain't for pickin' no box. I come to git some shells for my rifle. Sorta figgered on uh wild turkey or two. *(He comes up on the porch and starts in the store.)*

DAISY: If Dave go git me dat big ole turkey an' you go git me one too—gee! Won't I have uh turkey fit?

LINDSAY: Lord, Daisy, you gointer have dese boys killin' up every turkey in Orange County.

WALTER: You mean *Dave*. Jim couldn't hit de side of uh barn wid uh brass fiddle.

JIM: *(Hitching up his trousers)* Who can't shoot? *(To Clarke)* Come on an' gimme uh box uh shells. I'll show yuh who kin shoot! *(He exits into store with Clarke behind him.)*

DAVE: *(To Daisy)* You wait here till Ah git back wid yo' turkey.

DAISY: Ah'm skeered.

DAVE: Whut you skeered of? Jim? He ain't no booger boo, if his ears do flop lak uh mule.

DAISY: Naw. Ah ain't skeered uh no Jim. Ah got tuh git back tuh de white folks an Ah'm skeered tuh go 'round dat lake at night by myself.

*(Enter Jim from store and stands in door with box of shells in his hand.)*

JIM: No girl look like you don't have to go home by yo'self, if it was midnight.

DAVE: *(Gun in hand and ready to exit)* Naw, 'cause Ah'm right here—

JIM: Daisy don't you trust yo'self round dat lake after dark, wid dat *(Points at Dave)* breath-and-britches. You needs uh real man to perteck you from dem 'gators and moccasins.

DAVE: Let somethin' happen and she'll find out who got rabbit blood and who ain't. Well, Ah'm gone. *(He steps down off the steps but looks back at Daisy.)*

JIM: Ah'm goin' too—git you uh great big ole turkey-rooster.

*(Dave takes a step or two towards left exit.)*

DAISY: Jim, ain't you gointer knock off a lil tune fo' you go? Ah'm lonesome for some music.

*(Dave stops in his tracks and looks wistful. Jim sets down the shells on the bench and picks up his box with a swagger and tunes a bit.)*

WALTER: Georgy Buck!

*(Jim plays the air through once then starts to sing. Dave leans his gun against the fence and stands there.)*

JIM:

Georgy Buck is dead, last word he said
I don't want no shortenin' in my bread.

Rabbit on de log—ain't got no dog
How am I goin' git him, God knows.

*(Dave walks on back near the step, and begins to buck a wing. Daisy comes down the step admiring both the playing and the dancing. All the men join in singing and clapping.)*

Rabbit on de log—ain't got no dog
Shoot him wid my rifle, bam! bam!

Oh Georgy Buck is dead, last word he said
Never let a woman have her way.

*(The tempo rises. As Dave does a good break he brings up directly in front of Daisy. He grabs her and swings her into a slow drag. The porch cheers. Jim stops abruptly. Enter two women [Lulu and Jenny] right. [They] hurry up to the porch.)*

LULU: Don't stop, Jim! Hit dat box a couple mo' licks so some of dese men kin scorch us in de store and treat us.

JIM: Aw, I don't feel lak no playin'.

DAVE: *(Grinning triumphantly)* Ah'm gone dis time to git dat turkey. Daisy run tell yo' ma to put on de hot water kittle. *(He exits left with gun on shoulder.)*

DAISY: Oh lemme see if I got a letter in de post office. *(She exits into store.)*

JIM: He better git for home 'fore ah bust dis box over his head.

LULU:[11] *(Grabbing Lige)* Aw, don't worry 'bout Dave Carter. Play us some music so I kin make Lige buy me some soda water. *(She is playfully dragging Lige towards the door.)* Jenny you grab Walter.

*(Walter makes a break to jump off the porch and run. The woman [Jenny] catches him and there is a very gay bit of tussling as the men are dragged towards the door.)*

I bet if this was Daisy, they'd uh done halted inside and toted out half de store.

JENNY: Yeah. *(Gets Walter to the door.)* Everything you hear is Daisy, Daisy, Daisy! Just 'cause she got a walk on her like she done gone crazy through de hips! *(Yanks Walter into the door.)* Yeah, y'all goin' treat us. Come on!

WALTER: Yeah, but Daisy's uh young pullet and you gittin' gray headed.

JENNY: Thank God I ain't gray elsewhere! Come right on. You gointer buy me some soda water, nigger. *(To Jim)* Play us some music, Jim, so we kin grand march up to de counter.

JIM: I can't play nothin'—mad as I is. I'm one minute to boilin' and two minutes to steam. I smell blood!

LULU: You don't want to fight, do you?

JIM: Sho do. You ain't never seen a Weston yet dat wouldn't fight, have you?

LIGE: That's whut they all got run outa town for—fightin'. *(Calls into store)* Hey, Joe, give Jenny and Lulu some soda water and ground peas on me so they'll turn us loose. *(To Jim)* Yeah, y'all Westons b'lieves in fightin'.

JIM: Ah'd ruther get run out for fightin' than to be uh coward. *(He slings the guitar 'round his neck an' picks up his box of shells.)* Well, Ah reckon Ah'll go git Daisy her turkey 'cause she sho won't git none 'less Ah go git it. Here come Elder Simms anyhow so 'tain't no mo' pickin' de box. *(To Daisy)* Don't git lonesome whilst Ah'm gone.

*(Enter Daisy from the store smiling, and walks down to where Jim is standing.)*

DAISY: Whut's all dis talk about fightin'?

JIM: Lige throwin' it up to me 'bout all my folks been run outa town for fightin'. But I don't keer!

DAISY: Mah mouf done got lonesome already. Buy me some chewing gum to keep mah mouf comp'ny till y'all gits back wid dat turkey.

JIM: Don't hafta buy none. *(Reaches in his pocket and pulls out a stick.)* What it takes tuh satisfy de ladies, Ah totes it. *(He hands her the gum tenderly.)* 'Bye, Daisy. *(He walks to left exit.)*

DAISY: *(Coyly)* 'Bye, till you come back.

*(Enter Reverend Simms right.)*

SIMMS: Good evenin' everybody.

ALL: Good evenin', Elder Simms.

LUM: *(Getting up from his seat on the porch)* Have mah seat, Elder.

*(Simms takes it with a sigh of pleasure. Lum steps off the porch and sets his hat over one eye.)*

Say, Daisy, you ain't goin' to sprain yo' lil mouf on dat tough chewin' gum, is yuh? Not wid de help *you* got. Better lemme kinda tender dat gum up for yuh so yo' lil mouf won't hafta strain wid it.

*(He places himself exactly in front of her. She glances up coyly at him.)*

DAISY: Ain't you crazy, now?

*(Lum tries to snatch the gum but she pops it into her mouth and laughs as he seizes her hands.)*

LUM: You don't need no gum to keep yo' mouf company wid me around. Ah'm all de comp'ny yo' mouf need. Ah'm sweet papa chewin' and sweetness change.

DAISY: Tell dat to Bootsie Pitts, you can't fool me. *(Turns right.)* Guess Ah better go home and see mama. Ah ain't been 'round since Ah come from de white folk. You goin' walk 'round there wid me?

LUM: Naw, Ah ain't gointer *walk*. When Ah'm wid de angels Ah puts on mah hosanna wings and flies round heben lak de rest. *(He falls in beside her and catches her elbow.)* Less go! *(To the porch)* See you later and tell you straighter.

LINDSAY: Don't stay 'round to Daisy's too long, Lum, and get run out from under yo' hat!

LUM: Who run?

HAMBO: 'Tain't no use in you hollerin' "who." Yo' feet don't fit no limb.

*(General laughter. Exit Lum and Daisy right.)*

WALTER: Lawd! Daisy sho is propaganda. She really handles a lot of traffic. Ah don't blame de boys. If Ah was uh single man Ah'd be 'round there myself.

LIGE: Ah'm willin' tuh serve some time on her gang as it is, but mah wife won't lissen to reason. *(Laughter)* Ah tries to show her dis deep point where 'tain't right for one woman to be harboring uh whole man all to herself when there's heaps uh po' young girls ain't got no husband atall. But Ah just can't sense her into it. *(Laughter)*

HAMBO: Now take Jim and Dave for instant. Here they is, old friends, done fell out and ready to fight—all over Daisy.

WALTER: Thass me all over. I don't want no partnership when it comes to my women. It's whole hawg uh none. Lawd, what wimmen makes us do!

LINDSAY: What is it dey don't make us do[?] Now take for instant Jim Weston. He know he can't hunt wid Dave—Dave is uh sworn marksman, but jes' so as not to be outdone here he go trying to shoot turkeys—wild turkeys mind you—'ginst Dave.

JOE CLARKE: I God, I hope he finds 'em too. If he get to killin' turkeys maybe he'll stay 'way from my hen house. I God, I done lost nine uh my best layin' hens in three weeks. *(General laughter)*

WALTER: Did Jim git 'em?

CLARKE: I ain't personatin' nobody but I been told dat Jim's got uh powerful lot uh chicken feathers buried in his back yard. I know one thing, if I ever ketch his toenails in my chicken yard, I God, he's gointer follow his pappy and his four brothers. He's got to git from dis town of mine.

*(Enter a little girl right, very neat and starchy. She runs up to Reverend Simms.)*

GIRL: Papa, mama say send her dat witch hazely oil she sent you after right quick.

LINDSAY: Whuss matter wid Sister Simms—po'ly today?

SIMMS: She don't keep so well since we been here, but I reckon she's on de mend.

HAMBO: Don't look like she never would be sick. She look so big and portly.

CLARKE: Size don't mean nothin'. My wife is portly and she be's on de sick list all de time. It's "Jody, pain in de belly" all day. "Jody, pain in de back" all night.

LIGE: Besides, Mrs. Simms ain't very large. She wouldn't weigh more'n two hundred. You ain't seen no big woman. I seen one so big she went to whip her lil boy an' he run up under her belly and stayed up under dere for six months. (General laughter)

WALTER: You seen de biggest one. But I seen uh woman so little till she could go out in uh shower uh rain and run between de drops. She had tuh git up on uh box tuh look over uh grain uh sand.

SIMMS: Y'all boys better read yo' Bibles 'stead of studyin' foolishness. (He gets up and starts into the store. Clarke and the little girl follow him.) Reckon Ah better git dat medicine.

(The three exit into store.)

HAMBO: Well, y'all done seen so much—bet y'all ain't never seen uh snake big as de one Ah seen down 'round Kissimmee. He was so big he couldn't hardly move his self. He laid in one spot so long he growed moss on him and everybody thought he was uh log layin' there, till one day Ah set down on him and went to sleep. When Ah woke up Ah wuz in Middle Georgy.

(General laughter. Two women enter left and go in store after everybody has spoken to them.)

LINDSAY: Layin' all sides to jokes now, y'all remember dat rattlesnake Ah kilt on Lake Hope was 'most big as dat one.

WALTER: (Nudgin' Lige and winking at the crowd) How big did you say it was, Joe?

LINDSAY: He mought not uh been quite as big as dat one—but jes' 'bout fourteen feet.

HAMBO: Gimme dat lyin' snake! He wasn't but fo' foot long when you kilt him and here you done growed him ten feet after he's dead.

(Enter Simms followed by the girl with an all day sucker. Simms has a small package in his hand.)

SIMMS: (Gives the package to the child and resumes his seat.) Run 'long home now. Tell yo' ma to put on uh pot uh peas.

(Child exits right trotting and sucking her candy.)

WALTER: They's some powerful big snakes 'round here. We was choppin' down de weeds in front of our parsonage yistiddy and kilt uh great big ol' cotton mouf moccasin.

SIMMS: Yeah, look like me or some of my fambly 'bout to git snake-bit right at our own front do'.

LIGE: An' bit by uh Baptist snake at dat.

LINDSAY: How you make him out uh Baptist snake?

LIGE: Nobody don't love water lak uh Baptist an' uh moccasin. *(General laughter)*

HAMBO: An' nobody don't hate it lak de devil, uh rattlesnake an' uh Meth'dis.

*(General laughter. Enter Joe Clarke from store. [He] stands in [the] door.)*

SIMMS: Dis town needs uh cleanin' in more ways than one. Now if this town was run right, when folks misbehaves, they oughter be locked up in jail and if they can't pay no fine, they oughter be made to work it out on de streets—chopping weeds.

LINDSAY: How we gointer do all dat when we ain't got no jail?

SIMMS: Well, you orta *have* uh jail. Y'all needs uh whole heap of improvements in dis town. Ah ain't never pastored no town so way back as this one here.

CLARKE: *(Stepping out before Simms)* What improvements you figgers we needs?

SIMMS: A whole heap. Now for one thing, we really does need uh jail, Brother Mayor. 'Tain't no sense in runnin' people out of town that cuts up. We oughter have jails like other towns. Every town I ever pastored had uh jail.

CLARKE: *(Angrily)* Now hold on uh minute, Simms! Don't you reckon uh man dat knows how to start uh town knows how to run it? You ain't been here long enough to find out who started dis town yet. *(Very emphatic, beating his palm with other fist.)* Do you know who started dis town? *(Does not pause for an answer.)* Me! I started *dis* town. I went to de white folks and wid *dis* right hand I laid down two hundred dollars for de land and walked out and started dis town. I ain't like some folks—come here when grapes was ripe. I was here to cut new ground.

SIMMS: Well, 'tain't no sense in one man stayin' mayor all de time, nohow.

CLARKE: *(Triumphantly)* So dat de tree you barkin' up? Why, you ain't nothin' but uh trunk man. You can't be no mayor. I got roots here.

SIMMS: You ain't all de voters, though, Brother Mayor.

CLARKE: *(Arrogantly)* I don't hafta be. I God, it's my town and I kin be mayor jes' as long as I want to. *(Slaps his chest.)* I God, it was *me* dat put dis town on de map.

SIMMS: What map you put it on, Brother Clarke? You musta misplaced it. I ain't seen it on no map.

CLARKE: 'Tain't on no map, hunh? I God, every time I go to Maitland de white folks calls me Mayor. Otherwise, Simms, I God, if you so dissatisfied wid de way I run dis town, just take yo' Bible and flat foots and git younder cross de woods.

SIMMS: *(Aggressively)* Naw, Ah don't like it. You ack lack 'tain't nobody in de corporation but you! Now look. *(Points at the street lamp)* 'Tain't but one street light in town an' you got it in front of yo' place. We pays de taxes an' you got de lamp.

CLARKE: I God, nobody can't tell me how to run dis town. I 'lected myself and I'm gonna run it to suit myself. *(Looks all about)* Where is dat marshall? He ain't lit de lamp!

WALTER: Scorched Daisy Blunt home and ain't got back.

CLARKE: I God, call him there, some of you boys.

LIGE: *(Steps to edge of porch left and calls)* Lum! Lum!

LUM: *(At a distance)* What!

LIGE: Come on and light de lamp—it gittin' dark.

SIMMS: Now, when I pastored in Ocala you oughter seen de lovely jail dey had.

HAMBO: Thass all right for white folks. We colored folks don't need no jail.

WALTER: Aw, yes we do too. Elder Simms is right. We ain't a bit better'n white folks. *(Enter [Lulu and Jenny].)* You wimmen folks been in dat store uh mighty long time.

LULU: We been makin' our market.

HAMBO: Looks mighty bad for some man's pocket. But y'all ain't had no treat on me. Go back and tell Mrs. Clarke tuh give you some candy.

LINDSAY: Have somethin' on me too. Money ain't no good lessen de women kin help you use it. *(Hollers inside.)* Every lady in there take a treat on me.

JENNY: Ain't y'all comin' in tuh help us eat de treat? Come on, Elder Simms!

*(Hambo [gets] up quickly. Lindsay and Joe Clarke also get up. They go inside laughing.)*

HAMBO: Here, lemme git hold of somebody.

*(Grabs one of the women by the arm as they exit into the store.)*

LIGE: *(Pointing his thumb after the women)* Ah wouldn't way lay nothin' lak dat. Too old even tuh chew peanuts if Ah was tuh buy it.

WALTER: Preach it, Brother. But they's all right for mullet heads like Lindsay and Hambo. *(Sings)*

When they git old, when they git old
Old folks turns tuh monkeys
When they git old.

*(Looks off right)*

Lawd! They must be havin' recess in heben! Look at dese lil ground angels! *(Yells off right)* Hello Big 'Oman, an' Teets an' Bootsie! Hurry up! My money jumpin' up and down in my pocket lak uh mule in uh tin stable.

*(Enter three girls right, dressed in cool cotton dresses. They are all lock-armed and giggling.)*

LIGE: Hello, folkses.

BOOTSIE: *(Coquettishly)* Hello yo'self—want uh piece uh corn bread look on de shelf.

*(Great burst of laughter from inside the store.)*

LIGE: *(Catching Bootsie's arm)* Lemme scorch y'all inside an' treat yuh.

BOOTSIE: *(Looks at the other girls for confirmation)* Not yet, after while.

WALTER: Well, come set on de piazza an' les' have some chat.

TEETS: We ain't got time. We come tuh git our mail out de post office.

LIGE: Youse uh got-dat-wrong! You come after Dave an' Jim an' Lum. But Daisy done treed de las' one of 'em. She got Jim and Dave out in de swamp where de mule was drugged out huntin' her uh turkey. An' she got Lum at her house. Thass how come de light ain't lit.

BIG 'OMAN: Oh, Ah 'ain't worried 'bout Lum. Ah b'lieve Ah kin straighten him out.

WALTER: Some wimmen kin git yo' man so he won't stand uh straightenin'.

LIGE: Don't come rollin' yo' eyes at me an' gittin' all mad 'cause y'all stuck on de boys and de boys is stuck on Daisy. *(Makes a sly face at Walter.)*

TEETS: Who? Me? Nobody ain't studyin' 'bout ole Daisy. She come before me like a gnat in a whirlwind.

WALTER: *(In mock seriousness)* Better stop dat talkin' 'bout Daisy, do, I'll tell her whut you say. I think I better call her anyhow and see whether you goin-ter talk dat big talk to her face. *(Makes a move as if to call Daisy.)*

LIGE: *(Keeping up the raillery, grabs Walter)* Don't do dat, Walter. We don't want no trouble 'round here. But sho 'nuff, girls, y'all ain't go no time wid Daisy. Know what Lum say? Says Daisy is a bucket flower—jes' *made* to set up on de porch an' look pretty. I ast him how 'bout de rest an' he says "Oh de rest is yard flowers, jes' plant them any which a way."

BOOTSIE: I don't b'lieve Lum said no sich uh thing.

LIGE: You tellin' dat flat—Ah know. *(Looks off left)* Here come Lum, now, in uh big hurry jus' lak he ain't been gone two hours.

BIG 'OMAN: Less we all go git our treat!

*(They start up on the porch. At that moment Hambo, Lindsay, Clarke, Simms, [Jenny and Lulu] enter from the store.)*

CLARKE: *(To Lige)* Looka here, I God! Ain't Lum lit dat lamp yet?

*(Enter Lum left hurriedly. Clarke stands akimbo glaring at him. Lum fumbles for a match, strikes it and drops it. Gets another from his pocket and goes to the lamp and strikes it.)*

Somebody reach de numbskull uh box.

*(Walter hands Lum a box off the porch and he gets up on it and opens the lamp to light it.)*

LUM: *(To Clarke)* Reckon Ah better put some oil in de lamp. 'Tain't much in it.

CLARKE: *(Impatiently)* Oh, that'll do! That'll do. It'll be time tuh put it out befo' you git it lit, I God.

*(Lum lights the lamp. The men have resumed their seats and the women are on the ground and near right exit. Walter and Lige and the three girls [Bootsie, Teets and Big 'Oman] are at the door about to enter the store. Lum has the box in his hand and is still under the lamp. He walks slowly towards the step, box in hand. At the step he looks off left.)*

LUM: Here come Dave.

*(All look off left. Walter and Lige and the girls abandon the idea of the treat and wait for Dave.)*

HAMBO: But Ah ain't seen no turkey yet. Dat ole gobbler's too smart for Dave.

*(Enter Dave with gun over his shoulder and holding his head. A little blood is on his shoulder. He pauses under the lamp a moment, then comes to the step.)*

HAMBO: Whuss de matter, Dave? Dat ole turkey gobbler done pecked you in de head? Whut kind of a huntsman is you? *(General laughter)*

DAVE: Naw, ain't no turkey pecked me. It's Jim. Ah wuz out in de woods and had done squatted down before he got dere. Ah know jus' where dat ole gobbler roost at. Soon's he hit de limb an' squatted hisself, Ah let 'im have it. He flopped his wings an' tried to fly off but here he come tumblin' down right by dem ole mule bones. Jim, he was jus' comin' up when Ah fired. So when he seen dat turkey fallin', whut do he do? He fires off his gun an' make out he kilt dat turkey. Ah beat him tuh de bird and we got tuh tusslin'. He tries tuh make *me* give him *mah* turkey so's he kin run tuh Daisy an' make out he done kilt it. So we got tuh fightin' an' Ah wuz beatin' him too till he retched down an' got de hock bone uh dat mule an' lammed me over de head an' 'fore Ah could git up, he done took mah turkey an' went wid it. *(To Clarke)* Mist' Clarke, Ah wants tuh swear out uh warrant 'ginst Jim Weston. Ah'm gointer law him out dis town, too.

SIMMS: Dat wuz uh low-down caper Jim cut sho 'nuff.

CLARKE: Sho it's uh ugly caper tuh cut. Come on inside, Dave, an' Ah'll make out de papers. He ain't goin' to carry on lak dat in *my* town.

*(Exit Dave and Clarke into store.)*

LINDSAY: *(Jokingly to Simms)* See whut capers you Meth'dis' niggers'll cut—lammin' folks over de head wid mule bones an' stealin' they turkeys.

SIMMS: Oh you Baptist ain't uh lot better'n nobody else. You steals an' fights too.

LINDSAY: *(Still bantering)* Yeah, but we done kotched dis Meth'dis nigger an' we gointer run him right on outa town too. Jus' wait an' see. Yeah, boy. Dat Jim'll be uh gone 'gator 'fore tomorrow night.

WALTER: Oh, I don't know whether he's gointer be gone or not. We Meth'dis got jus' as much say-so in dis town as anybody else.

LIGE: Yeah. You Baptis' run yo' mouf but you don't run de town. Furthermo' we ain't heard nothin' but Dave's lie. Better wait till we see Jim an' git de straight of dis thing.

HAMBO: Will you lissen at dat? Dese half-washed Christians hates de truth lak uh bed-bug hates de light. God a'mighty! *(Rising)* Ah'm goin' in an' see to it dat de Mayor makes dem papers out right.

*(He exits angrily into the store. Simms and all the men rise too.)*

SIMMS: Come on Walter, you an' Lige. Less we go inside too. Dat po' boy got tuh git jestice. An' 'tween de Mayor an' dese Baptists he ain't got much chance. *(They exit into the store.)*

LULU: Come on you young gals, whut y'all wants be hangin' 'round de store an' it's way after black dark. Yo' mammies oughter take an' frail de las' one of yuh! Come along!

*(The girls come down off the porch and join the women. Loud angry voices inside the store.)*

JENNY: Lawd, lemme git home an' tell my husban' 'bout all dis. Umph! Umph!

*(The women and girls exit as the men all emerge from the store. Lum comes first with the warrant in his hand. Clarke emerges last.)*

CLARKE: Can't have all dat fuss an' racket in my store. All of you git outside dat wants tuh fight! *(He begins to close up.)*

SIMMS: But Brother Mayor, I said it, an' I'll say it agin, 'tain't righ—

CLARKE: *(Turns angrily)* I God, Simms, Ah don't keer whut you say. 'Tain't worth uh hill uh beans nohow. Jim is gointer be 'rested for hittin' Dave an' takin' his turkey, an' if he's found guilty he's goin' 'way from here. 'Tain't no use uh you swellin' up neither. *(To Lum)* Go get him, Lum, an' lock 'im in my barn an' put dat turkey under arrest too. I God, de law is gointer be law in my town.

*(Exit Lum with an important air.)*

WALTER: Where de trial gointer be, Brother Clarke, in de hall?

CLARKE: Nope, it's too little. It'll hafta be in de Baptist church. Ah reckon dat's de bigges' place in town. Three o'clock Monday evening. Now, y'all git on off my porch tuh fuss. Lige, outen dat lamp for Lum.

*(The stage goes black. The crowd is dispersing slowly. Angry voices are heard. The curtain is descending slowly. Offstage right the voice of Lum is heard calling Daisy.)*

LUM: Oh Daisy! Oh Daisy!

DAISY: *(At a distance)* What you want, Lum?

LUM: Tell yo' mama to put on de hot water kittle. I'll be 'round there before long.

*(Curtain.)*

## ACT TWO
### Scene 1

*Setting: Village street scene. Huge oak tree upstage center. A house or two on backdrop. When curtain goes up Sister Lucy Taylor is seen standing under the tree trying to read a notice posted on the tree. She is painfully spelling it out. Enter Sister Thomas, a younger woman in her thirties, at left.*

SISTER THOMAS: Evenin', Sis Taylor.

SISTER TAYLOR: Evenin'. *(Returns to the notice.)*

SISTER THOMAS: Whut you doin'? Readin' dat notice Joe Clarke put up 'bout de meetin'? *(Approaches tree.)*

SISTER TAYLOR: Is dat whut it says? I ain't much on readin' since I had my teeth pulled out. You know if you pull out dem eye teeth you ruins yo' eye sight. *(Turns back to notice.)* Whut it say?

SISTER THOMAS: *(Reading notice)* The trial of Jim Weston for assault and battery on Dave Carter wid a dangerous weapon will be held at Macedonia Baptist Church on Monday November 10, at three o'clock. All are welcome—by order of J. Clarke, Mayor of Eatonville, Florida. *(Turning to Sister Taylor)* Hit's makin' on to three now.

SISTER TAYLOR: *(Looks up at sun to tell time)* You mean it's right *now*. Lemme go git ready to be at de trial—'cause I'm sho going to be there and I ain't goin' to bite my tongue neither.

SISTER THOMAS: I done went and crapped a mess of collard greens for supper—I better go put 'em on—'Cause Lawd knows when we goin' to git outa there—and my husband is one of them dat's gointer eat don't keer whut happen. I bet if Judgment Day was to happen tomorrow, he'd speck I orter fix him a bucket to carry 'long. *(She moves to exit right.)*

SISTER TAYLOR: All men favors they guts, chile. But whut you think of all dis mess they got going on 'round here?

SISTER THOMAS: I just think it's a sin and a shame before de livin' justice de way dese Baptis' niggers is runnin' 'round here carryin' on.

SISTER TAYLOR: Oh they been puttin' out they brags ever since Sat'day night 'bout whut they gointer do to Jim. They thinks they runs this town. They tell me Rev. Singletary[12] preached a sermon on it yesterday.

SISTER THOMAS: Lawd help us! He can't preach and he look like ten cents' worth of have-mercy, let 'lone gittin' up dere tryin' to throw slams at us. Now all Elder Simms done was to explain to us our rights—Whut you think 'bout Joe Clarke running 'round here takin' up for these ole Baptist niggers?

SISTER TAYLOR: De puzzle-gut rascal—we oughter have him up in conference and put him out de Meth'dis' faith. He don't b'long in there—Wanta run dat boy outa town for nothin'.

SISTER THOMAS: But we all know how come he so hot to law Jim outa town—hit's to dig de foundation out from under Elder Simms—

SISTER TAYLOR: What he wanta do dat for?

SISTER THOMAS: 'Cause he wants to be a God-knows-it-all an' a God-do-it-all and Simms is de onliest one in this town whut will buck up to him.

*(Enter Sister Jones, walking leisurely.)*

SISTER JONES: Hello Hoyt, hello Lucy.

SISTER TAYLOR: Goin' to de meetin'?

SISTER JONES: Done got my clothes on de line and I'm bound to be dere—

SISTER THOMAS: Gointer testify for Jim?

SISTER JONES: Naw, I reckon—Don't make much difference to me which way de drop fall—'Tain't neither one of 'em much good.

SISTER TAYLOR: I know it. I know it, Ida. But dat ain't de point. De crow we wants to pick is, is we gointer set still and let dese Baptist tell us when to plant and when to pluck up?

SISTER JONES: Dat *is* something to think about when you come to think about it. *(Starts to move on)* Guess I better go ahead—See y'all later and tell you straighter.

*(Enter Elder Simms right, walking fast, Bible under his arm, almost collides with Mrs. Jones. She nods and smiles and exits.)*

SIMMS: How you do, Sister Taylor, Sister Thomas.

BOTH: Good evenin', Elder.

SIMMS: Sho is a hot day.

SISTER TAYLOR: Yeah, de bear is walkin' de earth lak a natural man.

SISTER THOMAS: Reverend, look like you headed de wrong way. It's almost time for de trial and youse all de dependence we got.

SIMMS: I know it. I'm trying to find de marshall so we kin go after Jim. I wants a chance to talk wid him a minute before court sets.

SISTER TAYLOR: Y'think he'll come clear?

SIMMS: *(Proudly)* I *know* it! *(Shakes the Bible)* I'm going to law 'em from Genesis to Revelation.

SISTER THOMAS: Give it to 'em, Elder. Wear 'em out!

SIMMS: We'se liable to have a new mayor when all dis dust settle. Well, I better scuffle on down de road. *(Exit Simms left.)*

SISTER THOMAS: Lord, lemme gwan home and put dese greens on. *(Looks off-stage left)* Here come Mayor Clarke now, wid his belly settin' out in front of him like a cow-catcher. His name oughter be Mayor Belly.

SISTER TAYLOR: *([Arms] akimbo)* Jus' look at him! Trying to look like a jigadier Breneral.

*(Enter Clarke hot and perspiring. They look at him coldly.)*

CLARKE: I God, de bear got me! *(Silence for a moment.)* How y'all feelin', ladies?

SISTER TAYLOR: Brother Mayor, I ain't one of these folks dat bite my tongue and bust my gall—whut's inside got to come out! I can't see to my rest why you cloakin' in wid dese Baptist buzzards 'ginst yo' own church.

CLARKE: I ain't cloakin' in wid *none.* I'm de mayor of dis whole town. I stands for de right and against de wrong. I don't keer who it kill or cure.

SISTER THOMAS: You think it's right to be runnin' dat boy off for nothing?

CLARKE: I God! You call knockin' a man in de head wid a mule bone nothin'? 'Nother thing—I done missed nine of my best-layin' hens. I ain't sayin' Jim got 'em—but different people has told me he buries a powerful lot of feathers in his back yard. I God, I'm a ruint man! *(He starts towards the right exit, but Lum Bailey enters right.)* I God, Lum, I been lookin' for you all day. It's almost three o'clock. *(Hands him a key from his ring.)* Take dis key and go fetch Jim Weston on to de church.

LUM: Have you got yo' gavel from de lodge room?

CLARKE: I God, that's right, Lum. I'll go get it from de lodge room whilst you go git de bone an' de prisoner. Hurry up! You walk like dead lice droppin' off you!

*(He exits right while Lum crosses stage towards left.)*

SISTER TAYLOR: Lum, Elder Simms been huntin' you—he's gone on down 'bout de barn. *(She gestures.)*

LUM: I reckon I'll overtake him. *(Exit left.)*

SISTER THOMAS: I better go put dese greens on—my husband will kill me if he don't find no supper ready. Here come Mrs. Blunt. She oughter feel like a penny's worth of have-mercy wid all dis stink behind her daughter.

SISTER TAYLOR: Chile, some folks don't keer. They don't raise they chillen, they drags 'em up. God knows if dat Daisy was mine, I'd throw her down and put a hundred lashes on her back wid a plow-line. Here she come in de store Sat'day night *(Acts coy and coquettish, burlesques Daisy's walk)* a-wringing and a-twisting!

*(Enter Mrs. Blunt left.)*

MRS. BLUNT: How y'all, sisters?

SISTER THOMAS: Very well, Miz Blunt, how you?

MRS. BLUNT: Oh, so-so.

SISTER TAYLOR: I'm kickin' but not high.

MRS. BLUNT: Well, thank God you still on prayin' ground and in a Bible Country—me, I ain't many today. De niggers got my Daisy's name all mixed up in dis mess.

SISTER TAYLOR: You musn't mind dat, Sister Blunt. People just *will* talk. They's talkin' in New York and they's talkin' in Georgy and they's talkin' in Italy.

SISTER THOMAS: Chile, if you talk after niggers they'll have you in de graveyard or in Chattahoochee one. You can't pay no 'tention to talk.

MRS. BLUNT: Well, I know one thing—de man or woman, chick or child, grizzly or gray that tells me to my face anything wrong 'bout *my* chile—I'm going to take *my* fist (*Rolls up right sleeve and gestures with right fist*) and knock they teeth down they throat. (*She looks ferocious.*) 'Cause y'all know I raised my Daisy right 'round my feet till I let her go up north last year wid them white folks. I'd ruther her to be in de white folks' kitchen than walkin' de streets like some of dese girls 'round here. If I do say so, I done raised a lady. She can't help it if all dese men get stuck on her.

SISTER TAYLOR: You'se telling de truth, Sister Blunt. That's what I always say— don't confidence dese niggers, do, they'll sho put you in de street.

SISTER THOMAS: Naw indeed. Never syndicate wid niggers—do, they will distriminate you. They'll be an *anybody*. You goin' to de trial, ain't you?

MRS. BLUNT: Just as sho as you snore, and they better leave Daisy's name outer dis too. I done told her and told her to come straight home from her work. Naw, she had to stop by dat store and skin her gums back wid dem trashy niggers. She better not leave them white folks today to come praipsin' over here scornin' her name all up wid dis nigger mess—do, I'll kill her. No daughter of mine ain't going to do as she please long as she live under de sound of my voice. (*She crosses to right.*)

SISTER THOMAS: That's right, Sister Blunt—I glory in yo' spunk. Lord, I better go put on my supper.

(*As Mrs. Blunt exits right, Reverend Singletary enters left with Dave and Deacon Lindsay and Sister Lewis. Very hostile glances from Sisters Thomas and Taylor towards the others.*)

SINGLETARY: Good evening, folks.

*(Sister Thomas and Sister Taylor just grunt. Sister Thomas moves a step or two towards exit. Flirts her skirts and exits.)*

LINDSAY: *(Angrily)* Whut's de matter, y'all? Cat got yo' tongue?

SISTER TAYLOR: More matter than you kin scatter all over Cincinnati.

LINDSAY: Go 'head on, Lucy Taylor, go 'head on. You know a very little of yo' sugar sweetens my coffee. Go 'head on. Everytime you lift yo' arm you smell like a nest of yellow hammers.

SISTER TAYLOR: Go 'head on yo'self. Yo' head look like it done wore out three bodies. Talking 'bout *me* smelling—you smell lak a nest of grand daddies yo'self.

LINDSAY: Aw, rack on down de road, 'oman. Ah don't wantuh change words wid yuh. You'se too ugly.

SISTER TAYLOR: You ain't nobody's pretty baby yo'self. You so ugly I betcha yo' wife have to spread uh sheet over yo' head tuh let sleep slip up on yuh.

LINDSAY: *(Threatening)* You better git 'way from me while you able. I done tole you I don't wanta break a mouth wid you. It's a whole heap better tuh walk off on yo' own legs than it is to be toted off. I'm tired of yo' achin' 'round here. You fool wid me now an' I'll knock you into doll rags, Tony or no Tony.

SISTER TAYLOR: *(Jumping up in his face)* Hit me! Hit me! I dare you tuh hit me. If you take dat dare you'll steal a hawg an' eat his hair.

LINDSAY: Lemme gwan down to dat church befo' you make me stomp you. *(He exits right.)*

SISTER TAYLOR: You mean you'll *git* stomped. Ah'm going to de trial too. De nex' trial gointer be *me* for kickin' some uh you Baptis' niggers around.

*(A great noise is heard offstage left. The angry and jeering voices of children. Mrs. Taylor looks off left and takes a step or two towards left exit as the noise comes nearer.)*

CHILD: [*(Offstage)*] Tell her! Tell her! Turn her up and smell her. Yo' mama ain't got nothin' to do wid me.

SISTER TAYLOR: *(Hollering off left)* You lil Baptis' Haitians, leave them chillun alone. If you don't, you better!

*(Enter about ten children struggling and wrestling in a bunch. Mrs. Taylor looks about on the ground for a stick to strike the children with.)*

CHILD IN CROWD: Hey! Hey! He's skeered tuh knock it off. Coward!

SISTER TAYLOR: If y'all don't git on home!

MARY ELLA: *(Standing akimbo)* I know you better not touch me, do, my mama will tend to you.

SISTER TAYLOR: *(Making as if to strike her)* Shet up, you nasty lil heifer, sassing me! You ain't half raised.

*([Mary Ella] shakes herself at Mrs. Taylor and is joined by two or three others.)*

SISTER TAYLOR: *(Walking towards right exit)* I'm going on down to de church an' tell yo' mammy. But she ain't been half raised herself. *(She exits right with several children making faces behind her.)*

WILLIE: *(To [Mary Ella])* Aw haw! Y'all ol' Baptis' ain't got no book case in yo' church. We went there one day an' I saw uh soda cracker box settin' up in de corner so I set down on it. *(Pointing at Mary Ella)* Know whut ole Mary Ella say? *(Jeering laughter)* Willie, you git up off our library! Haw! Haw!

MARY ELLA: Y'all ole Meth'dis' ain't got no window panes in yo' ole church.

METHODIST GIRL: *(Takes center of stage and hands akimbo shakes her hips)* I don't keer whut y'all say. I'm a Meth'dis' bred an' uh Meth'dis' born an' when I'm dead there'll be uh Meth'dis' gone.

*(Mary Ella snaps fingers under other girl's nose and starts singing. Several join her.)*

MARY ELLA:

Oh Baptis', Baptis' is my name
My name's written on high
I got my lick in de Baptis' church
Gointer eat up de Meth'dis' pie.

*(The Methodist children jeer and make faces. The Baptist camp make faces back for a full minute. There is silence while each camp tries to outdo the other in face making. [A] Baptist makes the last face.)*

WILLIE: Come on, less us don't notice 'em. Less gwan down to de church an' hear de trial.

MARY ELLA: Y'all ain't the onliest ones kin go. We goin' too.

WILLIE: Aw haw! Copy cats! *(Makes face)* Dat's right, follow on behind us lak uh puppy dog tail.

*(They [Methodist children] start walking toward right exit switching their clothes behind. Baptist children stage a rush and struggle to get in front of the Methodists. They finally succeed in flinging some of the Methodist chil-*

*dren to the ground and some behind them and walk towards right exit
haughtily switching their clothes.)*

WILLIE: *(Whispers to his crowd)* Less go 'round by Mosely's lot and beat 'em
there!

OTHERS: All right!

WILLIE: *(Yelling to Baptists)* We wouldn't walk behind no ole Baptists!

*(The Methodists turn and walk off towards left exit switching their clothes
as the Baptists are doing. Slow curtain.)*

Scene 2

*Setting: Interior of Macedonia Baptist Church, a rectangular room, win-
dows on each side, two "Amen Corners,"*[13] *pulpit with a plush cover with
heavy fringe, practical door in pulpit, practical door in front of church, two
oil brackets with reflectors on each side wall with all lamps missing but one,
one big oil lamp in center.*
    *Action: At the rise, church is about full. A buzz and hum fills the church.
Voices of children, angry and jeering, heard from the street. The church bell
begins to toll for death. Everybody looks shocked.*

SISTER LEWIS: Lawd! Is Dave done died from dat lick?

SISTER THOMAS: *(To her husband)* Walter, go see.

*(He gets up and starts down the aisle to front door. Enter Deacon Hambo
by front door.)*

WALTER: Who dead?

HAMBO: *(Laughing)* Nobody—jus' tollin' de bell for dat Meth'dis' gopher dat's
gointer be long long gone after dis trial. *(Laughter from Baptist side)*

WALTER: Y'all sho thinks you runs dis town, dontcher? But Elder Simms'll
show you somethin' t'day. If he don't, God's uh gopher.

HAMBO: He can't show us nothin' 'cause he don't know nothin' hisself.

WALTER: He got mo' book-learnin' than Rev. Singletary got.

HAMBO: He mought be unletter-learnt, but he kin drive over Simms like a road
plow.

METHODISTS: Aw, naw! Dat's a lie!

*(Enter Reverend Simms by front door with open Bible in hand. A murmur of
applause arises on the Methodist side, grunts on the Baptist side. Immediately
behind him comes Lum Bailey leading Jim Weston. They parade up to the*

*right Amen Corner and seat themselves on the same bench, Jim between [Lum] and the preacher. A great rooster-crowing and hen-cackling arises on the Baptist side. Jim Weston jumps angrily to his feet.*

*Enter by front door Reverend Singletary and Dave. Dave's head is bandaged, but he walks firmly and seems not ill at all. They sit in the left Amen Corner. Jeering grunts from the Methodist side.)*

SISTER THOMAS: Look at ol' Dave trying to make out he's hurt.

LIGE: Everybody know uh Baptis' head is harder'n uh rock. Look like they'd be skeered tuh go in swimmin', do, they heads would drown 'em.

*(General laughter on Methodist side. Enter Brother Nixon with his jumper jacket on his arm, [who] climbs over the knees of a bench full of people and finds [a] seat against the wall directly beneath [an] empty lamp bracket. He looks around for some place to dispose of his coat. Sees the lamp bracket and hangs up the coat, hitches up his pants and sits down.)*

SISTER LEWIS: *(Rising and glaring at Nixon)* Shank Nixon, you take yo' lousy coat down off these sacred walls. Ain't you Meth'dis' niggers got no gumption in de house of Wash-up!

*(Nixon mocks her by standing akimbo and shaking himself like a woman. General laughter. He prepares to resume his seat but looks over and sees Deacon Hambo on his feet, and glaring angrily at him. He quickly reaches up and takes the coat down and folds it across his knees.*

*Sister Taylor looks very pointedly at Sister Lewis then takes a dip of snuff and looks sneering at Lewis again.)*

SISTER TAYLOR: Some folks is a whole lot more keerful 'bout a louse in de church than they is in they house. *(Looks pointedly at Sister Lewis.)*

SISTER LEWIS: *(Bustling)* Whut you gazin' at me for? Wid your pop-eyes looking like skirt ginny-nuts.

SISTER TAYLOR: I hate to tell you whut yo' mouf looks like. I sho do—you and soap and water[14] musta had some words.

SISTER LEWIS: Talkin' 'bout other folks being dirty—yo' young 'uns must be sleep in they draws 'cause you kin smell 'em a mile down de road.

SISTER TAYLOR: 'Tain't no lice on 'em though.

SISTER LEWIS: You got just as many bed-bugs and chinches as anybody else, don't come trying to hand me dat rough package 'bout yo' house so clean.

SISTER TAYLOR: Yeah, but I done seen de bed-bugs marchin' out yo' house in de mornin', keepin' step just like soldiers drillin'. An' you got so many lice I seen 'em on de dish-rag. One day you tried to pick up de dish-rag and put it in de dish water and them lice pulled back and tole you "Aw naw, damned if I'm going to let you drown me." *(Loud laughter from the Methodist side.)*

SISTER LEWIS: *(Furious—rises [with arms] akimbo)* Well, my house might not be exactly clean, but there's no fly-specks on my character! They didn't have to git[15] de sheriff to make Willie marry *me* like they did to make Tony marry *you.*

*(Sister Taylor jump[s] up and starts across the aisle. She is pulled back out of the aisle by friends.)*

SISTER TAYLOR: Yeah, they got de sheriff to make Tony marry me, but he married me and made a good husband, too. I sits in my rocking cheer on my porch every Sat'day evening and say "Here come Tony and them"—

SISTER LEWIS: Them what?

SISTER TAYLOR: Them dollars. Now you sho orter go git de sheriff and a shot-gun and make some of dese men marry yo' daughter Ada.

*(Sister Lewis jump[s] up and start[s] across the aisle. She is restrained, but struggles hard.)*

SISTER LEWIS: Lemme go, Jim Merchant! Turn me go! I'm going to stomp de black heifer till she can't sit down.

SISTER TAYLOR: *(Also struggling)* Let her come on! If I get my hands on her I'll turn her every way but loose.

SISTER LEWIS: Just come on out dis church, Lucy Taylor. I'll beat you on every-thing you got but yo' tongue and I'll hit dat a lick if you stick it out. *(To the man holding her)* Turn me go! I'm going to fix her so her own mammy won't know her. She ain't going to slip *me* into de dozens and laugh about it.

SISTER TAYLOR: *(Trying to free herself)* Why don't y'all turn dat ole twist mouth 'oman loose. All I wants to do is hit her one lick. I betcha I'll take her 'way from here faster than de word of God.

SISTER LEWIS: *(To man holding Mrs. Taylor)* I don't see how come y'all won't[16] let ole flat-behind Lucy Taylor aloose—make out she so bad, now. She may be red hot but I kin cool her. I'll ride her just like Jesus rode a jack-ass.

*(They have subsided into their seats again, but are glaring at each other. Enter Mayor Clarke through the pulpit door. [He] is annoyed at the clamor going on. He tries to quell the noise with a frown.)*

SISTER TAYLOR: Dat ain't nothin' but talk—you looks lak de devil before day, but you ain't so bad—not half as bad as you smell.

CLARKE: Order, please. Court is set.

SISTER LEWIS: You looks like all hell and de devil's doll baby, but all I want *you* to do is to hit de ground and I'll crawl you. Put it where I kin git it and I'll sho use it.

CLARKE: *(Feeling everywhere for the gavel)* Lum Bailey! Where's dat gavel I told you to put here?

LUM: *(From beside prisoner)* You said *you* was going to git it yo'self.

CLARKE: I God, Lum, you gointer stand there like a bump on a log and see I ain't got nothin' to open court wid? Go 'head—fetch me dat gavel. Make haste quick before dese wimmen folks tote off dis church house.

*(Lum exits by front door.)*

SISTER TAYLOR: *(To Lewis)* Aw, shet up, you big ole he-looking rascal you! Nobody don't know whether you'se a man or a woman.

CLARKE: You wimmen, shut up!

SISTER LEWIS: *(To Taylor)* Air Lawd! Dat ain't *yo'* trouble. They all *knows* whut *you* is—eg-zackly!

LINDSAY: Aw, why don't you wimmen cut dat out in de church-house! Jus' jawin' and chewin' de rag!

SISTER TAYLOR: Joe Lindsay, if you'd go home and feed dat raw-boned horse of yourn you wouldn't have so much time to stick yo' bill in business that ain't yourn.

LINDSAY: You ain't got nairn to feed—you better go hunt another dead dog and git some mo' teeth. Great big old empty mouf, and no cheers in de parler.

SISTER TAYLOR: I kin git all de teeth I wants—I'd ruther not have no cheers in my parlor than to have them ole snags you got in yo' mouf. I'd ruther gum it out.

LINDSAY: You don't *ruther* gum it out, you *hafta* gum it out. You ain't got no teeth. Dey better send out to dat ole mule and git you some teeths.

SISTER LEWIS: Joe Lindsay, don't you know no better than to strain wid folks ain't got sense enough to tote guts to a bean? If they ain't born wid no sense you can't learn 'em none.

LINDSAY: You sho done tole whut God love now. *(Glaring across the aisle)* Ain't got enough gumption to kill a buzzard.

*(Enter Lum by front door with gavel in one hand and mule bone in the other. He walks importantly up the aisle and hands Clarke the gavel and lays the bone atop the pulpit.)*

CLARKE: *(Rapping sharply with gavel)* Hear! You moufy wimmen shut up. *(To Lum)* Lum, go on back there and shut dem wimmen up or put 'em outa here.

*(Lum starts walking importantly down the aisle towards Mrs. Taylor. She almost rises to meet him.)*

SISTER TAYLOR: Lum Bailey, you fresh little snot you! Don't you dast to come here trying to put *me* out—many diapers as I done pinned on *you!* Git 'way from me befo' I knock every nap off of yo' head, one by one.

*(Lum hurries away from her apologetically. He turns towards Mrs. Lewis.)*

SISTER LEWIS: 'Deed God knows you better not lay de weight of yo' hand on *me*, Lum. Here you ain't dry behind de ears yet and come telling *me* what to do. Gwan 'way from here before I kick yo' clothes up 'round yo' neck like a horse collar.

*(Lum goes on back and takes his seat beside the prisoner.)*

CLARKE: *(Glaring ferociously)* This court is set and I'm bound to have some order or else. *(The talking ceases. Absolute quiet.)* Now less git down to business. We got folks in dis town dat's just like a snake in de grass.

MRS. BAILEY: Brother Mayor! We ain't got no business going into no trial nor nothin' else 'thout a word of prayer—to be sure de right spirit is wid us.

VOICE ON METHODIST SIDE: Thass right, Elder Simms, give us a word of prayer.

*(He rises hurriedly.)*

VOICE ON BAPTIST SIDE: This is a Baptist church and de pastor is settin' right here—how come he can't pray in his own church?

VOICE ON METHODIST SIDE: Y'all done started all dis mess—how you going to git de right spirit here? Go 'head, Rev. Simms.

VOICE ON BAPTIST SIDE: He can't pray over me. Dis church says one Lord, one faith, one baptism—and a man that ain't never been baptized atall ain't got no business praying over nobody.

CLARKE: *(Rapping with gavel)* Less sing! Somebody raise a tune.

*(Voice on Baptist side begins "Onward Christian Soldiers" and the others join in. Voice on Methodist side begins "All Hail the Power of Jesus' Name"*

*and the Methodists join in. Both shout as loud as they can to the end of the verse. Clarke raps loudly for order at the end of the verse and lifts his hands as if to bless a table.)*

CLARKE: *(Praying)* Lord be with us and bless these few remarks we are about to receive, Amen. Now this court is open for business. All of us know we came here on serious business. This town is 'bout to be tore up by back-biting and malice. Now everybody that's a witness in this case stand up. I wants the witness to take the front seats.

*(Nearly everybody in the room rises. Brother Hambo frowns across the aisle at Mrs. McDuffy, who is standing.)*

HAMBO: Whut *you* doing standin' up for a witness? I know you wasn't there. You don't know one thing about it.

SISTER MCDUFFY: I got just as much right to testify as you is. I don't keer if I wasn't there. Any man that treats they wife bad as *you* can't tell nobody else they eye is black. You clean round yo' *own* door before you go sweeping 'round other folks.

SISTER LINDSAY: *(To Nixon)* What you doin' up there testifying? When you done let yo' hawg root up all my p'tater patch.

NIXON: Aw shut up woman—you ain't had no taters for no pig to root up.

SISTER LINDSAY: Who ain't had no taters? *(To Lige)* Look here, Lige, didn't I git a whole crocus sack full of tater slips from yo' brother Sam?

LIGE: *(Reluctantly)* Yeah.

SISTER LINDSAY: 'Course I had sweet p'taters! And if you stand up there and tell *me* I ain't had no p'taters I'll be all over you just like gravy over rice.

NIXON: Aw shut up—we ain't come here to talk about yo' 'tater vines, we come—

SISTER LINDSAY: *(To her husband)* Joe! What kind of a husband is you? Set here and let Nixon 'buse me out lak dat!

WALTER: How is he going to give anybody a straightening when he needs straightening hisself. I bought a load of compost from him and *paid for it in advance* and he come there when I wasn't home and dumped a half-a-load in there and drove on off wid my money.

SISTER HAMBO: Aw, you ain't got no right to talk, Walter, not lowdown as you is—if somebody stump their toe in dis town you won't let yo' shirt-tail touch you till you bolt over to Maitland and puke yo' guts to de white folks—and God knows I 'bominates a white folks' nigger.

WALTER: Aw you just mad 'cause I wouldn't let your old starved-out cow eat up my cow-peas.

SISTER HAMBO: *(Triumphantly)* Unhumh! I knowed you was the one knocked my cow's horn off! And you lied like a doodle-bug going backwards in his hole and made out you didn't do it.

WALTER: I didn't do no such a thing.

SISTER HAMBO: I say you did and [I] belong to Macedonia Baptist Church and I can't lie.

WALTER: Yo' mouf is cut cross ways, ain't it? Well then, yo' mouf ain't no prayer-book even if yo' lips do flap like a Bible. You kin lie and then re-lie.

HAMBO: Walter Thomas, talk dat biggity talk to me, not to my wife. Maybe you kin whip her, but if you can't whip me too, don't bring de mess up.

CLARKE: *(Rapping)* Y'all men folks shut up before I put you both under arrest. Come to order everybody.

LINDSAY: I just wanta say this before we go any further. Nobody bet' not slur my wife in here—do, I'll strow 'em all over de county.

SISTER NIXON: Aw, youse de nastiest threatener in three states but I ain't seen you do nothin'. De seat of yo' pants is too close to de ground for you to be crowin' so loud. You so short you smell right earthy.

SISTER LINDSAY: De seat of yo' husband's britches been draggin' de ground ever since I knowed him. Don't like it dontcher take it, here's my collar come and shake it. *(She puts the palms of her hands together and holding the heels together, flaps the fore part of her hands like a 'gator opening and shutting its mouth. This infuriates Mrs. Nixon.)*

CLARKE: Shut up! We didn't come here to wash and iron niggers. We come here for a trial. *(Raps.)*

SISTER NIXON: *(To Clarke)* I ain't going to shut up nothin' of de kind. Think I'm going to let her low-rate me and I take it all? Naw indeed. I'm going to sack dis female out before we any further go.

SISTER LINDSAY: Aw, I done dished you out too many times. Go 'head on and try to keep yo' lil squatty husband away from down on de lake wid wimmens and you'll have *all* you can do. How does old heavy-hipted mama talk? *(Snaps her fingers.)*

SISTER NIXON: Nobody wouldn't have you if he could get anybody else. *(She makes a circle with her thumb and first finger and holds it up for Mrs. Lindsay to see.)* Come through—don't you feel cheap?

CLARKE: Sister Nixon, shut up!

SISTER NIXON: You can't shut me up, not the way you live. When you quit beatin' Mrs. Mattie and dominizing her all de time, then you kin tell other folks what to do. You ain't none of my boss. Don't let yo' wooden God and corn-stalk Jesus fool you now. Not[17] de way you sells rancid bacon for fresh.

NIXON: Aw, honey, hush a while, please, and less git started.

*(A momentary quiet falls on the place. [Clarke] glowers all over the place. Turns to Lum.)*

CLARKE: Lum, git a piece of paper and a pencil and take de names of all de witnesses *who was dere while de fight was going on.*

LUM: *(Pulling a small tablet and pencil out of his coat pocket)* I brought it with me.

CLARKE: Now everybody who was at de fight hold up yo' hands so Lum can know who you are.

*(Several hands go up. Sister Anderson puts up her hand.)*

CLARKE: You wasn't there, Sister Anderson, not at that time.

SISTER ANDERSON: I hadn't been gone more'n ten minutes 'fore Dave come in from de woods.

CLARKE: But you didn't see it.

MRS. ANDERSON: It don't make no difference—my husband heered every word was spoke and told me jes' lak it happen. Don't tell *me* I can't testify.

HAMBO: Nobody can't testify but de two boys 'cause nobody wuz at de fight but dem.

MRS. ANDERSON: Dat's all right too, Brother, but I know whut they wuz fightin' about an' it wudn't no turkey neither. It wuz Daisy Blunt.

MRS. BLUNT: Just you take my chile's name right out yo' mouf, Becky Anderson. She wuzn't out in dat cypress swamp. Leave her out dis mess.

SIMMS: You ain't got no call to be so touchous 'bout yo' girl, but you sho said a mouthful, Sister Blunt. Dis sho is a mess. Can't help from being uh mess. *(Glares at [Clarke])* Holdin' a trial in de Baptist church! Some folks ain't got sense enough to do 'em till four o'clock and it's way after half past three right now.

CLARKE: Shet up, dere, Simms! Set down! Who ast yo' pot to boil, nohow? Court is de best church they is, anyhow, 'cause you come in court. You better have a good experience and a strong determination. *(Raps vigor-*

*ously.)* Now lemme tell *y'all* something. When de mayor sets court—don't keer when I sets it nor where I sets it, you got to git quiet and stay quiet till I ast you tuh talk. I God, you sound lak a tree full uh blackbirds! Dis ain't no barbecue, nor neither no camp meetin'. We 'sembled here tuh law uh boy on a serious charge. *(A great buzz rises from the congregation. [Clarke] raps hard for order and glares all about him.)* Hear! Hear! All of us kin sing at de same time, but can't but one of us talk at a time. I'm doin' de talkin' now, so de rest of you dry up till I git through. I God, you sound lak uh passel uh dog fights! We ain't here for no form and no fashion and no outside show to de world. We'se here to law. *(To Lum)* You done got all de witnesses straight—Got they names down?

LUM: Yessuh, I got it all straightened out.

CLARKE: Well, read de names out and let de witnesses take de front seats.

LUM: Mr. Clarke, I done found out nobody wasn't at dat fight but Jim and Dave and de mule bones. Dere's de bone Dave got hit wid up on de rostrum and dere's Jim and Dave in de Amen Corners.

DAVE: *(Rising excitedly)* Mist' Clarke! Brother Mayor, I wants to ast uh question right now to git some information.

CLARKE: All right, Dave, go 'head and ast it.

DAVE: Brother Mayor, I wanted to know whut become of my turkey gobbler?

CLARKE: I God, Dave, youse in order. Lum! I God, I been layin' off to ast you whut you done wid dat turkey. Where is it? *(A burst of knowing laughter from the house.)*

LUM: *(Very embarrassed)* Well, when you tole me to go 'rrest Jim and de turkey, I took and went on 'round to his ma's house and he wudn't dere so I took and turnt 'round and made it t'wards Daisy's house an' I caught up wid him under dat Chinaberry tree jest befo' you gits tuh Daisy's house. He was makin' it on t'wards her house wid de turkey in one hand—his gun crost his shoulder when I hailed 'im. I hollered "Jim, hold on dere uh minute!" He dropped de turkey and wheeled and throwed de gun on me.

CLARKE: I God, he drawed uh gun on de city marshall?

LUM: Yessir! He sho did. Thought I was Dave. Tole me: "Don't you come another step unless you want to see yuh Jesus." I hollered back "It's me, I ain't no Dave Carter." So he took de gun offa me and I went up to him and put him under arrest, and locked him up in yo' barn and brought you de key, didn't I?

CLARKE: You sho did, but I God, I ast you whut become of de turkey?

LUM: De turkey wasn't picked or nothin', so I put him under 'rrest too, jus' lak you tole me. *(General laughter)*

CLARKE: I God, Lum, whut did you *do* wid de turkey after you put him under 'rrest?

LUM: Jim, he didn't want to come wid me till he could make it to Daisy's house to give her dat turkey but, bein' so close up on him till he couldn't draw his rifle, I throwed my .32-20[18] in his face an' tole him I said "Don't you move! Don't you move uh pig—do, I'll burn you down! I got my burner cocked dead in yo' face and I'll keer you down jus' lak good gas went up. Come on wid me!" So I took his rifle and picked up de turkey and marched him off to yo' cow-lot. Ast him didn't I do it. I tole him, I said "I know you Westons goes for bad but I'm yo' match." I said "you may be slick but you kin stand another greasing." Now sir! I ain't skeered uh no-body. I'll put de whole town under 'rrest.

CLARKE: I God, Lum, if you don't tell me whut you done wid dat turkey, you better! *(Draws back the gavel as if to hurl it at Lum.)* I'll lam you over de head wid dis mallet! Whut did you do wid dat gobbler turkey?

LUM: Being as he wasn't picked or nothin', I know you didn't want to be both-ered wid it, so I took and carried it over to Mrs. Blunt's house and she put on some hot water and we set up way Sat'day night pickin' de turkey and fixin' him so nex' day she cooked him off—just sorta baked him wid a lil stuffin an' such, so he'd keep.

CLARKE: Didn't you know my wife knowed how to cook? Go fetch dat turkey here, and don't let no dead lice fall off of you on de way.

LUM: *(Extremely embarrassed)* I don't speck he's dere now, Mist' Clarke.

CLARKE: *(Ferociously)* How come?

LUM: I passed by dere on Sunday and et a lil piece of shoulder offa him, an' being everybody else was eatin' turkey too, I et some breast meat an' uh mouf'ful or two of stuffin' an' uh drum stick wid de ham part of de leg hung on to it wid a lil gravy. *(General laughter.)* I thought I was doin' right 'cause de turkey was kilt for Daisy anyhow. So I jus' took it on to her. Dave was all hurt up and Jim was locked up so—

CLARKE: Dat'll do! Dat'll do! Dry up, suh! *(Turns to Dave)* Stand up, Dave. Since youse de one got hurted, you be de first witness and tell me just whut went on out dere.

*(Dave rises slowly.)*

SISTER TAYLOR: Dat's right, Dave. Git up dere and lie lak de cross ties from New York to Texas. You greasy rascal you! You better go wash yo'self before you go testifying on people.

DAVE: I'm just as clean as you.

SINGLETARY: *(Jumping to his feet)* Wait a minute! 'Tain't none of y'all got no call to be throwin' off on dis boy. He come here to git justice, not to be slurred and low-rated. He ain't 'ssaulted nobody. He ain't stole no turkeys *nor* chickens. He's a clean boy. He set at my feet in Sunday school since he was so high, *(Measures knee height)* and he come through religion under de sound of my voice an' I baptized him and I know he's clean.

SISTER TAYLOR: It'll take more'n uh baptizin' to clean dat nigger.

DAVE: I goes in swimmin' nearly every day. I'm just as clean as anybody else.

*(Clarke begins rapping for order.)*

SISTER TAYLOR: *(Shouts out)* Swimmin'! Dat ain't gointer clean de crust offa *you*. You ain't had a good bath since de devil was a hatchet. If you ain't been parboiled in de wash pot and scoured wid Red Seal lye, don't bring de mess up.

CLARKE: I'm goin' to have order here or else! Gwan, Dave.

DAVE: It's just lak I tole you Sat'day night.

CLARKE: Yeah, but dat wuz at de store. Dis is in court and it's got to be tole agin.

SIMMS: Just uh minute, Brother Clarke, before we any further go I wants to ast de witness uh question dat oughter be answered before he open his mouf.

CLARKE: Whut *kind* of a question is dat?

SIMMS: Dave, tell de truth. Ain't yo' heart full of envy and malice 'gainst dis chile? *(Gestures towards Jim. Dave shakes his head and starts to deny the charge but Simms hurries on.)* Wait a minute now! Wait till I git through. Didn't y'all used to run around everywhere playin' and singing and everything till you got so full of envy and malice and devilment till y'all broke up? Now, Brother Mayor, make him tell de truth.

DAVE: Yeah, I useter be crazy 'bout Jim, and we was buddies till he tried to back bite me wid, wid my girl.

JIM: Never *was* yo' girl. Nohow I ain't none of yo' buddy. I ain't got no buddy. They kilt my buddy tryin' to raise me. But I did useter lak you till you acted so low down tryin' to undermine me and root me out wid my girl.

CLARKE: Aw, table dat business an' less open up new business. We ain't here to find out whose girl it is. We wants to know 'bout dis fight and who hit de first lick and how come. Go 'head on, Dave, and talk.

DAVE: Well, jus' lak I tole yuh, Sat'day night, I been watchin' dat flock uh wild turkeys ever since way last summer roostin' in de ledge of dat cypress swamp out by Howell Creek, where Brazzle's ole mule was dragged out. It was a great, big ole gobbler leadin' de flock. So last time I seen him I said I was gointer git him for my girl if it taken me uh year. So Sat'day, kinda late, I grabs ole Hannah, my gun, I calls her Ole Hannah, and come to de store to buy some shells. Y'all know whut went on at de store. Well, it made me feel lak I wuz gointer git dat ole gobbler if I had to follow him clean to Diddy-Wah-Diddy or slap into Ginny-Gall.[19] But I didn't have to do nothin'. When I got out by de ole mule bones, I seen 'em flyin' 'round lak buzzards. So I loaded both barrels, squatted down on uh log where I had dead aim on dat big ole cypress pine where they roosts at. Sho 'nuff, soon's de sun had done set, here dey come followin' de leader! He lit way out on de end of de limb kinda off from de rest and I eased ole Hannah up on him. Man! I got so skeered I wuz gointer miss him till I got de all overs. He gobbled two three times to see if all his fambly was safed den he settled down and bam! I let him have it! He spread his wings lak he wuz gointer fly on off an' I *cried* lak a chile! But I got him all right and down he come floppin', and me grabbin' him before he quit kickin'. Gee, I was proud. He felt lak he weighed forty pounds. Whilst I was kinda heftin' him in my hands I heard uh rifle fire and I looked and dere was Jim firin' into de turkey flock dat was flyin' 'round skeered. He didn't hit a God's thing, but he seen me wid my gobbler and come runnin' up talking 'bout give him his turkey. I ast him "who turkey you talking 'bout?" He says dat one of his'n I had done grabbed. I tole him he must gone crazy in de head. He says, I better give him his turkey before he beat my head off. I tole him I wasn't gointer give nobody but Daisy Blunt dat turkey. Otherwise, if he wanted to try my head, I wasn't runnin' uh damn step. Come on. So he jumped on me and tried to snatch de turkey. We fi't all over de place. First we was just tussling for de bird, but when he found out he couldn't take it he hit me wid his fist. Den I ups wid my African soup bone[20] and I bet I plowed up uh acre uh bushes wid his head. He hit ker-bam! right in dat pack uh mule bones and I turnt and started off, when lo and behold, he gits up wid dat hock bone and lams me in de head and when I come to, him and my turkey was gone. So I come swore out uh warrant aginst him 'cause he didn't fight fair. I ain't mad. I always lakted Jim, but he sho done dirty—lammin' me wid uh mule bone and takin' my turkey.

*(Dave resumes his seat and Jim drops his head for a moment, then snatches it up arrogantly and glares at the Baptists. The whole place is very silent for*

*a moment. Then Mayor Clarke clears his throat, raps with his gavel and looks sternly at Jim.)*

CLARKE: Jim Weston, stand up suh! *(Jim rises sullenly.)* Youse charged wid 'saultin Dave Carter wid uh dangerous weapon and then stealin' his lawful turkey gobbler. You heard de charge—guilty or not guilty?

JIM: *(Arrogantly)* Yeah, I hit him and I'll hit him agin if he crowd me. But I ain't guilty uh no crime. *(He hitches up his pants and sits down arrogantly.)*

CLARKE: *(Surprised)* Whut's dat you say, Jim? *(Raps sharply)* Git up from there sir! Whut's dat you say?

JIM: *(Rising)* I say, heah, I lammed ole Dave wid de mule bone, but I ain't guilty uh nothin'.

*(There is a stark silence for a few seconds. Then Clarke raps nervously.)*

CLARKE: How come you ain't guilty?

*(Jim sits down amid jubilant smiles of Methodists. Simms chuckles out loud and wipes his face with his handkerchief. He gets to his feet still gloating.)*

SIMMS: *(To Jim)* Set down, Jim, and lemme show dese people dat walks in de darkness wid sinners an' Republicans de light.

SINGLETARY: You just as well tuh hush up befo' you start, then, Simms. You can't show nobody uh light when you ain't got none tuh show.

HAMBO: Ain't dat de gospel?

NIXON: Aw, let de man talk. Y'all sound lak uh tree full uh blackbirds. Go 'head on, Elder Simms.

WALTER: Yeah, you can't teach 'em nothin' but talk on. We know whut you talkin' about.

CLARKE: *(Raps once or twice)* I God, tell it. Whut ever 'tis you got tuh tell.

SISTER LEWIS: Aw yeah, hurry up and tell it. I know it ain't goin' tuh be nothin' after you git it told but hurry up and say it so yo' egg-bag kin rest easy.

WALTER: Aw shet up an' give de man uh chance.

SISTER LEWIS: My shetters ain't workin' good. Sposin' you come shet me up, Walter. Den you'll know it's done right.

LIGE: Aw, whyn't y'all ack lak folks an' leave de man talk.

CLARKE: *(Rapping repeatedly)* Order in dis court, I God, jus' like you was in Orlando! *(Silence falls.)* Now, Simms, talk yo' chat.

SIMMS: (*Glances down into his open Bible, then looks all around the room with great deliberation. It is evident he enjoys being the center of attraction. He smiles smugly as he turns his face towards the pulpit. He speaks slowly and accents his words so that none will be lost on his audience.*) De Bible says, be sho you're right, then go ahead. (*He looks all around to collect the admiration he feels he has earned.*) Now, we all done gathered and 'sembled here tuh law dis young lad of uh boy on uh mighty serious charge. Uh whole passle of us is rarin' tuh drive him 'way from home lak you done drove off[21] his daddy an' his brothers.

HAMBO: We never drove off his pappy. De white folks took an' hung him for killin' dat man in Kissimmee for nothin'.

SIMMS: Dat ain't de point, Brother Hambo.

HAMBO: It's jes' as good uh point as any. If you gointer talk—tell de truth. An' if you can't tell de truth, set down an' leave Rev. Singletary talk.

SIMMS: Brother Mayor, how come you let dese people run they mouf lak uh passle uh cow-bells? Ain't I got de floor? I ain't no breath-and-britches. I was *people* in Middle Georgy befo' I ever come to Floridy. Whut kind of Chairman is you, nohow?

CLARKE: (*Angrily*) Heah! Heah! Don't you come tryin' show yo'self 'round me! I God, I don't keer whut you wuz in Georgy. I God, I kin eat fried chicken when you cain't git rain water tuh drink. Hurry up an' say dat mess you got in yo' craw an' set down. We needs yo' space more than we needs yo' comp'ny.

NIXON: Don't let him skeer you, Elder Simms. You got plenty shoulders tuh back yo' fallin'.

HAMBO: Well, each an' every shoulder kin hit de ground an' I'll git wid 'em. Don't like it dontcher take [it], here['s] my collar come an' shake it.

WALTER: Hambo, everybody in Orange County knows you love tuh fight. But dis is uh law hearin'—not no wrassle.

HAMBO: Oh you Meth'dis' niggers wants tuh fight bad enough, but youse skeered. Youse jus' as hot as Tucker when de mule kicked his mammy. But you know you got plenty coolers.

SISTER TAYLOR: Aw, 'tain't nobody skeered uh you half-pint Baptists. God knows Ah'm ready an' willin'.

(*She glares at Mrs. Lewis. Sister Lewis jumps to her feet but is pulled back into her seat. Mayor Clarke raps for order and the room gets quiet.*)

CLARKE: Aw right now, Simms. I God, git through.

SIMMS: *(Pompously)* Now, y'all done up an' took dis po' boy an' had him locked up in uh barn ever since Sat'day night an' done got him 'ccused uh assault an' stealing uh turkey an' I don't know whut all an' you ain't got no business wid yo' hands on him atall. He ain't done no crime, an' if y'all knowed anything 'bout law, I wouldn't have tuh tell you so.

CLARKE: I God, he is done uh crime and he's gointer ketch it, too.

SIMMS: But not by law, Brother Mayor. You tryin' tuh lay uh hearin' on dis boy an' you can't do it 'cause he ain't broke no law—I don't keer whut he done, so long as he don't break no law you can't tetch him.

SINGLETARY: He committed assault, didn't he? Dat sho is breakin' de law.

SIMMS: Naw, he ain't committed no 'sault. He jus' lammed Dave over de head an' took his own turkey an' come on home, dat's all. *(Triumphantly)* Yuh see y'all don't know whut you talkin' 'bout. Now, I done set in de court house an' heard de white folks law from mornin' till night. *(He flips his Bible shut.)* I done read dis book from lid tuh lid an' I knows de law. You got tuh have uh weepon tuh commit uh 'sault. An' 'tain't in no white folks' law and 'tain't in dis Bible dat no mule bone is no weepon.

CLARKE: *(After a moment of dead silence)* I God, whut's dat you say?

SIMMS: *(Sitting down and crossing his legs and folding his hands upon his Bible)* You heard me. I say you ain't got no case 'ginst dis boy an' you got tuh turn him go.

SINGLETARY: *(Jumping up)* Brother Chairman—

CLARKE: *(Raps once and nods recognition)* You got de floor.

SINGLETARY: I ain't book-learnt an' I ain't rubbed de hair offen my head agin' no college wall, but I know when uh 'sault been committed. I says Jim Weston did 'sault Davie. *(He points at Dave's head.)* An' steal his turkey. Everybody knows Jim can't hunt wid Dave. An' he 'saulted Dave too.

SIMMS: *(Arrogantly)* Prove it!

*(Singletary stands there silent and puzzled. The Methodist side breaks into a triumphant shout of "Oh Mary, Don't You Weep, Don't You Moan, Pharaoh's Army Got Drownded." Singletary sinks into his seat. When they have shouted out three choruses, Simms arises to speak.)*

I move dat we sing doxology and bring dis meetin' to uh close. We's all workin' people, Brother Mayor. Dismiss us so we kin gwan back to our work. De sun is two hours high yet. *(Looks towards the Methodist side)* I move dat we adjourn.

WALTER: I second de motion.

SINGLETARY: *(Arising slowly)* Hold on there uh minute wid dat motion. Dis ain't no lodge meetin'. Dis is uh court an' bofe sides got uh right tuh talk. *(Motions towards Simms' Bible)* Youse uh letter learnt man but I kin read dat Bible some too. Lemme take it uh minute.

SIMMS: I ain't uh gointer do it. Any preacher dat amounts to uh hill uh beans would have his own Bible.

CLARKE: I God, Singletary, you right here in yo' own church. Come on up here an' read out yo' pulpit Bible. I God, don't mind me being up here. Come on up.

*(A great buzzing breaks out all over the church as Singletary mounts the pulpit. Clarke raps for order. Simms begins to turn the leaves of the Bible.)*

SIMMS: Brother Mayor, you oughter let us outa here. You ain't got no case 'ginst dis boy. Don't waste our time for nothin'. Leave us go home.

CLARKE: Aw, dry up, Simms. You done talked yo' talk. I God, leave Singletary talk his. *(To Singletary)* Step on out when you ready, Rev.

SINGLETARY: *(Reading)* It says here in Judges 18:18 dat Samson slewed three thousand Philistines wid de jawbone of an ass.

SIMMS: *(On his feet)* Yeah, but dis wasn't no ass. Dis was uh mule, Brother Mayor. Dismiss dis meetin' and less all go home.

SINGLETARY: Yeah, but he was half-ass. A ass is uh mule's daddy and he's bigger'n uh ass, too. *(Emphatic gestures)* Everybody knows dat—even de lil chillun.

SIMMS: *(Standing)* Yeah, but we didn't come here to talk about no asses, neither no half asses, nor no mule daddies. *(Laughter from the Methodists)* We come to law uh boy for 'sault an' larceny.

SINGLETARY: *(Very patiently)* We'se comin' to dat pint now. Dat's de second claw uh de sentence we'se expoundin'. I say Jim Weston did have uh weepon in his hand when he 'saulted Dave. 'Cause y'all knows if de daddy is dangerous, den de son is dangerous too. An' y'all knows dat de further back you gits on uh mule de more dangerous he gits an' if de jawbone slewed three thousand people, by de time you gits back tuh his hocks, it's pizen enough to kill ten thousand. 'Tain't no gun in de world ever kilt dat many mens. 'Tain't no knives nor no razors ever kilt no three thousand people. Now, folkses, I ast y'all whut kin be mo' dangerous dan uh mule bone? *(To Clarke)* Brother Mayor, Jim didn't jes' lam Dave an' walk off. *(Very emphatic)* He 'saulted him wid de deadliest weepon there is in de world an' while he was layin' unconscious, he stole his turkey an' went. Brother Mayor, he's uh criminal an' oughter be run outa dis peaceful town.

*(Great chorus of approval from Baptists. Clarke begins to rap for order.)*

SIMMS: *(Standing)* Brother Mayor, I object. I have studied jury law[22] and I know what I'm talkin' about.

CLARKE: Aw dry up, Simms. Youse entirely out of order. You may be slick, but you kin stand another greasing. Rev. Singletary is right. I God, I knows de law when I hear it. Stand up dere, Jim.

*(Jim rises very slowly. Simms rises also.)*

CLARKE: Set down, Simms. I God, I know where to find you when I want you. *(Simms sits.)* Jim, I find you guilty as charged an' I wants you to git outa my town and stay gone for two years. *(To Lum)* Brother Marshall, you see dat he gits outa town befo' dark. An' you folks dat's so anxious to fight, git on off dis church grounds befo' you start. And don't use no knives and no guns and no mule bones. Court's dismissed.

*(Curtain.)*

### ACT THREE
Scene 1

*Setting: Curtain goes up on a stretch of railroad track with a luxurious Florida forest on the backdrop. Entrances left and right. It is near sundown.*
*Action: When the curtain goes up there is no one on the stage, but there is a tremendous noise and hubbub offstage right. There are yells of derision, shouts of anger. Part of the mob is trying to keep Jim in town and a part is driving him off. After a full minute of this, Jim enters with his guitar hanging around his neck and his coat over his shoulder. The sun is dropping low and red through the forest. He is looking back angrily and shouting back at the mob. A small missile is thrown after him. Jim drops his coat and guitar and grabs up a piece of brick and threatens to throw it.*

JIM: *(Run[s] back the way he came and hurls the brick with all his might.)* I'll kill some of you ole box-ankled niggers—*(grabs up another piece of brick)* I'm out yo' ole town—now jus' some of you ole half-pint Baptists let yo' wooden God and corn-stalk Jesus fool you to hit me! *(Threatens to throw. There are some frightened screams and the mob is heard running back.)* I'm glad I'm out yo' ole town, anyhow. I ain't never comin' back no more, neither. You ole ugly-rump niggers done ruint de town anyhow. *(There is complete silence offstage. Jim walks a few steps then sits down on the railroad embankment facing the audience. Jim pulls off one shoe and pours the sand out. He holds the shoe in his hand a moment and looks wistfully back down the railroad track.)* Lawd, folks sho is deceitful. *(He puts on the shoe and looks back down the track again.)* I never woulda thought people woulda acted lak dat. *(Laces up the shoe)* Specially Dave Carter, much as me an' him done proaged 'round together goin' in swimmin' and playin' ball an' serenadin' de girls an' de white folks. *(He sits there gloomily silent for a while, then looks behind him and picks up his guitar and begins to pick a tune. It is very sad. He trails off into "You May Leave an' Go to Halimuhfack."*[23] *When he finishes he looks back at the sun and picks up his coat also.*[24] *He looks back again towards the village.)* Reckon I better git on down de road an' git somewhere, Lawd knows where. *(Stops suddenly in his tracks and turns back towards the village and takes a step or two.)* All dat mess and stink for nothin'. Dave knows good an' well I didn't mean to hurt him much.

*(He takes off his cap and scratches his head thoroughly, then turns again and starts on down the road towards left. Enter Daisy left walking briskly.)*

DAISY: Hello, Jim.

JIM: Hello, Daisy. *(Embarrassed silence.)*

DAISY: I was just coming over to town to see how you come out.

JIM: You don't have to go way over there to find dat out—you and Dave done got me run outa town for nothin'.

DAISY: *(Putting her hand on his arm)* Dey didn't run you outa town, did dey?

JIM: *(Shaking her hand off)* Whut you reckon I'm countin' Mr. Railroad's ties for—just to find out how many ties between here and Orlando?

DAISY: *(Hand on his arm again)* Dey *cain't* run you off like dat!

JIM: Take yo' hands off me, Daisy! How come they can't run me off wid you and Dave an'—*everybody* 'gainst me?

DAISY: I ain't opened my mouf 'gainst you, Jim. I ain't said one word—I wasn't even at de old trial. My madame wouldn't let me git off. I wuz just comin' to see 'bout you now.

JIM: Aw, go 'head on. You figgered I was gone too long to talk about. You was haulin' it over to town to see Dave—dat's whut [you] was doin'—after gittin' *me* all messed up.

DAISY: *(Making as if to cry)* I wasn't studying 'bout no Dave.

JIM: *(Hopefully)* Aw, don't tell me. *(Sings)*

Ashes to ashes, dust to dust,
Show me a woman that a man can trust.

*(Daisy is crying now.)*

Whut you crying for? You know you love Dave. I'm yo' monkey-man. He always could do more wid you than[25] I could.

DAISY: Naw, you ain't no monkey-man neither. I don't want you to leave town. I didn't want y'all to be fightin' over me, nohow.

JIM: Aw, rock on down de road wid dat stuff. A two-timing cloaker like you don't keer whut come off. Me and Dave been good friends ever since we was born till you had to go flouncing yourself around.

DAISY: What did I do? All I did was to come over town to see you and git a mouf'ful of gum. Next thing I know y'all is fighting and carrying on.

JIM: *(Stands silent for a while)* Did you come over there Sat'day to see me sho 'nuff, sugar babe?

DAISY: Everybody could see dat but you.

JIM: Just like I told you, Daisy. I'll say it before yo' face and behind yo' back. I could kiss you every day—just as regular as pig-tracks.

DAISY: And I tole you I could stand it too—just as regular as you could.

JIM: *(Catching her by the arm and pulling her down with him onto the rail)* Set down here, Daisy. Less talk some chat. You want me sho 'nuff—honest to God?

DAISY: *(Coyly)* 'Member whut I told you out on de lake last summer?

JIM: Sho 'nuff, Daisy?

*(Daisy nods smilingly.)*

JIM: *(Sadly)* But I got to go 'way. Whut we gointer do 'bout dat?

DAISY: Where you goin', Jim?

JIM: *(Looking sadly down the track)* God knows. *(Offstage from the same direction from which Jim entered comes the sound of whistling and tramping of feet on the ties. Brightening)* Dat's Dave! *(Frowning suspiciously)* Wonder whut he doin' walking dis track? *(Looks accusingly at Daisy)* I bet he's goin' to yo' work-place.

DAISY: Whut for?

JIM: He ain't goin' to see de madame—must be goin' to see you.

*(He starts to rise petulantly as Dave comes upon the scene. Daisy rises also.)*

DAVE: *(Looks accusingly from one to the other)* Whut y'all jumpin' up for? I—

JIM: Whut you got to do wid us business? 'Tain't none of yo' business if we stand up, set down or fly like a skeeter hawk.

DAVE: Who said I keered? Dis railroad belongs to de *man*—I kin walk it good as you, can't I?

JIM: *(Laughing exultantly)* Oh yeah, Mr. Do-Dirty! You figgered you had done run me on off so you could git Daisy all by yo'self. You was headin' right for her work-place.

DAVE: I wasn't no such a thing.

JIM: You was. Didn't I hear you coming down de track all whistling and every-thing?

DAVE: Youse a big ole Georgy something-ain't-so! I done got my belly full of Daisy Sat'day night. She can't snore in my ear no more.

DAISY: *(Indignantly)* Whut you come here low-rating me for, Dave Carter? I ain't done nothin' to you but treat you white. Who come rubbed yo' ole head for you yestiddy if it wasn't me?

DAVE: Yeah, you rubbed my head all right, and I lakted dat. But everybody say you done toted a pan to Joe Clarke's barn for Jim before I seen you.

DAISY: Think I was going to let Jim there 'thout nothing fitten for a dog to eat?

DAVE: That's all right, Daisy. If you want to pay Jim for knockin' me in de head, all right. But I'm a man in a class—in a class to myself and nobody knows my name.

JIM: *(Snatching Daisy around to face him)* Was you over to Dave's house yestiddy rubbing his ole head and cloaking wid him to run me outa town—and me locked up in dat barn wid de cows and mules?

DAISY: *(Sobbing)* All both of y'all hollerin' at me an' fussin' me just 'cause I tries to be nice—and neither one of y'all don't keer nothin' 'bout me.

*(Both boys glare at each other over Daisy's head and both try to hug her at the same time. She violently wrenches herself away from both and makes as if to move on.)*

Leave me go! Take yo' rusty paws offen me. I'm going on back to my work-place. I just got off to see 'bout y'all and look how y'all treat me.

JIM: Wait a minute, Daisy. I love you likes God loves Gabriel—and dat's His best angel.

DAVE: Daisy, I love you harder than de thunder can bump a stump—if I don't—God's a gopher.

DAISY: *(Brightening)* Dat's de first time you ever said so.

DAVE AND JIM: Who?

JIM: Whut you hollering "who" for? Yo' foot don't fit no limb.

DAVE: Speak when you spoken to—come when you called, next fall you'll be my coon houn' dog.

JIM: Table dat discussion. *(Turning to Daisy)* You ain't never give me no chance to talk wid you right.

DAVE: You made *me* feel like you was trying to put de Ned book on me all de time. Do you love me sho 'nuff, Daisy?

DAISY: *(Blooming again into coquetry)* Aw, y'all better stop dat. You know you don't mean it.

DAVE: Who don't mean it? Lemme tell you something, mama, if you was mine I wouldn't have you counting no ties wid yo' pretty lil toes. Know whut I'd do?

DAISY: *(Coyly)* Naw, whut would you do?

DAVE: I'd buy a whole passenger train and hire some mens to run it for you.

DAISY: *(Happily)* Oo-ooh, Dave.

JIM: *(To Dave)* De wind may blow, de door may slam—Dat whut you shootin' ain't worth a damn. *(To Daisy)* I'd buy you a great big ole ship—and then baby, I'd buy you a ocean to sail yo' ship on.

DAISY: *(Happily)* Oo-ooh, Jim.

DAVE: *(To Jim)* A long train, a short caboose—Dat lie whut you shootin', ain't no use. *(To Daisy)* Miss Daisy, know what I'd do for you?

DAISY: Naw, whut?

DAVE: I'd like uh job cleanin' out de Atlantic Ocean jus' for you.

DAISY: Don't fool me now, papa.

DAVE: I couldn't fool *you*, Daisy, 'cause anything I say 'bout lovin' you, I don't keer how big it is, it wouldn't be half de truth. I'd come down de river riding a mud cat and leading a minnow.

DAISY: Lawd, Dave, you sho is propaganda.

JIM: *(Peevishly)* Naw he ain't—he's just lying—he's a noble liar. Know whut I'd do if you was mine?

DAISY: Naw, Jim.

JIM: I'd make a panther wash yo' dishes and a 'gator chop yo' wood for you.

DAVE: Daisy, how come you let Jim lie lak dat? He's as big a liar as he is a man. But sho 'nuff now, laying all sides to jokes, Jim there don't even know how to answer you. If you don't b'lieve it, ast him something.

DAISY: *(To Jim)* You like me much, Jim?

JIM: *(Enthusiastically)* Yeah, Daisy, I sho do.

DAVE: *(Triumphant)* See dat! I tole you he didn't know how to answer nobody like you. If he was talking to some of them ol' funny looking gals over town he'd be answering 'em just right. But he got to learn how to answer *you*. Now you ast *me* something and see how I answer you.

DAISY: Do you like me, Dave?

DAVE: *(Very properly in a falsetto voice)* Yes ma'am! Dat's de way to answer swell folks like you. Furthermore, less we prove which one of us love you de best right now. *(To Jim)* Jim, how much time would you do on de chain-gang for dis 'oman?

JIM: Twenty years and like it.

DAVE: See dat, Daisy? Dat nigger ain't willing to do no time for you. I'd *beg* de judge to gimme life. *(Both Jim and Dave laugh.)*

DAISY: Y'all doin' all dis boo-kooing out here on de railroad track but I bet y'all crazy 'bout Bootsie and Teets and a whole heap of others.

JIM: Cross my feet and hope to die! I'd ruther see all de other wimmen folks in de world dead than for you to have de tooth-ache.

DAVE: If I was dead and any other woman come near my coffin de undertaker would have to do his job all over—'cause I'd git right up and walk off. Furthermore, Miss Daisy, ma'am, also ma'am, which would *you* ruther be, a lark a-flying or a dove a-settin'—ma'am, also ma'am?[26]

DAISY: 'Course I'd ruther be a dove.

JIM: Miss Daisy, ma'am, also ma'am—if you marry dis nigger over my head, I'm going to git me a green hickory club and season it over yo' head.

DAVE: Don't you be skeered, baby—papa kin take keer a *you*. *(To Jim)* Counting from de finger *(Suiting the action to the word)* back to de thumb—start anything I got you some.

JIM: Aw, I don't want no more fight wid you, Dave.

DAVE: Who said anything about fighting? We just provin' who love Daisy de best. *(To Daisy)* Now, which one of us you think love you de best?

DAISY: 'Deed I don't know, Dave.

DAVE: Baby, I'd walk de water for you—and tote a mountain on my head while I'm walkin'.

JIM: Know whut I'd do, honey babe? If you was a thousand miles from home and you didn't have no ready-made money and you had to walk all de way, walkin' till yo' feet start to rolling, just like a wheel, and I was riding way up in de sky, I'd step backwards offa dat airyplane just to walk home wid you.

DAISY: *(Falling on Jim's neck)* Jim, when you talk to me like dat I just can't stand it. Less us git married right now.

JIM: Now you talkin' like a blue-back speller.[27] Less go!

DAVE: *(Sadly)* You gointer leave me lak dis, Daisy?

DAISY: *(Sadly)* I likes you, too, Dave, I sho do. But I can't marry both of y'all at de same time.

JIM: Aw, come on, Daisy—sun's gettin' low. *(He starts off pulling Daisy.)*

DAVE: *(Walking after them)* Whut's I'm gointer do?

JIM: Gwan back and hunt turkeys—you make out you so touchous nobody can't tell you yo' eye is black 'thout you got to run git de law.

DAVE: *(Almost tearfully)* Aw Jim, shucks! Where y'all going?

*(Daisy comes to an abrupt halt and stops Jim.)*

DAISY: That's right, honey. Where *is* we goin' sho 'nuff?

JIM: *(Sadly)* 'Deed I don't know, baby. They just sentenced me to go—they didn't say where and I don't know.

DAISY: How we goin' know how to go when we don't know where we goin'?

*(Jim looks at Dave as if he expects some help but Dave stands sadly silent. Jim takes a few steps forward as if to go on. Daisy makes a step or two, unwillingly, then looks behind her and stops. Dave looks as if he will follow them.)*

DAISY: Jim! *(He stops and turns.)* Wait a minute! Whut we gointer do when we git there?

JIM: Where?

DAISY: Where we goin'?

JIM: I done tole you I don't know where it is.

DAISY: But how we gointer git something to eat and a place to stay?

JIM: Play my box for de white folks and dance just like I been doing.

DAISY: You can't take keer of me on dat, not where we hafta pay rent.

JIM: *(Looks appealingly at Dave, then away quickly.)* Well, I can't help *dat,* can I?

DAISY: *(Brightly)* I tell you whut, Jim! Less us don't go nowhere. They sentenced you to leave Eatonville and youse almost a mile from de city limits already. Youse in Maitland now. Supposin' you come live on de white folks' place wid me after we git married. Eatonville ain't got nothin' to do wid you livin' in Maitland.

JIM: Dat's a good idea, Daisy.

DAISY: *(Jumping into his arms)* And lissen, honey, you don't have to be beholden to nobody. You can throw dat ole box away if you want to. I know where you can get a *swell* job.

JIM: *(Sheepishly)* Doin' whut? *(Looks lovingly at his guitar.)*

DAISY: *(Almost dancing)* Yard man. All you have to do is wash windows, and sweep de sidewalk, and scrub off de steps and porch and hoe up de weeds and rake up de leaves and dig a few holes now and then with a spade—to plant some trees and things like that. It's a good steady job.

JIM: *(After a long deliberation)* You see, Daisy, de mayor and de corporation told me to go on off and I oughter go.

DAISY: Well, I'm not going tippin' down no railroad track like a Maltese cat. I wasn't brought up knockin' 'round from here to yonder.

JIM: Well, I wasn't brought up wid no spade in my hand—and ain't going to start it now.

DAISY: But sweetheart, we got to live, ain't we? We got to git hold of money before we kin do anything. I don't mean to stay in de white folks' kitchen all my days.

JIM: Yeah, all dat's true, but you couldn't buy a flea a waltzing jacket wid de money *I'm* going to make wid a hoe and spade.

DAISY: *(Getting tearful)* You don't want me. You don't love me.

JIM: Yes, I do, darling, I love you. Youse de one letting a spade come between us. *(He caresses her.)* I loves you and you only. You don't see *me* dragging a whole gang of farming tools into us business, do you?

DAISY: *(Stiffly)* Well, I ain't going to marry no man that ain't going to work and take care of me.

JIM: I don't mind working if de job ain't too heavy for me. I ain't going to bother wid nothin' in my hands heavier than dis box—and I totes it 'round my neck most of de time. I kin go out and hunt you some game when times gits tight.

DAISY: Don't strain yo'self huntin' nothin' for me. I ain't goin' to eat nobody's settin' hen.[28]

JIM: Whut ole sittin' hen? Ain't you and Lum done et up de turkey I—I—brought?[29]

DAISY: You might of brought it, but Dave sho kilt it. You couldn't hit de side of uh barn wid uh bass fiddle.

DAVE: 'Course I kilt it, and I kilt it for you, but I didn't kill none for Lum Bailey. De clean head hound!

DAISY: *(Turns to Dave finally)* Well, I reckon you loves me the best anyhow. You wouldn't talk to me like Jim did, would you, Dave?

DAVE: Naw, I wouldn't say whut he said atall.

DAISY: *(Cuddling up to him)* Whut would *you* say, honey?

DAVE: I'd say dat box was too heavy for me to fool wid. I wouldn't tote nothing but my gun and my hat and I feel like I'm 'busing myself sometime totin' dat.

DAISY: *(Outraged)* Don't you mean to work none?

DAVE: Wouldn't hit a lick at a snake.

DAISY: I don't blame *you*, Dave, *(Looks down at his feet)* 'cause toting dem feet of yourn is enough to break down your constitution.

DAVE: They carries me wherever I wants to go. Daisy, you marry Jim 'cause I don't want to come between y'all. He's my buddy.

JIM: Come to think of it, Dave, she was yourn first. You take and handle dat spade for her.

DAVE: You heard her say it is all I can do to lift up dese feets and put 'em down. Where I'm going to git any time to wrassle wid any hoes and shovels? You kin git 'round better'n me. You done won Daisy — I give in. I ain't going to bite no friend of mine in de back.

DAISY: Both of you niggers can git yo' hats an' yo' heads an' git on down de road. Neither one of y'all don't have to have me. I got a good job and plenty men begging for yo' chance.

JIM: Dat's right, Daisy, you go git you one them mens whut don't mind smelling mules—and beating de white folks to de barn every morning. I don't wanta be bothered wid nothin' but dis box.

DAVE: And I can't strain wid nothin' but my feets and my gun. I kin git mo' turkey gobblers, but never no job.

*(Daisy walks slowly away in the direction from which she came. Both watch her a little wistfully for a minute. The sun is setting.)*

DAVE: Guess I better be gittin' on back—it's 'most dark. Where you goin', Jim?

JIM: I don't know, Dave. Down de road, I reckon.

DAVE: Whyncher come on back to town? 'Tain't no use you proagin' up and down de railroad track when you got a home.

JIM: They done lawed me 'way from it for hittin' you wid dat bone.

DAVE: Dat ain't nothin'. It was my head you hit. An' if I don't keer, whut dem ole ugly-rump niggers got to do wid it?

JIM: They might not let me come in town.

DAVE: *(Seizing Jim's arm and facing him back toward the town)* They better! Look here, Jim, if they try to keep you out dat town we'll go out to dat swamp and git us a mule bone apiece and come back and boil dat stew down to a low gravy.

JIM: You mean dat, Dave? *(Dave nods his head eagerly.)*

DAVE: Us wasn't mad wid one 'nother nohow. Come on less go back to town. Dem mullet heads better leave me be, too. *(Picks up a heavy stick)* I wish Lum would come tellin' me 'bout de law when I got all dis law in *my* hands. An' de rest of dem 'gator-face jigs—if they ain't got a whole set of mule bones and a good determination they better not bring de mess up.

CURTAIN

# THE SERMON IN THE VALLEY (1931)

> Oh, I love my religious material. Some of it is priceless. Know what I am
> attempting? To set an entire Bapt. service word for word and note for note.
> —ZORA NEALE HURSTON TO LANGSTON HUGHES, APRIL 20, 1929

The figure of the folk preacher stands tall in Hurston's work. Her own father was an itinerant Baptist minister, and growing up in Eatonville, as we see in *De Turkey and De Law,* she was surrounded by churchgoers of both the Baptist and Methodist faiths. The language of the folk sermon, exhortatory, eloquent, and colloquial by turns, clearly captivated Hurston, and she not only included many preachers as characters in her work (most notably, John Pearson, based on her father, the central character in *Jonah's Gourd Vine*), but incorporated the rhythms and rhetorical patterns of folk preaching throughout her writing. Deborah Plant writes that for Hurston and other African Americans, the folk preacher spoke in a "liberatory voice," and "through the antiphonal dynamics of the folk sermon, preacher and congregation merged in a ritual of spiritual renewal and empowerment. . . transforming silenced objects into speaking subjects" (93).

The structure of the sermon, as we see in this play, is as follows: the preacher announces the text, the biblical passage on which the sermon is to be based, provides a brief gloss on the passage, and then launches into the sermon itself. The two prefatory segments are rendered in prose; the sermon itself, in verse. Hurston's decision to render the sermon in free verse indicates her indebtedness to James Weldon Johnson's *God's Trombones: Seven Negro Sermons in Verse* (1927), which contains Johnson's best-known poem, "The Creation," based on the Genesis creation story.[1] In his preface to the volume, Johnson wrote,

> These poems would be better intoned than read. . . . The intoning practiced by the
> old-time preacher is a thing next to impossible to describe; it must be heard, and it
> is extremely difficult to imitate even when heard. . . . The tempos of the preacher I
> have endeavored to indicate by the line arrangement of the poems. . . . There is a
> decided syncopation of speech—the crowding in of many syllables or the
> lengthening out of a few to fill one metrical foot, the sensing of which must be left to
> the reader's ear.

The text included here is based on a transcription made by Hurston of a sermon given by the Reverend C. C. Lovelace to his congregation in Eau Gallie, Florida, on May 2, 1929. It was performed by Cleveland's Gilpin Players as a Theatre of Nations entry on March 29, 1931, and was later revived on December 12, 1934, and on December 7, 1949, where it played in repertory for a month. While Hurston's transcription makes up the vast majority of the work, it contains significant additions and revisions made by Rowena Jelliffe, the (white) co-founder, with husband Russell Jelliffe, of the Karamu settlement house in Cleveland, which hosted the Gilpin Players.

Although the theater at Karamu House played to white audiences, it was devoted to encouraging and producing plays by black playwrights, including Langston Hughes and Willis Richardson. And Jelliffe had played an editorial role with some of these productions, helping with revisions of Countee Cullen and Arna Bontemps's *St. Louis Woman* and Hughes's *Emperor of Haiti*. A comparison between *The Sermon in the Valley*, Hurston's transcription (published as "The Sermon" in Nancy Cunard's 1934 *Negro* anthology), and *Jonah's Gourd Vine* indicates that Jelliffe created the characters of Brother Ezra and Caroline, as well as reframing the sermon itself into one that emphasizes redemption rather than betrayal. Whereas Sister Caroline, in *Sermon in the Valley*, declares that Brother Ezra's sermon will "bring us strength and easement," John Pearson, in *Jonah's Gourd Vine*, stresses instead that his sermon will show that "it is not your enemies that harm you all the time. Watch that close friend." The redirection of the sermon toward redemption is consistent with the integrationist aims of Karamu House.

The script on which our edition is based was located at the Western Reserve Historical Society in Cleveland, Ohio.

# The Sermon in the Valley
## With Rowena Woodham Jelliffe

CAST:

BROTHER EZRA, leader of the flock, the preacher

CAROLINE, one of the flock, a young woman

THE FLOCK, a group of some eighteen or twenty people, both men and women, young and old, workers from the field

CAROLINE: (*Hurrying in and dropping to her knees, begins her prayer*) Oh, Lord—Is You there, Lord? This is me, Caroline. I come runnin' 'long 'head of the rest of 'em 'cause I want to tell You just how 'tis. The folks is awful tired, Lord. The day been powerful hot, the cotton rows been long. And seem like we's all kinda troubled in mind. So they's comin' here to the Valley—and they's bringin' Brother Ezra. Many times Brother Ezra done talked to us here. You heard us, Lord. I know You goin' to help him find de words that'll bring us strength and easement. Amen.

(*[Enter] Brother Ezra[. He] is a large, powerfully built man, with vibrant voice which ranges from a whisper to a thunder crash or a trumpet. There [is] majesty and dignity in his bearing, which marks him [as] the wise man, the counselor of the group who are his flock.*)

BROTHER EZRA: We are gathered this evening in the valley after the toil and heat of the day to say a few words about Jesus.[2]

Our theme this evening is the wounds of Jesus, Zachariah 13:6. When the Father shall ask, "What are these wounds in thine hand?" He shall answer, "Those are they with which I was wounded in the house of my friends." We read in the fifty-third chapter of Isaiah where He was wounded from our transgressions and bruised for our iniquity. And the apostle Peter affirms that His blood was shed from before the foundation of the world.[3]

He heard 'em when they cried and God ran up the shade in glory.
He pulled back the curtain and looked out the window in Heaven
And the light shone down. (*Pause*)
He threw back the curtains of the world so the angel could see the way.
He slammed shut the gates of Hell.
(*Whisper*) Old Satan tried to slip out past the Archangel, but,
But hark, Hallelujah, Old Gabriel drawed back his mighty sword.

[FLOCK:] Ah, git back, git back.

BROTHER EZRA:

> I kin see the heavenly hosts as they drove old Satan down.
> Down, down, down into the deepest pits of Hell—
> And they tied him down.
> They slammed shut the mighty portals of Hell
> And on the hinges is written
> "Eternity, Eternity."

FLOCK: (*Respon[ding] in tones of fervent prayer*)

> Eternity, eternity.
> Down in the pits of Hell, Lord.
> Ah yes, Lord.

BROTHER EZRA:

> Oh, grave, where is thy victory? (*Pause*)
> Oh, death, where is thy sting? (*Pause*)
> When God stepped out on the apex of His power.
> Before the hammers of creation fell
> Upon the anvil of time
> And hammered out the ribs of the earth.
> Before He made ropes by the breath of fire
> Set the boundaries of the waters
> By the gravity of His power.
> When God said, "Let us make man."
> The elders upon the altar cried out,
> "If yo' make man . . . if yo' make man . . . Ah, he will sin."

> (*Responses from the flock*)

> Then yo' friend Jesus said, "Father, dear Father, Oh, Father,
> I am the teeth of time that comprehended the dust of the earth,
> That weighed the hills in scales,
> Painted the rainbow that marks the end of the departing storm,
> Measured the seas in the hollow of my hand,
> Held the elements in a unbroken chain of controlment.
> Make man, Oh, make man
> And if he sin, I will redeem him

> (*Responses from the flock*)

> I'll break the mighty chasm of Hell.

> (*Rising in tempo, building*)

> Where the fire's never quenched,
> I'll go down in the dark grave where the worm never dies.

CAROLINE: (*Sings "Prayer is the Key to Heaven"—leads the flock*)

> Prayer is the key to Heaven
> Prayer is the key to Heaven
> Prayer is the key to Heaven
> Prayer is the key.

BROTHER EZRA:

> So God A'mighty got his stuff together.
> He dipped some water out of the mighty deep.
> He reached down and got him a handful o' dirt,
> From the foundation sills of the earth.
> He seized a thimbleful o' breath
> From the drums of the wind.
> Now I'm ready to make a-a-a-ah
> Ready to make man.
> Who shall I make him after? Who?

FLOCK: (*Repeats the chant*)

> Who shall I make him after?
> Who shall I make him after?

BROTHER EZRA:

> Worlds within worlds begin to reel and roll.

(*Rapid rise in tempo*)

> The Sun—ah . . .
> The Sun gathered up the fiery skirts of her garments
> And wheeled around the throne saying,—
> "Ah, make man after me."
> God gazed upon the Sun and sent her back to her blood-red socket
> And shook His head.
> The Moon seized the reins of the tides
> And dragged a thousand seas behind her
> As she walked around the throne,
> "Ple—es—ease make man after me."
> But God said "No."
> The Stars, the beautiful little stars,
> Bust out from their diamond sockets
> And circled the glittering throne crying,
> "Oh, please make man after us."
> But God said, "No, no, no. I'll make man,
> I'll make man in my own image and I'll put him in the garden."

FLOCK: (*[In] response*) Hallelujah, hallelujah, Lord have mercy.

BROTHER EZRA:

> And Jesus said, "If he sin I'll go his bond before the mighty throne."
> Ah . . . He was always yo' friend.
> He done make us all delegates to that judgment convention.
> Sinner you know you're born to die.

FLOCK: [(*Singing*)]

> Sinner you know you're born to die
> Sinner you know you're born to die
> Sinner you know you're born to die
> Sinner you know you're born to die.

CAROLINE:

> Just as the tree fall so shall it lie
> Just as the sinner lives so shall he die.

FLOCK:

> Sinner you know you're born to die
> Sinner you know you're born to die. (*Fades out*)

BROTHER EZRA:

> Faith ain't got no eyes but she can go far.
> Just take the spy glass of faith and look in that upper room,
> When yo' are all alone to yo' self,
> And yo' heart is burnt with fire and
> The blood is loping through yo' veins
> Like iron monsters on the rail,
> Look into that upper chamber.
> We notice at the supper table
> As He gazed upon His friends,
> His eyes a-flowin' with tears,
> "My heart is exceedingly sorrowful unto death,
> For this night one of you shall betray me."

FLOCK: (*Protesting moans and cries*) No, Lord. No—no—

BROTHER EZRA:

> "It were not a Roman officer
> It were not a centurian soldier
> But one of you who I have chosen my bosom friend
> That sops in the dish with me
> Shall betray me." (*Pause*)
> I . . . I want to draw a parable.
> I see Jesus leaving Heaven and all His glory,
> Disrobin' Hisself of His matchless honor,

Yieldin' up the scepter of revolvin' worlds,
Puttin' on the garments of humanity,
Comin' into the world to rescue His friends.
Two thousand years have gone by on their rusty ankles.
But with the eye of faith I kin see
Jesus look down from His tall, high tower of elevation.
I kin hear the golden pavements ring under His footsteps . . . sol-me,
     sol-do, sol-me, sol-do. (*Expand*)
I see Jesus when He step out on the rim bones o' nothin' cryin',—
"I am the truth, the light and the way."
I see Him grab the throttle o' the well ordered train of mercy.
I see kingdoms crush and crumble,
Whilst archangels held the winds in the corner chambers.
I see Him arrive on this earth
And walk the streets thirty and three years.
I see Him walkin' beside the sea of Galilee wid His disciples,
This declaration 'gendered on His lips.
"Let us go upon the other side."
God, my master! They entered the boat
With the oars stuck in the back
And their sails unfurled to the evenin' breeze.
But the ship was not sailin' as dey reached the center of the lake.
Jesus was asleep on a pillow in the rear of the boat.
And the dynamic powers of nature become disturbed.
And de mad winds broke de heads of de western drums
And fell down upon the sea of Galilee
And buried themselves behind the gallopin' waves,
And the white caps mobilized themselves like an army
And walked our like soldiers goin' to battle.
The flyin' clouds threw their wings into the channels of the deep,
And bedded the waters like a road plow
And faced the current of the chargin' billows.
The zigzag lightnin' licked out her fiery tongue,
The terrific bolts of thunder bust in the sky.
God a'mighty! The ship begin to reel and rock.
One of the disciples called Jesus.
"Master, carest thou not that we perish?"
And Jesus arose and the storm was in its pitch.
The lightnin' played on His rainment
As He stood in the prow of the ship
And He placed His foot upon the neck of the storm
And spoke to the howlin' winds.
The sea fell at His feet like a marble floor.
The thunders went back to their dim caverns.
Then Jesus sat down on the rim of the ship,

Took the hooks of His power and lifted the billows into His lap,
Rocked the winds to sleep on His arm saying,—"Peace, be still."
And the Bible says there was calm.
He said He would calm the ocean.

CAROLINE: (*Sings*)

He said He would calm the ocean

FLOCK: (*Sings*)

Oh yes He would

CAROLINE:

He said He would calm the ocean

FLOCK:

Oh yes He said he would

CAROLINE:

He said He would calm the rollin' seas

FLOCK:

He said He would.

BROTHER EZRA:

Wid the eye of faith I kin see Him
When He went from Pilate's house
With the crown of seventy-two wounds upon His head.
I see Him as He toiled up rugged Calvary
And hung upon the bitter cross fo' our sins.
I see—e-e-e . . .
The mountains fall to their rocky knees
When He cried: "My God, why hast thou forsaken me?"

(*Moan from flock*)

When the mountains fell to their rocky knees
And trembled like beasts
Under the strokes of the Master's whip—
One Angel that stood at the gate wid a flamin' sword
Was so pleased wid His power
Until He took His sword and pierced the Moon.
And the Moon ran down in blood.
The Sun batted her fiery eyes,
Put on her judgment robe
And laid down in the cradle of eternity
Where she rocked herself to sleep and slumber.

He died, and the great belt in the wheel of time
And the geological strata fell a-loose.
A thousand angels rushed the canopy of Heaven
Wid flamin' swords in their hands
And placed their foot upon blue ether's bosom,
And looked back toward the dazzlin' throne.
But the archangels had veiled their faces,
The throne was draped in mournin',
The orchestra had struck silence for the space of half an hour.
The angels had lifted their harps to the weepin' willow.
God A'mighty had looked off towards Immensity,
And blazin' words fell from His lips.
And just about that time Jesus groaned upon the cross
And said: "It is finished."

FLOCK: (*Chants*) And He never said a mumblin' word.

BROTHER EZRA:

The chambers of Hell explode and the damnable spirits come up from
    the Sodomistic world
And rushed into the smokey camps of eternal night:
Crying,—"Woe, woe, woe.
Woe, woe, woe."
Then it was the Centurian cried out,—
"Surely, this man is the son of God."

FLOCK: (*Repeats*) Surely this man is the son of God.

BROTHER EZRA:

And about that time the angel of justice
Unsheathed his flamin' sword
And ripped the veil of the Temple
And the High Priest vacated his office
And the sacrificial energy penetrated the mighty strata
And quickened the bones of the Prophets
And they arose from their graves
And walked about the streets of Jerusalem.

FLOCK: (*Repeats*)

The golden streets.
The streets of Jerusalem.

BROTHER EZRA:

I heard the whistle of the damnation train
That pulled out from the Garden of Eden
Loaded with cargo goin' straight to Hell,

Dat ran at breakneck speed all the way through the lan',
All the way through the reign of Kings and Judges
All de way through the prophetic age,
Flowed her way through the Jordan River
And on the way to Calvary when she whistled for the switch.
Jesus stood out on her track like a rough back mountain.
She thowed her cow-catcher[4] in His side and His blood ditched the train.
Ah . . . He died for our sins, wounded in the house of His friends.

(*Gently—change of mood*)

Dat's where I got off the damnation train
And dat's where you better get off.

(*Rising cadence*)

For in dat mornin' when we shall all be delegates
To dat judgment convention,
When old Gabriel shall lift the trumpet to his lips and blow,
To waken de quick and de dead,
When de two trains of time
Shall meet on de trestle of eternity,
And wreck de burnin' axles of de unformed ether,
When the mountains shall skip like lambs,
When Jesus shall place one foot on the bosom of the sea
And one foot on dry land,
When His chariot wheels shall be runnin' hub-deep in fire,
He shall take His friends
Through de open bosom of a unclouded sky,
Place in their hands de hosanna fan
And dey shall stand around and around de beatific throne
Praisin' His holy name forever.
Amen. (*He ends in a whisper*)

FLOCK: [(*Members sing lines simultaneously*)]

The Lord bless you
The Lord go with you, my children
Let Jesus take your hand
And walk with you into the cool of the night

CAROLINE: (*Leads singing*)

Jesus, Jesus take all my sins away
Jesus, Jesus take all my sins away
(*Repeat and fade away*)

CURTAIN

# FOUR PLAYS FROM *FAST AND FURIOUS* (1931)

The following plays, *Woofing*, *Lawing and Jawing*, *Forty Yards*, and *Poker!*, all appeared in some form in an all-black review entitled *Fast and Furious*. The show premiered on September 15, 1931, at the New Yorker Theatre and ran for seven performances—until the box office ran dry. Hurston was not surprised at either the critical drubbing the production received or its subsequent failure to catch on. She put the blame squarely on the shoulders of producer and director Forbes Robinson, who, Hurston wrote in a September 1931 letter to her patron, Charlotte Osgood Mason, allowed composer/performer Rosamond Johnson to select "both cast and material" and "steered him too often off the high way to success." She complained that Johnson chose his cast for personal reasons rather than for their theatrical talent, and "discouraged anything that spoke the real Negro."

The show was a mixed bag of acts, from Hurston's sketches to a musical number populated by a group of dancing pansies to a scene from *Macbeth*. Most of the music was written by black composer Porter Grainger and white composers Mack Gordon and Harry Revel, which led one reviewer to write: "the darkies . . . most of the time are forced to sing second-rate Broadway-Hebraic songs with dismal consequences," and were allowed only "about twenty minutes . . . to be themselves."[1] Hurston made $75 from the venture, all of which she used to pay debts, and chalked up the production to experience: in the same letter to Mason quoted above, she wrote, "I have learned a lot about the mechanics of the stage, which will do me good in playwriting."

*Woofing* and *Lawing and Jawing* both take place in Waycross, Georgia, a real town about ninety miles from Jacksonville, Florida, where Hurston lived after leaving home in her teens. *Woofing* is a slice of African American life, where playful banter and insults are as much a game as a round of checkers. Even the possible physical confrontation between the characters Cliffert and Skanko is merely a comic extension of "playing the dozens." The only glimpse of the world outside this neighborhood is mentioned by Bertha, nagging her husband to help her carry the washing to the "white folks she works for," a chore he refuses to do.

*Lawing and Jawing* is Hurston's version of a vaudeville favorite, the courtroom sketch. By the time *Fast and Furious* was presented, it apparently had become a familiar—even expected—device in all-black musicals, having appeared in *Darktown Jubilee* (1922), *Africana* (1927), *His Honery,* and *The Judge* (1927). The character of Judge Dunfumy can be seen as part of tradition of black comedy that includes Pigmeat Markham, Sammy Davis Jr., and Flip Wilson, all of whom adapted the wacky judge persona in their acts. Hurston pays homage in *Forty Yards* to her alma mater, Howard University, by portraying a dance-filled football game between Howard and rival Lincoln University. Unfortunately, no production photo exists to show how this exuberant production number was staged. *Poker!* finally, shows the darker side of "woofing" as a form of aggression that explodes into violence among the poor denizens of a "shotgun house." However, the stage business of all of the players cheating at the same time and a humorous tag line suggests that Hurston is winking at her audience.

# *Woofing*

CAST:
GOOD BLACK
BERTHA, his wife
CLIFFERT
LONNIE
SKANKO
BEA ETHEL
GIRLS
MAN 1
MAN 2
MAN 3
MAN 4
OTHER MEN
BOY
LITTLE GIRL
WOMAN

*Time: Present.*
*Place: Negro street in Waycross, Georgia.*

*Setting: Porch and sidewalk, etc.*
*Action: Through the open window of one of the shacks a woman [Bertha] is discovered ironing. A man [Good Black] is sitting on the floor of the porch asleep. She hums a bar or two, then comes to the window and calls to the man.*

BERTHA: Good Black, why don't you git up from dere and carry dese white folks' clothes home? You always want money but you wouldn't hit a lick at a snake!

GOOD BLACK: Aw, shut up woman. I'm tired of hearin' 'bout dem white folks' clothes. I don't keer if dey never git 'em.

BERTHA: You better keer! Dese very clothes took and brought *you* out de crack. 'Cause de first time I saw you, you was so hungry till you was walkin' lap-legged. Man, you had de white-mouf, you was so hungry.

*(Enter another man [Cliffert] leisurely. Good Black sees him and calls.)*

GOOD BLACK: Hey, Cliffert, where you headed for?

CLIFFERT: Oh, nowhere in particular.

GOOD BLACK: Come here then, fish, and lemme bend a checker game over yo' head. Come on, youse my fish.

CLIFFERT: *(Comes to the porch and sits.)* Git de checkers and I'll have you any, some or none. I push a mean chuck-a-luck myself.

BERTHA: *([From] inside, quarreling)* Dress up and strut around? Yes! Play checkers? Yes! Eat? Yes! Work? No!!

*(The game starts. A period of silence in which they indicate their concentration by frowns, cautious moves, head scratching. Good Black is pointing his index finger over the board indicating moves. He wig-wags, starts to move, scratches his head thoroughly, changes his mind and fools around without moving.)*

CLIFFERT: Police! Police! Come here and make dis man move!

GOOD BLACK: Aw, I got plenty moves. *(Scratches his head)* Jus' tryin' to see which one I want to make. But when *I* do move, it's gointer be just too bad for you.

*(A guitar is heard offstage and Cliffert brightens. He cups his hand and calls.)*

CLIFFERT: Hey Lonnie! Come here! Ha, ha, ha! I got me a fish.

*(Enter Lonnie picking "East Coast"[2] on his box and stands watching the game. He ceases to play as he stops walking.)*

Ha, ha! You see ol' Good Black goes for a hard guy. He tries to know more than a mule and a mule's head longer'n his'n. Ha, ha! I set a trap for him and he fell right in it. Trying to ride de britches! *Now* look at him.

GOOD BLACK: Aw, shut up! You tryin' to show yo' grandma how to milk ducks. You can't beat me playin' no checkers. *(Scratches his head again)* Just watch me show my glory.

BERTHA: *(Leans out of window)* Good Black! When you gointer come git dese clothes!

*(He does not answer. He is trying to concentrate.)*

LONNIE: You got him Cliffert. You got him in [the] Louisville Loop. He's yo' fish all right.

CLIFFERT: *(Boastfully)* Man, didn't I push a mean chuck-a-luck dat time! I'm good, better, and best. *(To Good Black)* Move, man! I told you not to do it.

GOOD BLACK: All dat noise ain't playin' checkers. You just wait till I make my move.

BERTHA: All right, now, Mr. Nappy-Chin! I don't want to have to call you no mo' to come keer dese white folks' clothes! I'm tired of takin' and takin' affa you! My belly's full clear up to de neck. I don't need no lazy coon lak you nohow. I'm a good woman, and I needs somebody dats gointer give aid and assistance.

GOOD BLACK: Aw, go 'head on, woman, and leave me be! Every Saturday it's de same thing! Yo' mouth exhausting like a automobile. You worse than Cryin' Emma. You kin whoop like de Seaboard and squall lak da Coast Line.[3] *(Taps his head)* You ain't got all dat b'long to *you*, and nothin' dat b'long to nobody's else. You better leave me 'lone before you make a bad man out of me. Fool wid me and I'll go git me somebody else. I'm a much-right man.

BERTHA: Now you ain't no much-right man neither. You didn't *git me* wid no saw-mill license—You went to de court house and paid a dollar and a half for me. 'Tain't no other woman got as much right to you as I got. De man got to tell you youse divorced befo' yo' kin play dat much-right on me!

GOOD BLACK: De man don't have to tell me nothin'! I got divorce in my heels.

BERTHA: You ain't de only one dat knows where de railroad track is. I done made up my mind, and I done promised Gabriel and a couple of other men dat if yo' don't do no better than yo' been doin,' I'm gointer pack me a suit-case and grab de first smoky thing I see. I'll be long gone.

GOOD BLACK: Aw, yo' ain't no trouble! Yo' can be had. Yo' ain't never gointer leave me.

BERTHA: How come I won't? Just 'cause I been takin' keer of yo', don't make a park ape out yo'self. I'll leave yo', just as sure as yo' snore!

GOOD BLACK: *(Rises and hitches up his trousers)* Aw, yo' ain't gointer leave me, and if yo' go, yo' wouldn't stay, 'cause I'm a damn sweet man, and yo' know it!

LONNIE: Hey, hey!

*(He begins to pick and Good Black sings.[4] Lonnie sings a line now and then.)*

GOOD BLACK:

Yo' may leave and go to Hali-muh-fack
But my slow drag will—uh bring yo' back
Well yo' may go, but this will bring yo' back

I been in de country but I moved to town
I'm a tolo-shaker from my head on down
Well, yo' may go, but this will bring yo' back

Some folks call me a tolo-shaker
It's a doggone lie I'm a back-bone breaker
Well, yo' may go, but this will bring yo' back

Oh, ship on de sea, boat on de ocean
I raise hell when I take a notion
Well, yo' may go, but this will bring yo' back

Oh, who do, who do, who do wackin'
Wid my heels[5] a-poppin' and my toenails crackin'
Well, yo' may go, but this will bring yo' back

BERTHA: Dat's all right too, pap, but if yo' can't make me tote dese clothes home, don't bring de mess up. Yo'se abstifically a humbug.

CLIFFERT: Man, come on back here and move, or else own up to de folks yo' can't push no checkers wid me.

*(He sits and begins to lay out moves with his fingers and scratch his head. Enter another man [(Skanko), who] stands [arms] akimbo looking over Cliffert's shoulder.)*

CLIFFERT: *(Looking up)* Don't stand over me lak dat, ugly as yo' is.

SKANKO: You ain't nobody's pretty baby yo'self!

CLIFFERT: Dat's all right, I ain't as ugly as yo'—youse ugly enough to git behind a Simpoon[6] weed and hatch monkeys.

SKANKO: And youse ugly enough to git behind a tombstone and hatch hants.

CLIFFERT: Youse so ugly dey have to cover yo' face up at night so sleep can slip up on yo'.

SKANKO: You look like ten cents worth of have-mercy. Yo' face look lak ole Uncle Jump-off. Yo' mouth look lak a bunch of ruffles.

CLIFFERT: Yeah, but yo' done passed me. Yo' so ugly till they could throw yo' in de Mississippi River and skim ugly for six months.

SKANKO: Look here, Cliff, don't yo' personate me! Counting from de little finger back to de thumb—yo' start anythin', I got yo' some.

CLIFFERT: Go 'head and grab me buddy, but if yo' don't know how to turn me loose too, don't bring de mess up! If yo' hit me, I may not beat you, but yo'll be so dirty when St. Peter git yo' dat he can't use yo'.

SKANKO: Don't call *me* buddy. Yo' buddy is huntin' coconuts. Don't yo' try to throw me for a nap. Do, I'll kill yo' so stiff dead they'll have to push yo' down. Yo' gointer make me do some double cussin' on you. *(He picks up a heavy stick and walks back towards Cliffert.)* Now I got dis farmer's choice in my hands, yo' better git outa my face.

CLIFFERT: Yo' wanta fight?

SKANKO: Yeah, I wanta fight. Put it where I kin use it and I'll sho' use it. I'll fight anybody. I git so hot sometimes I fights de corner of de house. I'm so hot I totes a pistol to keep from getting' in a fight wid myself. I prints dangerous every time I sit down in[7] a chair.

CLIFFERT: Man, this ain't no fighting weather. Ha, ha, ha! Did yo' think I was mad sho' nuff? Yo' can't fight me. They's got to be runnin' before fightin' and they's got to be plenty *good* runnin' before dis fight comes off.

SKANKO: All right now. Yo' leave me alone and I'm a *good* man. I'm just like an old shoe. If yo' rain on me and cool me off I'm soft! If yo' shine on me and git me hot, I'm hard.

*(He drops the stick and exits. Cliffert is shaking all over. He looks after [Skanko] to be sure he is gone.)*

GOOD BLACK: [*Laughing*] Kah, kah, kah. Whut yo' so scared about? De way yo' was talkin' I thought yo' was mad enough to fight.

CLIFFERT: I was. I gits hot real quick! But I'm very easy cooled when de man I'm mad wid is bigger'n me. *(He drops into his seat, wiping his face.)* Man did yo' see how he grabbed up dat check? He done skeered me into a three-week's spasm!

BERTHA: Good Black, dese clothes is still waiting.

GOOD BLACK: Well, let 'em wait on, I done tole yo' once. Yo' kin run yo' mouf but yo' can't run my business.

*(Enter a pretty girl [Bea Ethel]. She strolls happily across without stopping. Good Black pretends to cough.)*

Who is dat?

BEA ETHEL: *(Turns and glares at him.)* My old man got something for dat cough yo' got.

CLIFFERT: Dat's right, tell dese old mullet head married men to mind they own business. Now, take *me* for instance. I'm a much-right man. *(Gets up and approaches her flirtatiously)* I didn't quite git yo' name straight. Yo' better tell it to me again.

BEA ETHEL: My name is Bea Ethel, turned 'round to Jones.

CLIFFERT: *(Flirtatiously)* Yo' pretty lil ole ground angel yo'! Where did yo' come from?

BEA ETHEL: Detroit. Yo' like me?

CLIFFERT: Do I lak yo'? I love yo' just lak God loves Gabriel, and dat's his best angel. Go 'head and say somethin'. I jus' love to hear yo' talk.

BEA ETHEL: Gimme five dollars. I need some stockings.

CLIFFERT: *Now* mama, dis ain't Gimme, Georgia. Dis is Waycross. I'm just lak de cemetery. I takes in but never no put out. I ain't puttin' out nothin' but old folks' eyes—and I don't do that till they's dead. Run 'long, mama. (*[Bea Ethel] exits and he resumes his seat.*) Come on, Good Black, lemme wrap dis checker 'round yo' neck.

GOOD BLACK: Gimme time, gimme time! Don't try to rush me.

(*He begins same business of figuring out moves and scratching his head. Enter three[8] girls and fellows. The girls are dressed in cool summer dresses, but nothing elaborate.*)

LONNIE: I know I'm gointer play something now.

(*He tunes and plays "Cold Rainy Day."[9] He begins to sing and the others join in. Not all. But all start to dancing. They couple off as far as possible and Lindy.[10] The men unmated do hot solo steps. The men cry out in ecstasy.*)

MEN: Shimmy! If you can't shimmy, shake your head. Look, baby, look! Throw it in de alley. Look, if you can't look, stick out, and if you can't stick out, git out.

(*At the end of the song and dance, one of the girls exclaims.*)

GIRL: Aw, we got to go. Mama's looking for me.

(*The three girls exit, walking happily. The men watch them go.*)

CLIFFERT: Oh, boy, look at 'em! Switching it and looking back at it. (*He imitates the girls' walk.*)

GOOD BLACK: Yeah Lawd, ain't they specifyin'! They handles a lot of traffic.

CLIFFERT: (*Seating himself again*) Yeah, but dat don't play no checkers. Come on here, Good Black and lemme finish wearing your ant.

BERTHA: Good Black, yo' better come git dese clothes.

LONNIE: Good Black, yo' wife kin cold whoop for what she want.

GOOD BLACK: Yeah and if she don't git [it], she keep right on whoopin'. B'lieve I wants a drink of water. Wisht I knowed where I could slip up on me a drink.

CLIFFERT: Aw man, come on back here and move. Yo' doin' everythin' [but] playin' checkers. You'd ruther move a mountain wid a [*missing text*] bar than to move (*Points*) dat man.[11]

GOOD BLACK: *(Seats himself)* Lemme hurry up and beat dis game befo' yo' bust yo' britches.

*(He wags his finger to indicate moves, scratches his head, but doesn't move. Several men enter and group around the players. All offer suggestions.)*

MAN 1: You got him, Cliffert. He's locked up just as tight as a keyhole.

MAN 2: Aw, man, he kin break out!

MAN 3: Yeah, but it'll cost him plenty to git out of dat trap.

CLIFFERT: Police! Police! He won't move!

MAN 4: Aw, leave go de checkers and less shoot some crap.

*(Enter a woman in a house dress, head rag on, run down house shoes. She goes to the edge of the porch and calls inside.)*

WOMAN: Hi there Bertha, what yo' doin'[?]

BERTHA: Still bumpin' de white folks' clothes — hittin' for de sundown man. Come on in and have some sit down.

WOMAN: Ain't got time. Got a house full of company. I took a minute to see if yo' could let me have a little skeeting garret.

BERTHA: How come yo' didn't git yo'self some snuff whilst yo' was at de store? De man ast yo' what else. I ain't no Piggly Wiggly.[12] Reckon I kin spare yo' a dip, though.

*(She hands out the box and the woman fills her lip and hands it back.)*

WOMAN: Much obliged, I thank yo'. Reckon I better heel and toe it on back, to see how de comp'ny is makin' out.

BERTHA: Step inside a minute—I want to put a bug in yo' ear.

*(She makes an urgent gesture and the other woman goes inside. Lonnie is sitting off to himself and picking "Rabbit on de Log" softly. A small boy dashes on with a lollipop in his hand. He is licking it and laughing. He is pursued by a little girl yelling "you gimme my all day sucker! Johnny! You gimme my candy, now!" They run all over the stage. The men take notice of them and one of them seizes the boy and restores the candy to the girl. She pokes out her tongue at the boy and says "goody, goody, goody, goody, goody!" She notes the guitar playing and begins to dance. The boy makes faces back at her and dances back at her. The music gets louder, dancing faster, the checkerboard gets upset. General laughter at that. When dance is over, boy snatches the lollipop again and races away and the girl runs behind him yelling "Johnny! You gimme my candy! Johnny!" The music stops and the craps game gets under way. Furious side bets for five and ten cents*

*each. Loud calls on Miss "Daisy Dice," snake eyes, "Ada from Decatur." Somebody suggests a soft roll, others object on the ground that it's too easy for the experts to cheat.)*

GOOD BLACK: Gimme de dice! I'm gointer play 'em like John Henry.

LONNIE: John Henry didn't bother wid de bones. He used to play Georgy Skin.

GOOD BLACK: He shot crap too. He played everythin' and everythin' he played, he played it good. Just like he uster drive steel. If I could whip steel like John Henry, I wouldn't stay here and nowhere else.

CLIFFERT: Whut would yo' do?

GOOD BLACK: I'd go somewhere and keep books for somebody.

LONNIE: I know how to play "John Henry."

GOOD BLACK: Well, turn it on and let de bad luck happen.

*(As Lonnie plays through a verse warming up, all the men get interested and start to hum. Cliffert shouts out.)*

CLIFFERT: Lawd, Lawd, what evil have I done?

*(They sing "John Henry."*[13] *At the close, the woman who came to borrow snuff emerges from the house still talking back at [Bertha].)*

WOMAN: He ain't no trouble. I tole him, I says, "yo' must think youse de man dat made side meat taste lak ham." See yo' later.

*(She exits hurriedly. The crap game goes on until a band is heard approaching.)*

LONNIE: Who dead?

CLIFFERT: Nobody. Don't you know de Imperial Elks[14] is goin' to New York to de Elks Grand Lodge? Yeah, bo, and they's takin' they band. Dat's supposed to be de *finest* band in de United States.

*(The band approaches followed by a great crowd. The craps game is instantly deserted and all follow the band.)*

[*Curtain.*]

# Lawing and Jawing

CAST:
JUDGE DUNFUMY
CLERK
GIRL
BOY
OFFICER SIMPSON
SECOND OFFICER
JEMIMA FLAPCAKES
CLIFF MULLINS
CLIFF'S WIFE
DE OTIS BLUNT
LAWYER 1
LAWYER 2

*Time: Present.*
*Place: Waycross, Georgia.*

> *Scene: Judge Dunfumy's court.*
>
> *Setting: Usual court-room arrangement, except that there is a large red arrow pointing offstage left, marked "To Jail."*
>
> *Action: At rise everybody is in place except the Judge. Suddenly the Clerk looks offstage right and motions for everybody to rise. Enter the Judge. He wears a black cap and gown and has his gavel in his hand. The two police-men walk behind him holding up his gown. He mounts the bench and glares all about him before he seats himself. There is a pretty girl in the front row left, and he takes a good look at her, smiles, frowns at her escort. He motions the police to leave him and take their places with the spectators and he then raps vigorously with his gavel for order.*

JUDGE: Hear! Hear! Court is set! My honor is on de bench. You moufy folks set up! *(He glares at the boy with the pretty girl)* All right, Mr. Whistle-britches, just keep dat jawing now and see how much time I'll give you!

BOY: I wasn't talking, your honor.

JUDGE: Well, quit looking so moufy. *(To Clerk)* Call de first case. And I warn each and all dat my honor is in bad humor dis mawnin'. I'd give a canary bird twenty years for peckin' at a elephant. *(To Clerk)* Bring 'em on.

CLERK: (*Reading*) Cliff Mullins, charged with assault upon his wife with a weapon and disturbing the peace.

(*As Cliff is led to the bar by the officer, the Judge glares ferociously at the prisoner. His wife, all bandages, limps up to the bar at the same time.*)

JUDGE: So youse one of dese hard-boiled wife-beaters, huh? Just a mean old woman-jessie![15] If I don't lay a hearing on you, God's a gopher! Now what *made* you cut such a caper?

CLIFF: Judge, I didn't go to hurt her. Saturday night I was down on Dearborn Street in a buffet flat—

JUDGE: Buffet flat?

CLIFF: Aw, at Emma Hayles' house.

JUDGE: Oh, yes. Go on.

CLIFF: Well, (*Points thumb at wife*) she come down dere and claim I took her money and she claimed I wuz spending it on Emma.

CLIFF'S WIFE: And dat's just whut he was doing, too, Judge.

CLIFF: Aw, she's tellin' a great big ole Georgia lie, Judge. I wasn't spendin' no money of her'n.

CLIFF'S WIFE: Yes he was, Judge. There wasn't no money for him to git *but* mine. He ain't hit a lick of work since God been to Macon. Know whut he 'lowed when I worry him 'bout workin'? Says he wouldn't take a job wid de Careless Love Lumber Company, puttin' out whut make you do me lak you do, do, do.

JUDGE: So, you goes for a sweet-back, do you?

CLIFF: Naw suh, Judge. I'd be glad to work if I could find a job.

JUDGE: How long you been outa work?

CLIFF: Seventeen years—

JUDGE: Seventeen years? (*To Cliff's Wife*) You been takin' keer of dis man for seventeen years?

CLIFF'S WIFE: Naw, but he been so mean to me, it seems lak seventeen years.

JUDGE: Now you tell me just where he hurt you.

CLIFF'S WIFE: Judge, tell you de truth, I'm hurt all over. (*Rubs her buttocks*) Fact is I'm cut.

JUDGE: Did you git cut in de fracas?[16]

CLIFF'S WIFE: *(Feeling the back of her left thigh below her buttocks)* Not in de fracas, Judge—just below it.

*(She starts to show the Judge where she has been cut. He motions to stop her.)*

JUDGE: Stop! *(To Officer Simpson)* Grab him. Put him in de shade.

CLIFF: Judge, I'm unguilty! I ain't laid de weight of my hand on her in malice. You got me 'cused of murder and I ain't harmed a child.

JUDGE: Lemme ast *you* something. Didn't you know dat all de women in dis town belongs to me? Beat my women and I'll stuff you in jail. Ninety years. Take 'im away. *(Cliff is led off to jail. Judge looks angrily at the boy who is holding hands with the pretty girl.)* You runs me hot and I'm just dyin' to sit on *yo'* case. Whut you in here for?

BOY: Nothin'.

JUDGE: Well, whut you doin' in my court, you 'gator-faced rascal?

BOY: My girl wanted to see whut was goin' on, so I brought her in.

JUDGE: Oh yeah! *(Smiles at girl)* She was usin' good sense to come see whut I'm doin', but how come *you* come in here? You gointer have a hard time gittin' out.

BOY: I ain't done a thing. I ain't never done nothin'. I'm just as clean as a fish, and he been in bathin' all his life.

JUDGE: You ain't done nothin', hunh? Well den youse guilty of vacancy. Grab 'im, Simpson, and search 'im —and if he got any concealed weapons, I'm gointer give 'im life-time and eight years mo'. *(The Officer seizes the boy and frisks him. All he finds is a new deck of cards. The Judge looks at them in triumph.)* Uhn hunh! I knowed it, one of dese skin game jelly-beans. Robbin' hard workin' men out they money.

BOY: Judge, I ain't used 'em at all. See, dey's brand new.

JUDGE: Well, den youse charged wid totin' concealed cards and attempt to gamble. Ten years at hard labor. Put him in de dark, Simpson, and throw de key away. *(He looks at the girl and beams.)* Don't you worry 'bout how you gointer git home. You gointer be took home right, 'cause I'm gointer take you myself. Bring on de next one, Clerk.

CLERK: Jemima Flapcakes, charged with illegal possession and sale of alcoholic liquors.

*(She is a fat, black, belligerent looking woman. Judge looks coldly at her.)*

JUDGE: Well, you heard whut he said. Is you guilty or unguilty? And I'm tellin' you right now dat when you come up befo' *me* it's just like youse in church. You better have a strong determination, and you better tell a good experience.

JEMIMA: *(Arms akimbo)* Yes, I sold it and I'll sell it again. *(Snaps fingers and shakes hips)* How does ole booze-selling mama talk?

JUDGE: Yes, five thousand dollars and ten years in jail. *(Snaps fingers and shakes hips)* How does ole heavy-fining papa talk?

*(She is led away, shouting and weeping.)*

CLERK: De Otis Blunt, charged wid stealin' a mule.

*(Lawyer 1 arises and comes forward with the prisoner.)*

LAWYER 1: You can't convict this man. I'm here to represent him.

JUDGE: Yo' mouf might spout lak a coffee pot but I got a lawyer *(Looks at other lawyer)* dat kin beat yours segastuatin'. *(Looks admiring at girl)* How am I chewin' my dictionary and minglin' my alphabets?

LAWYER 1: Well, I kin try, can't I?

JUDGE: Oh yeah, you kin try, but I kin see right now where he's gointer git all de time dat God ever made dat ain't been used already. From now on. *(To Lawyer)* Go 'head, and spread yo' lungs all over Georgy, but he's goin' to jail! Mules *must* be respected.

LAWYER 1: *(Striking a pose at the bar)* Your Honor, *(Looks at the pretty girl)* Ladies and Gentlemen—

JUDGE: Never mind 'bout dat lady. You talk yo' chat to *me*.

LAWYER 1: This is a clear case of syllogism! Again I say syllogism. My client is innocent because it was a dark night when they say he stole the mule and that's against all laws of syllogism.

JUDGE: *(Looks impressed and laughs.)* Dat ole fool do know somethin' 'bout law.

LAWYER 1: When George Washington was pleading de case of Marbury vs. Madison, what did *he* say? What *did* he say?

Scintillate, scintillate, globule orific.
Fain would I fathom thy nature's specific.
Loftily posed in ether capacious,
Strongly resembling a gem carbonaceous.

What did Abraham Lincoln say about mule-stealing?

When torrid Phoebus refuses his presence
And ceases to lamp with fierce incandescence,
Then you illume the regions supernal,
Scintillate, scintillate, semper nocturnal.

Syllogism, again I say syllogism.[17]

*(He takes his seat amid applause.)*

JUDGE: Man, youse a pleadin' fool. You knows yo' rules and by-laws.

LAWYER 2: Let me show my glory. Let me spread my habeas corpus.

JUDGE: 'Tain't no use. Dis lawyer done convinced me.

LAWYER 2: But, lemme parade my material—

JUDGE: Parade yo' material anywhere you want to exceptin' befo' me. Dis lil girl wants to go home and I'm goin' with her and enjoy de consequences. Court's adjourned.

*Curtain.*

# Forty Yards

CAST:

HOWARD MOB
LINCOLN MOB
HOWARD BAND
CHEER LEADERS
HOWARD TEAM
LINCOLN TEAM

*Time: Present.*
*Place: Washington, D.C.*

*Scene: The ball park.*
    *Setting: The park with grandstands on either side and upstage.*
    *Action: At rise, the grandstands are full, the cheer leaders are violently gyrating to whip up the mob. The Lincoln colors fly from the right. The Howard [colors] from the left. Both have cheer leaders. First is heard the Lincoln mob singing "Didn't He Ramble, Ramble."*

LINCOLN MOB:

And didn't he ramble, ramble, ramble all around, in and out of town
He rambled, he rambled, rambled til Ol' Lincoln cut him down

HOWARD MOB:

There'll be nothing but sweetmeats for our football team
There'll be nothing but sweetmeats for our football team
Baked Hampton, boiled Shaw, fried Union, Lincoln slaw,[18]
There'll be nothing but sweetmeats, for our football team.

*(Enter the Howard band, led by a hot-strutting drum major. They parade the field and the men students pile down and fall in behind the team. They sing and shout the team song.)*

This is the T-E-A-M team
On which the hopes of Howard lean
Beat Ol' Hampton, beat Ol' Union
Sweep Ol' Lincoln clean.

We are the B-E-S-T best
Of the R-E-S-T rest

Come and watch us put Ol' Howard
On top of Lincoln's chest.

We'll hit the L-I-N-E line
For a hundred ninety-nine
For we love Ol' Howard, yes we love her
All the T-I-M-E time.

*(At the conclusion the teams take the field. The ball is put into play and Lincoln kicks off to Howard. As the ball is caught and when the player who is carrying the ball plunges, followed by his team, the Lincoln players fall on their knees and begin to sing "I Couldn't Hear Nobody Pray."*[19] *The Howard team charges down shouting "Joshua Fi't the Battle of Jericho." Whenever there is a player tackled there is a duet of dancing. Every step is a dance. Finally the grandstand catches fire and the dancing and shouting runs riot up there. When the ball is on Lincoln's ten-yard line, they hold Howard there by rounding up both teams into a huddle and the bunch shout and sing to a quick curtain.)*

# Poker!

CAST:
NUNKIE
AUNT DILSEY
TOO-SWEET
TUSH HAWG
BLACK BABY
PECKERWOOD[20]
SACK DADDY

*Time: Present.*
*Place: New York.*

*Scene: A shabby front room in a shotgun house. A door covered by dingy portieres upstage center. Small panel window in side wall left. Plain center table with chairs drawn up about it. Gaudy calendars on wall. Battered piano against wall right. Kerosene lamp with reflector against wall on either side of room.*

*[Action:] At rise of curtain Nunkie is at piano playing. Others at table with small stacks of chips before each man. Tush Hawg is seated at table so that he faces audience. He is expertly riffing the cards. [He] looks over his shoulder and speaks to Nunkie.*

TUSH HAWG: Come on here, Nunkie—and take a hand! You're holding up the game. You been woofin' 'round here about the poker you can play—now do it!

NUNKIE: Yeah, I plays poker. I plays the piano and Gawd knows I plays the devil.

BLACK BABY: Aw, you can be had! Come on and get in the game! My britches is cryin' for your money!

NUNKIE: Soon as I play the deck I'm comin' and take you all's money! Don' rush me.

Ace means the first time that I met you
Deuce means there was nobody there but us two
Trey means the third party—Charlie was his name
Four spot means the fourth time you tried that same old game—
Five spot means five years you played me for a clown
Six spot means six feet of earth when the deal goes down

217

Now I'm holding the seven spot for each day of the week
Eight means eight hours that she Sheba-ed with your Sheik—
Nine spot means nine hours that I work hard every day—
Ten spot means [the] tenth of every month I brought you home my
    pay—
The Jack is Three-card Charlie who played me for a goat
The Queen, that's my pretty mama, also trying to cut my throat—
The King stands for Sweet Papa Nunkie and he's goin' to wear the crown,
So be careful you all ain't broke when the deal goes down!

*(He laughs [and] crosses to table, bringing piano stool for [a] seat.)*

TUSH HAWG: Aw now, brother, two dollars for your seat before you try to sit in
    this game.

*(Nunkie laughs sheepishly—puts money down—Tush Hawg pushes stack
of chips toward him. Business.)*

NUNKIE: I didn't put it down because I knew you all goin' to be puttin' it right
    back in my pocket.

PECKERWOOD: Aw, y'all go ahead and play. *(To Tush Hawg)* Deal!

*(Tush Hawg begins to deal for draw poker. The game gets tense. Sack Daddy
is the first man at Tush's left—he throws back three cards and is dealt three
more.)*

SACK DADDY: My luck sure is rotten! My gal must be cheatin' on me. I ain't had
    a pair since John Henry had a hammer!

BLACK BABY: *(Drawing three new cards)* You might be fooling the rest with the
    cryin' you're doin' but I'm squattin' for you! You're cryin' worse than
    Cryin' Emma!

TOO-SWEET: *(Studying his three new cards. Sings)*

When yo' cards gets lucky, oh partner,
You oughter be in a rollin' game.[21]

AUNT DILSEY: *(Enters through portieres—stands and looks disapprovingly)* You
    all oughter be ashamed of yourself, gamblin' and carryin' on like this!

BLACK BABY: Aw, this ain't no harm, Aunt Dilsey! You go on back to bed and
    git your night's rest.

AUNT DILSEY: No harm! I know all about these no-harm sins! If you don't
    stop this card playin', all of you all goin' to die and go to hell.

*([She] shakes a warning finger [and] exits through portieres. While she is
talking the men have been hiding cards out of their hands and pulling aces*

*out of sleeves and vest pockets and shoes—it is done quickly, one does not see the other do it.)*

NUNKIE: *(Shoving a chip forward)* A dollar!

SACK DADDY: Raise you two!

BLACK BABY: I don't like to strain with nobody but it's goin' to cost you five. Come on, you shag-nags!

TOO-SWEET: You all act like you're spuddin'! Bet some money! Put your money where your mouth is!

TUSH HAWG: I'll [put] my fist where *yo'* mouf is! Twenty-five dollars to keep my company! Dog-gone, I'm spreadin' my knots!

SACK DADDY: And I bet you a fat man I'll take your money—I call you. *(Turns up his cards—he has four aces and [a] king.)*

TUSH HAWG: *(Showing his cards)* Youse a liar! I ain't dealt you no aces. Don't try to carry the Pam-Pam to me 'cause I'll gently chain-gang for you!

SACK DADDY: Oh yeah! I ain't goin' to fit no jail for you and nobody else. I'm to get me a green club and season it over your head. Then I'll give my case to Miss Bush and let Mother Green stand my bond! I got deal them aces!

NUNKIE: That's a lie! Both of you is lyin'! Lyin' like the cross-ties from New York to Key West! How can you all hold aces when I got *four*? Somebody is goin' to West Hell before midnight!

PECKERWOOD: Don't you woof at Tush Hawg. If you do, I'm goin' to bust hell wide open with a man!

BLACK BABY: *(Pulls out razor. Business.)* My chop-axe tells me I got the only clean aces they is on this table! Before I'll leave you all rob me outa my money, I'm goin' to die it off!

TOO-SWEET: I promised the devil one man and I'm goin' to give him five! *(Draws gun.)*

TUSH HAWG: Don't draw your bosom on me! God sent me a pistol and I'm goin' to send him a man! *(Fires. Business for all.)*

AUNT DILSEY: *(Enters after shooting business. Stands. Business. Drops to chair.)* They wouldn't lissen—*(Looks men over. Business.)* It sure is goin' to be a whole lot tougher in hell now!

CURTAIN

# THE FIERY CHARIOT (1932)

Hurston included this slight bit of comedy, which she described as an "Original Negro Folk Tale," in *From Sun to Sun,* the revised version of *The Great Day* (1932), the concert program that received widespread critical notice. It received a single performance at the New School for Social Research in New York on Tuesday, March 29, 1932.

According to biographer Valerie Boyd, Hurston was compelled to write the sketch in order to flesh out *From Sun to Sun,* which had to excise significant portions of *The Great Day* due to the agreement she had made with Charlotte Osgood Mason in January 1932 not to use the folk material she had collected on trips Mason had financed in 1928 and 1929. If one compares the program notes from the two performances (see Appendix), one can see that *The Fiery Chariot* replaces the "Conjure Ceremony" portion of *The Great Day;* Mason had specifically barred Hurston from staging any of the conjure and voodoo material she had collected in New Orleans in 1929.

The story of *The Fiery Chariot* originates in 2 Kings 2, where Elijah is taken to heaven in "a chariot of fire, and horses of fire." The figure of the chariot had particular significance to African Americans during the antebellum period, as it represented their deliverance from slavery; it was not simply a fiery chariot, but a sweet one, "coming for to carry me home." In this sketch, however, the notion of deliverance is turned on its head; given the opportunity to escape slavery through death (represented in the figure of "Ole Massa" dressed in a costume reminiscent of a Ku Klux Klansman), Ike does everything he can to outwit him when he realizes he does not actually want to die.

Hurston reproduced this story in *Mules and Men* as "Ole Massa and John Who Wanted to Go to Heaven." In both cases, she appears to rely heavily on stereotypes of blacks as being superstitious, gullible, and cowardly. However, as Susan Meisenhelder writes, the tale is rife with "complex ambiguity"; "While the tale seems to poke fun at the Black man through a series of racist stereotypes, a different kind of humor derives from the depiction of John as a trickster who not only outruns the Lord [in reality, his master] but also verbally outwits him" (272).

Our edition is based on the script held in the Play Script Collection at the Schomburg Center for Research in Black Culture in New York. Another copy is held in the George A. Smathers Library Special Collections at the University of Florida.

# The Fiery Chariot

CAST:
  DINAH, a plump black slave woman, wife of
  IKE, a tallish black man religiously inclined
  THEIR SON, a child of seven or eight
  OLE MASSA, the plantation owner

*Time: Before surrender.*
*Place: On a Florida plantation.*

*Setting: One half of the stage (left) shows the interior of a cabin in the slave quarters of the plantation. Upstage center is a rude bed against the wall. At the extreme left is a fireplace with a fire. The only light in the room comes from this. There is a small window in the rear wall closed by [a] rude wooden shutter. At the extreme right there is a practical door. A few garments hang against the wall near the bed at the left. There is a dilapidated rocker near the fireplace. A crude straight chair stands nearer the door. The other half of the stage (right) shows the quarters. More cabins are seen on the backdrop.*

*Action: At the rise, Dinah is discovered seated in the rocker facing the door. The child squats on the floor beside her playing with an empty spool. Dinah is mending a pair of jeans britches and singing a little. Ike squats before the fire and pulls out a roasted sweet potato, feels it to see if it is done, satisfies himself that it is and leaves it on the hearth to cool. This done, he crosses to the straight chair, clearing his throat, moaning and humming as he does so. Dinah looks up at him very irritated. She stops sewing and glares at him. He sees her but belligerently ignores her. He places the chair near the fire and starts to kneel. Then he remembers his potato and goes to see if it is cool yet. He blows [on] it, then goes back to his chair and ostentatiously kneels to pray. Dinah is plainly disgusted.*

SON: Mama, kin Ah have piece dat tater, please ma'am?

IKE: Yo' maw ain't got no tater heah. (*Lookin' back at the potato, kneels defiantly to pray.*)

DINAH: (*To son*) Honey you better go git some sleep befo' yo' pappy start his disturbance.

SON: Yessum, but Ah wants some tater. (*She ignores him in glaring at Ike.*)

[DINAH:] Looka heah, Ike, is you gointer start worryin' God agin 'bout takin' you tuh heben?

IKE: *(On his knees, looks up angrily at her)* I ain't worryin' God, but look lak Ah'm worryin' *you.*

DINAH: *(Very annoyed)* Yeah you bothers me! Every night heah, down on yo' rusty knees beggin' God to come git yuh and take you to heben in His fiery chariot. You know you don't want tuh die a bit more'n Ah do.

IKE: *(Taunting)* Ah, you jes' mad 'cause Ah'll git tuh heben befo' you will.

DINAH: If whoopin' an' hollerin' would git yuh dere, you would be dere way 'head uh me, but thang God, dat ain't whut counts. Ah betcher God gits so tired uh yo' noise dat when He see you gittin' down, He gwan in His privy house and slam de door. Dat's whut He think about you and yo' prayers.

IKE: Aw shut up 'oman! You lemme and God tend to us business. You ain't got a thing to do wid it. Ah'm a prayin' man, and long as Ah kin feel de spirit Ah'm gointer pray.

SON: Mah-mah! Ah'm slee-ee-py.

DINAH: *(Turns to child)* Awright, lemme pull off yo' things. *(Child steps out of pants and is in underwear. Dinah leads him to bed and tucks him in.)*

IKE: O Lawd, here 'tis once mo' and agin Yo' humble servant is knee-bent and body bowed wid mah heart beneath mah knees and mah knees in some lonesome valley cryin' for mercy whilst mercy kinst be found—

DINAH: Ah wisht you would shut up an' leave dat chile git his night rest.

IKE: Come Lawd, come in a good time and git Yo' humble servant and keer 'im to heben wid you. Come in Yo' fiery chariot and take me 'way from dis sin-sick world. Massa work me so-oo hard and Ah ain't got no rest nowhere. Come in Yo' fiery chariot and take dis po' nigger home wid You to Yo' rest. Where I kin walk up and down de golden streets—

OLE MASSA: *(Approaches right through quarters to cabin door and listens)* Every time I come through these quarters I hear Ike in here prayin' for God to come take him to heaven. I'm going to try him out and see if he means what he prays. *(He turns and exits right hurriedly.)*

DINAH: *(Who has resumed her seat)* Umph! Umph! Umph!

IKE: And O—when Ah kin stand 'round and 'round Yo' be-atific throne, and when You shall place in mah hand de hosanna fan—

*(Reenter Ole Massa with a white sheet. He stands on Ike's step and throws the sheet over his head and knocks on the door.)*

IKE: *(Looks up from his prayers)* Who dat? *(Turns to Dinah)* Who dat at de do' you reckon?

OLE MASSA: *(Sing-songing)* It's me, Ike, the Lord, I come in my fiery chariot to take you to heaven with me. Come right now, Ike.

IKE: *(Tiptoes to the bed and creeps under it. To Dinah)* Tell 'im Ah ain't heah, Dinah.

DINAH: *(Full of awe)* Oh Lawd, Ike ain't heah right now. Come 'round some other time and Ah reckon You might ketch 'im.

*(A slight silence.)*

OLE MASSA: Well then, Dinah, you'll do.

*(Dinah registers great consternation. Ike is hopeful of being spared and sticks his head out from under the bed. Dinah signals for him to go on with God. He shakes his head and motions for her to go.)*

OLE MASSA: *(Who is peeping through the hole in the door all the time and sees the situation)* I say Dinah, you'll do.

DINAH: *(In whisper)* Ike, why don't you gwan wid God. You hear Him callin' you.

IKE: Why don't *you* go wid 'im? He done called you too.

DINAH: You was de one been whoopin an' hollerin' for Him to come git you an' take you to heben. I ain't prayed de first lick.

IKE: Still He say you'll do.

OLE MASSA: Come on Dinah, and ride in my fiery chariot.

DINAH: *(Tearful)* Ike, if you don't come on and go wid God, He's gointer take *me*.

IKE: *(Nonchalantly)* Ah can't stop God from doin' what He want to do. Gwan if He call you.

DINAH: *(Desperately)* Ike, youse de one begged God to come git you and if you don't come out from under dat bed and go wid God, Ah gointer tell 'im where you is.

*(Ike shakes his head for her not to do it.)*

OLE MASSA: For the last time I say, Dinah you'll do.

DINAH: God, Ike ain't gone nowhere. He's right here under dis bed.

OLE MASSA: Ike, O Ike. Why do you try to fool me? Come out from under that bed and go with me.

*(Ike comes trembling forth, but turns upon Dinah and shakes his fist.)*

DINAH: You better not hit me. Ah'll holler and tell God on you.

*(Ike desists.)*

OLE MASSA: Come on Ike, my chariot is tired of waiting.

IKE: *(Drags to the door as slowly as possible and opens it. He visibly starts when he sees the white being outside.)* O Lawd, You so white and clean, Ah know You don't want me to go to heben wid You in dese ole dirty clothes. Gimme time to put on my Sunday shirt.

OLE MASSA: All right, Ike, go put on yo' Sunday shirt.

*(Ike turns slowly and closes the door. He looks longingly at the window but sees again that it is too small. He starts to look under the bed as if he thinks his shirt could be under there.)*

DINAH: *(Jumps up and snatches the shirt off the wall and throws it to him angrily.)* You know no shirt ain't under dat bed. You jes' tryin to wear God out.

IKE: *(Angrily)* Who ast *you* to be so fast—findin' my shirt befo' I do? Ah got a mind to maul yo' knot for you. *(Threatening)*

DINAH: Aw, ole cuffy, you better gwan to heben while God want you.

IKE: *(Puts on the shirt as slowly as possible, but finally he gets it on and drags to the door and cracks it to see if Ole Massa is still there. He recoils when he sees him still.)* O Lawd, Yo' heben is so high, and Ah'm so low, Ah know You don't want me ridin' in Yo' fine chariot in dese ole greasy britches. Gimme time to put on mah Sunday pants.

OLE MASSA: All right, Ike, go put on yo' Sunday pants.

IKE: *(Starts to filibuster about finding his pants. Dinah has been patching them and hurls them to him. He hurls them to the floor and can hardly restrain himself from jumping on Dinah.)* Whut Ah tell you 'bout mindin' mah business? You lemme hunt my own pants. *(Starts to draw on the pants)* If you don't look out you gointer be in hell befo' Ah git tuh heben.

OLE MASSA: Come on Ike.

IKE: Yessuh, Jesus. *(He creeps to the door sadly and opens it slightly and stares awhile. Then he opens it wide.)* Oh Lawd, the radiance of Yo' countenance is *so* bright, Ah can't come out by Yuh. Stand back jes' a lil' bit please.

*(Ole Massa takes one step backward.)*

IKE: *(Measuring the space with his eye)* O Lawd, heben is so high and Ah'm so humble in Yo' sight, and Yo' glory cloud is so bright and Yo' radiance is so compellment, be so kind in Yo' tender mercy as to stand back jes' a lil bit mo'.

*(Ole Massa steps back another step.)*

IKE: *(Measures the distance again)* O Lawd, You humble servant is knee-bent and body bowed, mah heart beneath mah knees and mah knees in some lonesome valley cryin' for mercy whilst kinst be found, hear me one mo' time whilst still Ah'm on pleadin' terms wid mercy. Grant me one mo' favor befo' de zig zag lightnin' goes to join de mutterin' thunder. Come wid peace in one hand and pardon in de other and be so pleased as to stand back a lil teeny bit further.

*(Massa takes another step backward and Ike leaps past him out of the door. Massa grabs up the tail of his sheet and starts in hot pursuit. They dash off right with Ike in the lead and steadily gaining. Ike looks back and seeing that he is gaining challenges Massa.)*

IKE: If Thou be a running death, ketch me! *(They exit right swiftly.)*

SON: *(Sits up in bed crying)* Mah-mah, you reckon God gointer ketch papa and take 'im off in His fiery chariot?

DINAH: *(Who has resumed her mending, looks scornfully at her son)* Hush up dat foolishness and gwan back to sleep. You know God ain't got no time wid yo' pappy and him barefooted too.

QUICK CURTAIN

# SPUNK (1935)

Although it was never produced, *Spunk* is arguably Hurston's most crafted play, next to *Polk County* (1944). It also functions as a bridge between the earliest successes of Hurston's career and her culminating achievement, *Their Eyes Were Watching God* (1937). The play began as the short story of the same title, which won Hurston second prize in the inaugural 1925 *Opportunity* literary contest as well as attracting the notice of the Harlem intelligentsia. The story was later published in the June 1925 issue of *Opportunity,* and Alain Locke included it in the same year in his seminal anthology, *The New Negro.*

The play retains the basic plot elements of the original story, including the love triangle between Jim (Joe in the short story), Spunk, and Evalina (Lena), Spunk's killing of Jim, and the element of conjure. However, the play is quintessentially comic, while the story ends in tragedy. In the earlier work, Spunk kills Jim and is acquitted of his murder, but is eventually killed by the lumber mill's huge circular saw; in his final moments, Spunk tells one of the onlookers that he believes Jim's ghost has pushed him in retribution. The final scene is desolate, yet strangely devoid of affect: "The cooling board consisted of three sixteen-inch boards on saw horses, a dingy sheet was his shroud," Hurston writes. "The women ate heartily of the funeral baked meats and wondered who would be Lena's next. The men whispered coarse conjectures between guzzles of whiskey." In contrast, in the play, it is Jim who dies at the hands of the saw, and Evalina and Spunk who are left to live their life of "love from on high."

More significantly, the character of Spunk himself undergoes a complete transformation. In the story, Spunk is described as "a giant of a brown skinned man," "skeered of nothin'," a crack shot who would "beat you full of button holes as quick as he's look atcher." By the time he appears in the play, he is a "box-picking fool" rather than a gunslinging one; a large man, but "sweet-smelling and clean, like magnolias." He bears a strong resemblance to Hurston's most memorable hero, Tea Cake of *Their Eyes Were Watching God,* a man who "looked like the love thoughts of women . . . Crushing aromatic herbs with every step he took."

Between the publication of the short story and beginning work on the dramatic version, Hurston had spent years collecting stories, songs, and dances in the South; she had been trained by Franz Boas and funded in her research by Charlotte Osgood Mason. The play is thus infused with a variety of folk elements almost wholly absent from the short story. One of the strengths of the play is the way in which Hurston weaves together song, story, and ethnography, retaining the fundamental dramatic structure of the story's plot while also incorporating cultural practices such as the toe party, croquet matches, lining songs, voodoo rites, and of course, the idiomatic expressions for which Hurston is best known. The song's chants and ballads, in turn, play a strong role in conveying the emotions of the characters and are thus a fundamental aspect of the play's development. It is worth noting that parts of *Spunk*—specifically, several of the musical and dance interludes—may have been staged as part of *The Great*

*Day* and *From Sun to Sun,* which were both described as programs of "Original Negro Folklore" (see Appendix). Both works include lining songs ("Can't You Line It?") as well as a ring play; *The Great Day* also has a "Pea-vine Candle Dance" as part of the program that may very well have been inserted as act 3, scene 2 of this play.

# Spunk

## ACT ONE
### Scene 1

*Setting: All action from spectators' viewpoint. A railroad track through the Florida woods. Luxuriant foliage on the backdrop. A hand car with tools is standing on the track at extreme left.*

*Action: The white boss of the extra gang is leaning on the car. The gang is "lining" a rail downtage, center. The singing-liner[1] is moving about downstage, right. He dramatizes every utterance. Half dances every step. He chants and the men grunt rhythmically as they pull on the lining bars.*

SINGING-LINER: Ah Mobile!

MEN: Hanh!

SINGING-LINER: Ah, in Alabama!

MEN: Hanh!

SINGING-LINER: Ah, Fort Myers!

MEN: Hanh!

SINGING-LINER: Ah, in Florida!

MEN: Hanh!

SINGING-LINER: Ah, let's shake it!

MEN: Hanh!

SINGING-LINER: Ah, let's break it!

MEN: Hanh!

SINGING-LINER: Ah, let's shake it!

MEN: Hanh!

SINGING-LINER: Ah, just a hair! *(Men straighten up from their strain, mop their faces and start for the hand car.)*

BOSS: Line another one before you spike. Come on, bullies!

SINGING-LINER: All right. Nine hundred pounds of steel in place! Let's go. *(Men grab up bars and jump into place.)* Come on if you're coming, let's go if you're going! *(He struts to center and begins to sing.)*

> When I get in Illinois
> I'm going to spread the news about the Florida boys
> Shove it over! Hey! Hey! Can't you line it?
> Ah, shack-a-lack, a-lack, a-lack, a-lack, a-hunh!
> Can't you move it?
> Hey! Hey! Can't you try?[2]

*(The men grin and work furiously. He sings five verses and men join in chorus.)*

BOSS: *(Peering down the rail to see if it is lined correctly)* All right, boys, that gets it. Hammers!

*(The men all start towards the car with the bars to exchange them for snub-nosed hammers. Singing-liner is humming "This Old Hammer"[3] and two or three others are harmonizing the hum. Offstage right can be heard the picking of a guitar and a baritone voice singing sketchily. All stop and look that way.)*

NUNKIE: Who you reckon that is giving that box that nasty fit? If he can't play that guitar there ain't a hound dog in Georgia, and you know that's de puppy's range.

SINGING-LINER: Wished I knowed myself. He sure is propaganda.

*(Enter Spunk walking energetically down the track. His hat is far back on his head. His shirt collar thrown wide open. He stops playing as he reaches the gang.)*

ORAL: *(In admiration)* Hey, box-picking fool, where you come from?

SPUNK: *(Pleased with the compliment)* From Polk County, where the water taste like cherry wine. *(He plays a few bars of "Polk County."[4] The men are in high glee. The Boss frowns.)*

BOSS: All right, boys, get to work. You killing up the company's time.

BLUE TROUT: *(Cajoling)* Us going to work, Cap'n. Leave him play just a little bit, please. We could work twice as good then. *(To Spunk)* Hit dat box, Big Boy.

*(Spunk starts to smile, then frowns. Advances threateningly on Blue Trout.)*

SPUNK: Who you calling Big Boy? You must be want to see your Jesus. Elephant is bigger than me, and they call him Elephant. I got a name.

ORAL: Tell a dumb man something! He know better than to be calling folks Big Boy. When these white folks say it you can excuse they ignorance 'cause they don't know no better. Blue just trying to be cute.

BLUE TROUT: Aw, y'all blowin' a mole hill into a rocky mountain! I didn't mean no harm. I beg your pardon, mister.

SPUNK: *(Mollified)* It's granted. Ain't nobody mad no more. *(Crosses to Boss)* Say, Cap'n, don't you need another man on this job?

BOSS: Yeah, I sure do. But I can't take you because I got all this breath-and-britches on the pay-roll. If some of them don't do better you can start to work Monday morning.

NUNKIE: Cap'n, you're getting good service. Look what we done done since morning.

SPUNK: Anybody know where I can get a job of work 'round here? I ain't used to doing nothing. I got to work.

BOSS: *(Thoughtfully)* It's hard to tell exactly. Times is hard. You just follow the track into town—'bout three miles, I reckon. It's a sawmill there and they 'most always taking on men.

ORAL: They got a job right there now, but they can't get nobody to take it.

SPUNK: How come? They make pay-day, don't they?

ORAL: Yeah, good pay, too. But folks 'round here done got scared of that job.

SPUNK: What's the matter with it?

ORAL: Well, looks like everybody that takes it gets killed sooner or later.

SPUNK: What's it doing?

ORAL: Running the big circle saw at the sawmill. Somehow or 'nother they gets killed.

SPUNK: I'll ride that saw till it's bow-legged. All I want them to do is to pay me. I'll ride it till it wear clean out. Boys, I'm gone like a turkey through the corn.

BOSS: *(Impatiently)* All right, boys! What you all trying to do—make me mad? Fool with me, I'll have a brand new crew out here after pay-day.

SINGING-LINER: Yassuh!

*(Spunk hurries to the exit left. Singing-liner pretending to sing for the boys chants after him)*

Hey, you guitar picker, play it some more
Big toe party over town tonight, and I know you want to go!

Let's spike it, boys!

SPUNK: *(Calls back over his shoulder)* I heard you buddy! *(His guitar and voice come back)*

Oh I don't want no cold corn bread and molasses
Oh I don't want no cold corn bread and molasses
Gimme beans, Lawd, Lawd, gimme beans
I got a woman, she shake like jelly all over
I got a woman, she shake like jelly all over
Her hips so broad, Lawd, Lawd, her hips so broad.[5]

*(Curtain.)*

## Scene 2

*[Action:] Group singing "All Ye Sins." At the rise Mrs. Georgia Watson is presiding behind the refreshment stand. Admiral is beating out a rhythm on a soda crate and Blue Trout is trying to "buck and wing." People stand around in easy poses, eating, talking or just looking on.*

MRS. WATSON: Hey there, Blue! Did anybody hit you to start you? 'Cause if they did I'm going to hit you to stop you.

BLUE TROUT: *(Attempting a fancy break and botching it)* What's the matter with my dancing, Mrs. Watson?

MRS. WATSON: Don't ask me. I ain't never seen none of it. That what you doing ain't *nothing*. If you was dancing for peanuts you wouldn't even get the hulls. You ain't no trouble. Git out there Oral and do some sure enough dancing.

ORAL: *(Sitting on the ground)* Wait! I don't want to spread my [mess][6] till Maggie Mae git here. Then I'll dance up camp meeting, dust off associations and strut Jordan dry. Hello!

MRS. WATSON: She's liable not to pay *you* no mind when she come. All I can hear is the girls screaming over that new fellow that's working at the sawmill. I can't hear nothing but Spunk.

TEAZIE: From what I heard he got some stuff for all you fellows 'round here. I wish he would come on so we could see if he's like they say.

ORAL: Oh, he's sort of over average built with oakobolic hair.

ADMIRAL: Let's squat that rabbit and jump another one. I'm a business man. Who wants to go for a boat ride? I got my boat there. Only ten cents a ride.

MRS. WATSON: *(Laughs)* Now Admiral, you know ain't nobody here going to go out on the lake in that boat of yours. It's got so many cracks it looks like somebody worked it full of button-holes. We'se assembled for a toe party tonight. Not no swimming match. *(General laughter)*

ADMIRAL: It don't leak so much. Come one, come all! Ten cents a ride!

WILLIE JOE: Aw, shut up, Admiral, about your old beat up boat! Lemme tell you all what else that Spunk done today. Men, you ought to seen him! Soon as he got the hang of that saw he begin to talk to it just like a man would to his dice.

ORAL: *(Gleefully)* What he say to it?

WILLIE JOE: First he didn't say nothing. You know how a saw sound when it's cutting a log. A high moaning *(imitates sound)*. Well, Spunk leaned his head down and listen to the saw till it got through. Then he answered the saw back in a kind of singing way. Man, everybody stopped to listen, even the boss. And all the time he was really milling the lumber.

BLUE TROUT: Hurry up and tell us what he *say.*

WILLIE JOE: Oh, I can't remember exactly. Something about how that old saw had done chewed up a thousand million trees and spit out the dust, and had done chopped down men just like they was trees but it wouldn't never get him.

ORAL: Do it. Go 'head on, Willie Joe, and show us how he done it.

WILLIE JOE: Oh, I can't do it like him. Wait till he get here. He'll do it for you.

DAISY: Come on, Teazie! Let's me and you go find him and bring him on to the party.

BLUE TROUT: You all don't need to bother. Ruby Jones done grabbed him. He was eating his supper at her house just now. She done got him all sewed up.

DAISY: Aw, she ain't no trouble. That old beat-looking gal! All she can do is sing.

BLUE TROUT: Now here! Ruby ain't got nobody so it's all right for her to pull after the new man. But the rest of you girls belong to us. Better leave him alone. Eh, boys?

ORAL: Them girls know better. They just trying us out. Don't pay 'em no mind. Come on, Willie Joe. *You* go on and show us. Spunk and Ruby might not come atall.

WILLIE JOE: All right, you all help me out some with the saw. You got to moan high like the saw while I'll talk like Spunk. (*He places Oral, Blue Trout, and Admiral together in a line and close together.*) Now you all is the saw. Go 'head on and sound like one.

(*They get pitch and hum. He begins to chant.*)

Oh, you done cut trees into lumber and—

(*There is the sound of a group talking off left and they all look that way.*)

Here come Spunk and them now. Hey, Ruby, rush your frog to the frolic!

(*Ruby enters proudly on Spunk's arm. Two other couples are with them. Spunk has his guitar slung across his back. Everyone looks at him with interest.*)

SPUNK: I heard you before I got here, but that ain't what I said.

WILLIE JOE: That's what I told 'em. I knowed I couldn't say what you said. They all wants to hear it.

SPUNK: 'Tain't nothing much to tell, but if you all so desire, I'll tell you and show you the best I can.

ORAL: We'se already the saw for you.

SPUNK: All right, let's go. Wait a minute. Do you know what the saw says?

ORAL: Naw.[7] Do it say anything besides noise?

SPUNK: Yeah, man. Before the log gets there the saw is grumbling to itself and saying "I done cut a tree into a board, done cut a board into a box." By that time the log is there. And the saw is glad so it can go to cutting. That's what it loves. Cutting. Filling up its jaws with trees. Spitting out sawdust and lumber. So when it hits the log it laughs like the horse in the valley of Jehoshophat. It says

*(Boys begin hum of saw)*

"I'm going to make me a graveyard of my own
I'm going to make me a graveyard of my own
I carry 'em down a smoky road
Bring 'em back on a cooling board
I'm going to make me a graveyard of my own."

So I listened good and answered it back:

"You done gaped your jaws
You done rolled your eyes
You done cut a coffin
But it ain't my size
You can growl and thunder
You can howl and sigh
But I'll wear you out, Lawd, before I die.
Cut your timber, cut your ties
Cut your timber, cut your ties
Show your teeth, Lawd, roll your eyes."

ORAL: Gee, youse powerful! Wish I could be there to hear you talking to that old saw. It's done killed several 'round here.

*(They crowd around Spunk for a moment. Ruby seizes his arm and stands there in ecstasy. Enter Blue Trout,[8] Maggie Mae and two or three others.)*

WILLIE JOE: Blue, I know you ain't been by Maggie Mae's house and brought her. Oral say he ain't going to hear that.

BLUE TROUT: Naw, I ain't no trouble 'round there. We met up on the road. *(To Spunk)* Hello, buddy! I see you got here.

SPUNK: Oh yeah, I always likes to be where the ladies and the music and the fun is. You ain't sold out all the toes is you? 'Cause I got some money to buy some toes too.

BLUE TROUT: Nope, you know our people never hold nothing on time. They just coming now.

MRS. WATSON: *(Beating on a skillet)* All you young pullets and all you all hens go behind the curtain. We're going to sell off the toes. Everybody come on. Hurry up!

*(There is a lot of bashful giggling as the girls haltingly make their way to the quilts. Ruby stands by Spunk without moving.)*

Hey, Ruby, ain't you taking no part in the party? What you come here for?

RUBY: *(Coyly)* I don't know whether my gentlemen friend want me to play that or not. He might choose for me to just stay with him. *(She looks coyly into his face.)*

SPUNK: Oh, that's all right with me, baby. Don't let me stop your fun. The boys might think hard of me if they didn't get a chance at your toe.

*(Ruby is chagrined and goes slowly to join the others behind the quilts. Spunk pulls his guitar from behind him and plays a chord or two in an absent-minded way.)*

MRS. WATSON: Whilst the girls is getting their toes ready to show, maybe our new friend will favor us with a guitar selection.

*(Everyone begins to clap hands and Spunk plays "Polk County." His hearers are delighted.)*

MRS. WATSON: *(In admiration)* That's a box-picking fool! Gwan, play us some march music for the boys to march up and choose by.

SPUNK: I wants to march, too. I aims to buy a toe myself.

MRS. WATSON: *(Arranging line)* Get on the tail end of the line and play and march at the same time, like a nice boy. Don't make nobody beg you to play.

*(Spunk goes to the end of the line and begins to pick softly. The sale of toes begins. There is much laughter and shouting as the girls come from behind the curtain and the men see whom they have bought. Some are proud and strut up to the table, others hang back. Willie Joe pretends that he will jump in the lake to get away from his. Spunk buys the last toe and finds he has Ruby.)*

DAISY: *(Sneering)* I see how come [she] never put her toe out till the last!

RUBY: *(Seizing Spunk's arm triumphantly)* Young coon for running, old coon for cunning! Ha! Ha! Come on y'all, let's play a ring play.[9]

DAISY: *(Gladly)* I'm in the ring!

*(They begin to organize around Daisy. Enter at left Jim Bishop and Evalina [who] stand a moment looking about.)*

ORAL: The very person we need to make this play go good. *(Calls out)* Come on, Evalina! We fixing to play "Baby Child"!

*(Evalina brightens and takes a step. Jim catches her elbow.)*

JIM: *(Turning towards refreshment stand)* You better come on here and get this little treat while I'm in the notion of buying it!

EVALINA: *(Pulling away slightly)* I don't choose no treat yet awhile. I just got here. *(She advances towards the game a step or two.)*

JIM: Don't think you going to keep me up here half the night. I'm a working man. By the time we walk 'round the place and see it all we going on back home. Come on here and get some sweeten water.

EVALINA: *(Coldly)* I ain't in no hurry atall and I done told you I don't want no lemonade yet awhile. *(She turns again towards the circle, and finds herself looking straight into Spunk's eyes.)*

JIM: *(At the stand)* Two glasses of that sweeten water y'all call lemonade and make it good and cold.

*(Evalina hesitates a moment, undecided whether to follow her husband or to join the ring.)*

ORAL: Come on here, Lina! You can get a treat any old time. Quit acting scared.

*(She turns smiling towards the game. Jim drinks his lemonade and follows Evalina with a glass for her.)*

JIM: Here your treat, Lina. Here, take it before I spill it.

EVALINA: Spill it, then! Nobody don't care. I don't aim to drink nothing unless I want it. *(He catches her arm and tries to hold it to her lips. She pulls away.)* Don't you spill that mess on me and ruin up my good clothes.

JIM: *(Tries to thrust it into her hands)* Aw, here, take this lemonade and drink it, Lina. You ain't going to make me waste up my money for nothing.

EVALINA: Nobody didn't ask you to buy it, did they? You always trying to put your mind in my head.

JIM: Fool with me, I'll leave you here. Get home the best way you can.

EVALINA: *(Over her shoulder)* Go on then. Nobody don't care. *(Exit Jim left, furiously)*

WILLIE JOE: You better go on with him, Evalina. He going to tell his papa what you done done. He'll be working some more of his roots on you.

ORAL: Yeah, that's where he gone. He figger his old man can hit a straight lick with a crooked stick. Watch out. It won't be long before Old Hodge Bishop will be here.

EVALINA: Let him go and get his pappy! I don't care. Come on, let's dance!

*(She hurries to break into the circle. Ruby sees the look on Spunk's face as he watches Evalina.)*

RUBY: Aw naw, this game is for young folks. This ain't for no old married women. They ought to go class off to theirselves.

*(Evalina draws back quickly with a hurt "oh" on her lips.)*

ORAL: Who you calling old? Evalina is a whole heap younger than you, Ruby.

RUBY: That's all right. She's married, ain't she? We'se all courting couples. She ain't got no business in with us.

*(She looks up at Spunk in triumph. His eyes follow Evalina.)*

SPUNK: I don't believe I choose no ring play. B'lieve I'll just stroll around and look things over. *(He starts to break his hand clasp.)*

RUBY: *(In panic)* Aw, come on and play, Lina. Can't you take a joke? Meet my gentleman friend. Mrs. Lina Bishop, Mr. Spunk. *(Rolls her eyes in admiration)* Papa tree-top, tall.

EVALINA: Pleased to meet you, Mr. Spunk.

SPUNK: My compliments, Mrs. Lina. Hope to be better acquainted.

ORAL: *(Jumping and clapping)* Come on, let's go, people. *(Clapping gets hot. He begins to sing)*

Eh, yeh, Lollie Lou,
Eh, yeh, Lollie Lou.

*(Daisy chooses Oral and he chooses [a girl]¹⁰ and she chooses Blue Trout and Blue chooses another girl and she chooses Admiral and he chooses Evalina. The rhythm has grown terrific and Oral begins to chant "Baby Chile."¹¹ Evalina dances it to a high pitch and chooses Spunk and they end the dance in a frenzy of rhythm. Everyone is over-heated and tired. Some drop laughing on the grass. Others rush over for a cooling drink. Spunk raises Evalina from their final dance position and stands holding her hands. Oral hands him his guitar.)*

SPUNK: Miss Lina, would you do me the favor to step over to the refreshment stand and choose your ruthers on me?

EVALINA: *(Coyly)* Much obliged, Mr. Spunk, and my mouth is a little parched from all this dancing. I'll choose some lemonade.

*(They stroll towards the table with Ruby and several others staring hard. While Evalina drinks the lemonade he quietly buys her a huge stick of peppermint candy and places it in her hand. She accepts it gladly and they cross near the water.)*

SPUNK: Whilst we's so hot from dancing, we ought to try one of them boat-rides. I loves to pull a boat.

EVALINA: Them boats is full of leaks. Admiral ain't fooling nobody on his boat-rides. *(They laugh lightly.)*

SPUNK: *(Earnestly)* Well, anyhow, we can git in one of them and sit down, can't us?

EVALINA: *(Nodding yes)* Uh, huh, I reckon.

*(He helps her to a seat in the prow and seats himself on the rower's bench and picks up an oar. Everybody begins to stare silently.)*

SPUNK: Must I shove off, Miss Lina?

EVALINA: *(Nervously)* We better not get out into deep water, Mister Spunk. It's dangerous, in the dark too.

*(Enter Hodge Bishop, left. An ominous silence falls as he looks all about him. He walks slowly to center and stands glaring at Evalina and Spunk. Then he lifts his hat, fumbles in the band and puts it on again, but backwards this time and exits again, left, insolently.)*

SPUNK: Nothing can't be dangerous when you with me. I can swim real good. I could take the Mississippi River for a dusty road if I had to. I'd love to be out on that lake.

EVALINA: *(Looks about nervously)* We better not, though. Not out on the water. Let's just set in the boat.

SPUNK: *(Seating her facing the audience and he facing her)* Whatever you say, Miss Evalina. But I done found out it ain't no use being scared of things. If you feel to do a thing, do it. You can't die but one time nohow.

*(She looks at him softly. He gets back into position.)*

I got a song made up in me for you.

EVALINA: For me? You must have made it up awful quick. This the first time you ever seen me.

SPUNK: It don't seem that way. Seem like I always been knowing you. When I seen you come walking in just now it seem like you had been off somewhere and just got back home.

EVALINA: You don't seem strange to me neither. Look like I been knowing you, too. And that's a nice feeling. I don't like to feel strange 'round people. And that's the way I been.

SPUNK: I know how that is by my own self. That's how come I already got your song made up. But anyhow it ain't hard for me to make up songs. If I get to feeling real strong inside a song makes itself up and all I have to do is sing it. Like this one I'm going to sing right now.

EVALINA: I'll be glad. Your compliments is nice.

(*He begins to sing "Halimuhfack"*[12] *and people listen amazed and then burst into a thudding monotone and pantomime of gossip as a comment on the situation. He sings two verses.*)

EVALINA: Let's see! I can make up some to go with that.

(*She sings a verse to him. The rumble and the gestures keep up. They sing the fourth verse together. While it is being sung Hodge Bishop reenters with Jim and glares ominously in the direction of Spunk and Evalina. As the song ends Jim struts over and stands glaring at her.*)

JIM: Get yourself out that boat, Lina! Anybody would think you was some courting girl, sitting up there! We going home.

(*She alights with deliberation as the rumble rises to a thudding tempo. She haughtily strides across the stage behind Jim to left. Spunk rises too and walks slowly after her to center stage. As Evalina reaches the left exit she stops and gives Spunk a long dragging look. He returns it in kind. Then she is gone. He continues to stare after her. Ruby creeps to him and hugs his left arm. He is impatient.*)

RUBY: What's the matter, daddy? Look like you thunder-struck by lightning.

SPUNK: (*Staring and straining like a dog on a leash to keep from following Evalina*) Aw, naw! I done got a letter from love and so help me I'll go to hell but what I answer it.

(*Curtain.*)

## ACT TWO
### Scene 1

*Action: At the rise there is the crack of mallet against ball and Nunkie rushes across the [croquet] court from upstage left to downstage right. His ball rests very near another. He stoops to arrange the balls.*

DAISY: (*Approaching him*) What you doing, Nunkie? You never hit my ball.

NUNKIE: (*Indignantly*) Who never hit it? I almost sent it to Georgia.

ORAL: Aw, you never hit it. Stop cheating.

NUNKIE: I don't have to cheat you when I'm beating you. Talking about I didn't hit it! (*He goes on preparing to roquet the balls*) I bet you I'll send it to Diddy-Wah-Diddy.[13]

ORAL: That's all right, Daisy, let him roquet you. It's my next shot. I'm going to hit him and send him back to Ginny-Gall, where they eat cow-head, skin and all.

NUNKIE: I ain't from no Ginny-Gall. 'Tain't no such place nohow.

ORAL: Well, where is you from, then?

NUNKIE: I'm from Bandandy, Georgia. *(All laugh)*

ORAL: You can gum, Nunkie, but don't bite. You know there ain't no such a place. Bandandy! Where is that?

NUNKIE: I don't recollect. I was too small when we left there for me to remember, but I done heard mama speak [of] it many a time.

ORAL: That's a name your mama made up so she could claim you was born in a town. 'Tain't no Bandandy *no where.* Stop your cheating and let's play.

TEAZIE: Who cheating? You all the one trying to cheat us. I was looking right at you, Oral, shoving your ball into position at that last wicket.

ORAL: Teazie, youse a—er, er, Got-that-wrong! Girl, you can mold 'em. I ain't pushed my ball. Nothing of the kind. We going to beat you and have our correct amount of fun while we doing it. I mean to die bold.

MRS. WATSON: Aw, you-all hurry up and get through so somebody else can play. Me and Willie Joe going to take the winners.

RUBY: Naw, let all of 'em come off when they finish that game. Let four brand new ones get on there. I'm tired of waiting.

JIM: *(Pulls coin from his pocket)* Here, Admiral, run get me a cold Coca-Cola.

ADMIRAL: Yessir. Don't you want me to bring you some cigarettes, too? I need a smoke.

JIM: Well, all right. But I wasn't figgering on none right now.

*(Admiral darts off left running.)*

DAISY: *(To Nunkie, gloating)* Now, you dead on the game and ain't even made your center wicket. You ain't no trouble.

NUNKIE: Aw, shoot and shut up! You have to play this game. Your talk don't help none. I done belled the buzzard, crowned the crow; got the key to the bushes and I'm bound to go.

MRS. WATSON: *(Slams card down on the table)* High, low, Jack and the bend-wood tosser.[14] Roasting ears ripe and the corn's et offa. Gone from two! Out and gone!

WILLIE JOE: Gone out your head! Where you all get any two from?

*(Reenter Admiral [who] hands Jim Coca-Cola and change. He begins to open the cigarettes as Jim wipes the mouth of the bottle with his hand and places it to his lips.)*

RUBY: Aw, let it go. Nobody don't care, nohow. We ain't bet money. Let 'em have it. *(She looks about her absently and begins to hum.)*

Oh Lord, Oh Lord, let the words of my mouth, O Lord

*(The others begin to pick up.)*

Let the words of my mouth, meditations of my heart
Be accepted in thy sight, O Lord.

*(They sing it the second time in full harmony.)*

MRS. WATSON: Ain't y'all *never* going to get through with that game?

*(There is the sound of full guitar chords offstage. Jim starts violently, almost strangles himself and removes the bottle from his lips and listens painfully.)*

WILLIE JOE: Spunk and Evalina all set for their afternoon stroll. Listen! He's coming down the steps when he play like that.

*(Ruby drops her head upon the table.)*

NUNKIE: Yep. Every day, him and Evalina and the music going for a walk after work. Wonder how come they go walking every day.

ORAL: Why don't you ask him when he get here! Then you'll know. Betcha Spunk got a magnolia bloom in his hat!

ADMIRAL: Betcha he ain't!

ORAL: He is too! You ain't never seen them out walking 'less Lina had a magnolia stuck in his hat band.

ADMIRAL: I have.

ORAL: When was that?

ADMIRAL: Yesterday. They was out walking and he didn't have no magnolia in his hat band.

ORAL: I don't believe it.

ADMIRAL: He done been out a lot of times without a magnolia bloom in his hat. *(Laughs)* Man, don't you know magnolias ain't in bloom this time of the year? Ha! Ha! Lina's going to put some kind of a flower all over him every day. Magnolias is her preference, but she can't get 'em if they ain't on the tree.

*(They laugh. Guitar heard approaching.)*

WILLIE JOE: *(Winking broadly)* Jim, how you and Evalina making out these days?

JIM: *(Starts painfully)* We'd be all right, I reckon, if we—if—if somebody didn't come between us.

NUNKIE: You ain't no kind of a man or nobody couldn't come between you. Some things ain't decent for a man to take. You low-rates yourself if you do. So what you going to do?

WILLIE JOE: What's he going to do? Mildew! Do like the folks the other side of the creek—do without!

RUBY: *(Jumping up suddenly with wet eyes)* Why don't you-all leave him alone? You ain't got no gumption—teasing him 'bout a thing like that. If a person can't get the one they love, it's pitiful! It ain't nothing to be cracking over. Leave Jim be!

WILLIE JOE: How come he's got to be different from everybody else 'round here? Y'all laughed and made all manner of jokes when Pearl left me and went down the East Coast. Jim and all the rest of y'all cracked me *hard*. How come he can't take what he give?

ORAL: That ain't the first time a man's wife been took away from him. Jim is just a fool to keep hanging after Lina when she's done told him she don't want him and gone to living with Spunk.

NUNKIE: Yeah, I had a good woman. *(Shrugs resignedly)* The fool laid down and died.

JIM: *(Stands with hands in pockets)* Just like you say, Nunkie, I reckon it is my fault for being so easy. *(Strikes a belligerent pose)* But Spunk done gone too far. I stopped by here today just in order to tackle 'em when they pass. I'm going to know from him today what he means by coming between me and Lina. I love that girl! I love her! If I don't love her, God's a gopher! *(All but sobs)*

WILLIE JOE: That's right, Jim. Make him tell you something. Man ain't nothing but a man.

*(There is a tinkle of music and Evalina enters, left, clinging to Spunk's arm. He touches the guitar now and then. His broad-brimmed Stetson is full of honeysuckle. A bit hangs from his shirt pocket.)*

SPUNK: Hellow, Oral! Hello Nunkie and Willie Joe! How you making it, Teazie?

ALL: Hi, there Spunk and Lina. Y'all sho looks good to this world. Red hot!

MRS. WATSON: Say, Spunk, they all wants to know how come you and Lina go for a walk to the woods every day the Lord sends. How come that?

SPUNK: *(Laughing)* Lina, you know, is wild about her flowers, and she done made me make her a flower garden. So she always want to hear whatever new song I done made up setting out in the flower yard under the tree. But just as soon as I get to playing my song she begin to point out more work for me to be doing in the yard. So I just take her off into the woods where God done planted all the flowers she want and I don't have to work 'em. *(Everybody laughs.)*

WILLIE JOE: Women folks don't love to see a man sitting down. If you stay 'round the house they'll find plenty for you to do.

SPUNK: And ain't you noticed you can't never chop more stove[15] wood than a woman needs? If you chop six pieces she'll get the meal. If you chop a hundred pieces she'll burn every last stick of it just the same. *(Laughter)*

EVALINA: *(Scolding tenderly)* Now, honey, you know I don't burn wood like that.

SPUNK: Yes you do, cuteness. But if I didn't let you burn it the way you want to I'd be so mad with myself till I'd have to tote a pistol to bed to keep me from getting up and beating myself to death for worrying you. So I done made arrangements 'bout the whole thing. The boss is sending me a load of slabs every week from the sawmill and I done got Admiral to keep plenty chopped up. Burn *all* the wood you want, baby. Youse all I'm working for.

JIM: *(Swallowing convulsively)* Spunk, I want to speak to you.

SPUNK: *(Cool)* Well, I'm standing in front of you.

JIM: Spunk, I done told Lina, and I done told her mama and now I'm telling you. I want you to leave my wife alone.

SPUNK: Who do you call your wife?

JIM: Lina, there. That's my wife.

SPUNK: That's a big old Georgia lie! You multiplied roach, you! She's mine!

JIM: How come she's yourn? I know you-all is living together like man and wife, but I got *papers* for her. I went to the big court house and got the papers and stood up in her mama's house and married her. Tell *me* that ain't my wife!

SPUNK: *(Laughs shortly)* Court house! Papers! Standing up on the floor! Humph! That don't make a woman yours. That don't mean nothing. Evalina is *mine*. God took and made her special for me. When I was a lad of a boy I seen her in a vision standing 'round the throne waiting for me and I been hunting for her ever since. You the one shoved yourself out of place when you went and got them papers. She's mine!

JIM: *(Doggedly)* Naw she ain't neither. She is so my wife.

SPUNK: She is not! All right, you say she's yours. A woman know who her boss is and she'll go when he call. There Lina is. You call her and see if she'll come to your command.

JIM: *(Nervously)* Lina, Evalina, why don't you come on back home and quit this living like you is? Got everybody in town talking about you like you was a dog. Come on home!

EVALINA: *(Impatiently)* I'm living home now. All the I home I ever expect to have. Spunk ain't took me away from you. I went to him. And furthermore ain't nobody talking about me like a dog excepting you and your meddlesome old root-working papa! *(Draws away scornfully)* Leave me be! I loose you.

SPUNK: *(Involuntarily puts his arm about her)* All right now, Jim. That's the word with the bark on it. Now as long as a mule go bareheaded don't you stop my wife on the streets no more and be nam-namming at her and trying to crumple her feathers. You talk your big talk to me. If you was a man my size I would have done stopped you.[16] I ignores men your size. If there's anything I hate worse'n no fight it is a poor fight. I hates to look imposing and bull-dozing. But you leave her be. I'm telling you. Let's go, doll-baby. Bye, everybody. See you later. *(They exit with admiring glances of all following.)*

ADMIRAL: *(Looking after Spunk)* I hear you crowing, rooster! *(To others)* You have to give the man credit. He got grit in his craw.

*(Jim stumbles back to his seat and sits with his head in his hands.)*

RUBY: I don't give him no credit. Many single girls as it is 'round here he got to take a man's wife away from him. It's low-down!

NUNKIE: *(In mock sympathy)* I know just how you feel, Ruby. Here you was all set to love Spunk yourself and Evalina took and taught him the amendment to love. It's tough! You gets just as hot as jail-house coffee every time you see 'em.

RUBY: I ain't got Spunk and his woman to study 'bout.

WILLIE JOE: Oh yes you is, Ruby. We all see you every afternoon all primped up and sitting out on your steps waiting for Spunk to pass by. Oh yeah, you still loves him.

RUBY: I don't neither.

WILLIE JOE: Oh yeah, you do. But why not take *me*, Ruby? I know I ain't nothing but you could use me till a real man come along. Lawd, that would be swell! Me coming home from work and find you singing all over the house with that pretty voice! 'Course you got that oakobolic hair, but I'd make it a habit to listen to you, baby. I wouldn't rest my love on looking at you.

RUBY: Your head looks like a pepper patch itself so you ain't got no cause to talk about nobody else. Looks like policement on a beat.

WILLIE JOE: All right, let's don't talk about hair, then. Let's talk about something else. How about love?

RUBY: Rock on down the road, Willie Joe. I don't want to talk about no love with you.

WILLIE JOE: What's the matter with me? Nobody didn't tell me but I heard that I'm a mighty sweet man to have around a house.

RUBY: Umph! I hope you ain't trying to call yourself a pimp! That face of yours would handcuff a devil-fish and he got eight arms. (*Laughter*)

WILLIE JOE: Naw, indeed. I make a payday every week. And baby (*exaggerated*) I'm crazy about you. You know it. (*Gesture of pretended affection*) I'll do anything for you except work for you and give you my money. Anything else you just let papa know. I know I ain't no Spunk.

RUBY: (*Shoving him off*) I ain't studying about you and Spunk neither. He ain't nothing.

BLUE TROUT: Oh yes, he is some good, too. He's plenty trouble. Most any man I know would be glad to be in his place. I know I don't fault him atall.

ORAL: Yeah, Spunk's all right! Jim, thought your papa was such a good hoodoo man he could make a crooked road straight? That's what folks been saying 'round here. Your papa worked roots and made Lina marry you. How come he can't work 'em and keep Spunk from biting you in the back? Your papa must be losing his stroke.

MRS. WATSON: I don't believe he ever had none. He just been going 'round here fooling up anybody that would pay him any mind. Making out he know every chinch in China! I don't b'lieve a thing!

WILLIE JOE: (*Fearfully*) Well, I do. I done seen some mighty[17] funny things happen. I know things *can* be done. Spunk better watch out.

ORAL: Maybe things can be done, but I don't b'lieve old man Bishop can do none of it. I useter b'lieve, but since he done talked and prophesied all he was going to do to Spunk and ain't none of it come to pass, I don't b'lieve a thing. I don't even b'lieve that lard is greasy. Let's sing off of it according common meter. I'm going to line it out. Y'all sing! (*[To the] tune of "Get on Board that Ship of Zion, It Has Landed Many a Thousand."*)

Oh, Spunk ain't scared of Bishop's conjure
Oh, Spunk ain't scared of Bishop's conjure
Oh, Spunk ain't scared of Bishop's conjure
He ain't scared, Lawd, he ain't scared.

*(The others join in the spirit of fun. Full harmony.)*

Oh, he done made sweet Lina love him
Oh, he done made sweet Lina love him
Oh, he done made sweet Lina love him
Wish 'twas me, Lawd, wish 'twas me.

NUNKIE: Let me line out a verse, there. One done come to me:

He told me the boss's head a mess, Lawd
Told that boss's head a mess, Lord *(Oh sing it children)*
Oh yes, he told his head a mess, Lawd
Ain't I glad, Lawd, ain't I glad.

MRS. WATSON: *(Smiling)* Ain't they crazy? *(Laughing)* If you all ain't the biggest fools I ever seen!

WILLIE JOE:

What made sweet Lina take and love him
What made sweet Lina take and love him
What made sweet Lina take and love him
Wish I knowed, Lawd, wish I knowed.

JIM: *(Jumps up jerkily)* Whilst you all carrying on like a passle of fools, I'm going out in them woods and bring my wife back.

WILLIE JOE: *(Rising seriously and catching Jim's arm)* Jim, sit down. I wouldn't go out there if I was you.

JIM: Yes, I'm going and I'm going to bring Lina back with me, too. *(Draws a razor from his hip pocket and tests the edge)* And Spunk better not fool with me neither. I done took and took until I'm sick and tired.

ORAL: Spunk got a gun. He always totes one.

JIM: *(Twisting the blade)* Yes, and I got this razor, too. And I got a way to get him. And a firm determination. I'm going out there and he sho God better not gripe me today. *(Dashes off right)* I'm out and gone! *(All look behind him.)*

MRS. WATSON: Why don't some of you men go catch that gump and bring him back?

NUNKIE: Mrs. Watson, you know that fool ain't going out there after Spunk sho 'nough! There have to be some running before that fight come off. *(Laughs)* Yes ma'am! Some darn good running before any fighting between them two. Jim's got a willing mind, but too light behind. He just bluffing us. He'll hide that razor behind the first palmetto bush he come to and sneak back here and lie 'bout all he done. He ought to know that Spunk will kill him if he come drawing any razor on him or Lina.

ORAL: Spunk wouldn't hurt him, I don't believe. I done seen him pass up the chance to fight two or three runts like Jim. If he push him, Spunk might cut a switch and whip his can for him, but he wouldn't knock him around with his fist.

WILLIE JOE: (*Gloomily*) I don't know, now. Remember he ain't 'round the sawmill. He's off with Evalina. A man don't take much when he's 'round women folks that he prize. I wouldn't push him, if 'twas me. (*Pause*) I wonder what make him think he can out-do Spunk?

ADMIRAL: Maybe he's peeping through his liquor. His whiskey told him to go fight and he's gone.

RUBY: Aw naw, he ain't drunk, neither! You all drove him to that with your cutting capers and carrying on. You ain't got no sense, none of you.

MRS. WATSON: (*Looking off left*) Ain't that Jim's papa coming yonder?

RUBY: Yes, ma'am. It sure is. I'm glad, too.

(*Enter Hodge Bishop.*)

BISHOP: Good evening everybody.

MRS. WATSON: I'm mighty glad that you come along, Mr. Bishop. Jim is gone behind Spunk and Lina with a razor. Says he's going to fetch Lina and get Spunk. You ought to stop him. Maybe he will listen to *you*.

BISHOP: (*Shortly*) Naw, I wouldn't move out of my tracks to stop him from killing that Spunk. Jim's got *my* wisdom teeth in him. That's what he ought to have done six months ago. No jury in the world would convict a man for protecting his home. Let him kill the varmint. Loping up and down the road, taking off folkses wives.

MRS. WATSON: *Your* wisdom teeth! Humph. Some folks is just like a possum — the older they get the less sense they got. If anybody got sense to see you won't pay no attention to that laugh of Spunk's. He's a man that gives 'em hard and stops 'em short. Youse better go call that son of yours.

NUNKIE: Why, you told me long time ago that you was protecting Jim's home with roots. It must not have worked 'cause Spunk got the girl, the best job 'round here and done gone to house-keeping. Your conjure must be getting all beat up. You ain't no trouble *atall*.

BISHOP: I got him set for still bait. I'm just waiting for a certain thing to come about, then I'll make him gimme a back view. I'm slow walking him down. (*Murmur of disbelief.*)

ORAL: Sing it boys!

It may be so, but I'm 'bliged to doubt it
It may be so, but I'm 'bliged to doubt it

Oh it may be so, but I'm 'bliged to doubt it
Sounds like a lie, Lord, just like a lie.

*(They pretend to shout, talk the unknown tongues and grow boisterous. Shouting "Peace," "Thank you, Father," and "It's truly wonderful." There is the report of a gun, and everyone stops still and listens for a moment. Ruby shudders and begins to sob quietly.)*

WILLIE JOE: Gosh a'mighty! You reckon anything done come off? I feel like I'm running in my skin.

NUNKIE: Come on, Oral and Admiral. Less we go see.

ADMIRAL: *(Timidly)* We don't have to run see, do we? We'll get there quick enough walking.

*(They start off hesitantly. Before they can get off there is the sound of sobbing approaching. In a minute Spunk enters with Evalina sobbing beside him. Everybody stares and he stands there a moment before he speaks.)*

SPUNK: Well, that creeping cat come out there and made me kill him. *(He whirls and shows his back.)* See where he cut my clothes? Yeah, instead of coming to my face if he wanted to fight and fight me like man, naw, he got down on his hands and knees and crawled up behind the log where we was setting and tried to cut me in the back. So before I could think, I wheeled and shot him, so he's dead. Somebody better go get him and bury him. I never meant to kill him, though. He made me do it.

*(Oral, Nunkie and Admiral bolt off right. Hodge Bishop crouches and comes close to Spunk from the rear.)*

WILLIE JOE: Jim was just naturally death struck. I tried to get him not to go out there. Well, I reckon we better swear ourselves in, kind of deputize ourselves, and form a posse to place Spunk under arrest and turn him over to the high sheriff.

SPUNK: *(Angrily)* If anybody puts their hands on me, just like God sent me a pistol I'll send him a man! That's the reason I always tried to stay out of trouble—so nobody wouldn't be tying me up like I was some cow! I'll go on over and tell the white folks what I done and how come I done it and everybody can come testify. But don't touch me.

*(He puts his arms about Evalina and they walk downstage center. Hodge creeps after him threateningly.)*

Lina, don't cry like that. I'm not gone for good. I ain't done no hanging crime. I'll be back sometime. Maybe not very long. And no matter what come, I'll be back. Even if they was to kill me, in twenty minutes after I was dead my spirit would be in the house with you. Go home, honey. You know where everything is. *(Takes his guitar from around his neck and places it on hers.)* You know next to you I love my box. Take good care of it and come see me as much as they let you. Oh God, I wish I didn't have to go! Go on home, now, before I move out my tracks.

*(He kisses her and watches her exit left. Then he glances around and sees Hodge gesturing behind him and wheels to defend himself. As he does so, Hodge retreats, snarling. As soon as Spunk turns to walk off right, he rushes up behind him again.)*

HODGE: Took my son's wife and then kill him like a dog! I curse you! I put bad mouth on you!

*(Spunk turns and glares and Hodge retreats in fear to a safe distance. As Spunk turns, left, he rushes up behind him again.)*

I point my dog-finger at you!

*(Spunk turns and he is so close that Hodge thinks Spunk has seized him. He almost falls in fright.)*

I'm picking up your track! Ah *(gloatingly)* now I got you in the go-long. I put bad mouth on you!

*(Each movement takes Spunk closer to left exit, until finally he goes off with old Hodge following after with his right arm pointed menacingly. [He] stoops and takes sand out of Spunk's track and straightens up gloating and full of malice and hate.)*

You won't never get out of this! I done put my mark on you! The white folks will hang you! I got you now and I'm going to throw you away! I'm going to nail you up in a tree! You'll die!!

*(Curtain.)*

## Scene 2

*Action: At the rise about a dozen convicts are working on the highway in their stripes. The guard with a rifle in his arms walks slowly back and forth. The men are singing.*

CHAIN GANG:

Please don't drive me because I'm blind
B'lieve I can make it if I take my time
Lift up the hammer and let it fall down
It's a hard rocky bottom and it must be found.

CAPTAIN HAMMER: Can't you all find nothing to sing besides that damn mournful tune?

*(All look from one to the other but say nothing, except Spunk who is work-ing near center. He pauses and rests on his shovel.)*

SPUNK: I could sing plenty more if I had my guitar here with me. But I ain't. Left it with my wife. Didn't know what was liable to happen and I want it taken good care of.

CAPTAIN HAMMER: You reckon she'll do it?

SPUNK: Why certainly! She'll do just what I say, no matter what it is. I'm sure glad I ain't got to be away from her but thirty more days. *(Pauses a mo-ment and thinks.)* Cap'n, is you got a cigarette you could gimme? I don't know how come Evalina didn't come bring me some yesterday. It was vis-iting day. She must be sick or something.

CAPTAIN HAMMER: *(Pulls out a pack and hands it to Spunk. Looks at other con-victs and scowls)* Hey, you bastards, get to work! What the hell you two doing whispering? Get away from one 'nother! *(He fingers his rifle sug-gestively.)* Here's[18] a match, Spunk. I don't mind obliging you atall. You been a good prisoner. Ain't gimme one mite of trouble the two months you been here.

SPUNK: *(Lighting cigarette and returning pack to guard)* I ain't come here for no trouble. I wants to get through with this the quickest way possible and get back home. I ain't no conzempt! This the first time I ever been on a gang and I wouldn't be here now if that Jim hadn't of tried to kill me with a razor. *(Sadly)* I just don't know how come Lina never come to see me yesterday. She know she can't see me but once a month and look like she wouldn't miss. *(Begins to work hard and hum. Then sings. Others join.)*[19]

Got on the train didn't have no fare
But I rode some, I rode some
Got on the train, didn't have no fare
But I rode some, I rode some
Got on the train, didn't have no fare
Conductor asked me what I'm doing there
But I rode some, I rode some.

*(Men begin to get in a happier mood.)*

Well, he grabbed me by the hand and he led me to the door
But I rode some, I rode some
He grabbed me by the hand and he led me to the door
Hit me over the head with a forty-four
But I rode some, I rode some.

*(Everybody begins to laugh, even the guard. Spunk stops abruptly and stands brooding.)*

Look like she could have sent me some kind of a word if she didn't come herself. *(Begins to hum and sing again.)*

All day long, you heard me moan, don't tell my cap'n which way I gone
I'm going to loose this right hand shackle from 'round my leg

*(Others join and harmonize.)*

Cap'n, Cap'n, can't you see, this work you got is killing of me.
I'm going [to] loose this right hand shackle from 'round my leg.

*(Spunk wipes his brow and laughs.)*

Lord, Lord, Lord! Where'll I be thirty days from now? Oh sitting up beside Evalina! Lord, Lord!

CONVICT: If some other man ain't done tee-rolled you with her. Ha! Ha! Maybe it's another mule kicking in your stall.

*(Spunk goes cloudy and his chest begins to swell slowly as he glares coldly and fixed until his chest has reached its limit.)*

SPUNK: Now you done got me just as hot as the alligator when the pond went dry. You son of a conbunction! Evalina's name don't come in your conversation. When I call her name out here I'm talking to myself. Now you just crack *one more* time and you're going to make a *bad* nigger out of me. *(He tenses his muscles ominously.)*

CAPTAIN HAMMER: Nixon! You leave Spunk be! Work more and talk less. *(Gently)* Here, take another smoke, Spunk.

*(Spunk is fumbling a cigarette out while Captain Hammer holds the pack. Suddenly he thrusts the pack into Spunk's hand and starts walking left rapidly. Spunk turns and sees Willie Joe walking through the gang staring at each prisoner as if he is searching for someone. Captain Hammer gets his rifle ready to fire as he crosses.)*

Halt there! Hey, stray nigger, what you doing 'round here?

WILLIE JOE: *(Lifts both hands in the air trembling. He has a letter in one hand.)* Ah just come here to bring Spunk a letter. Yessuh, somebody done sent me with it.

CAPTAIN HAMMER: Why didn't you take it to camp and leave it? Fetch it here! *(Willie Joe advances.)* Know this nigger, Spunk?

SPUNK: Yessir, Cap'n. I know him well.

*(His eyes burn with eagerness as he fixes them on the letter. Captain Hammer feels it for any concealed object and reaches it towards Spunk.)*

CAPTAIN HAMMER: Now the next time anybody send you with a letter, you take it where it belongs.

WILLIE JOE: Yessir, Cap'n. I sure will. *(To Spunk)* I reckon I won't wait 'round for no answer. I'll tell 'em you can write later. *(He hurries off left, looking back fearful of being shot. )*

SPUNK: Cap'n, can I glance through it, please sir?

CAPTAIN HAMMER: *(Starts to refuse, but softens a bit. Spits tobacco juice and nods his head yes.)* I reckon so, Spunk, since youse a trusty. *( He glares at the others to maintain discipline. )*

SPUNK: *(Reads. Others sing a verse of song and work hard.)* Cap'n, I got to go. This letter come to me and it's telling a lie, Cap'n Hammer. I got to go.

CAPTAIN HAMMER: Spunk, is you gone crazy? You know you got twenty-nine more days to make. You can't leave the camp, and you know damn well you can't.

*(Other convicts work in listening pose.)*

SPUNK: *(As if he has not heard)* Cap'n, I got to go. *(Looks up at sun)* I'll be there by black dark. She say in the letter she done give me up. I got to go. *(Racks his tools beside the road)* Says she's never to be with me no more. I got a letter and it done told a lie. I got to go.

CAPTAIN HAMMER: Spunk! Grab up them tools and git to work! I'll kill you!

*(The others, sensing trouble, work furiously, looking fearfully over their shoulders at the guard.)*

SPUNK: *(Hitches up his pants and looks off left)* I'd rather to be dead than to be like this. *(Turns left)* You'll just have to kill me, Cap'n Hammer, 'cause I'm going. It's on the bill and it's got to be filled. I aim to go in the flesh, but if I don't make it I'll be there in the spirit. Bye, Cap'n.

*(He starts striding heedless towards the left. The others divide fearfully to let him pass.)*

CAPTAIN HAMMER: Halt there! I'll shoot you down! *(Softer)* Spunk! You Spunk! I hate to kill you!

*(Spunk never looks back. The others fall down fearful of being hit by stray bullets. As he reaches the exit the gun fires three times rapidly but Spunk strides off.)*

Missed him, dammit to hell! He's got clean away! *(Turns fiercely upon the others.)* Get up off that ground you damn dog-meat, you! Grab them tools. I'll shoot you just to see you jump.

SPUNK: (*Singing mournfully in the distance*)

> She used to rock me, rock me in the cradle by the window
> Rock me, rock me, Lord, rock me in the cradle by the window
> Poor gal, don't do it now, poor gal (*hums mournfully*)

> She used to put them sweet magnolias in my hat band
> She used to put them sweet magnolias in my hat band
> Hibiscus too, Lord, Lord, hibiscus too.

> I got a rainbow, wrapped and tied around my shoulder
> I got a rainbow, wrapped and tied around my shoulder
> It ain't going rain, Lord, Lord, it ain't going rain!

(*Mournful hum. Curtain.*)

## Scene 3

*Setting: Night time. At extreme left is the front of Ruby's house with practical door and steps. A wooden window stands wide open revealing an oilcloth-covered table, a wood-burning cook-stove. Bright little fixings about the place. A china-berry tree at left of house. At extreme right is Evalina's house beneath a magnolia tree at left. A white picket fence. Window beneath the tree with low-hanging limb across the window. The wooden shutter stands open. A light inside. Street is downstage before both houses.*

*Action: At the rise, Ruby is puttering around between the stove and table. Evalina sits by her window with Spunk's guitar in her lap. She touches it now and then and sings. Ruby listens and hums an obligato above Evalina's chorus.*

EVALINA:[20]

> Love come my way, stayed but a day
> Went and left me crying like a child
> It left me feeling sad, left me feeling bad
> Maybe things will straighten after while

> (*Chorus*)
> I'm going down the long lonesome road, oh
> I'm going down the long lonesome road
> I'm going down that long, lonesome road

> (*Sobbingly*)
> Oh weep like a willow, mourn just like a dove
> Weep like a willow, mourn just like a dove
> Oh, fly to the mountain, light on the man I love.

> All my dreams is dead, things ain't like he said
> I been leaning on a broken reed

He never meant to stay, just stopped by for a day
On his string of life I'm just a bead.

*(Chorus)*
I'll see you when your troubles get like mine, oh
I'll see you when your troubles get like me
I'll see you when your heart is broke like mine.

*(She sits there a moment touching the strings absent-mindedly. Enter Spunk left and crosses rapidly. He steps over the fence and rushes to the window. Evalina starts up.)*

EVALINA: Spunk!! What you doing here?

SPUNK: *(Reaching through the window to touch her)* A letter come. It had your writing on it and it said you was never to look for me back no more.

EVALINA: *(Scared)* Spunk, you done broke gang!

SPUNK: It ain't broke. I just left to see 'bout you. You done got religion like you say in the letter and done promised everybody to keep 'way from me?

EVALINA: *(Quietly)* Yeah, Spunk. They done prayed with me and laid me under conviction of my sins. They showed me that my sins done got Jim killed and you on the gang. It's time for me to turn. I want to live clean.

SPUNK: I never felt no dirtiness being with you. I didn't know you felt that way 'bout me. So you done promised, huh?

EVALINA: Yeah, Spunk. They all done made me see. *(There is a long silence. Spunk hangs his head.)* Your guitar is right here, Spunk. I took good care of it like you said. *(She hands it to him and he takes it slowly)* Hold up your head. You won't miss me long. Ain't that what you say?

SPUNK: You doing the talking, Lina. I'm struck dumb. Guess I better jolt on down the road.

*(He walks slowly out of the gate. She leans out of her window hungrily.)*

EVALINA: Better come in and hide yourself from the white folks, Spunk.

SPUNK: Oh, let 'em get me! I'm guilty!

*(He walks slowly towards left. Ruby steps out of the door and stands before him.)*

RUBY: Hello, Spunk! Where you bound for?

SPUNK: Oh, just trucking on down the road. God knows.

RUBY: *(Seizing his arm)* You can't go 'way from here like that. Mama got shrimp with okra and tomatoes! Dry rice, too. You got to come eat some. Come on now, big doll-baby.

*(He lets himself be carried inside and sits by the stove and rears back in a chair gloomily.)*

RUBY: *(Standing before him)* Take all them knots out your face. You got friends a-plenty. Where one door is closed, there's a thousand open. *(Calls loudly)* Mama! Come look who's here! *(To Spunk)* You big, old good-looking thing, you! Play me something on that box whilst I put the supper on the table.

SPUNK: I don't feel to play. *(Begins to tune)* But I reckon I will a little. Songs make themselves up in you and then you have to sing 'em. They got to come outside. *(Strums)* Never can tell what's going to come out. *(Strums)* Sometimes they got light with a brightness, but sometimes they sad. You could wring tears out of 'em. *(Laughs bitterly)* Maybe I been sleep-walking and just woke up.

RUBY: Sing, Spunk, but don't sing nothing sad. I hates blues!

SPUNK: How can I tell what I'm going to sing? We got the power to open our mouth, but God gives us our words.

RUBY: Play something you already know. Like that pretty song you played sitting in the boat at the toe-party that night.

SPUNK: *(Shakes his head sadly)* Wisht I could, Ruby. But I ain't the same man. To myself I looked like the king of the world that night. Now I'm 'round here looking like the figure of fun. I was in my element that night. A fish loves to swim in water, but he's dead when he's swimming in grease.

*(Begins to improvise. Strikes a definite tune.*[21] *Evalina listens hard.)*

RUBY: Play it, papa, play it! You got the business and you know it!

*(She cuts a caper or two. He begins to sing. Ruby senses the song is not for her and gets quiet. Evalina closes the window. Opens it again. Goes to the door and comes outdoors and creeps to Ruby's window. Ruby is sitting on the arm of the chair and puts her arm about Spunk's shoulders. He sings. Finally she pats his cheek.)*

EVALINA: Spunk!

*(She yells his name and runs home and takes her same seat at the window. Spunk jumps when he hears his name and looks all about him.)*

SPUNK: Look like I heard Evalina call my name.

RUBY: What would she be calling you for? She done stood up in church and told everybody she was through with you. Say she aims to live free from all sin till she die.

SPUNK: *(Crossing to door)* So she figger it's a sin to be with me, huh? I didn't know that. *(A short pause)* Still, she called me.

RUBY: *(Clings to his hand)* Nobody ain't called you, Spunk. Maybe it's a ghost. You better not answer. If you do you'll die soon.

SPUNK: *(Dragging Ruby as he goes)* Lina called me. And if she didn't her spirit did. I got to go and see. Loose me.

RUBY: *(Still clinging)* Aw, Spunk, stay here and get treated right. Somebody done told her you got a wife and child somewhere 'round Bartow and she b'lieves it. She don't want you no more. With anybody else I'd say the same thing myself, but with you I don't care. Don't go, Spunk. Hear?

SPUNK: *(Standing in the door. Pushes Ruby off.)* I couldn't have been mistook. She called me. *(He leaps the fence and rushes to the window.)* What you want with me, Lina? You called me.

EVALINA: What make you think I called you, Spunk?

SPUNK: 'Cause I heard you. And if your mouth was too stiff to say my name, your spirit called me. I heard it.

EVALINA: Maybe it was your wife and children down in Bartow calling you home.

SPUNK: Who told you that lie, Lina?

EVALINA: It wasn't told to me, but I heard it.

SPUNK: I swear to God that's a lie, Lina. A great big old Georgia lie. What you reckon I come back for if it wasn't 'cause I love you?

EVALINA: Oh, some comes for a reason and some comes for a season.

SPUNK: *(Shortly)* The capacity of your vocabulary ain't nothing but saw-dust, Lina. Stop talking foolishness. I swear I love you.

EVALINA: Don't swear to a lie, Spunk. That makes everything even worser than it is already.

SPUNK: I ain't never told you a lie, Lina. Why you doubt my word now?

EVALINA: First old man Bishop come told me that he met somebody from Bartow and they told him you had a family there you had done walked off and left. So I told him to get out of my face with his lies. Then somebody wrote me a letter with no name signed to it and told me the same thing. Then a man come hunting you. A strange man. Said he was right from there and come to take you home to your wife. He was asking everybody where you was so somebody pointed me out and he come here asking. Said you had a habit of going off like that to spend a while but you always come home whenever your wife sent for you. Said he had your railroad fare in his pocket. So then I told him where you was so he thanked me and left to go out there where you was. Didn't he come?

SPUNK: Je-sus! What a lie! Ain't no man been to see me 'cepting these boys from here. That's some of Old Hodge Bishop's doings. He still trying to hurt me. So that why you quit me, honey? Lawd, Lawd, it's just like the old folks say, "You can't make buckling tongues meet."

EVALINA: Yes. You see I worried and fretted a heap. I said I would just wait and see. Then the waiting got to be too tiresome for me. Waiting for you to come when maybe you'd be in Bartow done forgot all about me. It got to the place where I had done tasted all the food in the world. So I wasn't hungry no more. I didn't need no more sleep or nothing. I told myself it would be easier to quit waiting then it would be to wait for nothing. So I told 'em all I had done give you up. So they prayed over me and I joined the church Sunday and wrote you about it.

SPUNK: So the fight between me and them Bishops ain't over yet! And they all alike—underhand. He knowed that parting us would hurt me worse'n anything he could do, so he went to work and done it. I wished he had of killed me. Done experienced everything I hate to make my love come out right and love done throwed me down.

EVALINA: Hurry up and tell me, Spunk, if you got that wife or not.

SPUNK: What you want to know that for? You don't want me no more.

EVALINA: *(Bantering)* Maybe I don't, but you see the waves a long time after the ship done passed. Maybe I want to know just for old time's sake.

SPUNK: What you trying to do—put the hot-box to my head? You got me like a stepped-on worm. Half dead but still trying to crawl.

EVALINA: I done throwed up a highway in the wilderness for you to walk on. Answer me what I asked you.

SPUNK: I'll tell you with a parable, Lina. You know God got a long rail fence in Heaven, made out of gold. And when He makes the people out of clay He stand 'em up against that fence to dry. And when they's good and dry, He blows the breath of life in 'em and turns 'em go. Lina, soon as God breathed on me I knowed I was lonesome and I knowed you was somewhere looking for me. So I come straight from God's drying fence to you. I might have stumbled 'round examining a few girl babies to find out if it was you. But I am never even breathed marriage to no other woman in my life.

*(Evalina drops her head and sits silent.)*

I hope you did call me, Evalina. I needs calling. Ring the bells of mercy and call the sinner man home.

(*Evalina leans out of the window and breaks a bloom from the magnolia tree and sticks it in his hat-band. Then draws back shyly.*)

Move that chair out the way, Lina.

(*She moves the chair. He steps through the window and closes it behind him. There is the baying of bloodhounds in the distance. Curtain.*)

### ACT THREE
#### Scene 1

*Setting: Croquet court.*

    *Action: A game is in progress. It is late afternoon and all the young folks are out. Some playing, some sitting around. Enter Mrs. Watson, left, fanning with a palm leaf fan.*

DAISY: I know you want to play, Mrs. Watson. You can take my hand.

MRS. WATSON: Naw, indeed! All I want to do is get off my feet. (*Pulls off shoes as she sits.*) My feet so sore from so much standing I don't feel like I can wear nothing on 'em but a pillow-slip. The mess you all made at my house last night worked me nearly to death to get cleaned up. But wasn't that a reception, though? Old Spunk and Lina looked good on that floor! And when the preacher pronounced 'em man and wife I thought he would knock her down kissing her. (*Laughs*)

DAISY: I know she was tickled to death to get him. But I can't see what she go and have a big wedding for and everybody know how it come about.

MRS. WATSON: That's their own business. If they want to brag off of they feelings let 'em do it. They ain't trying to hide nothing. At least they know what they getting married for and that's more'n a lot of other folks know.

DAISY: Wonder how come they didn't take him back to the chain gang to finish out his time?

WILLIE JOE: 'Cause his boss talked to the high sheriff over the 'phone and told the sheriff he need Spunk in the mill so he could meet his contract to some lumber. Sheriff come on over to the mill and him and Wilkins set in the office and drunk liquor and laughed and talked. He wasn't arrested for killing Jim, nohow. That was self-defense. They give him them ninety days for toting a gun.

NUNKIE: He sure got off light. Kill a man, they give him ninety days and he don't even serve that out. He must be got roots.

MRS. WATSON: Aw naw! He didn't kill no white man, did he? The white folks don't care nothing 'bout one nigger killing another one. And then again Spunk is a good worker and Jim was lazy. So they figger they don't even miss him. *(Big laugh)*

NUNKIE: Yeah, they 'bout figger that Spunk saved them the trouble of killing him theirselves. *(More laughter)*

WILLIE JOE: Yeah man, the boss called Spunk into the office to talk with the sheriff. Know what he say? Says, "Well, Spunk, the country is running short of groceries so you'll have to get off the gang and go working for yourself." Then he laughed, one of them big blow-out laughs, and told Spunk not to give the boss no trouble.

ORAL: And to tell you the truth, white folks don't care nothing 'bout our moral doings. If you work good and don't give 'em no trouble youse a good nigger and they like you. Otherwise they don't give a damn. And you all know that the God's truth. So don't heat up your gums and lie. *(Laughter)* Naturally his old man feels bad 'bout Jim.

WILLIE JOE: Naturally. *(Looks at his watch)* Spunk and Lina is late today for their stroll.

MRS. WATSON: Late? They don't just have to get here no special time, do they? What you rushing 'em for? They looks just the same as ever.

WILLIE JOE: Oh, I just want to see and hear what new song he made up for today, being he makes a new one nearly every day. *(To Admiral)* Let's set up a *good* game of croquet. Me and Nunkie will play you and Oral. Let's go.

*(All rise. There is a heavy chord on the box and Spunk and Evalina enter. She carries a guitar made out of a cigar box. Both are beaming.)*

Hey Spunk! What you say? What you say? What is it today?

SPUNK: *(Beaming)* It's about the family this time. Me and Evalina and our baby boy.

MRS. WATSON: Where you all get any baby boy from? I ain't seen none.

SPUNK: Us got married last night, didn't we? It won't be long now. I done gone to fixing for him.

ORAL: What that you got in your hand, Lina?

EVALINA: *(Laughing)* That's the baby's guitar.

ORAL: The *baby's* guitar!

SPUNK: Yeah, man. I made it at the mill today. I'm not going to let my son sit up in the cradle and ask his daddy "Papa, how you let me come in this world without no instrument to play on?" So I done made it already. Man, by the time he's ten years old I'd be[22] shame to play in front of him. And what make it so cool, he's going to look just like me.

MRS. WATSON: How you know that, Spunk? It's liable to take after Lina or some of her folks or some of yours. You never can tell.

SPUNK: Oh no! My first baby got to favor *me*. She can mold some of the others to favor our kinfolks, but that first one got to be the very spit of me.

(*Plays and sings "Evalina."*[23] *All join in chorus.*)

Yeah man, that boy of mine is going to be a whip!

EVALINA: (*Seriously*) If nobody don't do nothing to him.

SPUNK: Nobody better not do nothing to our son and stay on this earth. I'll run 'em as slick as a meat-skin.

EVALINA: They might not come out bold. Some folks takes undercurrents. Throw at you and hide they hand.

SPUNK: You talking about old man Bishop? I done told you ain't nothing to him.

EVALINA: (*Generally*) You know Spunk don't believe in nothing. He don't b'lieve folks can hurt you.

SPUNK: I b'lieve they can hurt me if they get something in my stomach and cut me or shoot me. But burying things for me to step over and things like that, naw! You cooks for me so he can't put no spider in my dumpling. I keep my eye on him 'round the mill so he can't steal me with a knife or a gun. And I watch them logs he loads on the carriage so he can't trick none to throw me on that saw. So what is it to worry about?

EVALINA: Still and all things can be done, can't they? (*Makes a general appeal.*)

WILLIE JOE: I know they can. I done seen things happen. Plenty things. I seen a hoodoo doctor up in Georgia put a man to barking like a dog.

SPUNK: Well, if these hoodoo doctors can do so much why don't they conjure these white folks and get hold of some money and some power? Why don't they hoodoo the bank? How come they don't put a spell on the jail house and keep colored folks out of it? These white folks is raw-hide to their backs and they 'round here throwing hoodoo at each other! Ain't nothing to 'em. Let me catch Old Bishop 'round my house and I'll let him hoodoo all he wants to while I run a railroad 'round he neck. He's abstifically a humbug! But I just got married so I feel like treating. *Every*body have something on me. Talk fast. (*There is a general clamor for various soft drinks, gum and cigarettes.*) Come on, Oral, and help me tote it. (*He exits right with Oral.*)

EVALINA: Spunk would get hurt if I listened to him. But I done sent down to Lakeland to that doctor down there. He's supposed to be better than Dr. Buzzard. He say anything Old Bishop try to do to Spunk, he'll throw it back on him.

MRS. WATSON: And, honey, he can do it, too. I know him. He has worked for me. He's good. He works with rattle-snakes. And you know the spirit they represent lives under God's foot-rest. 'Tain't nothing more powerful than that. Did he give you anything to keep in the house[?]

EVALINA: Yes. Some special dressed mustard seed. I told him about something like a cat coming in our bedroom every night. He give me some mustard seed to sprinkle by the door. If anybody get out of their skins to come through our keyhole he'll salt their hides. They'll never get back in it no more. They'll die.

(*She halts in fright. Enter Bishop, left. Stares about him and approaches Mrs. Watson.*)

MRS. WATSON: Howd'do, Brother Bishop?

BISHOP: I ain't none of your brother. Your brother is out hunting coconuts. I'm going to have you up in church and see can't they handle you.

MRS. WATSON: What for?

BISHOP: You know what for. Letting murdering infidels marry in your parlor and then you holding a reception for 'em! The church ought to handle you. I'm going to have you up.

MRS. WATSON: You grass-gut goat, you! I begged you to stop your son from tackling Spunk with that razor. You said leave him alone. Now don't come blaming me.

(*Enter Spunk and Oral, loaded down but running*)

SPUNK: Hey, folks! My lumber done come! Going to build us a new house under the magnolia tree. Made arrangements to get it yesterday and now the boss done sent it. Y'all drink! Come on, Evalina! Less me and you walk this off!

(*He drops the packages and crosses to Evalina in high spirits. All but bumps into Bishop. Looks grim as their eyes meet. And starts right with Evalina.*)

NUNKIE: (*Clapping*) Hey Spunk, you and Lina do the short walk.

*(Others clap. Spunk squats down, takes Evalina's hand and she leads him off in a rhythmic waddle that makes the others laugh.)*

MRS. WATSON: Bishop, Spunk ought to pay you good for working for him. Heh! Heh! You *say* you working against him, but look like you gives him the best of luck. Heh! Heh!

BISHOP: I ain't worked against him yet. I just been letting nature take its course but before long I mean to raise hell and put a chunk under it.

ORAL: That ain't what you said. You told us the *very* night that Spunk met Lina at the toe-party that you had done put travel-dust down for him and he couldn't stay here more'n three days. It's nearly a year now.

BISHOP: Oh, that's all right, it will get him to go. You just watch.

NUNKIE: Yeah, and you said you had done dressed that saw to kill him and that ain't happened, neither. He's making *good* money at it.

BISHOP: Oh 'tain't too late. Ten years ain't too long for a condor to wear a stiff bosom shirt.

*(Razzing noise)*

MRS. WATSON: And you put out your brags that he was going to be hung 'bout that shooting and look what happened! Sixty days. And come home, got his old job back and done married Lina and now building a brand new house. You sure have put him on the ladder. *(Laughter)* If you keep on working at him like you is we'll soon have a jig governor of Florida. *(Laughter)* You make out youse Old Man Jump-off. Make out you can peep through muddy water and see dry land.

ORAL: Thought you said that Spunk was going to die on the chain gang? Thought you said you had done parted him to Lina. You ain't no trouble! Just heating up your gums for nothing. Done made a big mess then fell in it. *(Laughter)* Hope it don't give you the protolapsis of the cutinary lining.

BISHOP: *(Angrily awesome)* That's right! Laugh, fools and show your ignorance! I ain't done nothing yet 'cause I ain't tried nothing yet. Not nothing serious. And how come I didn't? 'Cause the right elements ain't come together. I works with cats, the most powerful thing in God's world. So the cat-bone told me to wait. It's been hard, but I done waited. Now the cat-bone says next Friday night is my time. Then the seventeen quarters of the spirit will meet in the upper air. I'll meet 'em! *(They begin to be awed)* The black cat-bone will take the throne in power! I'm going to show you that ugly laugh. *(He exits in trembling anger. The others watch him go in awe. Curtain.)*

## Scene 2

*[Hurston's note:] Conjure scene can not be fully put on paper. Must be done in direction.*

*Time: One a.m. Friday.*
*Place: Hodge Bishop's altar room.*

*Setting: It is a small room with rafters and joists showing. There is a big altar upstage right. A small one in the corner, upstage left. Entrance, rude door, downstage left. Fastens with a bar. Altar set for a death ceremony. Ceremonial objects about the room.*

*Action: At the rise, six men, dressed in cat robes, stand around the pea-vine emblem on the floor. They stand silent and tense. Hands to the sides. Bishop is before the altar lighting the "earth candle" and the incense. He takes six blue candles from the altar and gives one to each of the men. They hold the candles in the left hand. Bishop returns to the altar and takes up a doll on it that is bound hand and foot and places it in the power spot. Takes a large black candle and lights it from the earth candle and begins to dance towards the first man. They join right hands and dance a step around each other. Bishop lights the man's candle from his and dances on to the next one and so on until all are burning. Then he dances back to the altar via the pea-vine and assaults the doll and cries out.*[24]

BISHOP: Death! Follow this man! Follow this Spunk. Take his body and his footsteps off the earth.

*(The men cry out like great angry cats. Bishop pours whiskey out before Death.)*

I'm paying you to follow that man!

*(They all cry out again. Bishop deposits a nickel and cries again and the others answer. He dances down the pea-vine with the others growling and snarling and dances back to the altar, more excited this time.)*

The great cat! Born of the cat! I ask you to follow this man.

*(Same business as before. He dances down the pea-vine once again. This time the tempo is increased. When he returns to the altar he beats and stabs the doll violently with the cat-men crying and snarling.)*

He is not to the north for we have been there
He is not to the south for we have searched there
He is not to the east for we have looked well.
So we hurry to the west for we shall find him.

*(There is a wild burst of gloating, crying, dancing.)*

Bring in the winds!

*(They make the gesture of sweeping the four winds in to the altar. They drop the cat robes and stand nude and shining black. They dance fiercely. Hodge takes the black cat-bone from the altar and places it in his mouth. The dance continues. They all rub him violently for a moment with their hands until he trembles violently, then leaps away in terror as far as possible. Bishop begins to writhe and his black skin begins to split at the top of his head.)*

CAT-MEN: Slip 'em and slip 'em again!

BISHOP: *(The skin peels down to the neck.)* Cat men! Guard my skin! Cat men! Guard my skin from evil.

CAT-MEN: It shall be protected from pepper and salt!

*(The black skin peels on down slowly and Bishop stands dripping blood as he steps out of his skin and picks it up and stretches it before the altar. That done, he creeps downstage center and glares all about him.)*

BISHOP: *(In a thundering voice)* Where is my saddle cat?

*(There is a great cat-call and the shadow of a huge bristling cat is seen on the back wall. Bishop makes to mount it. There is a great wail of cats. Darkness. Curtain.)*

Scene 3

*Setting: Street scene [from act 2, scene 3]. Late afternoon. Many homey flowers around both houses. A pile of new lumber beneath the magnolia tree. Evalina sits at her window humming and braiding her hair. She dresses it attractively and looks at herself well in the mirror. Ruby in a clean wash dress enters and sits on her steps but turns her back to Evalina pointedly. Evalina laughs and humming, comes outside to cut a red hibiscus bloom which she fixes in her hair and walks to the gate and leans over. Enter Mrs. Watson, right, [who] stops at Evalina's gate.*

EVALINA: How do you do, Mrs. Watson? You looking fine.

MRS. WATSON: Oh, so-so. Waiting for that husband, eh?

EVALINA: Oh, I just come out this minute. You know I got to have a flower to wear. Where you headed for?

MRS. WATSON: Right here. I want some flowers for my sitting room. I'm expecting company from way off. Presiding Elder.

EVALINA: *(Opens gate)* Come in. Get all you want of what you see. *(She enters and begins to pick flowers leisurely)* I'd pick 'em for you but I'm too busy looking up the road for my husband. *(Laughs)* That first glimpse is always so nice. Sort of like day-break. You know it's coming but it gives you a glad surprise every time. It's funny, ain't it?

MRS. WATSON: Oh, I reckon so. I done got past all that. Sometimes my husband come home and get in the bed with me and I don't know it till I wake up next morning.

EVALINA: You know, I'm worried 'bout Spunk. He makes good money and the boss is good to him, but I wish he'd quit that job. Old Bishop is working against him and he ain't never going to stop till Spunk is dead. I woke up screaming last night. Look like a great big tiger cat was springing on us in the bed.

MRS. WATSON: Do, Jesus! Umph! Umph! Umph!

EVALINA: Yes, honey, there was the howling and the growling of cats 'round this house last night from midnight till nearly daybreak when that big cat something jumped at us in the bed. But somehow it halted right in the air over us and vanished. *(Tearfully)* I want to leave here! That's why I haven't let Spunk start on the new house. I want us to go.

MRS. WATSON: Why don't you tell him, honey?

EVALINA: I done told him but he won't listen. He says he'll he a well-off man in five years if he keep on like he's going. But I'm afraid he won't be alive by then. He ain't got it to study about. It's me. *(They sit on the front steps.)* And today I can't sit nowhere in peace. Not after that dream I had. It still seem too plain for a dream.

MRS. WATSON: Oh, they say Friday night, dark of the moon, is the time for dreams and visions. Some say that whatever you see then is true. I don't know. *(More cheerfully)* What you got good for supper?

EVALINA: Spare-ribs and Hopping John.[25] It's seasoned down, too. Don't you want some of it?

MRS. WATSON: *(Laughs)* Lord, naw! I got the same thing. My husband buys five pounds of black-eye peas every Saturday. Only I got bacon instead of spare-ribs. *(Look of listening)*

EVALINA: *(Half rising in alarm)* Sounds like I hear some singing at a distance. *(She listens intensely.)* Songs and crying mixed.

*(Waits listening. Ruby rises and moves about restlessly like an animal sensing danger.)*

MRS. WATSON: *(Wide-eyed in apprehension)* Reckon I better get along home. Go inside, Lina, and set down. *(She coaxes Evalina to her gate tenderly. Then moves to left exit.)* I better go see. *(Exits)*

*(Ruby moves to left exit and back to her own door. Nervous, jerky movements. Evalina stands, violently a-tremble, near her gate. So far not a sound has been heard. Then the sound of chanting, mournful and high, comes faintly to them. They answer, Ruby in a high, keening²⁶ wail, Evalina a throaty, sustained moan.)*

RUBY: Oh, Lord, to never know! To never know!

*(The wailing comes nearer. A voice can be heard "lining out" "Hark from the Tomb A Doleful Sound Mine Ears Attend a Cry." This is sung by a chorus, mostly male. Muted, doleful. Evalina staggers to her step and sits down heavily and begins moaning to herself.)*

EVALINA: *(Raises her head bravely)* I ain't to cry. That wouldn't be right. It would look like I was sorry 'bout something when I ain't. *(Strangles a sob.)* He done filled every little corner in my heart. Ain't nothing been left out. He done showed his love in every way a man could do. *(Moans sadly, triumphantly)* I done had love from on high. *(Rises)* I got to pick some flowers for him to rest under because he was that kind of a man—big, and sweet-smelling and clean, like magnolias.

*(She enters gate and pulls down a limb and begins to break blooms hurriedly. Ruby sees her and begins to pick roses frantically. Both keep looking offstage left. The weird chant breaks out again right at hand. The group is about to enter, left. Evalina comes out of the gate with a large bunch of flowers and stands trying to be brave.)*

These flowers in my hand don't keep the water out of my eyes, though. *(Sings)*

Stand by me, Lord, stand by me
Stand by me, Lord, stand by me
Standing in the world, Lord, the world don't like me
Stand by me, Lord, stand by me.

*(The cortege enters. Six men bear a crumpled body on an improvised stretcher, a wide, new board with three short lengths of timber beneath it as handles. Ruby stops picking roses and starts downstage. Evalina walks resolutely to meet the group and wipes her eyes and looks lovingly down. Then [she] starts violently, puzzled for a moment. Then joyfully drops the flowers from her hand. A flower or two roll off onto the ground.)*

EVALINA: 'Tain't Spunk! It's old man Bishop!

WILLIE JOE: Yeah, death took the old man kind of sudden-like.

*(They move on. Evalina nearly bursts with joy. Ruby also expands. The sound of a guitar is heard off left. Joyful. Evalina's feet fly that way as Spunk comes walking fast and joyfully.)*

SPUNK: Hello, sugar! How's papa's lil ground angel!

(*Evalina does not answer. Catches hold of him and searches his face. Picks up a fallen flower and signals him to bow his head. He does so and she thrusts it in his hat-band.*)

SPUNK: What's the matter, honey? Look like you 'bout to cry. You really ought to be laughing. Old Hodge Bishop was so busy trying to get *me* onto that saw that he let a log fall on him. And when they moved it, there was the old conjure man pressed just as pretty as a flower. (*They both laugh.*)

EVALINA: (*Sniffing and tearing off into the house*) Come on in. I smell my supper burning! (*She dashes inside.*)

RUBY: (*Sidling up*) I'm so glad you ain't hurt, Spunk, I had to go pick some flowers. Bet mama going to kill me 'bout her flowers. (*Smells roses and gets ready to offer them.*) Yes, indeed, I'm real glad you ain't hurt.

SPUNK: (*Laughs*) Me, get hurt! Who going to hurt me? So long, Ruby. (*He dashes in after Evalina.*)

(*The guitar begins to sound gaily inside and Ruby tiptoes[27] to the window and peers in. They begin to sing "Evalina." After the first verse Ruby sings.*)

RUBY:

Me with flowers in my hand and love and me apart
Flowers withered like the house stretching on to break of heart
Roses scorned and drooping low to die
Empty hours weeping, creeping as they pass me by.

SPUNK AND EVALINA:

I squat beside the way of life where highways meet and part
With wilted flowers in my hand and trouble in my heart
The flowers ungiven in my hands to die
And life unmingled on my heart to lie.

(*[Ruby] walks slowly towards her step, the flowers dropping one by one from her hand. She hums sadly an obligato over Spunk and Evalina's song.*)

CURTAIN

# POLK COUNTY (1944)

Hurston spent several months at the Everglades Cypress Lumber Company in Loughman, Florida, in 1928, on a trip financed by Charlotte Osgood Mason. While there, she collected material that formed the basis of this play: the characters Big Sweet and Dicey Long were closely based on women she met in the lumber camp, and Leafy Lee is a fictionalized version of Hurston herself. Even before she wrote *Polk County,* however, the material had surfaced in many of her other works, including *De Turkey and De Law* (1930) and *The Mule-Bone* (1931), *Spunk* (1935), and *Their Eyes Were Watching God* (1937). She also used these experiences as the basis of a large section of *Mules and Men* (1934).

Loughman was just one county over from Eatonville, but was a completely different world. Unlike Eatonville, the lumber camp and its denizens "were ephemeral in every way"; they worked hard, loved hard, and resolved disputes with fists and knives rather than in courts of law. Yet the "refugees from life" who populated the camps, Hurston writes, "see nothing unlovely in the sordid camp. They love it and when they leave there, will seek another place like it." Although Hurston eventually fled Loughman after being attacked with a knife by a jealous rival, she clearly retained fond memories of the camp and for Polk County, where, as Big Sweet says, "the water. . . taste like cherry wine." The play, even more than her account in *Mules and Men,* attests to her deep love for the language and music of the sawmill and the jook. Despite their failings, Hurston writes, it is "these people" who "have given the world the blues."

*Polk County* is the first of Hurston's dramatic works to be embraced by the contemporary theater community. This "Negro folk opera," as it was described in a March 1944 newspaper item, never received its promised Broadway opening, dashing Hurston's last hopes for a professional production during her lifetime. After rediscovering her plays in the 1990s, the Library of Congress gave several informal readings that drew the attention of Arena Stage, Washington, D.C.'s premiere regional theater. Two concert readings given in December 2000 using actors from the theater were so well received that Arena Stage added the piece to their 2002 season. Director Kyle Donnelly and dramaturg Cathy Madison edited the script, reducing the running time from four hours to two-and-a-half, and musical historian Steven Wade located definitive versions of songs indicated in the script as well as composing original music.

Critics and audiences alike loved the show. The *Washington Times* called it a "sassy and dizzyingly high-spirited evening of music and mythic-sized characters," while *American Theatre* called it a "newly polished gem." The *New York Times* went so far as to declare it "a significant contribution to dramatic literature" that brought "a new musical sound to the theater."[1] The show ran from March 29 to May 12, 2002, and won the Charles MacArthur Award for Outstanding New Musical. After the run, Donnelly continued to streamline the script and reduced the number of characters from twenty-six to seventeen. In 2004, a new version was put forth with music by Chic Street Man, a jazz and blues composer who had previously written songs for the 1990 production of George C. Wolfe's adaptation of Hurston's short story "Spunk" at the Public Theatre. This joint venture between the McCarter Theater Center in Princeton and the Berkeley Repertory Theatre enjoyed successful runs at both venues. It remains to be seen if *Polk County* will become a regional theater staple.

# Polk County
## *A Comedy of Negro Life on a Sawmill Camp with Authentic Negro Music in Three Acts With Dorothy Waring*

CAST:

BIG SWEET, a handsome Negro woman around thirty. Physically very strong. She has a quick temper and great courage, but is generous and kind, and loyal to her friends. Sings well. Has the quality of leadership.

DICEY LONG, a homely narrow-contracted little black woman who has been slighted by nature and feels "evil" about it. Suffers from the "black ass." Her strongest emotion is envy. What she passes off as deep love is merely the determination not to be outdone by handsomer women. Yearns to gain a reputation as "bad" (the fame of a sawmill camp) to compensate for her lack of success with men. She is extremely jealous of Big Sweet. Being short, scrawny and black, a pretty yellow girl arouses violent envy in her.

LONNIE, a soft spoken man with a baritone voice. He loves and relies on Big Sweet because she is his opposite. He is loyal and kind. Tall, brown and well-made.

LEAFY LEE, a slim mulatto girl who wants to be a blues singer. Frustrated in her hopes of a career in the music halls, she takes to wandering aimlessly, and perhaps subconsciously comes to Lofton Lumber Mills in Polk County where blues are not only sung in the real manner, but are made. Simple, kindly and timid of life.

MY HONEY, a fairly nice-looking brown man in his mid-twenties who has no other love but his "box" (guitar) when the story opens, though Dicey has resolved to make him hers. He is gentle, and not apt to resist her by force as the other men would do. So she persists in chasing and hounding him. He is pals with Lonnie, and gives him a sort of adoration.

STEW BEEF, portly, witty, good humored. Dances and sings.

SOP-THE-BOTTOM, big appetite, a rather good gambler at Georgia Skin[2] but not above being sharp with less efficient players. Not really wicked, but considers himself smart.

LAURA B, just the average woman found on sawmill, turpentine[3] and railroad camps. No looks to speak of. Just taking what life has to offer one who has no more to offer life than she has. Not bitter nor looking for anything in particular.

BUNCH AND OTHER WOMEN, same type as Laura B.

Do-Dirty, Box Car, [of the] usual type found on such "jobs," the kind of men who would be misfits in other places. Rough, cheerful, careless of human life, including their own, used to prison, hard work, and danger. Come day, go day, God send Sunday.

Few Clothes, differs from the rest only in that he plays the mouth organ well.

Nunkie, a no-good gambler—shifty and irresponsible. His soul is as black as his face and his face is as black as the sins he commits. Any place with a dice table is his home.

Quarters Boss, a poor white who would[4] be a misfit outside of the job he holds, which is to keep order in the rough, lawless Negro quarters, where at least one person is killed every pay night. He is a little of a bully, but avoids trouble if he can. Tall, lanky, and looks poor white.

Piano Player, a good player who "jooks," that is, plays by ear.

Ella Wall,[5] though primitive and pagan, has the air of a conqueror. She is strutting and self-assured and accustomed to the favors of men which she in return grants freely. She practices voodoo and feels she leads a charmed life.

A Preacher, an old-time darkie—an aesthetic figure.

Maudella

Alwishus

Other children, about six or eight (boys and girls).

Male Chorus and Female Chorus, a male quartet and a female quartet—if necessary, a sextet.

Rooster

Hen 1

Hen 2

Other Hens

Dancers

Drummers[6]

## ACT ONE

*Scene and setting: The Lofton Lumber Company has its big mill and quarters deep in the primeval woods of south central Florida. Huge live oaks, pines, magnolia cypress, "sweet gum" (maple) and the like grow lush. Spanish moss drapes the trees. Tall cabbage palms tilt their crowns in clusters above the surrounding trees. Scrubby palmettos make a dense undergrowth.*

*The woods surround everything. Bull alligators can be heard booming like huge bass drums from the lake at night. Variegated chorus of frogs, big owls, and now and then the cry of a panther.*

*There are a hundred or more houses in the quarters. They are laid out in straight rows like streets. There is a main street, wider than the others called "The Square." On it are the public places like the Jook, or pleasure houses furnished by the management. There is a piano in it (sometimes a victrola also), tables for card games made of unpainted lumber, and a big table with a trip-string for dice. This is the life of the camp after work hours. There is a sort of cafe where soft drinks, tobacco, dried fish, chitterlings, etc. are sold. It is the second place in popularity.*

*The streets of the quarters are unpaved, sandy places. There are trees that have been left standing here and there.*

*The houses are of raw, second grade lumber, unpainted, each with a porch and two or three rooms. Each man with a "family" is allotted a house for which he is docked about fifty cents a week. The single men live with others or room at the rooming house next door to the cafe. No fenced in yards, few flowers, and those poorly tended. Few attempts at any kind of decoration or relief of ugliness. Everyone lives temporary. They go from job to job, or from job to jail and from jail to job. Working, loving temporarily and often without thought of permanence in anything, wearing their switch-blade knives and guns as a habit like the men of the Old West, fighting, cutting and being cut, such a camp where there is little law, and the peace officers of state and county barred by the management, those refugees from life see nothing unlovely in the sordid camp. They love it and when they leave there, will seek another place like it.*

*Such a place is the cradle of the blues and work songs. There they are made and go from mouth to mouth of itinerant workers from one camp to the other.*

*They are ephemeral in every way. The murderous fight of today is forgotten tomorrow and the opponents work together in utmost friendship inside of twenty-four hours. The woman of today may be forgotten tomorrow. Certainly it is remarkable for a love affair to survive a change of scene. There will be more women where they are going, and they say, "Let every town furnish its own. It's a damn poor town that can't furnish its own. Take no woman anywhere." Here and there an attachment becomes permanent, and they settle down together, or travel together from camp to camp.*

*The women are misfits from the outside. Seldom good looking, intelligent, or adjustable. They have drifted down to their level, unable to meet the competition outside. Many have made time in prisons also. Usually for fighting over men. They too pack knives. No stigma attaches to them for prison terms. In fact, their prestige is increased if they have made time for a serious cutting. It passes for bravery—something to give themselves a rating in their small world, where no intellectual activities exist. Hence the boastful song: "I'm going to make me a graveyard of my own, etc."*

*Rough fighting, drinking, loving, reckless, but at times a flash of religion comes to the top when they are very troubled or scared. Then for a short while, a spiritual will well up out of them and be much felt for the moment. Small churches have a hit-and-miss existence on the camps. They feel the*

*need of a preacher for funerals. He is more often a man of the same stripe
who reformed.*

*But these people have given the world the blues, work songs, guitar pick-
ing in the Negro manner, and the type of piano playing which made Fats
Waller famous, and is now being taken up by the world. Because it is typical, they call that type of piano playing "jooking."*

## Scene 1

*Scene: It is dawn. Birds twitter from the woods. A rooster crows lustily from
offstage, and is answered by another. The Square is silent and deserted.
Snores can be heard from the houses nearest the footlights.*

*Lonnie enters upstage left. He has a heavy stick and raps on the porch of
the house closest to where he enters and chants.*[7]

LONNIE:

Wake up, Jacob! Get on the rock!
'Tain't quite day, but it's five o'clock!

*(Raps again and crosses the stage and raps on the porch opposite)*

Wake up, bullies! Day's a-breaking.
Get your hoe-cake a-baking and your shirt-tail shaking!

*(Crosses back, raps again)*

Hey, you rowdy mule-skinners! You better learn how to skin.
Cap'n got a new job and needs a hundred men!

*(A drowsy hum of noise begins to rise inside the houses. Lights begin to ap-
pear, and there is movement behind the drawn shades. Lonnie crosses and
keeps rapping and chanting.)*

Wake up, bullies! I know you feel blue!
I don't want you, but the Bossman do!

*(The communal noises mount. More movement and lights and other signs
of waking.)*

What did the rooster say to the hen?
Ain't had no loving in the Lord knows when.

> *(In a bantering tone)* Git out from under them covers, Sop-The-Bottom!
> You could have been in the bed when you was skinning last night. Fall
> out! *(He turns away grinning)*

Wake up, bullies! Pull for the shore!
Big crap game on the other side, and I know you want to go!

*(Mounts a porch and listens at the window a minute)* Git up from there, Stew Beef! If you ain't made it by now, you better wait till night again. Git on up!

*(Leaps off porch grinning. A hum in harmony follows his chants now. The camp is stirring. Lonnie is down at the footlights. He makes a last general call.)*

All up, bullies! Unlessen you want some trouble with the bossman! *(Turns to exit right)* I done called you once! I done called you twice!

*(He holds the hum of his last syllable until he disappears off right. The lights have come up gradually, but not very much. Rooster crows, flaps wings, begins to strut as his flock of hens follow him on.)*[8]

HEN 1: Ground cold to my feet this morning. I wish I had some shoes.

ROOSTER: *(Doing a love dance around her)* What did the rooster say to the hen? Ain't had no loving in the Lord knows when.

HEN 1: *(Uninterested)* These Polk County roosters! They want plenty loving, but they don't buy you no shoes.

ROOSTER: *(Love dance around another hen)* How about a lil kiss?

HEN 2: *(Evading him)* I want some shoes!

ROOSTER: *(Dances around another)* Oh, gimme a lil kiss.

ALL HENS: *(Complaining in rhythm)* Well, I lay all the eggs, and I go barefooted! *(Rhythmic imitation of cackle)*

ROOSTER: *(Trying to evade the issue)* 'Tain't a man in Tennessee can make a shoe to fit your foot!

*(It is a well established chant-dance by this time.)*

ALL HENS: *(Chanting in imitation of cackle and dancing)* Well, I lay all the eggs and I go barefooted!

ROOSTER: *(Trying his luck with first one hen then another)* 'Tain't a man in Tennessee can make a shoe to fit your foot!

*(Same chants and business for duration of dance)*

ROOSTER: *(At end of dance)* Aw, cutta-cut cut! You Polk County hens always hollering for shoes! Why I have to buy you shoes to love you? You get just as much out of it as I do. Aw, cutta-cut cut!

*(He leads them off between the houses clucking disgustedly.*
*Lights are up in kitchens. The wooden shutters are open. Shades are up. There is a clatter of pots and pans. Breakfasts are being hurriedly eaten, and*

*buckets being packed with dinners. Men begin to drift out into the Square,*
*collecting in a bunch to go to work. Sop-the-Bottom comes out playing his*
*mouth organ and men begin singing.)*

MEN:

> I'm going to make me a graveyard of my own
> I'm going to make me a graveyard of my own
> Oh, carried me down on the smoky road
> Brought me back on the cooling board
> I'm going to make me a graveyard of my own.

> I'm going to live anyhow until I die
> I'm going to live anyhow until I die
> Sticks and stones may break my bones
> Talk all about me when I'm dead and gone
> But I'm going to live anyhow until I die.

DO-DIRTY: And that sure is the truth, man. I'm liable to make me a graveyard
all by myself. I'm so mean till I'll kill a baby just born this morning.

FEW CLOTHES: Me too. Man, I'm mean! I have to tote a pistol with me when I
go to the well, to keep from gitting in a fight with my own self. I got
Indian blood in me. Reckon that's how come I'm so mean.

*(They all admit to Indian blood and meanness.)*

DO-DIRTY: *(Yawning)* I sure ain't like Lonnie. I swear I wouldn't let nobody
beat me out my money like Nunkie done him last night. Stacking the
deck, and carrying the cub[9] and everything. I would have kilt Nunkie so
dead that he couldn't fall over. They would have to shove him over.

SOP-THE-BOTTOM: Lonnie didn't even know Nunkie was carrying the cub to
him. Lonnie can't skin worth a cent. He ought to quit trying to gamble.

FEW CLOTHES: I seen Nunkie what he was doing, but I ain't no bet-straight-
ener. It's more folks in the graveyard right now from straightening bets
than anything else. Blind man ain't got no business at the show.

DO-DIRTY: You done right. It wasn't none of your business. Blind man ain't got
no business at the show. But it is a good thing Big Sweet didn't come
along about then. She would have cut Nunkie a brand new one.

SOP-THE-BOTTOM: I told Nunkie he better leave Lonnie's change alone, and
then after he got it, I told him he better make it clean off this place before Big Sweet find out he got it.

FEW CLOTHES: Oh, she bound to find it out. My woman done found it out and
she wouldn't let her shirt-tail touch her till she run tell Big Sweet all she
know. If Nunkie ain't gone, he better be on his way.

SOP-THE-BOTTOM: He claim that his knife going to back Big Sweet off him. Claim he ain't scared, but I know better. He's talking at the big gate.

DO-DIRTY: *(Laughs aloud)* Did the fool talk like that? You just wait till Big Sweet get a hold of him. Before she turn him loose she'll make him tell her that she is Lord Jesus, and besides her there is no other.

STEW BEEF: I wouldn't exactly say Lonnie is blind. He ain't really dumb to the fact. He just ain't got his mind on no gambling. Lets folks talk him into the game. You know how he is—half the time his mind is way off on something else.

FEW CLOTHES: Yeah, them sort of visions he have. But I likes to hear him tell about 'em.

STEW BEEF: Me too!

LONNIE: *(Singing offstage)*

> I ride the rainbow, Amen
> I ride the rainbow, Amen
> I ride the rainbow, when I see Jesus
> Trouble will be over, Amen.

STEW BEEF: Here he come now. Sound like he been off on one of his trips.

*(There is an eagerness as Lonnie enters. They all want to hear what he has to say. Lonnie enters left, with a beatific smile on his face.)*

ALL: *(Very eager like children to hear a story)* Hi there, Lonnie!

*(Lonnie brings himself back to the present with a visible effort.)*

LONNIE: 'Lo, folks. *(They draw around him.)*

STEW BEEF: Sound like you been off this morning.

LONNIE: Fact of the matter is, I is been off.

STEW BEEF: Where was you at? Tell us so we can know.

LONNIE: *(Casually)* Oh, sort of knocking around heaven a while.

SOP-THE-BOTTOM: *(Intensely interested)* Tell us how you managed to git there. I ever wanted to see the place.

LONNIE: *(Illuminated)* On a great bird. A crow, diamond-shining black. One wing rests on the morning and the other one brushes off the sundown. He lights down out the sky, and I rides on his back.

FEW CLOTHES: How do you manages to git where he is, Lonnie?

LONNIE: He comes right here. You all just don't see him when he come.

STEW BEEF: How you know when he come?

LONNIE: A drum. A way off drum begins to throb. It gits closer and closer, and afterwhile, here come the Great Crow circling round to light down on the ground. I jumps on. Never do know where he going take me, but I don't care. I just goes.

STEW BEEF: Umph! Umph! Umph! Ain't that wonderful?

LONNIE: Sure is. This time, he took me 'crost a ocean, all made out of melted down pearls. And the shore was this coarse grainy gold. Wasn't no sand, no dirt-sand there at all. It was wonderful!

SOP-THE-BOTTOM: How come we don't miss you when you go?

LONNIE: *(Laughs in a superior way)* Oh, that's easy! I just leaves my hull around here making motions, and you all thinks that I am here.

SOP-THE-BOTTOM: That's a good thing, too, 'cause if the Boss ever figured you even got far enough off the ground to crack your heels, he sure would dock you for the time you was up in the air. *(They all agree to this and laugh)*

STEW BEEF: Aw, let the man tell us what heaven was like. That's what I wants to hear about. *(General clamor)*

LONNIE: Tell you when we get to work.

SOP-THE-BOTTOM: What you trying to do—make out youse High John de Conquer?[10]

LONNIE: I knows him well. Nothing can't git too bad when ole John de Conquer is around. *(Laughs)* Yeah, John de Conquer can find a way to beat out everything.

*(This makes a deep impression. Awe—can it be possible?—in their faces.[11])*

SOP-THE-BOTTOM: I know that High John was around in slavery days, but I thought he was gone back to Africa for good.

LONNIE: Supposing he was in Africa? What he care about distance? He could be right here in Lofton the next minute. He gits around right smart. Takes me off with him every occasionally.

SOP-THE-BOTTOM: No wonder you gits along so good. If you got the inside tracks on John de Conquer, youse something on a stick. Gimme some luck in a skin game.

LONNIE: It's too big to be brought down to that. It's for something big, like in your bosom.

SOP-THE-BOTTOM: Oh, to hell with it then. If it can't make me hold the last card I'm through with John de Conquer right now. You can have him. He got a willing mind, but too light behind.

DO-DIRTY: It's a fact. Why he don't distribute out whole hams?

LONNIE: Oh, he comes in handy. They got hams at the commissary if that's all in the world you wants.

FEW CLOTHES: That put me in the mind of something. *(Opens his dinner pail and looks in)* Looka here! Bunch done gimme the wrong thing in my dinner bucket. I done told her, I don't want no cold cornbread and molasses. I told her to fix to me some black-eyed peas with fat-back. She going to fix this bucket all over again, else hell is going to break loose in Georgy! *(Exits left in a hurry)*

DO-DIRTY: I don't blame Few a bit. Don't give me no half-handed dinner bucket. I don't want no stingy woman over my cook-stove.

SOP-THE-BOTTOM: Some women folks ain't exactly stingy, they's just contrary to that. I shacked up with a woman once that was so contrary she used to sleep humped up in the bed so you couldn't find no way to stretch out comfortable to sleep.

DO-DIRTY: Yeah, and I done been with some that pulls bed-covers. Won't let you stay covered up. Them kind of women don't look like they know what you bought a bed for. They think it's some place to lay up and study evil. *(All laugh)*

LONNIE: You telling the truth, I done seen 'em dreaming. They don't never dream about roses and scenery and sunshine like a sweet woman do. Naw, they dreams about hatchets and knives and pistols, and ice-picks and splitting open people's heads. I done seen 'em dreaming it! *(There is a wild burst of laughter at this.)*

SOP-THE-BOTTOM: Lonnie ain't lying. I had one like that down 'round Tampa one time. I tried hard to be good to that woman, but she wouldn't let me. Bought her shoes for her feet, and a brand new wig for her head. But she used to hump up in the bed and pull bed-covers right on. Lay up there and dream about killing folks every night. Go to bed evil and get up evil. Know what I done? One day I just told her, say, "Mary, gimme back the wig I bought you." She hollered and cried and ask-ed me, "What is I'm going to do for hair?" "Let your head go bald." Man, I grabbed it, and I was out and gone. Left her without a dust of meal or flour.

*(They all laugh in approval.)*

Dicey put me in the mind of Mary more than anybody I ever seen. Just won't agree with nobody or nothing. Why, I seen Mary get into a fuss

with a signboard one day. We was coming long the road and a signboard
said Sweetheart Soap. Mary stopped and called the signboard a liar! Said
it was Octagon Soap.[12] *(They all laugh loudly.)*

LONNIE: I better go see where My Honey is. I woke him up, but I don't hear that
guitar of his, so he might have dozed off again.

DO-DIRTY: Let's all go wake up the rascal. I know he ain't woke because he
tunes that box before he pulls on his pants. Let's go git him.

LONNIE: The Bossman is getting mighty tight about losing time. I don't want
us men that been together for a long time to get parted. That's why I most
in general wakes the camp ahead of time—to get everybody up and on
the job.

SOP-THE-BOTTOM: Yeah, look like the more money he make, the more he feel
like firing folks. But what can we do? He got us in the go-long.

LONNIE: *(Dreamily)* Old John de Conquer could always find a way. He could
make a way out of no-way. I'm gone to see about My Honey.

SOP-THE-BOTTOM: Come on, let's we all go 'long with Lonnie to My Honey's
house, and come on back with the music.

*(This meets with general favor, and there is a stir of them all heading off
left.)*

My Honey always got something good to be picking on his box.

*(There is a general, happy exodus.*
*The lights have come up further. Calls and answers can be heard from
different directions. Male and female voices, and general stir.*
*Big Sweet enters left, crosses quickly and stealthily to right and wedges
herself against the wall of a house. She has on a man's felt hat set rakishly
on the back of her head. She is smoking a cigarette, but she douses it, pushes
the hat far back, and listens carefully. She peeps around the corner of the
house on the alert in her ambush. She tenses as she hears stealthy footsteps,
and gets ready to spring.*
*Nunkie enters from between two houses, very close to Big Sweet but does
not see her as he steals along looking fearfully over his shoulder. Big Sweet
pounces on Nunkie, seizes him by the lapels of his coat and buttons him up.)*

BIG SWEET: Where you think you going?

NUNKIE: *(Scared, startled, but recovers and tries to appear defiant)* Take your
hands off of me!

BIG SWEET: Gimme that money back!

NUNKIE: *(Struggles to free himself, but vainly)* Take your hands out of my collar, woman! I don't allow no woman to button me up.

BIG SWEET: *(Tightens her grip firmly)* Well, I done done it, Mr. Nunkie, and look like there ain't no help for it. Gimme my Lonnie's money! You know I don't allow none of you low-life-ted gamblers to hook Lonnie out of his money. Give it here!

*(Nunkie starts his hand to his pocket nervously, but looking into Big Sweet's angry face, thinks better of it.)*

NUNKIE: I ain't supposed to teach Lonnie how to skin, is I? *(Tries to wrench free)* Naw, I ain't going to give you nothing! I ain't putting out nothing but old folks' eyes, and I ain't doing that till they dead. *(Struggles)* Let go!

*(Nunkie starts his hand to his pocket nervously, but looking into Big Sweet's angry face, thinks better of it. Big Sweet tightens his clothes around his neck until he is being choked.)*

BIG SWEET: *(Shakes him violently)* Gimme!

NUNKIE: *(Desperate)* Take your hand out my collar! *(It is half appeal.)*

BIG SWEET: I'll beat you till you slack like lime! Gimme that six dollars you beat Lonnie out of! *(Another twist)* Gimme!

NUNKIE: *(In desperate straits, tries to get to his pocket knife)* I'll cut your throat—

BIG SWEET: *(Lands a terrific blow to his stomach)* You going to cut me, eh? *(Another blow to his face, and Nunkie goes down. She kicks him hard.)* I'll kill you. Gimme!

NUNKIE: *(Trying to cover up)* Murder! Help!

BIG SWEET: *(Trying for another good place to kick)* You didn't die! You multiplied cockroach. *(Aims another kick)* I'll teach you to die next time I hit you! Die!

NUNKIE: Murder! Murder! Somebody come git this woman off of me!!

BIG SWEET: Shut up that racket! I mean to kill you. Beating my Lonnie out of his money. Gimme! If you don't, and that quick, they going to tote you through three yards—this yard, the churchyard, and the graveyard. Gimme!

*(Sop-The-Bottom, Do-Dirty, Laura B, Few Clothes and Bunch rush in and take in the scene.)*

LAURA B: Oooooh, Big Sweet done caught Nunkie!

SOP-THE-BOTTOM: *(With admiration)* Look at that lump on his jaw! Big Sweet, you sure hit him a lick.

BUNCH: You told that right.

LAURA B: *(To Big Sweet)* Did you all have some words before you fell out?

BIG SWEET: *(Hovering over Nunkie so that he cannot escape)* He better gimme Lonnie's money before I finish him. I asked him nice and kind to gimme Lonnie's money, but naw, he had to get up in my face with some of his big talk. I'm going to kill him!

DO-DIRTY: *(To Nunkie)* Give it to her, man, if you got good sense. 'Tain't nothing in the drugstore will kill you quicker than Big Sweet will about Lonnie Price. Give it to her.

SOP-THE-BOTTOM: You might as well give it to her. You can't whip her. She got them loaded muscles. Come on, hand it to her. Give her that little spending change.

*(Nunkie, sullen and silent, rolls his eyes hatefully at Big Sweet.)*

BIG SWEET: *(Looks from the spectators back to Nunkie on the ground all curled up like a worm. This sends her into a fresh frenzy)* Don't you lay there all curled up like that! *(Puts her foot on top of him and presses down to make him straighten up)* Straighten up and die right! *(She glares at him, then turns full of self-pity to the crowd)* See? That's how so many lies gets out on me. They twist theyselves all up and dies ugly, and then folks swears I kilt 'em like that. *(Kicks Nunkie)* You ain't going to die a lie on me like that. Straighten up!

LAURA B: *(Pleadingly)* Give him one more chance, Big Sweet. Maybe he's fixing to give you Lonnie's money right now.

*(They all look expectantly at Nunkie, but he is sullen and slyly looking for a chance to run.)*

DO-DIRTY: Why you want to die so young, Nunkie? Give her Lonnie's money and live to get old.

SOP-THE-BOTTOM: I know I don't aim to get hurt trying to hold Big Sweet off you when she start to finish you. Big Sweet is two whole women and a gang of men.

BUNCH: *(Disgusted, takes Few Clothes' arm)* Oh, leave her kill him! If he ruther to die than to part with Lonnie's money, let him have his ruthers. Come on Few, let's go. Hard head make sore behind, you know.

FEW CLOTHES: *(Disgusted)* Yeah, come on everybody, so we won't know nothing about it. Big Sweet can kill him dead for all I care. He ain't no kin to me.

BIG SWEET: And I am going to kill him too. Old trashy breath-and-britches ain't got no business beating folks out of money they done worked hard for. Run get me my gun, Bunch! If God send me a pistol, I'll send him a man!

NUNKIE: *(Terrified)* Here's them few little old dimes is. *(He flings a little roll of bills at Big Sweet's feet and jumps to his knees.)* I got plenty more.

BIG SWEET: *(Knocks him back down)* Pick it up! You didn't get it off the ground did you? You got it out of Lonnie's hands. Pick it up!

*(Nunkie grabs up the money.)*

You ain't going to discount me like that. Git up from there and place it in my hand.

*(Nunkie hurriedly hands Big Sweet the money.)*

BIG SWEET: *(Snatches it angrily)* Now, stand back and lemme see if it is all here. *(Counts it)* Yeah, this is it. *(Puts it in her dress pocket)* I ought to beat you till your ears hang down like a Georgy mule for putting me to all this trouble. You ain't no good for what you live, nohow. Just like your no-count brother, Charlie. Git! Sweep clean! Broom!

*(Nunkie dodges the blow Big Sweet aims at him to speed him and dashes off right. At the exit, he pauses.)*

NUNKIE: I'll get you for this. I ain't scared of you. I'll—

*(Quarters Boss rushes in right and seizes Nunkie who jumps in fright.)*

QUARTERS BOSS: What the hen-fire is coming off here?

*(He has his gun in his hand and his eyes on Big Sweet. Dicey and several more people, mostly men, enter left on the run attracted by the excitement.)*

NUNKIE: Big Sweet jumped me when I wasn't looking, and robbed me out my money.

QUARTERS BOSS: Big Sweet, ain't I done told you about your meanness? You ain't to cripple up everybody on the place. You hear me?

BIG SWEET: Youse a got-that-wrong. I wasn't bothering that thing. *(She indicates Nunkie with contempt)* It come here bothering *me*.

QUARTERS BOSS: *(Examining Nunkie's messed up condition)* Big Sweet—

DO-DIRTY: *(Giving Nunkie an unfriendly look)* He don't belong on this job, Mr. Pringle.

QUARTERS BOSS: *(Turning unfriendly eyes on Nunkie)* He don't? Then what is he doing in these quarters?

SOP-THE-BOTTOM: Come in here last night to gamble. Bothering Big Sweet about Lonnie's money.

QUARTERS BOSS: *(A great light)* Oh, he did, did he? She ought to have kilt him dead. Bulldozing the place and stealing, eh? *(Begins to frisk Nunkie roughly. Finds the knife and a greasy deck of cards)* Toting knives and weapons. *(Finds about a dollar's worth of small change and transfers it to his own pocket immediately)* Stealing honest people's money too! *(Examines the deck of cards, then fixes Nunkie with an accusing look)* Up to all kinds of meanness, too. *(Shakes the deck under Nunkie's nose as if it were a set of burglar's tools)* Unhunh! And toting concealed cards, highway shuffling, and attempt to gamble! *(Grabs Nunkie roughly)* You going down to Bartow to the big jail. Let's go!

NUNKIE: Don't take me to jail! Please, Cap'n! Lemme go this one time and I—

QUARTERS BOSS: *(Still glaring to intimidate Nunkie)* Well, I'm going to let you go this time. But you know no outside folks ain't allowed in these quarters. If I ever catch you on these premises again, I'll git you ninety-nine years and a jump-back in jail. Hit the grit!

NUNKIE: *(Pulling his hat down tight on his head)* Yassuh! *(Nunkie starts to walk rapidly towards right, watching nervously out of the corner of his eye for signs of threats to his escape.)*

DICEY: Poor Nunkie! It could be that he ain't harmed a soul. *(General growl of disagreement)*

SOP-THE-BOTTOM: *(Shortly)* Aw, Dicey, you always got to pull different from everybody else. You know Nunkie is a mink.

*(Nunkie, hearing Dicey defend him, thinks that things are improving for him, halts and decides to hit back at Big Sweet.)*

NUNKIE: Naw, I ain't stole nothing. Big Sweet—

QUARTERS BOSS: *(Firing off his gun into the air)* Git! Didn't I tell you to git?

*(Nunkie departs in a hurry, and all laugh but Dicey.)*

DICEY: *(Not daring to accuse Big Sweet directly, mutters out loud)* Some folks thinks they is a lord-god sitting on a by-god. They just loves to 'buke and boss.

BIG SWEET: Who you personating, Dicey? You must of woke up with the black-ass this morning.

DO-DIRTY: Just like usual. *(Sings)*

She got the blues, she got the black-ass too.
The blues don't hurt her, but the black-ass do.

*(Disapprovingly)* Always thinking evil.

DICEY: How come you all always get to take a pick-out after me? I can't break a breath without somebody got to hurt my feelings.

QUARTERS BOSS: Here! Here! Squat that rabbit and let's jump another one. *(To Big Sweet)* Big Sweet, not that I fault you for what you done this morning, but I been laying off to caution you for some time.

BIG SWEET: Caution *me?* Caution me about what?

QUARTERS BOSS: *(Placating)* Now, I ain't after no fuss. I gits paid to keep order in these here quarters, and I tries my level best to do it.

BIG SWEET: Well, who told you not to? I know it wasn't me.

QUARTERS BOSS: You been lamming folks a mighty heap 'round here.

SOP-THE-BOTTOM: Who? Big Sweet? Big Sweet don't bother nobody. You must be talking about somebody else.

BUNCH: I ain't heard nobody say nothing against Big Sweet. She's even nice.

DO-DIRTY: If folks leave her alone, she'll leave them alone. She just don't like to see nobody bulldozing the place and running the hog over other folks. She'll cold crawl you for that.

LAURA B: And nobody can't coldwater her for that. Some folks is too biggity and imposing.

*(Everybody but Dicey joins in the testimonial by noises of approval.)*

QUARTERS BOSS: *(Mocking)* Yeah, yeah, I know. That's all I can hear from most of you. Big Sweet ain't never done a thing but praise the Lord. Her mouth is a prayer-book and her lips flap just like a Bible. But where do all these head-lumps come from that the company doctor is always greasing? Somebody done told me. Big Sweet lumps your heads, and kicks your behinds for you, and you all lie and make out you don't know who done it. How can I keep order like that?

LAURA B: But we already got order! Lonnie don't like no rough stuff and Big Sweet, she—

QUARTERS BOSS: I'm the one getting paid to look after things. Big Sweet is too heavy with her hands. Now, take Lonnie Price for instance: Lonnie is a *good* man. No better conditioned man ever been on the place. Works hard and regular and don't git into no cutting scrapes. But I can count the pay-days on Lonnie's head. Big Sweet's got a lump up there for every pay-day. But will he tell *me* she done it? Naw, indeed! A piece of lumber flew up and hit him, or something like that.

BIG SWEET: *(Aroused)* I don't aim to let *nobody* tell me that I mistreats Lonnie. It's my lifetime pleasure to do what I know he want done. Lonnie, he's different. He don't like all this old rough doings and fighting, so I makes 'em live better 'cause what Lonnie says is right. *(Tenderly)* Lonnie is just a baby, in a way of speaking. He thinks everybody will just naturally do right, but I knows different. So I gets around to see to it that they do.

QUARTERS BOSS: Well, why you lam Lonnie? He don't act rough.

BIG SWEET: *(A self-conscious laugh)* I don't lam Lonnie. I just sort of taps him once in a while. You see, Lonnie got his mind way up in the air, and I taps him to make him know that the ground is here right on, and that there's minks on it trying to take advantage of him all the time. They can't fool *me.* Lonnie dreams pretty things. That's what make I love him so.

*(Quarters Boss, touched by Big Sweet's sincerity, looks at her a long time.)*

QUARTERS BOSS: I believe you do, Big Sweet. *(Back to his official manner)* No use in talking, I reckon. If the rest of you all don't care how much Big Sweet whips your heads and kicks your behinds, I don't give a damn. *(He turns shortly to leave, right)* But still and all, the company don't want all the help kilt off. You got to leave somebody to do the work on this job.

SOP-THE-BOTTOM: So far as that is concerned, more men makes time now than they used to do 'cause Big Sweet keeps a lot of 'em from cutting the fool and going to jail. She don't bother nobody.

BIG SWEET: *(Seriously)* No, I don't bother nobody. They bothers *me.* Looks like to me, folks ought to improve up some.

LAURA B: *(Triumphantly)* See that? Big Sweet—

QUARTERS BOSS: *(Exasperated)* All right! All right! Big Sweet is the bellcow, and to hell with it! *(Exits right quickly)*

*(The minute he is gone, they all break into boisterous laughter. They dance and caper. Few Clothes pulls out his harp and begins to play "Train." Big Sweet buck dances a few steps to a "break" then finishes off with a belly-wobble. They laugh and exclaim some more.)*

BUNCH: Big Sweet, youse a mess!

DICEY: *(Who has taken no part in the jubilation)* Reckon I better go see about My Honey's bucket. I baked a cake so he could have some to carry in his dinner bucket. *(She simpers, and goes off left quickly, walking as if she has some romantic secret.)*

LAURA: Is Dicey done shacked up with My Honey?

BIG SWEET: Aw, naw! He rooming with us right on.

BUNCH: What she doing fixing him a bucket, then?

BIG SWEET: Lord knows. I fixed My Honey's bucket last night just like always. He did mess with her for a day or so when he first come on the job, but that was long time ago. He don't mean Dicey no good, and she know it. She call herself fooling folks.

Sop-The-Bottom: I thought My Honey could do better than that. Me, I wouldn't have her for a Christmas gift.

Laura B: So contrary. What she got to take up for Nunkie for? Everybody know he ain't worth doodley-squat. Bet he will stay out of these quarters now. *(Laughs)* You sure give his head a straightening.

Do-Dirty: But I would watch out for him if I was you, Big Sweet. You heard him say he aimed to get you.

Big Sweet: I heard him, but I ain't scared of that trash. I'll finish him next time he mess with me. Specially with my Lonnie.

Do-Dirty: But he's the kind wouldn't come up and fight you a fair fight. He would lay 'way for you and try to steal you.

Sop-The-Bottom: And he hangs out around that Ella Wall in Mulberry all the time. She's jealous because you got such a swing around here. They're liable to try to gang you. They's dirty!

*(From offstage comes the sound of a guitar and men's voices singing "Jesus Going to Make Up My Dying Bed.")*

Do-Dirty: Listen at old My Honey! That fool can cold pick a box!

Big Sweet: *(Proudly)* You listen at *my* baby singing. Listen! That's Lonnie singing right in there. Listen!

Lonnie: *(Offstage)*

Well, I'm going down to the river.
Stick my sword up in the sand
Going to shout my troubles over, Lord
I'm going to make it to the Promised Land.

Male Chorus:

Well, well, well! I'm going to cross over
Well, well, well! I'm going to cross over
Well, well, well! I'm going to cross over
Jesus going to make up my dying bed.

Lonnie:

Oh, meet me, Jesus, meet me
Meet me up in the middle of the air
And if my wings should fail me, Lord
Won't You meet me with another pair!

BIG SWEET: *(In ecstasy)* Do it, Lonnie, do it!

*(The men come in singing the chorus. Lonnie and My Honey are walking side by side and the others are grouped close to keep the harmony straight. They are strutting, smiling and feeling anything but religious. They are carried away by melody and rhythm.*

*A loud-laughing cheer goes up from the spectators. They egg the others on. My Honey is conscious of the good finger work he is doing and is grinning about it.)*

LONNIE: *(Sings)*

And in my dying hour
I don't want nobody to moan
All I want you to do for me
Is just to fold my dying arms.

*(This manner of delivery pleases everyone. They show it by smiles and laughs. Men start on chorus.*

*Dicey enters running hard from left with an open switch-blade knife in her hands, leaps on My Honey and tries to button him up. He flings her off, but she attacks again grabbing hold of the pocket of his jumper and winding her hand in it and feinting at his middle with her knife. Everybody is struck dumb for a moment by the suddenness of the attack.)*

DICEY: Oh, yeah! *(Panting)* I got you! Trying to duck and dodge from me, but I got you!

*(My Honey recovering his faculties somewhat, struggles to break the hold.)*

MY HONEY: Git away from me, Dicey! Is you gone crazy in the head? *(Flings her off again so hard that she is off balance)* I don't want to hurt you. Why don't you leave me alone?

DICEY: *(Seeking an opening)* I'll fold your dying arms for you!

*(Big Sweet is tensing herself to seize Dicey from behind, and waiting for a favorable moment as she makes threatening motions with her knife at My Honey.)*

Trying to scorn me! I won't stand a quit. I mean to cut you just as long as I can see you.

*(Big Sweet darts in and grabs Dicey's uplifted right hand and wrests the knife away. Dicey gives a short scream of fright as she fears that Big Sweet means to cut her with it. But Big Sweet looks at it good, closes it, and puts it in her pocket.)*

DICEY: Gimme back my knife! I mean to stick my knife in him and pull it down. Gimme my knife! My money paid for it.

BIG SWEET: *(Calmly)* Naw, I better keep it. You doing too much talking about cutting folks to death these late days. You keep on flourishing that old free[13] around here, and somebody is going to hurt you.

*(Dicey rushes back and grabs hold of My Honey. She tries to hit him in his face but he blocks every blow, and keeps shoving her off.)*

DICEY: I mean to kill you and go to jail for you.

MY HONEY: Why don't you leave me be, Dicey? I done told you I don't want no parts of you. Behave yourself!

*(There is a strong growl among the males.)*

SOP-THE-BOTTOM: It's a good thing it ain't me she's pulling on. God knows I'd get her to go. She better not never draw no knife on *me*.

LONNIE: *(Angrily)* I don't believe in knocking lady people around like I would a man, but if I was God, I sure would turn Dicey into a hog, and then I would cement the world all over, so she wouldn't have a damn place to root.

DICEY: *(Furiously to Lonnie)* You keep your big mouth out of me and My Honey's business. That's what the matter now—me and him was getting along fine till you had to go tole him off and turn him against me. Yeah, I'm going to cut him, and a heap more 'round here if they mess with me.

LONNIE: Big Sweet, why don't you talk some sense into this crazy fool? You know My Honey ain't got no more use for her than he is for his baby shirt. She's just taking advantage because he won't knock her down like some mens would. *(To Dicey)* Turn My Honey go! Take your hands off of his clothes!

DICEY: Ain't a-going to do it till I get good and ready. He ain't going to quit me like I was some old dog.

MY HONEY: *(Tartly)* I ain't never said I wanted you yet. You better wait till somebody ask-es you before you go claiming 'em.

LONNIE: *(Distressed)* How come we got to have all this changing words and disturbment? How come everything can't go on nice and friendly?

*(Big Sweet looks at Lonnie's unhappy face, then interferes.)*

BIG SWEET: Lonnie is right. 'Tain't no use in all this who-struck-John. *(Approaches Dicey)* Me, myself, I done learnt better about a lot of things since I been with Lonnie. *(Kindly to Dicey)* Dicey, on the average, I am for the women folks, because the mens take so much undercurrents of us. But, Dicey, My Honey's case done come up in your court. He ain't fooled you and mistreated you. All he ever done was joke with you a time or two.

He done told you he don't want you. I wouldn't want no man that didn't want *me*. Pulling after a man that don't want you is just like peeping in a jug with one eye. You can't see a thing but darkness. Take a fool's advice and leave the man alone, like Lonnie say.

MY HONEY: *(Sullenly)* I done tried and tried to tell her that. But look like her head is hard.

STEW BEEF: I sure would soften it up for her, if it was me.

LONNIE: I never did choose no woman that run me down.

DICEY: *(Full of self-pity)* Why you all want to double-teen[14] on me? Always faulting me for everything. I can't even talk to my gentleman friend without everybody got to dip in.

MY HONEY: If you talking about me, you ain't got none. You'll never snore in my ear if I can help myself.

DICEY: I know I ain't yellow, and ain't got no long straight hair, but I got feelings just like anybody else. Go on, treat me mean if you want to, but someday, you all going to wish you had of treated me right. *(Exalted)* I'm going to be propaganda! Everybody going to be talking about me. Mens is going to scream over me more'n they ever did over Ella Wall, going to make up songs about me too and they going to talk about me more'n they do about Big Sweet.

LONNIE: How you going to bring all that about, Dicey?

DICEY: I'm going go git me a new, big knife. That kind you touch a button and the blade fly open, and I'm going to make me a graveyard of my own. *(As if visualizing)* I'm going to cut everybody that bother me. I'm going to stick 'em just to see 'em jump. Carry me down to Bartow to jail and folks will come running from way off just to look at me. They'll say, "There she is! That's Dicey, the one that kilt so many folks. Big Sweet? What you talking about, man? Big Sweet can't hold a light to Dicey Long. She'll kill you without a doubt. Slice you too thin to fry. Shoot until her gun jumps the rivets! Don't care who it is and where it is, that Dicey Long will fight. She'll shoot in the hearse, don't care how sad the funeral is. That's Dicey Long!"

*(In her reverie, she has released My Honey's coat and made gestures of exaltation. Now she comes out of it.)*

Then My Honey and a whole heap of mens will be pulling after me. I'm going to scorn him then. Tell him to come 'round another day. All of you all going to be trying to git in with me, but I aim to turn my nose up at you. I'll be Miss Dicey Long, with finger rings and things.

*(The whistle blows loud and long and the men respond automatically. Before Dicey realizes it, they are moving off and My Honey is out of her reach.)*

LONNIE: Come on boys! Another day! The work is hard, and the boss is mean. Can you make it?

MALE CHORUS: Yeah!

LONNIE: Can you break it?

MALE CHORUS: Yeah!

LONNIE: Can you shake it?

CHORUS: Yeah!!

LONNIE: All right, then! Follow me, bullies! *(Chants)* Cutting timber! Ha! Cutting ties!

DICEY: *(Plaintive)* My Honey! *(She moves towards him, but Lonnie blocks her.)*

MY HONEY: Aw, don't bother me woman. I'm going to leave this job just to get rid of you.

DICEY: I'll wait for you. How long you going to be gone?

MY HONEY: From since when till nobody knows!

DICEY: Going to take me with you?

LONNIE: Tell her, "no!" Let every town furnish its own.

DICEY: Where you figger on going?

MY HONEY: Way up in Georgy.

STEW BEEF: Man, is you crazy? Christ walked the waters just to go around Georgy, and you fool enough to go right in it!

DICEY: *(Almost sobbing)* My Honey, tell me sure enough, if you go, when you coming back?

MY HONEY: Not that it is any of your business, but I'll be back some old cold rainy day.

*(The second whistle blows short and sharp.)*

LONNIE: Let's go!

*(They all make motions of leaving.)*

STEW BEEF: Let's go! The work is hard and the boss is mean. *(Sings)*

Asked my cap'n what the time of day
He got mad and threw his watch away.

LONNIE: (*Entering into the spirit of kidding bossmen*)

> Cap'n can't read and cap'n can't write.
> How the hell do he know when the time is right?

MY HONEY:

> Cap'n got a pistol and he try to play bad
> But I'm going to take it if he makes me mad.

DO-DIRTY: My Honey, you better not take that box. Didn't Cap'n tell you not to bring it on the job no more?

MY HONEY: I ain't got that man to study about. I takes my music and my meanness everywhere I go.

STEW BEEF: Aw, you make the time, don't you? Play that box, man! Give us something to walk on. Git with him Few Clothes.

> (*The men wave and yell back at the women who wave and yell at them and go off singing "Cold Rainy Day."*[15] *The animation in the women dies as the singing fades out. They are drab again, and begin to make slow motions of dispersal to homes.*
> *Dicey stands looking forlorn after the men when all other women have turned away. Big Sweet looks at her and grows sympathetic. She approaches Dicey and starts to put her arms around her, but Dicey spurns her.*)

DICEY: You old destruction-maker! Taking My Honey away from me!

BIG SWEET: Nobody ain't took him because he never was yours.

DICEY: You did! You did! You and that Lonnie, and you more especial. Keeping him laying 'round your house night and day. I'm going to get even with you for it too. I'll put Ella Wall on you!

BIG SWEET: Ella Wall ain't my mama. I ain't a bit more scared of her than I is of you. And then again, what I got to be scared about? Ella Wall ain't no big hen's biddy, if she do lay gobbler's eggs.

DICEY: You'll find out. You done more than Lonnie think you done to git My Honey away from me, and keep him tied up 'round your house like a yard dog.

BIG SWEET: (*Angry*) That's a lie! *I called you a liar.* You don't like it, don't you take it. Here's my collar, come and shake it!

> (*The atmosphere becomes tense. The others crowd around expecting action. Dicey backs off cringing.*)

DICEY: Your time now, be mine after while.

BIG SWEET: So be it in the grand lodge. (*Curtain.*)

## Scene 2

*Scene: It is late afternoon. The sun is strong in the Square. Housework is done and suppers are cooked and waiting for the men to return. Women have changed into clean cotton housedresses, well starched, and [are] sitting around on porches. Several large boys and frying-size girls are out in the Square playing Chick Mah Chick Mah Craney Crow,[16] as the women sit around and patch, or here and there two or three "visit" on the porch of a neighbor. A boy about fifteen [Alwishus] is the crow. A girl about the same age [Maudella] is the hen.*

MAUDELLA: All right, Alwishus, you be the Crow. I'll be Mama Hen.

ALWISHUS: Okay, now, but don't make out I didn't catch you when I did.

MAUDELLA: Aw, go on and get ready.

*(Alwishus gets a stick about the size of a large pencil and squats in the center of the play area. The girls form in line behind the Mama Hen, each holding the girl in front around the body, or by her dress in the back, and start the march around the Crow chanting.)*

Chick mah chick mah craney crow
Went to the well to wash my toe
When I come back my chick was gone.
What time, Old Witch?

ALWISHUS: *(Making a mark on the ground)* One!

*(Same business till the count is three. The Crow gets up and assumes a predatory posture. The Hen and all her chicks go on the alert to avoid capture. The whole movement is a rhythmic dance with chanted words.)*

ALWISHUS: Chickie!

MAUDELLA: *(Dancing counter to Crow with all chicks with her)* My chickens 'sleep!

ALWISHUS: *(Wing and foot movement)* Chickie!

MAUDELLA: *(Foiling him)* My chickens 'sleep.

ALWISHUS: I shall have a chick!

MAUDELLA: You shan't have a chick.

ALWISHUS: My pot's a-boiling!

MAUDELLA: Let it boil!

ALWISHUS: *(Executing banking flight as if he is leaving)* I'm going home.

MAUDELLA: *(Undeceived)* There's the road!

ALWISHUS: I'm coming back! *(Suits action to words.)*

MAUDELLA: Don't care if you do!

*(Leafy Lee enters from right. A slim mulatto girl with a cheap suitcase in her hand. Walking slowly and looking about her as if searching. It is hot, and she wipes her face. She is not discovered immediately because of the excitement of the play-dance. She watches the dance with interest a minute, then advances more rapidly.)*

ALWISHUS: *(Working up to a high pitch)* My mama's sick!

MAUDELLA: Let her die!

ALWISHUS: *(Coming in closer for the kill)* Chickie!

*(Darts in suddenly and seizes one of the chicks to loud screams of mock terror. It is then that Leafy Lee is discovered. They all stop and look.)*

LAURA B: *(Under guise of a cough)* Who is that?

NEIGHBOR: Look like she is white. What you reckon she want in here?

LAURA B: Lord knows.

*(Dicey enters from her house and stands on porch staring at Leafy. Leafy approaches the girls and boys playing.)*

LEAFY: Hello.

MAUDELLA: *(Bashfully)* How de do.

LAURA B: *(Undertone to others)* Seem like she colored from the sound.

LEAFY: *(Exhibiting a small piece of white paper)* Can you tell me where I can find Miss Bunch?

LAURA B: *(Undertone)* She colored. Hear her put that handle to Bunch's name. *Miss* Bunch. *(To Leafy)* Who was it you wanted to see?

LEAFY: *(Approaching Laura's porch, setting down her bag and wiping her face.)* Miss Bunch. They told me at the office that she could let me have a room.

LAURA B: Oh, then you expecting to stay here a while? *(Catching herself)* Oh, where is my manners today? Won't you come up on the porch and have some set down? It's sort of hot out there today.

LEAFY: Much obliged to you. It *is* real hot in the sun.

*(Bunch enters from her house across the street and stands on her porch listening.)*

LAURA B: *(Raising her voice so that Bunch can hear)* You say you looking for Bunch? Is you some kin to her?

LEAFY: Oh, no. I never seen her in my life. The man at the office just give me her name on this piece of paper and said she might let me have a room to stay if she had one to spare.

LAURA B: Bunch ain't around home right now. Seems like I seen her going to the commissary awhile back. You say you aim to stay here? You going to teach the school? You sort of looks like a schoolteacher.

LEAFY: No ma'am. I'm not a schoolteacher at all. I just come to stay around awhile.

LAURA B: Is you married?

LEAFY: Oh, no ma'am. I haven't got no husband at all. All by myself.

LAURA B: Oh, I see, you got a man friend here, and you come to live with him.

LEAFY: *(Shocked)* Oh, no ma'am. I haven't got nobody likes that at all. I don't know a soul here so far.

*(All the women are out where they can listen and give each other significant glances on Leafy's answers.)*

DICEY: *(Calls over)* Er, Laura B, come here. Maybe I can tell you where Bunch went.

*(Laura B understands that Dicey wants to talk to her and gets up. Two or three other women head towards Dicey's porch at the same time, including Bunch.)*

LAURA B: *(To Leafy)* You better step in the house and have a seat. It may be a little cooler in there. Maudella, pick up the lady's suit-satchel and take it inside for her. She can set there until Bunch come home and let her know.

MAUDELLA: *(With eyes devouring Leafy in admiration)* Yassum. *(She picks up bag and precedes Leafy into the house.)*

LEAFY: *(Up on the porch)* That was a pretty game you all were playing. I wish you would teach it to me.[17]

MAUDELLA: *(Happily)* Sure will because I likes to play it my ownself. *(They exit into house.)*

LAURA B: *(As she joins the others at Dicey's porch)* You got a bug to put in my ear?

DICEY: Ain't got nothing different. Don't be pointing out Bunch to that gal. She ain't nothing! Bunch don't want nothing like that in her house causing disturbment.

BUNCH: Oh, you knowed her before?

DICEY: Not to speak to, but look like I seen her somewhere. But if I never seen her before, you can tell she ain't nothing. Just a old storm-buzzard out for what she can get. I wouldn't have her in *my* house. (*There is a thoughtful silence.*)

LAURA B: She don't seem like no fan-foot[18] to me. I figgered her out for sort of nice, didn't you, Bunch?

BUNCH: Sort of kind of. Wants to play ring play with the young'uns. That don't sound so bad.

DICEY: (*Heated*) That ain't nothing but a form and a fashion and a outside show to the world. She done heard about the money our mens makes on this job, and she done come in time to make a pay-day. Better git her on off from here before sundown and the mens come home from work. She'll be after all us men before you can turn around. Let's git her way from here.

LAURA B: The Quarters Boss must have figgered she was all right, else he wouldn't have let her in here.

DICEY: Aw, that white man don't know what he talking about. I has words with Big Sweet sometimes, but she ain't wrong all the time. She ain't going to like no stomp-down fan-foot 'round here tearing up peace and agreement. Let's call Big Sweet and tell her. She'll get her gone from here, Quarters Boss or no Quarters Boss. You know Big Sweet. Us ought to halt her right now before the mens gits a chance to see her and cut the fool over her. Don't let the 'gator beat you to the pond, do, he'll give you more trouble than the day is long. Send Alwishus after Big Sweet. She home.

(*The first lines of "Polk County" are heard offstage left.*)

BIG SWEET: (*Singing offstage*)

You don't know Polk County like I do
Anybody been there, tell you the same thing too.[19]

LAURA B: Here she come now. I sure is glad, because I sure don't know what to do.

BUNCH: Me neither. I was going to tell Laura B to bring her on over to my house, but if she is like Dicey say she is, I don't want no trouble with Few Clothes.

LAURA B: None of us don't want no kind of trouble like that. These mens don't want to half do nohow. It's just like pulling eye-teeth to git a pair of shoes out of 'em. They got a mouth full of gimme, and a hand full of much-obliged.

BIG SWEET: (*Enters left, still humming "Polk County"*) Say, what's the matter over there? You all got your head together like crows in a storm.

(*They all motion her to hurry over. Big Sweet crosses quickly and joins them without another word.*)

The law in here hunting somebody?

DICEY: (*Very friendly*) It's a woman. A fan-foot.

LAURA B: Oh, we ain't so sure about that part yet. But it's a young, real high yaller—I got her in my house till we can find out what to do about her. The Quarters Boss give her a note to Bunch to stay with her.

DICEY: A regular old strumpet making pay-days. Just somebody on the road somewhere. Color struck, too. Crazy about that little color she got in her face, and that little old hair on her head. You ain't going to like her a bit. And she'll be after Lonnie and My Honey and everybody else right off.

BIG SWEET: Come on, Laura B.

(*She turns resolutely towards Laura B's house. Big Sweet and Laura B lead the way with the others following slowly so as to appear just to happen up in time to see the show.*)

LAURA B: (*At her porch, and in a low tone*) She don't look bad to me. If Dicey hadn't of said—

BIG SWEET: (*Grimly*) Call her out.

(*She rests her left foot on the steps, and her left elbow on her left thigh. The voices of Leafy Lee and Maudella can be heard in gay talk and laughter inside.*)

LEAFY:

Well, I went up on that meat-skin
And I come down on that bone
And I grabbed that piece of cornbread
And I made that biscuit moan.

See, I got it right that time, didn't I?

(*They both laugh.*)

LAURA B: (*At door*) That Maudella is too fast and womanish. (*Proudly*) She ain't scared of nothing! (*She exits into house while Big Sweet waits grimly.*) Miss, er, you child, it's somebody out here wants to have a talk with you. Just step outside a minute.

(*The other women are drifting up and around the porch.*)

LEAFY: Leafy is my name. Leafy Lee. (*Coming to door*) Is it Miss Bunch done come?

*(Sees Big Sweet. Big Sweet looks Leafy over from head to foot slowly and deliberately, and back again. There is either hostility or cold indifference in the faces of every woman about her, as Leafy stands there on the porch and takes in the circle. Finally she meets Big Sweet dead in the eye. They eye-ball each other well, then Leafy breaks into a grin. Big Sweet tries to hold her solemn pose, but she also begins to grin. She purses her lips, but the chuckle gets bigger and bigger as she and Leafy expand their smiles. Finally Big Sweet gives in, takes her foot down, stands akimbo and [makes] an attempt to conceal her admiration under rough good humor.)*

BIG SWEET: You crazy thing!

LEAFY: *(Laughing, imitates Big Sweet's stance)* Crazy your ownself.

*(The women look from one to the other in amazement.)*

BIG SWEET: Youse all right, Little Bits. 'Tain't nothing wrong with you. I been told you was stuck up and color struck, but youse all right. You grins natural. If you was stuck up you would try to smile. *(They both laugh at that.)* Where you come from and where you going? *(All listen intently.)*

LEAFY: Well, I come from New York, but I wasn't born up there. Mama and Papa is both dead, so I had to go for myself. Folks always told me I could sing, and I ever wanted to sing like Ethel Waters.[20] But I haven't had no real good job yet. I got to sort of wandering around, and next thing I know, I was way down here. They told me if I wanted to learn to sing blues right, I ought to come learn how on a sawmill job, so I heard about here, and come on. The Bossman says I can stay here and learn all I want to. So he sent me to Miss Bunch to get myself a room. But she is away from home somewhere. I'm waiting for her to come.

BIG SWEET: *(Dawning happiness, though hard to believe)* You mean you want to sing blues—sure enough blues?

LEAFY: That's right. Maybe I can make something out of myself if I do. Go back to New York and make enough money to take care of myself.

BIG SWEET: Well, you done come to the right place. What name did you say you was going by?

LEAFY: *(Surprised)* What name I'm going by? The one my mama give me when I was born. Leafy, Leafy Lee.

BIG SWEET: That's a pretty name to have. Specially when it's yourn for real. Folks on these kinds of jobs uses different names at different times. I see what you come here for. You come here for a reason, and not for a season, and Leafy, you done come to the right place. Me and my man sings them blues every night at our house. And we got a friend man that cold picks 'em on a guitar. If he can't whip a box, 'tain't a hound dog in Georgy, and you know that's the puppies' range.

LEAFY: Well you all the very people I want to meet up with. I wants to sing the blues.

*(Big Sweet grabs Leafy by the hand and pulls her down off the porch.)*

BIG SWEET: Come on go home with me so we can talk some. You ain't got a bit more sense than me and Lonnie got. I loves to meet up with folks that loves good singing.

*(The whole atmosphere has changed to warmth. Everybody is beaming on Leafy, except Dicey, who is tragically disappointed.)*

LAURA B: And Big Sweet sure can sing them blues. When she gits hold of a good one, she turn it every way but loose. She's the one can help you out a lot.

LEAFY: *(Happily, then checks herself)* But if I go off with you, I'll miss Miss Bunch, then I won't have no place to stay.

BUNCH: Did you say Bunch? Here I is. I thought all the time you was asking for Lena Branch. But you said Bunch, didn't you? You can git your suit-satchel and come on 'cross the way right now. I got a good room you can use.

BIG SWEET: *(Picking up the bag)* She going home with me for awhile. This child ain't after nobody's man. Anyway, I don't figger on nobody taking Lonnie away from me. Come on Little Bits. You going home with me.

LAURA B: *(Calling after them as they start upstage left)* Me and Stew Beef will be on over there after supper.

BUNCH: And me and Few.

BIG SWEET: That's right, you all come on and make the poor child feel welcome. You see she's a orphan child. Everybody come on. Don't look to eat up none of our groceries, but we going to have plenty music, and cut Big Jim by the acre.

*(Big Sweet and Leafy go off chatting happily. The others watch them go. Dicey alone looks unhappy and stands looking after them grimly. Curtain.)*

Scene 3

*Time: Immediately after scene 2.*

*Scene: Interior of Big Sweet's house. Raw, unpainted lumber with rafters and uprights showing. Furniture cheap and the decor garish. Bright colored calendars and advertisements nailed on wall. Watermelon pink calico curtains at the two windows. White iron bedstand in one corner with starched lace fringed pillowslips and a cheap spread. Three kitchen chairs and a cheap wooden rocker with a lace doily.*

*At the rise, Big Sweet and Leafy are discovered in the front room. Big Sweet is seated on the bed, and Leafy in the rocker, She has removed her hat and dress, and is cooling off in her underwear. There is an easy air of old acquaintance between them.*

BIG SWEET: It's a wonder that your boy friend let you come off by yourself like this.

LEAFY: I haven't got no fellow.

BIG SWEET: What's the matter? You all had a falling out?

LEAFY: *(Shakes her head slowly)* Never had one—not no real one.

BIG SWEET: *(Astonished)* How you mean? You look 'round twenty years old to me.

LEAFY: Twenty-two.

BIG SWEET: What's the matter? Is you been sick, or something?

LEAFY: Oh, I had fellows to come take me out to the moving pictures and things like that once in a while. And one fellow, he liked me real well, but I didn't care nothing about him. He even went and asked Papa for my hand.

BIG SWEET: Your *hand?* What did he want with that?

LEAFY: Why, why, he wanted to marry me. So he asked my Papa for my hand.

BIG SWEET: How come he didn't say what he mean, instead of go asking for your *hand?*

LEAFY: That's what you say when you want to marry a girl.

BIG SWEET: *(Loud and embarrassed laughter)* Is that what they say when they want to shack up with a gal? When they feel they love come down?

LEAFY: That's the proper way.

BIG SWEET: *(Dumbfounded)* Umph! Umph! Umph! That just go to show you how bad it is to be ignorant. But, when you don't know, you don't know. Here, all this time these ignorant mens been[21] going 'round here asking folks for they *can* when they ought to be asking for they *hand*. The no-mannersted things! *(Indignant)* I better not hear no more of that kind of talk 'round here. They better not say "can" to me no more, even if it's got tomatoes in it. *(Deep respect and awe comes over Big Sweet and a wistfulness.)*

BIG SWEET: Youse wonderfly, Leafy. You knows a heap of good things.

LEAFY: Oh, that ain't nothing much to know.

BIG SWEET: I think it's fine. Wisht I had of knowed that long time ago. (*A minute of deep thought.*) You mean you ain't never knowed nothing about no man?

LEAFY: That's right. (*Apologetically*) Maybe it's because I have never been in love with nobody that was in love with me.

BIG SWEET: (*In awe*) You ain't joking?

LEAFY: (*Embarrassed*) No ma'am. I ain't never given to no man.

BIG SWEET: I never expected to find nothing like that sure enough. (*She leans her head against the bedpost with a far-off bitter look on her face and thinks.*) I'm glad for you, Leafy. 'Cause you done won the battle that I lost.

LEAFY: What do you mean by that?

BIG SWEET: I wanted to be a virgin my ownself. I always said that I was going to be one till I got married, when I was growing up, and I meant to, too. That was my firm determination. 'Course I didn't know what his name was going to be, but I knowed that I was going to find Lonnie some time or other. And I often wish that I could have come to him like you is now. (*A deep, long sigh.*) No use wishing now. Them years is behind the mountains. I think that I would have made it too, but you see, Papa died when I was fifteen, and times got mighty hard. It was too expensive for somebody in the fix I was. I couldn't afford to be a virgin. (*Pause*) Then, after that, I got to knocking around, and found out what folks mean by careless love. You mean good, and think maybe it will lead to something permanent. But he hits you a love-lick and be gone! So when you get through thinking and feeling, you try another one. Pretty soon, you be feeling again like you been drug through hell on a buzzard gut. You find out it's a lot of bulldozing, imposing and biggity folks in the world that loves to take advantage. They looks fine from the top of their heads down, but if you see 'em from the foot up, they's another kind of people. They sings and says that the water in Polk County taste like cherry wine. So I come pulling here like a heap more girls done done. (*A bitter laugh*) Well, after while, I met up with Lonnie, and then things was all right. But by that time, I had done got my craw full of folks doing they bullying and bulldozing and trompling on everything and everybody they could git they foot upon.

(*Leafy rushes across to Big Sweet and flings her arms about her.*)

LEAFY: You make me feel so little. Just being a virgin ain't a thing besides what you are, honey.

BIG SWEET: *(Wraps Leafy in a tight embrace)* Oh, you going to be a lot of help to me. You got more schooling than I got.

LEAFY: But you knows the most. Mama used to always tell me that study-ration beat education all the time.

BIG SWEET: *(Laughs heartily)* And that's right too in a way. We can sort of swap. You don't know a thing about this world, but I aim to put *my* wisdom tooth in your head. I mean to be your forerunner like John the Baptist. Fight everything from graybeard to battle height.

LEAFY: You mean you really fights?

BIG SWEET: Yeah, I has to sometimes. Some folks ain't going to do right un-lessen you do. I don't mean no harm, but one day about six years ago, me and God got to sort of controversing on the subject of how some folks loves to take advantage of everybody else. He said that sure was the truth, and He never had meant it to be that-a-way. Preaching and teaching didn't do some of 'em no good. Jailing 'em didn't help 'em none, and hanging was too good for 'em. They just needed they behinds kicked.

LEAFY: Did God tell you to kick 'em?

BIG SWEET: *(Laughing)* Well, He didn't exactly *tell* me to kick 'em, but He looked down at my big feets and smiled.

LEAFY: So you been kicking 'em, eh? *(Laughing)*

BIG SWEET: Sure is, and it's done a heap of 'em good. I done made over this place more nearly like Lonnie say it ought to be. No need in all this fight-ing and carrying on every pay night. Pole cats trying to make out they's lions!

LEAFY: Don't hurt yourself too much for other folks. Just like Mama used to say, "Good nature make nanny goat wear short tail."

BIG SWEET: *(Laughing heartily)* Youse crazy! You must of told God the same thing I did. When He ask-ed me, "Little angel, where do you want to go?" I told Him, "It matters [not] a difference where I go, just so I go laugh-ing."

*(There is a group noise of loud talk and laughter at a distance, and Big Sweet sits up and listens.)*

That's the men folks done come home from work. Git into your clothes right quick. You got to be ready when my Lonnie and My Honey git here. Everybody will come pulling in here to meet the new stranger. *(She jumps and opens the suitcase on the floor.)* I'll help you some.

*(Leafy goes to bag quickly and selects an attractive but inexpensive wash dress, and throws it over her head. Big Sweet pulls it down and helps fasten it. [She] gives Leafy a playful slap on her behind after the dress is adjusted.)*

BIG SWEET: My Lord, Little Bits, you ain't got a bit of meat on your bones! The man marry you, going to have to shake the sheets to find you. *(They both laugh.)*

LEAFY: Maybe nobody won't ever want me enough to marry.

*(There is a sound of footsteps at the outer door, and Big Sweet starts out of the room with a big smile on her face.)*

LONNIE: *(Outside)* Hey, in there! Housekeepers!

BIG SWEET: That's my baby! *(Calls)* Hey yourself! Want a piece of cornbread, look on the shelf!

*(She bolts out of the room, leaving the door wide open. Leafy hurriedly powders her face and puts on lipstick. The sound of a loud smack of a kiss comes to her as she applies the lipstick.)*

LEAFY: *(Half wishful)* I wonder if these men do any raping around here? *(Curtain.)*

## Scene 4

*Time: Two hours later.*

*Scene: Interior of Big Sweet's house. Big Sweet, Lonnie, Leafy, My Honey, Stew Beef, Laura B, Bunch, Few Clothes, Sop-The-Bottom, and Do-Dirty are all in the room. Lonnie, in a clean, starched shirt and overalls, is in the middle of the floor.*

LONNIE: We done took Leafy for a little sister. She want to sing blues, so we all got to help her out all we can. Each and every one of you teach her what you know.

BUNCH: I don't know none. I like to hear 'em, but I never did know too many of them old reels and things.

FEW CLOTHES: Youse the boss, Lonnie. We'se bound to do the best we can. I'll play one, and My Honey, you help me out with that guitar. The rest of you can sing the words. Big Sweet, you verse it out.

*(He wipes off his harp and begins to play "Nasty Butt," and My Honey falls in playing with him. They play through a verse with flourishes, and vamp for the voices.)*

STEW BEEF: (*Carried away by the swing, starts to sing*)

> Thought I heard somebody say
> You nasty-butt, you stinky butt
> Take it away! Oh, you—

BIG SWEET: (*Jumps up furious*) Stop it! Don't you sing nothing like that in front of Leafy. She's a lady.

STEW BEEF: Oh, excuse me. I didn't mean no harm.

(*The men all look from one to the other, puzzled.*)

BIG SWEET: Teach her another one. I'm going to pass out the lemonade whilst you all go ahead helping Leafy. (*She exits through door.*)

SOP-THE-BOTTOM: (*Brightly*) Us don't have to sing under the clothes of them Tampa fan-foots. Let's we sing about a man. (*Pats his foot to get the swing and begins*)

> Uncle Bud, Uncle Bud, Uncle Bud, Uncle Bud, Uncle Bud
> Uncle Bud is a man, a man like this
> Great big man with a great big fist.

LONNIE: (*Catches on fire*)

> *Refrain:*

> Uncle Bud's got gals that's long and tall
> And they rocks their hips from wall to wall.

(*It is their favorite song at work and they take up the refrain with great gusto.*)

STEW BEEF:

> Oh, little cat, big cat, little bit of kitten!
> Going to whip their backs if they don't stop spitting!

(*The enjoyment mounts. The men are putting plenty pep into it.*)

ALL:

> Uncle Bud's got gals that's long and tall
> And they rocks their hips from wall to wall.

LONNIE:

> Oh, little cat, big cat playing in the sand
> Little cat cuss like a natural man.

(*Shout of laughter as they tear into refrain*)

ALL:

> Uncle Bud's got gals that's long and tall
> And they rocks their hips from wall to wall.

LONNIE:

> Oh, who in the hell, the goddamned nation
> Put this trash on Pa's plantation?

*(Wild yell of approval)*

BIG SWEET: *(Bursting through door with tray of glasses full of lemonade)* Stop it! Don't you vip another vop on that.

LONNIE: *(Injured)* Good Lord, baby, how we going to teach the girl if you won't let us sing?

BIG SWEET: You can sing without singing that, can't you?

*(My Honey fools around with his box and drifts into "Angeline" and begins to sing it softly and absentminded. The men pick him up and make harmony.)*

MY HONEY:

> Oh, Angeline! Oh, Angeline!
> Oh, Angeline, that great, great gal of mine.

BIG SWEET: Now, that's a new one that I don't know, but it sound nice.

MY HONEY:

> And when she walks, and when she walks
> And when she walks, she rocks and reels behind.

BIG SWEET: *(The drinks are passed out, but she has the empty tray in her hand, which she brandishes)* Stop. That one ain't fitten' neither.

LONNIE: *(Disgusted)* Oh, go ahead and instrument the box, My Honey. Big Sweet won't let us sing nothing at all.

*(Great howl for My Honey to play.)*

LEAFY: Oh, please do, Mr. My Honey. I ever loved box-picking.

MY HONEY: *(So pleased at her interest that he gets all fussed)* Oh, thank you ma'am, Miss Leafy, er, my compliments, er, excuse me, of what you want me to pick for you?

LEAFY: Just anything you will or may.

LONNIE: Polk County! You know you does that thing.

ALL: Yeah, man! Polk County!

(*My Honey plays the piece excitedly and with extra flourish, and is acclaimed.*)

LEAFY: (*Deeply moved by his artistry*) That's great! I never thought to hear nothing as good as that. My Honey, you're an artist.

LONNIE: Don't be calling my buddy out of his name. What is a artist nohow?

LEAFY: It's somebody can do something real fine and high and noble. And My Honey is one from way back. If he was to go to New York and pick his box like that, he would be famous, and make a lot of money besides. I wish I could sing like he can pick.

LONNIE: My Honey, look like you done got to be somebody. You hear what Leafy say?

MY HONEY: (*Over modest*) Oh, she just joking me. I just fools with this box 'cause I loves it better than anything else in the world. Nobody wouldn't be fool enough to pay money to hear nobody pick a box. That's something done for pleasure.

LEAFY: Yes, they would, too.

BIG SWEET: I know you telling the truth, Leafy, 'cause I love to hear good picking so that I would give something to hear some if it wasn't 'round here free. And them white folks in New York *could* be even crazier than I is. (*Burst of laughter.*) Now, lemme tell you all something. Lemme tell your heads something in front. I don't want no slack talk over Leafy. She's trying to make something out of herself. And I *know* when mens gits to slack-talking, next thing it's something further. No loose talk and slack mouth around Leafy.

LONNIE: And that's right, too.

BIG SWEET: And, oh, yes. No more mention about "cans." I done learnt the right way, now. You all got to come up to time. You supposed to ask a lady for her *hand*, not her can. You hear me? That's stylish.

LONNIE: That a fact? I'm proud to know it.

BIG SWEET: You done all the asking you ever going to do, Lonnie, so this don't come before you. But tell everybody else on this job.

STEW BEEF: Well, sir! Hand! I done caught on New York style.

BIG SWEET: And don't be telling Leafy nothing about your after-ten-o'clock-at-night feelings, neither.

LONNIE: And my tongue is in Big Sweet's mouth. I say the same thing.

My Honey: And I string along with my buddy. I'll fight about her too.

Leafy: *(Quickly and brightly)* Will you, My Honey?

Lonnie: Will he? That's a true fact. Me and My Honey is buddies. Jack the Rabbit, Jack the Bear, two sworn buddies on the road somewhere. We backs one another up in everything.

*(There is a general murmur of confirmation.)*

Laura B: Let's we women teach Leafy a song.

My Honey: Go ahead, and I'll pick it off for you.

Laura B: *(Hesitates a minute)* Oh, we don't know just which one it is just yet. You all liable to laugh at us. Come on, let's we all go out in the kitchen and practice up. Then we'll come back and show you if we make it.

Big Sweet: That's a good idea. Come on, you gals!

*(They all exit to the kitchen hurriedly and the men are left alone. Few Clothes, warming up on his mouth organ, begins to play "The Fox Hunt," and the men egg him on to the end.)*

My Honey: That was real good, Few.

Few Clothes: Let's me and you practice on together.

My Honey: Just a minute. I want to speak with Lonnie private. Be back in a minute. Come over here Lonnie, where we can be to ourselves.

*(They cross over near the kitchen door. Few Clothes fumbles around blowing a chord here and there.)*

My Honey: You reckon Miss Leafy think I'm any good, sure enough?

Lonnie: *(Indignant)* Think you any good? How can she help it if she got any sense? Youse a good man. Work regular, save your money, don't gamble and don't git drunk, what more can a woman want out of anybody? And then, you got a cool kind disposition, and looks good in clothes.

My Honey: But do you reckon *she* believe it like that? You reckon—Oh, I wants you to talk to her for me. Tell her about me. Git Big Sweet to talk to her for me.

Lonnie: *(In great surprise)* My Honey! I ain't never seen you this way before. You claimed that the woman you wanted for a regular wasn't born yet, and her mama was dead. All you wanted was that box to pick.

*(My Honey stands silent while the voices of the female quartet comes from the kitchen singing "Careless Love."[22])*

WOMEN: *(Offstage)*

It was love, O love, O careless love
Love, O love, O careless love!
You caused me to weep, you caused me to moan
You caused me to leave my happy home.

When I wore my apron strings low
When I wore my apron strings low
When I wore my apron strings low
You were always standing at my door.

Now I wear my apron to my chin
Now I wear my apron to my chin
Now I wear my apron to my chin
And you pass my door and won't come in.

See what careless love has done
See what careless love has done
You've broken the heart of many a[23] poor gal
But you'll never break this heart of mine.

MY HONEY: Yeah, I know I said all of that, and I meant it too, when I said it. But Big Moose done come down from the mountain. *(Listens to the singing for a space.)* I done got a letter from Love, and I'll go to hell, but what I answers it.

LONNIE: *(Great admiration in his tones.)* You said that like a man.

*(The women burst in laughing triumphantly and all in good spirits.)*

BIG SWEET: Leafy is doing all right, I'm telling you.

LAURA B: Yeah, she going to sing good too, when she learn some songs.

LONNIE: Git your box fixed, My Honey, let's hear what she done learnt.

LEAFY: Oh, I don't believe I know it well enough just yet. Maybe in a day or so. Let Big Sweet sing something.

LONNIE: Big Sweet, why you don't teach her "John Henry"? That song they sings on the railroad camps?

BIG SWEET: My Honey plays that all the time. He can teach her and tell her.

MY HONEY: Be glad to. *(Begins to tune)* Lemme git it tuned in Vastopol. *(The Vastopol[24] tuning. He runs off a few scales and chords.)* But I can't handle the singing and the playing too. You sing it for her, Big Sweet, and I'll bottle-neck it off.

STEW BEEF: Now, you going to hear something, Miss Leafy. Big Sweet and My Honey is a mess on that.

BIG SWEET: Oh, nothing much. A woman ain't even supposed to sing it. But I messes around with it on every occasionally.

LONNIE: *(Proudly)* Aw, go ahead and sing, Big Sweet. You ain't had no complaints from nobody yet.

*(My Honey does a brilliant introduction, and Big Sweet takes the center of the floor and sings.*[25]*)*

BIG SWEET:

John Henry driving on the right hand side
Steam drill driving on the left
Says 'fore I'll let your steamdrill beat me down
I'll hammer my fool self to death, Lord!
I'll hammer my fool self to death.

*(All join in the chant)*

ALL:

Anhhanh! Aaaahahah! Anhhanah! *(Etc.)*

BIG SWEET:

John Henry told his captain
When you go to town
Please bring me back a nine-pound hammer
And I'll drive your steel on down, Lord!
I'll drive your steel on down. *(Same business)*

John Henry had a little woman
The dress she wore was red
Says I'm going down the track, and she never looked back
Says I'm going down the track, and she never looked back
I'm going where John Henry fell dead, Lord!
I'm going where John Henry fell dead!

The captain asked John Henry
What is that storm I hear?
He says captain that ain't no storm
'Tain't nothing but my hammer in the air, Lord!
Nothing but my hammer in the air.

Who's going to shoe your pretty lil feet?
And who's going to glove your hand?
Tell me who's going to kiss your dimpled cheek
And who's going to be your man? Lord!
Who's going to be your man?

My father's going to shoe my pretty lil feet
My brother's going to glove my hand
My sister's going to kiss my dimpled cheek
John Henry's going to be my man, Lord!
John Henry's going to be my man!

Where did you get your pretty lil dress?
The shoes you wear so fine?
Lord, I got my shoes from a railroad man
My dress from a man in the mines, Lord!
My dress from a man in the mines.

*(The crowd comes in on the hum, pat their feet for drums, and in the last choruses, they clap hands on it as the excitement rises to a high pitch. It ends on a sort of frenzy. They cheer Big Sweet and My Honey and themselves when it is over.)*

STEW BEEF: We did that thing! Man, we whipped that thing to a cold jelly.

BIG SWEET: *(Proudly)* And did you hear Leafy coming in just like a old timer towards the end? *(General clamor of praise for Leafy)* I done got me something fine when I friended with Leafy. I mean to go with her, and stand by her, and prop her up on every leaning side.

LONNIE: I hope you do. It something I'd love to see. Women folks don't stand with one another like men friends do. Not on the average, they don't.

BIG SWEET: I mean this. I'm promising God and a couple of other responsible characters to stand by Leafy through thick and thin. Anybody that picks a fight with her, if they can't whip me too, they better not bring the mess up. You all can strow that around. I'm backing Leafy up. She's green as grass, and then she don't know nothing. But I'm with her in *everything*.

LAURA B: We hear you. And then again, we going to tell it around.

BIG SWEET: Don't miss. Some folks like to take advantage of weak folks. Tell 'em in front, so they can know that Leafy ain't by herself in the world.

*(There is a sharp knocking on the door, and Big Sweet goes and opens it quickly.)*

Oh, hello, Dicey. You coming in?

DICEY: *(In the door)* Naw. I didn't come here to come in. *(She does come far enough to take in the whole scene and looks around the room with a grim expression. Sees Leafy seated next to My Honey, and the general happy air in the room.)* Big Sweet, I'll thank you to give me back my knife.

*(Big Sweet studies Dicey's face for a long minute. Sees the challenge there. Comes to a decision, and reaches in her pocket and hands Dicey the knife*

*without a word. Everyone in the room except Leafy realizes that a challenge has been flung, and accepted. Dicey goes quickly, and Big Sweet shuts the door sharply.)*

LONNIE: Poor Dicey, she sure is set on cutting out her own coffin. But me and High John ain't going to let her. Are we, Big Sweet?

*(Curtain.)*

ACT TWO
Scene 1

*Scene: The following Saturday night. The Jook. The interior of the Jook is a large rectangular room. The piano is against the wall upstage center. The long sides of the room are parallel with the footlights. The room is lighted by naked bulbs hanging from cords. There are entrances right and left in the ends of the building, and one at right of the piano. A few streamers of crepe paper hang from the ceiling, fragments of a past celebration that have not been removed. There is a table for dice, green top, string across the center for tripping the dice to the right of center and a rough pine table for cards to the left. There is a third table pulled out untidily from the left wall with un-painted kitchen chairs haphazard around it where the occupants of the night before have left them. There is a deck of cards on it.*

*At the rise, Do-Dirty and Sop-The-Bottom are at the dice table practic-ing throws. The piano player is playing a hot stomp and Stew Beef, Laura B, Bunch, Few Clothes are dancing. The women have on hats of their men. Box Car is dancing alone and cutting steps and cheering himself with every "break."*

*Dicey enters left and begins to work her way across the room to a seat on one of the benches against the wall at right. When she starts to pass Box Car, he grabs her and tries to dance with her. She snatches away rudely.*

BOX CAR: *(Annoyed)* Aw, come on and dance, why don't you?

DICEY: *(Proceeding)* 'Cause I don't want to.

BOX CAR: Well, what you come here for if you don't want to be sociable?

DICEY: *(Tartly)* I didn't come here to dance. I come for a reason and not for a season. *(She switches on across the room.)*

BOX CAR: *(Looking at her angrily for a moment, then shakes his head, rolls his eyes up and sighs)* My people, my people![26] I likes folks that's nice and friendly.

DICEY: *(Tightening her skirts up to sit)* It matters a difference to me if you likes me or if you don't. None of you old mullet heads ain't studying about *me* nohow. I ain't yellow, and ain't got no long straight hair. Go dance with some of them you screams over. If Big Sweet and that Leafy was in here you wouldn't know I was even in here.

Box Car: *(Maliciously)* You told that right.

*(He goes back into his dancing and laughing at himself, and Dicey settles herself into a pose that indicates she is there but not of the place. The dance music mounts to a climax and ends abruptly. The dancers all exclaim cheerfully.)*

Laura B: Hello there, Dicey. Look like you ain't having yourself no fun.

Dicey: Maybe not right this minute, but I will be. *(Laughs unpleasantly.)* Oh yeah! Before the night is far spent, I'll be having my proper amount of fun. *(Mysteriously)* Some that goes for a great big stew will be simmered down to a low gravy. *(Laughs again.)* Then I'm going to show 'em my ugly laugh. *(They all look puzzled, one to the other, for a moment but Dicey laughs again.)*

Stew Beef: Dicey laugh like she done found a mare's nest and can't count the eggs.

Box Car: *(Impatiently)* Oh, squat that rabbit, and let's jump another one. *(To Laura B)* Laura B, you always 'round Big Sweet, tell me something about that pretty little frail eel Big Sweet got at her house. Is she from New York sure enough?

Laura B: That's what she say, and she sure is got them kind of clothes.

Box Car: And she sure do become her clothes too. I really would like to git in there. How come you don't tell her about me? I ain't got nobody.

Stew Beef: *(Scoffing)* Oh, oh! With nearly every man on the job after her? Boy! You sure going to get a plenty hindrance on that job.

Dicey: *(Mysteriously)* I know one won't be pulling after her. You mean that stray, half dead-looking yeller gal that drug in here a few days back? Shucks! She ain't no trouble.

Sop-The-Bottom: Which one ain't going to pull after her? I know it ain't me. She sure can git every cent I make, just like I make it.

Dicey: *(Coquettishly)* My Honey ain't.

Box Car: You better say "Joe" 'cause you don't know. *(Significantly)* He could be worser off than anybody else around here.

Sop-The-Bottom: Yeah, he been buying a mighty lot of ice cream lately, and toting it to Big Sweet's house. He could be guilty.

Dicey: I don't see nothing on her to scream over.

FEW CLOTHES: That's natural. (*General laughter*) Who did you say was the crazy fool that wouldn't have that pretty little doll baby if he could git her?

DICEY: You heard me. I say My Honey wouldn't. He got somebody he like more better.

BOX CAR: (*Scornfully*) Maybe you got some inside information on My Honey that the rest of us don't know about.

DICEY: (*Taking him literally*) I don't have to tell you all me and My Honey's business.

FEW CLOTHES: I ain't never heard nobody say you and My Honey had no business together. You must have dreamt it.

DICEY: (*Stung*) I'll show you if My Honey is mines or not. You just let that yaller consumpted thing, or anybody else get to messing around My Honey now.

FEW CLOTHES: What can you do if they do?

DICEY: I'll take my knife and go 'round the ham-bone looking for meat. That's what I'll do. I'll slice her too thin to fry. (*She crosses quickly over to table, snatches a chair and drags it over to the bench.*)

DO-DIRTY: Don't take that chair off, Dicey. We fixing to git up a game.

DICEY: Git it up then. You won't git this chair. I'm saving it for My Honey when he come. He got to have a chair to sit in when he pick his guitar.

DO-DIRTY: (*Sarcastically*) Oh, excuse me. I didn't know that My Honey had done bought any chairs in here, no more'n anybody else. I thought it was first come, first serve. (*Growing angry*) And then again, I ain't heard nothing about My Honey making you no guardeen over him, to be saving him no chairs.

FEW CLOTHES: The first of my knowing it too. (*General agreement*)

DICEY: How come every time I open my mouth all you all got to jump down my throat? I got friends in Mulberry that wouldn't spit on this old low-life-ted place. I friends with Miss Ella Wall. She could buy all the trash in this place and sell 'em. In fact she could pay for 'em and give 'em away.

STEW BEEF: Oh, is that who you cracking off of? Ella Wall is a used-to-be. Good gun, but she done shot.

DICEY: (*Jumping to her feet angrily*) Who? Who you talking about?

STEW BEEF: Aw, sit down! What you hollering "who" for? Your feet don't fit no limb.

*(There is the sound of a guitar offstage and the voice of My Honey singing "Had a Good Woman, but the Fool Laid Down and Died." There is a general stir in the place at the sound.)*

SOP-THE-BOTTOM: Here come old My Honey now! *(There is a stir of anticipated pleasure.)* He can evermore pick that box.

*(My Honey enters upstage right, with his hat set recklessly, his guitar around his neck and strumming.)*

STEW BEEF: Do that thing, My Honey! Have a fit! You got a fitten place to have it in.

*(He [My Honey] creates a pleasant stir as he walks slowly down towards center stage. Dicey jumps up and offers the chair she has been holding.)*

DICEY: Have some set down. I been saving this chair for you baby boy.

MY HONEY: *(Unpleasantly affected by her too intimate address, halts and recoils)* Baby? Boy? How big do men grow where you come from?

DICEY: I mean youse my boy.

MY HONEY: *Your* boy? My mama is dead. *(He starts to turn away left)*

DICEY: *(Still trying to save face as she sees the grins on the faces of the men)* Set down and play me something on that box.

MY HONEY: Don't believe I cares to set down just at present. I ain't tired the least bit. And my box ain't tuned to play nothing in particular.

*(He crosses to where Stew and the others are grouped around the table. Some sit on the benches, some in the chairs.)*

STEW BEEF: Where Lonnie at?

MY HONEY: *(Looks elaborately in all of his pockets.)* Don't believe that he's here.

LAURA B: *(Laughing)* You crazy thing!

STEW BEEF: But sure enough. You always be's together.

MY HONEY: *(Seriously)* That's what I want to know my ownself. I figured he might have come on here. He's acting kind of funny and I wanted to find out what was the matter with him.

BOX CAR: Aw, Lonnie is a man just like me. I ain't going to waste no breath asking about no jar-heads. What I wants to know is, where is that pretty little doll baby from New York? How come you ain't scorching her tonight?

MY HONEY: I ain't got no deeds to Miss Leafy.

BOX CAR: *(Happy)* Tell a blind man something! If you can't do no good, git out the way and give somebody else a chance.

MY HONEY: *(Soberly)* Suppose us don't handle her name so careless like. Anyhow, her and Big Sweet will be on afterwhile. They putting they trunks on they backs tonight and they tray on they heads. Shoved me and Lonnie on out. Said they had to git dressed particular. *(Smiles pleasantly to himself)* Don't know who they gitting dressed so for.

STEW BEEF: But you hope it's you. *(Comes around the table and begins to rub My Honey all over his chest to the amusement of the others.)* Good gracious! *(Snatches his hand away as if he got burned)* Poor My Honey! His heart is about to burn a hole in his undershirt.

MY HONEY: *(Snatches away and backs downstage, fending his teasers off)* Git away from me! I don't want no mens feeling all over me, like I was a woman. Gwan!! *(Worried)* Wonder where Lonnie is sure enough?

SOP-THE-BOTTOM: Oh, don't you worry about Lonnie. He's all right. Bet he's off somewhere having one of his visions. Nothing don't worry that Lonnie. He's just like High John de Conquer. Don't care what trouble it is. He can always find a way.

LAURA B: That's the truth, now. Just listen to Lonnie talk awhile, and he can make your side-meat taste like ham.

*(Somebody begins to hum)*

Troubles will be over, Amen
Troubles will be over, Amen
Troubles will be over, when I see Jesus
Troubles will be over, Amen.

DO-DIRTY: That's old Lonnie's song, all right.

*(Lonnie steps in the door and stands. He has a wild look in his eye, and a fixed smile on his face.)*

LONNIE: Yeah, this old Lonnie. *(Advances from right to left a few steps)* Otherwise, Old Peter Rip-Saw, the Devil's High Sheriff and son-in-law![27] Hello, people!

*(There is a great gust of welcome, but all look at him curiously.)*

LAURA B: What's the matter with you, Lonnie? You got a grin on you like a dead dog in the sunshine.

LONNIE: *(Coming to center stage)* Who said anything was the matter with me? Nobody ain't heard me complaining is they?

STEW BEEF: Naw, but anybody can see you looks like you been drug through hell on a buzzard gut.

MY HONEY: *(Goes to Lonnie and takes his arm)* What's wrong? You know you can git the last cent I got, and if you needs any backing up otherwise, you know so well I'm already dressed to die standing by you.

*(General clamor from the men to the same effect. Lonnie drags the table a little away from the group by the wall towards center stage and stands leaning heavily on it with both hands while he laughs and laughs without mirth. My Honey stands looking at him and listening for a moment then shoves a chair up behind Lonnie.)*

MY HONEY: Why you don't stop that laughing? You know you ain't tickled.

LONNIE: *(Drops loosely into chair)* Naw, I ain't tickled. *(Puts his hand in the side pocket of his jumper-jacket)* I got a letter. Yeah man, somebody done wrote me a letter. *(Laughs)* And I'm so outdone, till I just opened my mouth and laughed.

*(The place breaks into a big hum. Everybody is conjecturing and wondering. Curiosity and sympathy are mingled. It goes on and gets higher. Dicey falls all over herself in a happy, gloating laugh.)*

BOX CAR: *(Angrily)* What you laughing at, Dicey? This ain't your fun.

DICEY: Do I have to tote a coffin in my pocket because Lonnie is feeling sad? Everybody don't have to cry at one time. Nobody 'round here don't cry when *I* cry. I cries all by my ownself. How come I can't laugh the same way? *(She bursts into loud, taunting laughter)* Aye, Lord! A heap sees, but a few knows. God don't love ugly.

BOX CAR: Well He must be ain't got a bit of use for *you.*

DICEY: Maybe He ain't. Maybe He's just like you. But that don't stop me from having my proper amount of fun when them that goes for pretty, and you all washes up so much, gets put outdoors. *(She laughs gloatingly all over herself.)* Oh, me! I sure got something funny to tell Ella Wall when she gits here.

*(They all look at her in an unfriendly way, and gather 'round Lonnie in an attempt to soothe him.)*

LAURA B: Lemme go git you a piece of that fried rabbit we had for supper, Lonnie.

MY HONEY: Would you choose a piece of barbecue?

SOP-THE-BOTTOM: How about a big drink of likker? That will make you forgit anything you got on your mind.

LONNIE: Naw, I thank you. I done had all I want to eat, and likker won't do my case no good. Naw, I thank you.

*(They all look from one to the other in puzzlement, and Lonnie picks up the deck of cards and begins to fumble with it aimlessly.)*

STEW BEEF: Did you and the Bossman have some words?

LONNIE: *(Nervously lights a cigarette)* Naw. And I don't never expect to have no words with him, long as I stay here, neither. He may be lying, but he make out he can't git along without me.

BOX CAR: And he told that right. Youse the best man on the job, without a doubt. *(They all agree to that.)*

LONNIE: I tries to do what's right.

STEW BEEF: So it's something else, and look like you could tell us what's wrong? Did I hurt your feelings?

LONNIE: Oh, no. Not to give you no short answer, but this don't come before nobody but me. If my heart is beneath my knees, and my knees is in some lonesome valley crying for mercy where mercy can't be found, it's just me. No help can come to the place where I'm at.

LAURA B: *(With deep feeling)* I reckon us all knows the feeling of that. Everybody is by theyselves a heap of times, even when they's in company.

DO-DIRTY: So what can you do? Just open your mouth and laugh.

STEW BEEF: Aw, we been sad long enough. Let's git up a skin game and laugh.

*(He reaches for the deck of cards, but Lonnie clutches them to him and shakes his head.)*

SOP-THE-BOTTOM: *(Fishing another deck out of his pocket)* Here, I got a deck. Let's git on the other table.

BOX CAR: *(Grabbing for them)* Is they star-back?[28]

SOP-THE-BOTTOM: *(Showing them)* Sure.

BOX CAR: That's all right then. I don't want nobody carrying the cub to me for my money I done worked for.

SOP-THE-BOTTOM: *(Arrogantly)* Aw, man, I don't have to cheat you when I can beat you. *(Coaxingly to Lonnie)* Come on man, and git in the game.

LONNIE: You know I don't much gaming nohow, and tonight more especial, I don't.

SOP-THE-BOTTOM: Come on, My Honey.

MY HONEY: You know my money ain't going on no cards. Chew my tobacco and spit my juice. Save my money for another use.

*(The crowd moves to the other card table noisily, and My Honey begins to pick absently on the box. Lonnie keeps his seat and fumbles with the cards. The pianist notes that My Honey is chording "Daisies Won't Tell" and joins in. As the game is being organized, the crowd sings it first spottily, and then intensely on the chorus. All of the men except Lonnie and My Honey are in the game. The women stand around behind them very interested and rooting for their own men. Lonnie is doing something with the cards that interests him. Dicey rocks her hips exultantly over to the game and looks on. My Honey starts that way, but on seeing Dicey going, he turns and walks towards the piano and sits on the seat. The pianist has gotten up.)*

PIANO PLAYER: *(Hurrying across to the game)* Gimme a card.

SOP-THE-BOTTOM: *(Dealer)* I'm ready to deal out your cards.

BOX CAR: *(Stops him abruptly)* Don't deal me none. I want to scoop one in the rough.

SOP-THE-BOTTOM: That will cost you a dollar.

*(He offers the deck to Box Car and he selects one far down in the deck and turns it down beside him and places a dollar on the card.)*

SOP-THE-BOTTOM: *(Deck in hand)* All right you pikers, I'm dealing. *(Looks all around the table and stops abruptly.)* I don't see no bets down. It's a quarter. Put your money on the wood and make the bet go good. And then again, put it in sight and save a fight.

*(All put down a quarter. Few Clothes gets his from Bunch, who goes down in her stocking to get it on his request by gesture. They are all set. )*

STEW BEEF: Let the deal go down, Sop-The-Bottom!

ALL: *(In chorus)* Let the deal go down!

SOP-THE-BOTTOM: *(Sings)*

When your card gets lucky, Oh, partner!
You ought to be in a rolling game.
Let the deal go down, boys![29]

ALL: *(In chorus with harmony)* Let the deal go down!

*(Sop-the-Bottom turns every card off the deck with deliberation and hits it on the table with a smack. All eyes watch eagerly to see who "falls.")*

SOP-THE-BOTTOM:

I ain't had no money, Lord, partner! *(Card smacks)*
I ain't had no change. *(Card smacks)*
Let the deal go down, boys! *(Card smacks)*

ALL: Let the deal go down!

SOP-THE-BOTTOM: *(Turning another card and looking around the board)* That's you, Stew Beef! You head-pecked shorty! Pay off!

STEW BEEF: *(Shoving in money and card)* I can't catch a thing tonight. Can't even catch nobody looking at me. Gimme another card.

SOP-THE-BOTTOM: *(Takes one from the discard)* Here! Take this queen. It's clean.

STEW BEEF: *(Positively)* Aw, naw! Gimme another card. I don't play them gals till way late at night.

*(Sop-The-Bottom hands him another card. Stew Beef puts down another quarter and the game goes on.)*

SOP-THE-BOTTOM:

I ain't had no trouble, Lord, partner!
Till I stopped by here.
Let the deal go down, boys!

ALL: Let the deal go down!

SOP-THE-BOTTOM: That's you, Few Clothes! Pay off!

*(Few Clothes does so sadly.)*

Here, you want another card?

FEW CLOTHES: *(Feeling in his pockets)* I'm clean as a fish, and he been in bathing all his life. *(Looks around at Bunch suggestively)* Bunch, lemme have another two-bits.

BUNCH: Naw! You wasted up seven dollars pay night skinning. You gimme this to keep, and I'm a-going to do it too.

FEW CLOTHES: I worked for that money. How come I can't spend it like I please?

BUNCH: Naw! You wouldn't have doodly-squat if I leave you have your way. Naw!

SOP-THE-BOTTOM: Lady people sure is funny about money. *(To the table)* I'm raising the bet. Another two-bits. I likes long sitters and strong betters. Put down! My pockets is crying for your money.

*(The others all put down another quarter.)*

DICEY: *(Putting down money)* Four bits on Box Car's nine!

*(Stew Beef looks around and sees that Dicey is directly behind him and has her foot on his chair.)*

STEW BEEF: Take your foot off my chair, Dicey! You holding me down.

BOX CAR: And a dollar my nine is the best.

SOP-THE-BOTTOM: (*Covers it*) Let the deal go down, boys.

ALL: Let the deal go down!

> (*Big Sweet enters left, followed by Leafy Lee. Big Sweet has a new hair-do, and is dressed very becomingly if a little loud. Leafy looks very chic in a low-priced silk dress.*)

BOX CAR: (*Leaping up from the table*) Look a-yonder! Whooeee! (*Slams his hat down on the floor in pretended ecstasy.*) Must be a recess in heaven—all these little ground angels out and walking around.

SOP-THE-BOTTOM: (*Also jumping up*) Big Sweet, youse sharp! You so sharp in that dress, that if you didn't have but one eye, I would swear that you was a needle.

MY HONEY: (*Advancing quietly to meet them with a chair*) Miss Leafy, ma'am, also ma'am, will you be so condescending as to stoop without bending, and have this chair?

> (*Big Sweet and Leafy advance leisurely to center stage, smiling and conscious that they look well.*)

BOX CAR: (*Seizing a chair*) Miss Leafy, you don't want that old nasty chair My Honey got. Take this here nice one I got for you, Miss Leafy.

LEAFY: (*Accepting My Honey's chair with a self-conscious smile*) I thank you, but I reckon this one will do. I wouldn't want to deprive you. (*To My Honey with a sweet smile*) You sure I ain't depriving you?

MY HONEY: (*Overcome*) What would I look like setting down with er, pretty ladies standing up? (*There is a howl from the crowd.*)

BOX CAR: Listen at old bashful My Honey! Done found his tongue.

STEW BEEF: Yeah, he's getting on some stiff time.

SOP-THE-BOTTOM: Big Sweet, you got to accept this chair from me. The rest of these jar-heads is scared to tell you how pretty you is on account of Lonnie. (*Throws Lonnie a pseudo-challenging look.*) Me, I ain't got Lonnie to study about. I'll fight him about you right here and right now.

> (*Big Sweet casts an adoring look at Lonnie.*)

BIG SWEET: Oh, you bad, eh? You must be the guy that killed Jesse James. (*General laughter*)

SOP-THE-BOTTOM: I hates to tell you how really bad I is. I'm so bad till my spit turns to concrete before it hits the ground. *(General laughter.)* Fact is, I'm worser than that snake that was so poison that he crawled up and bit the railroad track, and he was so poison that it killed a train when it come 'long past. *(Great shout of laughter.)*

STEW BEEF: *(Laughing)* Stop your lying, Sop!

SOP-THE-BOTTOM: *(Chuckling)* Man, I ain't lying.

STEW BEEF: Naw, you done quit lying and gone to flying. *(Gets behind Big Sweet's chair and bends over her confidentially)* But all joking aside, Miss Big Sweet. You evermore looks good tonight. You got on drygoods! It would take ten doctors to tell how near you is dressed to death.

BIG SWEET: *(A concerned look at Lonnie)* Much obliged for your compliments, but you all go on and woof at Leafy. I done heard all them lies too many times.

BOX CAR: That's right you is. So us can just tell Miss Leafy how much us loves her. *(Tries to suppress a grin)* 'Cause then that will be the truth. Miss Leafy, is your little feets resting good in My Honey's no-count chair? You better git up and take mines.

MY HONEY: Oh, she's doing all right where she is.

BOX CAR: Oh, it'll do in a rush. But what you reckon a pretty girl child like she is would want with your old chair when she can git mine? Take my chair, Miss Leafy. This is the first time I had a real good look at you, but I declare, already, I would rather all the rest of the women in the world to be dead than for you to have the toothache. *(There is a room-wide howl at the big lie and the audacity to tell it.)*

SOP-THE-BOTTOM: Man, how come you don't quit your lying?

BOX CAR: *(Suppressing a grin)* That ain't no lie. Miss Leafy, if that ain't so, God is gone to Tampa, and you know He wouldn't fool around a place like that. *(They all laugh, and this time Box Car laughs himself.)* Take my chair and show those no-count jar-heads who you really love. *(Laughter)*

SOP-THE-BOTTOM: *(Pretended disgust)* What you want to waste up the girl's time woofing at her for? Why you don't give the girl something to prove how much you love her? *(Tenderly to Leafy)* Miss, just tell me what it is your little heart crave and desire. I sure will git it for you. 'Course, I aim to give you a passenger train just for a sort of remembrance—*(A howl of laughter)* And then I aims to hire some mens to run it for you.

DO-DIRTY: *(Shoves Sop-The-Bottom roughly aside)* Git away, Sop! A passenger train! Is that all you aims to give a pretty girl baby like this? A little old passenger train? Miss Leafy, I aims to buy you one of them big ocean lin-ers, and then I aims to buy you a ocean of your own to run it on. *(Scornfully)* Passenger train!

BOX CAR: Some these mens around here is too cheap to live. *(Sighs heavily and rolls his eyes up)* My people, my *people!* *(Laughter)*

DO-DIRTY: *(Shoving in between Leafy and Box Car)* Miss Leafy, Old Maker didn't give you all them looks you got to be talked to any which a way. Youse something special. You hear these jigs woofing at you and telling you about all they going to give you, and they don't even know how to talk to a girl like you.

BOX CAR: Come on! Come on! Pick up your points.

DO-DIRTY: Oh, I'm going to pick 'em up.

LEAFY: *(Smiling in the spirit of the game)* And how would you talk to me, Do-Dirty?

DO-DIRTY: You just ask me something and see. *(He makes an ornate gesture of getting ready to answer.)*

LEAFY: Mr. Do-Dirty, are you having a good time tonight?

DO-DIRTY: *(Screws his face all up in a grimace that is meant to be very ingrati-ating and pleasing)* Yes ma'am. *(The crowd howls as he does his act. Then he comes out of it)* That's the way to talk to a pretty girl like you with all that Nearer-My-God-to Thee hair. *(Makes a gesture of combing long, silky tresses)* If they answers you any other way they is sassing you. *(Laughter)* That's how come you ought not to be setting in that old chair My Honey stuck under you. *(Offers chair)* Move into this nice setting-chair that I got for you.

LEAFY: *(Laughing)* Reckon I'll have to humor you, Do-Dirty.

MY HONEY: *(Rushing forward with a gesture of restraint)* No, no, Miss Leafy. Don't move out that chair I give you. *(He is very earnest about it, and it is noticed by all.)*

STEW BEEF: Look like old My Honey done got thunder-struck by lightning. *(Looks at My Honey's face seriously)* Don't move out his chair for good-ness shake. It will throw him into a three-weeks spasm.

DICEY: *(Thrusting into the center of the group)* How come she can't move? My Honey needs that chair more than she do. He got to set down to play, ain't he?

MY HONEY: *(Quickly to defend Leafy)* Aw, she ain't keeping me from setting down if I want to. I can play if I wants to, but there ain't no compellment about it. Just set and rest yourself, Miss Leafy. I loves to stand up anyhow.

*(There is a tense feeling and silence for a minute. Everybody looks to Lonnie.)*

LONNIE: Aw, table that talk. Leafy can set in any chair she will or may. They all belongs to the Bossman. If My Honey feels to stand up and let her set, that's his privilege. No need for all this who-struck-John about it.

STEW BEEF: *(Indicating Dicey)* That's what I told her.

DICEY: *(Significantly)* Some folks better sweep around they own door before they go trying to clean around mine. They got plenty to worry about they ownself.

*(She throws Lonnie a triumphant look, and then purses her mouth in a knowing way. All look at Lonnie to see if that is the answer to his strange behavior.)*

BIG SWEET: *(Crossing to Lonnie happily and with self assurance)* What you setting off by yourself for, sugar, like youse somebody throwed away?

*(Lonnie, laying out the cards carefully, looks up at her briefly then down again without speaking.)*

SOP-THE-BOTTOM: *(Worried, but trying to be light)* Oh, leave the man alone. Maybe he's just dreaming up something like he always do.

STEW BEEF: It can't be that, 'cause he always dream laughing. Something to make everybody feel good. He ain't laughing now, and none of us don't feel right.

SOP-THE-BOTTOM: Maybe it's something deep this time. He might be way out on ether's blue bosom somewhere travelling around. Then he going to come back and tell us something to make our work seem easy, and our burdens seem light.

DO-DIRTY: Sure is the truth. This old sawmill job seem just like New York with Lonnie around. I wouldn't stay here a day if he was to leave. *(General agreement with this)*

DICEY: *(Laughs)* If some folks would mind they own business instead of meddling with mine, they wouldn't be in the fix they's in.

MY HONEY: Aw, you always saying something nobody don't want to hear!

BOX CAR: *(To Dicey)* Shut up!

DICEY: *(With hand thrust suddenly into dress pocket)* You better come shut me up, then you'll know it's done right. My shutters ain't working so good.

BOX CAR: Keep on cackling when Lonnie feel bad and I will.

DICEY: I wish to God you would put your hands on me. I'll cut everything off you but quit it.

BOX CAR: Aw, don't be so public. Draw that knife and I'll draw my gun. *(Ominously)* And my gun don't lie to me. I'll shoot till my gun jumps the rivets.

BIG SWEET: *(Turns impatiently from her observation of Lonnie)* Aw, you all stop that racket in my ear!

BOX CAR: Well you make old ugly Dicey leave me be. Looking like some old phantassle!

DICEY: If I'm ugly, God made me ugly.

BOX CAR: That's a lie! God ain't never made nobody ugly. They gits that way they ownself. Thinking evil.

BIG SWEET: Hush!! I got to see about Lonnie. It's something wrong with him. *(Tenderly)* What's wrong, pudding-pie? You ain't going to keep nothing from *me,* I know.

*(Lonnie looks carefully at the arrangement of cards, but does not look up at Big Sweet, who tries to get into his line of vision.)*

PIANO PLAYER: *(Begins to play softly and sing)*

I'd rather see my coffin come rolling in my door
Than to hear my baby say she don't want me no more.

BIG SWEET: Lonnie, why you! You ain't even told me if I look good in my clothes or not.

*(Piano keeps on in undertone. Lonnie picks up a card and regards it intently. Everybody crowds about him and Big Sweet. There is a dramatic wait, then Lonnie begins to read the deck.)*

LONNIE:

Ace means the first time that I met you.
Deuce means there was nobody there but us two.
Trey means the third party —Charlie was his name
Four means the fourth time you tried that same old game
Five means *five years* you played me for a clown
Six means six feet of earth when the deal goes down.
Now, I'm holding the seven spot for each day in the week
Eight, means eight hours you sheba-ed with your sheik
Nine spot, nine hours I worked hard every day
Ten spot, the tenth of every month I brought you home my pay
The Jack, that's Three-Card Charlie *(Sensation)*[30] who played me for a
    goat
And the queen, that's *you,* pretty mama, also trying to cut my throat.

*(Rises to his feet)*

> The king, that's me, old Lonnie, and I'm going to wear the crown.
> So you better be sure you're ready when the deal goes down!

*(There is a moment of stunned silence as Lonnie and Big Sweet stand facing each other. Dicey breaks into raucous laughter which convulses her.)*

DICEY: Whatever goes over the devil's back is bound to buckle under his belly.

*(People are so intent on Big Sweet and Lonnie that they do not notice Dicey's antics, so she desists. Big Sweet approaches and tries to take Lonnie's arm, but he jerks away.)*

BIG SWEET: What make you mention Three-Card Charlie?

LONNIE: *(Hurt and belligerent)* Because you make me do it, that's why. That bed-bug!

BIG SWEET: Bed-bug? Even so, what is Charlie being a bed-bug got to do with you and me?

LONNIE: *(Vehement)* That is all he is, the scoundrel-beast, a bed-bug. *(Mimics stoop-shouldered posture)* He is flat, he crawls, he bites in the secret of darkness, and he stinks!

BIG SWEET: *(Bewildered and alarmed)* Is you done gone crazy? What the hell is the matter with you?

LONNIE: I'm a straight man, and believe in doing right. So, I ain't got no time to fool with you, and neither take up no time with you. I'm going down to the railroad station and grab the first thing smoking.

*(There is a general sigh and cry of dismay from all. Leafy thrusts through and faces Lonnie.)*

LEAFY: What *is* done got the matter with you, Lonnie?

LONNIE: I'm hurted. I'm hurt-ed to my very heart. *(Bows his head)* I loves Big Sweet, but she can't snore in my ear no more.

STEW BEEF: *(Desperate)* Lonnie, you can't go off and leave us like that.

LAURA B: Him and Big Sweet been gitting 'long too good to bust up and fall out.

BUNCH: It makes us all feel bad. What would us *do*?

*(There is a general feeling of helplessness and dismay. Big Sweet, resolute, steps forward, waving the others back. She raises Lonnie's chin and forces him to look at her.)*

BIG SWEET: Don't you all worry. Lonnie is just talking, for some reason or another. *(To Lonnie)* You ain't through with *me*, Lonnie Price.

LONNIE: *(Trying to resist her)* Oh, yes I is through with you. Why you think I can't quit you?

BIG SWEET: *(Growing confidence)* Because you belonged to me when they lifted you out of your cradle, and you going to be mine when they screw you down in your coffin.

LONNIE: Still and all, how come I can't git through with you?

BIG SWEET: *(Sensing his yielding)* Because I'm a damned sweet woman and you know it, too. *(Kisses him tenderly, which he does not resist.)* Now, tell me what I done.

DICEY: *(On edge of crowd)* What she done, she been doing that.

*(There is a general snarl from the crowd which has been anxiously watching the progress of agreement with expressions of hope and pleasure.)*

SOP-THE-BOTTOM: Hush up!

MY HONEY: *(Intense)* I wish thunder and lightning would kill you!

BIG SWEET: *(Gestures for quiet)* Tell me, Lonnie, what is I done?

LONNIE: What is you done? You done fooled me. You done cut the ground from under my feets. You done put out the sun and muddied up all the water in the world. You done took off all my dreams. You done stuck my foot in the mire and clay, so I can't fly no more. You done drove off the Great Crow.

*(There is a sob and a sigh from the crowd.)*

BIG SWEET: I never meant to do nothing like that to you. Tell me how I done it. *(She is deeply moved.)*

LONNIE: *(Looks at her searchingly)* You and Charlie been playing me for a fool. *(He explodes on "fool.")* And I don't intend to put up with it no more. I didn't choose you for that. Never no more.

BIG SWEET: No *more?* You got to have *some*, Lonnie, before you can have *more*. And you ain't had none up to now.

LAURA B: *(Very partisan)* Somebody done told a big old sway-back-ted lie. Big Sweet ain't harmed a soul.

BIG SWEET: Lonnie, I don't know as yet where you got this mess from, but it certainly is a lie.

LONNIE: I got a letter right here in my pocket say you been giving him my money. Say you been meeting him down in Mulberry.

BIG SWEET: *(Indignant)* That's another lie! *(Suddenly remembers and begins to laugh)* Shucks! I thought you was mad with me about something. I did meet Charlie once, but it wasn't nothing.

LONNIE: Nothing? You mean meeting another man on me ain't nothing? *(He shoves her away from him again.)*

BIG SWEET: *(Smiling and hugging him again)* That was way year before last.

LONNIE: That don't excuse you none. Year before last I was working for you and bringing you home my pay just like I got it from the man, just like I been doing ever since.

BIG SWEET: But, pudding-pie, what evil have I done? Since some old sea-buzzard had to go tell a lie on me, I reckon I better tell you how it was.

LONNIE: And you better git it fixed, too.

BIG SWEET: Baby, you know old Charlie always did have a pick at me.

LONNIE: That I know is so. But you always made out to me you didn't want him.

BIG SWEET: And I done neither. Never did. Well, about two years back, he took to picking at me, and sending me messages how he love me so hard, and all that money he had in his pocket was for me, till I got up a real good feeling for Charlie.

LONNIE: *(Groans)* Do, Jesus!

BIG SWEET: So one time when he begged me so hard, I thought I might as well go down there and git all that money he had for me.

*(Lonnie groans and almost collapses on table, but Big Sweet makes him sit up again.)*

Wait a minute, sugar, lemme finish telling you how it was. So I went down to Mulberry, and met him where he told me to come. He was there waiting with his hair all slicked down and everything. Soon as my toe-nails crossed the doorsill, I told Charlie, "Gimme what you got for me." He look like he didn't git the right understanding because he come telling me about all the love he had for me. So I asked him plain, "Is you got anything besides yourself?" *(Emphatic with rage)* And baby, you know that mink didn't have a dime to cry. When he told me that, honey, you know that good feeling I had for Charlie took and left me right then and there, and I ain't had it since. I turnt right 'round and come on home to you.

LONNIE: *(Jerks her roughly to him)* I dare him to send you any more messages. I'll give him a straightening if he do.

BIG SWEET: *(Drops down in his lap and begins to fondle him.)* Which one would you rather believe—your baby, or that old lying letter?

LONNIE: I rather to believe *you,* baby. I loves you harder than the thunder can bump a stump.

BIG SWEET: *(Snuggles down, and Lonnie's hand unconsciously begins to caress her legs.)* You see, sugar, I didn't fly hot and go accusing *you* when I found out that Ella Wall was sending for you all the time like she been doing for the last longest.

LONNIE: You don't need to worry about Ella Wall and no other woman God ever made. You got the keys to the kingdom.

STEW BEEF: *(Triumphant)* There now! The mule done kicked Rucker!

BIG SWEET: *(Hands on her hips, self-assured and smiling)* What I put on you, brother, soap and water won't take off.

LONNIE: All right, I admits to the truth. You done put me on the linger. And I even went so far as to ask you for your, your hand. How come you won't marry me like I ask-ed you to?

BIG SWEET: *(Recoils in hurt)* Now, *my* feelings is hurted, Lonnie.

LONNIE: I don't see how come. I been good to you as any man could be and I'm asking you to be my wife. I aims to go with you and stand by you till I press a dying pillow.

BIG SWEET: And I loves you just as hard as you love me. But, Lonnie, you want us to be running and gitting married like common folks. Us got this big love that nobody ain't never had *be*-fore. Us don't have to run to the courthouse and git papers and witnesses to prove if we is guilty. Us got that big-feeling love for one another. If I go dragging you to the white folks, it won't look like I believe what you say. I ain't never going to leave you, and I don't aim to let you leave me, neither. So what we got to act scared about?

LONNIE: *(Happy)* I'm mighty glad to hear you say we is never to part, baby. I just figured me and you ought to make a example out of ourselves for Leafy and My Honey and the rest of these folks 'round here.

BIG SWEET: Oh, it's going to be plenty marrying going on 'round here first and last. *(She looks pointedly at Stew Beef and Few Clothes.)* Some of these womens is been good to they mens, and they going to git ast-ed for they hands. Things got to be different on this job.

BUNCH: Lord knows it's time. I ain't seen a marriage on this job since I been here, and that's going on seven years.

BIG SWEET: It's going to be plenty marrying going on pretty soon now. This place got to be fitten for somebody like Leafy to live in.

STEW BEEF: How come you can't lead off, then?

BIG SWEET: Don't try to do as I do. You do as I *say* do. Most of you all won't tell the truth. Just like I told Leafy—she ain't to believe a thing you all say after ten o'clock at night, and nothing you promise no time on pay-day. I know you. Youse a gang of minks. I ought to know you. I done summered and wintered with you, ain't I? And then again, I hauled the mud to make you. I know just exactly what's in you.

FEW CLOTHES: But, Big Sweet, these womens—

BIG SWEET: I don't want to hear it. If you will hang after 'em you going to marry 'em. You going to ask for *hands*. Not cans.

LONNIE: And me and you can stand on the floor with each and every couple, can't we, baby? See the thing well done.

BOX CAR: I reckon we better start considering, if that's the way it's going to be. But it sure is taking a lot of fun out of pay-day.

STEW BEEF: *(Sighs heavily)* Just 'cause you shack up with a woman now, you got to give her money. Umph! Umph! Umph!

SOP-THE-BOTTOM: It's hard, but it's fair. *(Looks at Leafy)* I might as well git married now and git used to things.

LONNIE: *(With an air of command and finality)* Yeah, the time done come when big britches got to fit little Willie. *(Takes Big Sweet's arm affectionately)* Now, I can dream some more. Listen! I hear the drums of High John de Conquer. I can fly off on the big wings. I can stand on ether's blue bosom. I can stand out on the apex of power. Nobody can beat me doing what I'm supposed to do, and nothing can't keep me down. I got my wings. I rides the rainbow.

*(He stands exalted, and his mood touches all. The faint throb of a distant drum permeates the silence, and gradually draws nearer. First Lonnie smiles beatifically, then good humor and laughter spreads over the place.)*

STEW BEEF: Lonnie, youse a pistol! You can make anybody feel good. You can make a way out of no-way, and hit straight with a crooked stick.

BIG SWEET: That is how come I ever loves Lonnie. *(To Lonnie)* Come on, let's we go home and get our night rest.

LONNIE: *(Eagerly)* That's the very corn I wants to grind. *(Rushes Big Sweet towards exit right, downstage.)* I got to speak to you pointedly about your hand.

*(They stride towards exit, with the others clapping time with their hands, and exit. The others come out of the mood and begin spreading over the place.)*

Box Car: *(Passing Dicey, puts his hand on her head)* Well, Dicey, you took and laughed too quick. Big Sweet and Lonnie didn't bust up like you was hoping.

Dicey: *(Snatching away)* Keep your old nasty hands off my head! I ain't got Big Sweet and Lonnie to study about.

Sop-The-Bottom: Oh, yes you is. You was cackling to beat the band, and urging it on. That's how come I don't like you—always for a fuss.

Dicey: Oh, nobody on this job don't like me nohow.

Box Car: Look like you don't want nobody to like you, the way you do.

Dicey: Yes, I do too. I wants folks to like me just like anybody else. That's how come I likes to visit down at Mulberry. Ella Wall, and two three more likes me fine down there.

Laura B: That's the place you ought to live then, Dicey—where folks friends with you. How come you don't move down there?

Dicey: Naw, I ain't going to move down there nothing of the kind. They will turn against me too. *(Musing)* It's a funny thing—them that don't know me good is just crazy about me, but them that knows me well ain't got no use for me at all.

Stew Beef: *(Chuckling)* Maybe it's because they know you. *(There is a spontaneous burst of laughter.)*

Dicey: *(Instantly riled)* That's right! Laugh! Like a passle of jackasses. You just wait till I see Ella Wall and my other friends. You'll be laughing out the other side of your mouth, then. *(She starts furiously towards left exit. At the door she halts.)* I'll give you something to cackle over—you self-conceited dogs! *(She vanishes out of the door instantly. There is a light sprinkle of laughter after her exit.)*

Stew Beef: Let's dance this thing off. Play that piano, boy! I feels like a waltz. Miss Leafy, can I scorch you 'round the hall?

Leafy: *(Hugging herself as if with cold, perches on the side of the table and looks nervously about her.)* Not just now. Dicey—the way she looks at me—she gives me the weak-trembles.

Box Car: *(Crosses to table and stands admiring Leafy)* Pay it no mind. Dicey been talking about cutting up everybody for the last longest. She ain't crazy sure enough to think anybody is going to let her cut 'em and do nothing. Pay it no mind.

LEAFY: *(Still nervous)* You sure about that, now? The way she looks at me, nothing in the drugstore would kill me quicker than she would.

MY HONEY: *(Trying to get closest to Leafy)* I wouldn't stand 'round and let her hurt you, even if she had that in mind.

LEAFY: *(Not too sure)* I hope you know what you talking about.

BOX CAR: Let's table this talk on Dicey and open up the house for new business. *(Diffidently)* My Honey, is Miss Leafy your best-goodest lady friend?

MY HONEY: If you want to know who going to scorch Miss Leafy home tonight, I'm doing it. Anything else you want to know there she is, ask her! She can tell you what she want you to know.

SOP-THE-BOTTOM: Oh, you don't have to git mad because somebody else want to talk with the lady. She's a much-right, ain't she? Much-right for me as she is for you.

MY HONEY: There she is. Ask her your ownself.

BOX CAR: *(Diffident)* Miss Leafy, which would you ruther be, a lark a-flying, or a dove a-setting?[31]

SOP-THE-BOTTOM: He mean would you ruther be married or single?

LEAFY: *(Bridling)* Oh, you done asked me a hard question, Box Car. It all depends.

BOX CAR: Depends on what?

LEAFY: *(With an under-eye at My Honey)* It depends on whether I was in love or not. If I was in love, I would want to be a dove a-setting like Big Sweet. If I wasn't in love, I would choose to be a lark a-flying like I been doing.

BOX CAR: Now, we gitting deep. Is you seen anybody around here up to now that you figger you could nest with?

MY HONEY: Oh, leave Miss Leafy alone! She don't want to be bothered with you into her private business.

BOX CAR: I can't pick no box, My Honey, but I got a right to talk, ain't I? Good Lord! I'm looking out for my ownself. I ain't breaking into none of *your* arrangements, is I? *(Turns back to Leafy)* You ain't answered me yet.

LEAFY: *(Sits thoughtful)* Well, and then again, I can't say. *(The piano begins a waltz, and the couples begin to dance.)* But I did have a dream last night. *(My Honey strolls over to the piano and stands. Box Car and Sop get partners and dance.)* No, it wasn't true. It was just a dream. He came right into my room last night. The moonlight was tropic-white. He kissed me. He pressed me there on my bed. But it was just a dream. A shadow thrown by the moonlight. *(Sings)*

The moonlight came into my room
With his laugh
With his light
With his loom
He brought your face so near to me
I could feel
I could touch
I could see
I could seem
I could dream in the spell of the moon
In my room
Ah, the moon!

It was the full moon with his light
That brought you
And brought love
In the night.
He wove your wish right into mine.
With a kiss
That was bliss
So divine
Made you near
Ever dear, ever true—Ah that moon!
In my room
Ah, the moon!

*(The dancers keep on waltzing softly as Leafy sings in a sort of picturization of her dream-desires, there on the edge of the table. My Honey approaches her, puts down his guitar, she steps into his arms and they waltz into the crowd as the curtain falls.)*

## Scene 2

*Scene: One month later. Interior of Big Sweet's house.*[32] *At the rise, it is early night, and Big Sweet is in a loose wrapper arranging her hair for the street. She sings a light song as she dresses. She puts on her street shoes and stockings, adding proudly a pair of beribboned red garters. A silk dress is laid out on the bed, and she throws off her wrapper to put it on. But she whiffs under her arms, reaches over on the window sill and gets her wash cloth and wipes again, dusts herself with talcum, and arranges the dress carefully to go over her head without wrinkling. Lonnie bursts in, his face lit up with happy excitement.*

LONNIE: Sugar! Sugar! What you reckon? *(He grins delightedly.)* Old My Honey done got it out at last!

BIG SWEET: *(Dress still in her hands)* What?

LONNIE: He done got up the nerve and ask-ed Leafy for her hand. They's going to git married sure enough!

BIG SWEET: *(Glorified)* No! Well, the old slow thing got it out at last, eh? I sure is glad.

LONNIE: Yeah, and everything is going to be up to time, too. Bought license, a finger-ring and everything. Ain't that something?

BIG SWEET: *(Pulling dress over her head)* When did you find it out?

LONNIE: He just told me a while ago at the commissary. I come quick as I could to let you know. I wouldn't take a play-pretty for that.

BIG SWEET: Me neither. I'm so glad for Leafy. The poor thing wanted My Honey so bad, and look like the fool never was going to ask her. So bumble-tongued! I felt like zotting him over the head two three times.

LONNIE: He was scared she wouldn't have him. So pretty, and from New York and everything. But look like he done talked up a breeze now. Everything is copasetty.

BIG SWEET: *(Smiling)* That sly little hussy! She must of knowed he was due to ask. No wonder she went off from here around sundown dressed to death. Where they at, now?

LONNIE: Down at the cafe. Eating ice cream out the same spoon and grinning at each other like two glad dogs in a meat house.

BIG SWEET: *(Laughs heartily)* They's in heaven now, baby. They can't help it.

LONNIE: And My Honey done bought out the place with chocolate bars, and I reckon done started on the chewing gum by now.

*(They both laugh heartily, but proudly.)*

BIG SWEET: *(Fully dressed)* You wasn't much better when we first got together. *(Crosses and kisses him lightly.)* Remember that first time down behind the sawmill?

LONNIE: Aw, quit bragging on yourself! You knowed right then you had done laid me under conviction. And you meant to do it too.

BIG SWEET: Of course I did. I seen right away I was going to love you. Man, I threwed you some waves the ocean ain't never seen. *(Lonnie gives her an affectionate shove, and slaps her on her hips.)* And I hopes that Leafy do the same by My Honey.

LONNIE: You women always setting 'round figuring out how to take the undercurrents on some man. But us likes it, though.

BIG SWEET: But Lonnie, not changing the subject, us can't let Leafy and My Honey go get a house and live all by theyselves.

LONNIE: Why not? They'll be man and wife then, and he'll have all privileges. You can't—

BIG SWEET: Oh, I ain't talking about that. Them two will starve to death if we leave them do like that.

LONNIE: Like what? My Honey makes good money all the time.

BIG SWEET: Leafy is crazy about singing and dancing and she will forgit all about cooking something to eat. And My Honey he's carried away with picking that box and he won't think to say nothing to her about it. They'll sit 'round and starve just as stiff as a board. *(Both laugh.)*

LONNIE: Oh, I don't know, when that big gut reach and grab that little one, they'll scrabble up something to eat.

BIG SWEET: But it would be more better if they stayed right here with us.

LONNIE: *(Delighted)* You do git hold of the *best* notions! They got to stay right here. Anyhow, they going to be going to New York before long if Leafy have her way. She'll die the death of a doodle-bug if them folks in New York don't hear My Honey play that guitar.

BIG SWEET: Oh, yeah, she done talked my ear-flaps[33] down about how famous My Honey will be when he gits up there. Somebody of note like Booker T. Washington. She claim I and you ought to go up there and sing for money too. *(Laughs)* She must figure them white folks up there is crazy—paying folks good money just to sing.

LONNIE: She swears they does it, though. Maybe white folks ain't as smart as some folks thinks they is. Paying out good money to folks for having they fun. *(Chuckles)* I hope I meets up with some like that.

BIG SWEET: Well, us got money in the post office. If Leafy and them go up there, or if things was ever to go wrong 'round here, us could go up there and look around.

LONNIE: We could, at that. *(Gets up hurriedly)* The skitter man[34] is ill-sick in the hospital. Got to go put somebody else on the job till he gits better. *(He hurries to door and opens it.)* I'll be looking for my ground-rations tonight. *(He exits quickly.)*

BIG SWEET: *(Calls after him)* Okay, papa! I'll meet you at the Jook. *(She smiles to herself as she rubs powder on her face with a rubber sponge.)* What I tell that lie for? I know I ain't particular about going to no New York. I likes it here. I done come to be something here. I got Lonnie, and everybody puts they dependence in him and me. It's nice. Wonder who wrote that mean letter to Lonnie? Sure do wisht I knowed. I'd fix 'em.

*(There is a loud rapping at the door.)*

BIG SWEET: *(Listens)* Is that him doubling back? He must think I'm going to run off sure enough. *(Calls over her shoulder)* Come on back in Lonnie. I know it ain't nobody but you.

*(The door is thrown open roughly and the Quarters Boss enters, with his pistol hanging loosely in his hand. Big Sweet stares at him in surprise. He shoves his hat far back on his head, and with legs apart stands looking Big Sweet over sternly.)*

Oh, er, was you wanting to see Lonnie about something?

QUARTERS BOSS: Naw, I come here to—

BIG SWEET: Oh, you wanted to see me.

QUARTERS BOSS: I don't want to see you half as bad as the sheriff do, I reckon. *(He pauses to let that sink in.)* Vergible Thomas wasn't able to go to work today.

BIG SWEET: *(Offhand)* He don't do too much work no day.

QUARTERS BOSS: *(Losing his temper)* Never mind about how much work he do. I been told that you jumped him.

BIG SWEET: They told you right.

QUARTERS BOSS: Ain't I done told you and told you about stomping people and knocking 'em around?

BIG SWEET: *(Calm)* Vergible brought that on his ownself. I told him to hush his mouth. Talking all under folkses clothes and a whole lot of dirty, slack talk.

QUARTERS BOSS: *(Sneering)* Now, ain't that just too bad? Slack talk in sawmill quarters! Humph! Well, I aims to put a stop to you bulldozing these quarters. You act like you're some lord-god sitting on a by-god. Doing just as you damn please. Do you know you done kilt three men since you been on this job? Three men!

BIG SWEET: *(Nonchalantly)* I know it. I kilt 'em my ownself, didn't I? *(Boss almost explodes with anger, but cannot find words. Big Sweet sits in rocker and makes herself comfortable.)* And not a one of them minks died a day too soon, neither. They was low and mean and bulldozing, and had done kilt folks they own selves. They wouldn't do for they selves—they wouldn't do for nobody's else. They ought to been dead ten thousand years, the no-count things!

QUARTERS BOSS: So you mean to keep your meanness up, eh? Keep it up, and see what happens to you, then. The judge down to Bartow told me the last time you was there for a killing, that the very next time you come up before him for a killing, he was going to go hard on you. He's going to lay ninety days on you in the county jail!

BIG SWEET: *(Undisturbed)* Getting tough in his old age, eh? I bet you when lightning strikes him, it goes off through the woods limping.

QUARTERS BOSS: Smart, eh? Well, you done done your last big talk around here. Folks been bringing me news about your doings for the last month or so. I got plenty on you now. I git sick and tired of some coming to me telling me how you runs over folks. Well, one person will tell me things, anyhow. I'm telling you, you got to leave off this job.

BIG SWEET: *(Stunned)* Me leave here?

QUARTERS BOSS: Yes, you leave here. And no later than next pay day. *(He strides sullenly to the door.)*

BIG SWEET: *(Hard to comprehend the blow)* You mean *I* got to go? I—er, what's that you said?

QUARTERS BOSS: *(At door)* You heard me what I said. By next pay day.

*(He slams the door hard and is gone. She is stunned and disorganized. She gets up slowly and moves about aimlessly. Finally, she sinks on the side of the bed with her hands in her lap.)*

BIG SWEET: But how can I leave here? I won't have no home no more. Be like I was before. Just on the road, somewhere. *(Overcome)* No! No! I just can't leave. I'm somebody now. Folks needs me. I can't go off feeling like nothing no more. And everybody here will feel like nothing again when me just sawdust. Some more sawdust piled up like that behind the mill with the rain and the storm beating on it. *(She clenches her hands and suppresses a sob.)* Poor Lonnie! He's going to follow me off and he ain't never going to be satisfied no more. *(In helpless appeal)* Jesus! *(Begins to chant)*

Jesus, Jesus, Jesus, Jesus, Jesus!

*(She sings the melody with a distant drum rhythm under her. Then the strings in the orchestra take up the melody while she talks and chants against it.)* I ain't nothing. None of us ain't nothing but dust. Sawdust. Piled up round the mill. What is left over from standing trees. Sometimes, when Lonnie talks, the sawdust shines like diamonds, and glints like gold. Then the light goes out, and we are dust again. Dust from God's big saw. *(Sings)*

Jesus, Jesus, Jesus, Jesus, Jesus.

*(She gets hold of herself and the music fades. She gets up and goes resolutely to the door.)* Lonnie said meet him at the Jook. So I'm going and laugh and dance and sing. *(Quick exit. Curtain.)*

## Scene 3

*Scene: The following night. Interior of the Jook. At the rise, Sop-The-Bottom, Box Car and Do-Dirty are at the dice table playing. The pianist is playing, but in an experimental manner. Bunch and Laura B are sitting against the wall to the left, conversing in low tones and laughing quietly. Stew Beef and Few Clothes are in the center of the floor chatting inaudibly.*

BOX CAR: *(To Sop-The-Bottom)* Six is your point.

DO-DIRTY: Two bits you don't six.

BOX CAR: What's your come-bet?

FEW CLOTHES: *(Shoving Stew affectionately and laughing)* Aw, man, I wouldn't believe that lie if I told it my ownself.

STEW BEEF: Yeah it is so. Monkeys can talk when they want to. *(Laughs)*

FEW CLOTHES: Youse crazy! *(Laughs)* After that, I'm going to coon some with your old woman. *(Lifts voice as he goes to card table.)* Come on, Laura B, let's coon.

LAURA B: *(Getting up briskly and going to table)* All right, I'll play you.

FEW CLOTHES: *(Braggadocio)* You reckon you know the game?

LAURA B: *(Bragging)* If I ain't a coon-can player, I'm a 'leven card layer.[35] *(Shoves the deck towards Few Clothes.)* Strip it! *(Chants)*

Before I'll lose my rider's change
I'll spread short deuces and tab the game.

*(Few Clothes offers her the deck to cut. She shoves it back in disdain.)*

LAURA B: Deal! I don't cut green wood.

BUNCH: (*Coming over to watch*) Naw, no need to cut a rabbit out when you can twist him out.

LAURA B: That's right. (*Sings*)

Give my man my money to play coon-can
He lost all my money but he played his hand.

(*Stew Beef wanders over to dice game.*)

SOP-THE-BOTTOM: (*Starts singing*)

Oh, Angeline! Oh, Angeline!
Oh, Angeline, that great, great gal of mine.

(*The four about the table form a quartet and sing.*)

And when she walk, and when she walk
And when she walk she rocks and reels behind.
You feel her legs, you feel her legs
You feel her legs then you want to feel her thighs
You feel her thighs, you feel her thighs—

(*Leafy enters downstage left, locked arms with My Honey, both are radiant.*)

STEW BEEF: (*Seeing them enter*) Shhhhh! Here come Miss Leafy. (*The song ceases instantly.*) How you do, Miss Leafy? Hello My Honey.

(*Both respond and stroll towards piano. Box Car, Sop-The-Bottom and Do-Dirty all regard Leafy with hungry admiration as she swishes along with My Honey.*)

BOX CAR: (*Turning completely from the game*) Oh, will I ever? Will I ever?

MY HONEY: (*Over his shoulder*) No, you'll never, no, you'll never! (*All laugh at this passage.*)

BOX CAR: Well, you sure can't keep me from hoping.

MY HONEY: (*Rests his guitar on piano and turns. Laughs good natured.*) That's right. I can't keep the sight out of your eyes, but I sure God will keep the taste out your mouth. (*Takes Leafy's arm again.*) Come on, sugar, lemme find you a good seat.

(*They head downstage.*)

BOX CAR: (*Half in fun, half serious*) You don't care if us walk behind you do you, whilst you scorch Miss Leafy to a chair?

MY HONEY: (*Laughing*) You can walk behind and wish all you want to.

*(Box Car, Sop-The-Bottom, and Do-Dirty leave the table and fall in behind Leafy and My Honey with the most yearning and beseeching expressions in face and body and follow them along.)*

BOX CAR: *(Feigning utmost desire)* Oh, I wish it was me!

DO-DIRTY: *(Same business)* Oh, don't I wish it was me!

SOP-THE-BOTTOM: Lord knows, I wish it was me!

BOX CAR, SOP-THE-BOTTOM and DO-DIRTY: I wish it was me! I wish it was me!

*(They follow My Honey and Leafy all around the room in a parade lamenting, while the others laugh at the show. Finally, My Honey and Leafy shoo them off and sit down.)*

DO-DIRTY: *(To Sop-The-Bottom and Box Car)* Oh, well, look like he got us barred. We done let the 'gator beat us to the pond. We might as well give up.

SOP-THE-BOTTOM: Yeah, My Honey got the business. *(To My Honey)* When you all figger on jumping over the broomstick? I know Big Sweet ain't going to stand for no commissary license.

MY HONEY: We don't want none. We going to do it up brown.

STEW BEEF: Yeah man, he got them license in his pocket right now. I done seen 'em myself.

LAURA B: Yeah. And we done fixed up to give 'em a big woods dance and all. Just waiting for Big Sweet to make the arrangements.

BUNCH: This marriage is got to be fine. It's the first one, and it will be setting the style for the rest of us.

FEW CLOTHES: *(Groans)* I reckon nothing can't stop the rest of you womens after this one come off.

BUNCH: That's right. Me and you is going to marry. You heard what Big Sweet said.

STEW BEEF: *(Looking at Laura B)* And I guess I'm dead on the turn.

LAURA B: If you expect me to do for you anymore.

STEW BEEF: Well, we better give My Honey a big send off. Plenty to eat and drink, and cut Big Jim by the acre. Then they will do the same by us. Anyhow, this one got to be fine. It's the first one to come off since here on this job I been. I'm gitting so I likes the notion.

LAURA B: It's about time.

*(Big Sweet enters upstage, right with Lonnie. She is greeted with enthusiasm.)*

LONNIE: How ye folkses!

BIG SWEET: (*Coming down to center stage and looking all around her*) Well, people! I thought you all was teaching Leafy some more songs.

STEW BEEF: Leafy ain't got her mind on no singing. Look at her.

LEAFY: (*Coming out from under a long kiss*) Yes, I do want to know some more songs, too.

BIG SWEET: (*Seriously*) And I want you to learn all there is just as quick as you can. (*Meaningly*) It might git so you wouldn't be here to learn no more.

LEAFY: Why?

(*Everybody looks puzzled.*)

BIG SWEET: Oh, you just might not be here, that's all. (*To the room*) You all learn Leafy some more.

STEW BEEF: We done learnt her about all we know. Me and Laura B was just saying we couldn't think up no more. Lonnie, how about that thing you and My Honey was messing with today down in the swamp?

LONNIE: Oh, if she wants to learn it, we can do the best we can. Come on My Honey, and git in quotation with the piano so we can show the girl.

(*My Honey rushes to piano and gets guitar. A chord or two is struck and Lonnie begins.*)

Mama, Mama, who is Jack?
Where's his horse and where is his shack?
Was he true a sawmill man?
Did he skin and play coon-can?

(*Drums dominate*)

This is the house that Jack built.
This is the malt that lay in the house that Jack built.
This is the rat that ate the malt, that lay in the house that Jack built.
This is the cat that killed the rat that ate the malt that lay in the house that Jack built.

(*All begin to join the rhythm, clap hands, stomp with the drums.*)

This is the maiden all forlorn
That milked that cow with the crumpled horn
That tossed the dog that worried the cat
That killed the rat, that ate the malt
That laid in the house that Jack built.

(*Drum interval.*)

My Honey:

> This is the cock that crowed in the morn
> That woke that priest all shaven and shorn
> That married the man all tattered and torn
> That kissed the maiden all forlorn
> That milked that cow with the crumpled horn
> That tossed the dog that worried the cat
> That killed the rat, that ate the malt
> That laid in the house that Jack built.
>
> *(Drum interval.)*

Big Sweet:

> Oh, this is Jack with his hound and horn
> That caught the fox that lived under the thorn
> That stole the cock that crowed in the morn
> That woke that priest all shaven and shorn
> That married the man all tattered and torn
> That kissed the maiden all forlorn
> That milked that cow with the crumpled horn
> That tossed the dog that worried the cat
> That killed the rat, that ate the malt
> That laid in the house that Jack built.
>
> *(Drum interval.)*

Leafy:

> Oh, Mama! Mama! Look at sis
> Out in the yard trying to do that twist.
> Come in here, and I mean now!
> You're trying to be a rounder
> But you don't know how.
> Let your Mama show you.
>
> Oh, this is the horse of the beautiful form
> That carried Jack with his hound and horn
> That caught the fox that lived under the thorn
> That stole the cock that crowed in the morn
> That woke that priest all shaven and shorn
> That married the man all tattered and torn
> That kissed the maiden all forlorn
> That milked that cow with the crumpled horn
> That tossed the dog that worried the cat
> That killed the rat, that ate the malt
> That laid in the house that Jack built.

*(The others have worked up to a high pitch and are on their feet for the most part, dancing, clapping, etc. to the drums.)*

LONNIE:

> This is Sir John Barleycorn
> That owned the horse of the beautiful form
> That carried Jack with his hound and horn
> That caught the fox that lived under the thorn
> That stole the cock that crowed in the morn
> That woke the priest all shaven and shorn
> That married the man all tattered and torn
> That kissed the maiden all forlorn
> That milked the cow with the crumpled horn
> That tossed the dog, that worried the cat
> That killed the rat, that ate the malt
> That lay in the house that Jack built.

*(Every "that" is accented with drum and voice. The drums continue and finally die away like the end of a rainstorm.)*

BIG SWEET: Did you git that one, Leafy? Git it right?

LEAFY: *(Happily)* Oh, yeah. I got it good. And I like it too.

BIG SWEET: *(Very subdued)* As I before said, git all you can just as quick as you can. I might not be here always to see to things.

LONNIE: You been saying that all day. What you mean by that?

*(Big Sweet, with her eyes down, hesitates, while all hang on what she might say in explanation. Dicey enters downstage, left, with a triumphant flourish with Ella Wall, who has the air of a conqueror and struts towards center stage.)*

SOP-THE-BOTTOM: Ella Wall, Lord! Hi there Ella!

ELLA WALL: *(With a flourish)* I'm folks.

DICEY: I'll say youse folks. You was folks up in Middle Georgia before you ever come to Polk County. Youse folks in Mulberry, and youse folks in Lofton. Fact of the matter is, youse folks wherever you go.

*(Ella Wall has advanced to center stage confidently expecting Big Sweet, Leafy, and Lonnie who are still there to give way. She is brought to a halt when she sees that Big Sweet does not move, and the others take their cue from her. Ella stops abruptly as she comes against them. She halts and looks Big Sweet up and down in a sneering way.)*

ELLA: Hello, there, Big Sweet. Look like you got changing clothes, now.

BIG SWEET: It do look like it, don't it?

ELLA: You sure done improved up from what you used to be. I knowed you when you was just as naked as a jay-bird in whistling time.

*(She laughs excessively and Dicey joins her in the slur by laughing.)*

BIG SWEET: *(Quietly)* You sure telling the truth, Ella. *(Cruelly)* But that was before I *got* the man that you was trying to git. Lonnie don't let me want for nothing. Every pay day I sits on my porch and rock and say, "Here come Lonnie and them."

ELLA WALL: Them? What them?

BIG SWEET: *(Arrogantly)* Them dollars! You hear me. You ain't blind.

ELLA WALL: Lonnie? I just let you have him because I seen you was in need. I can git any man I wants.

LONNIE: Excepting me. Not since I come to know Big Sweet anyhow.

SOP-THE-BOTTOM: *(Woofing)* Pay Lonnie Price no mind, Ella. What you care about him when you can git me? If you handles the money you used to handle about ten years back and let me spend it like I please, I'm yours any time.

*(There is a big laugh and Ella is taken [a]back.)*

DICEY: Who? Ella don't have to give no mens her money. They gives her. She's just like the cemetery. She ain't putting out. She's taking *in.*

BIG SWEET: *(With a catty smile)* I see you got something too, Ella, that you didn't used to have.

ELLA: What is it? *(Displays her hands full of cheap jewelry)* I always had jewelry and things.

BIG SWEET: *(Indicating Dicey)* You got you a yard dog now to do your barking for you.

BOX CAR: *(Pretending sympathy for Dicey)* Aw, aw! Big Sweet, what make you play so rough? Dicey, I wouldn't take that if I was you.

STEW BEEF: *(Egging the fight on)* Now, what you want to try to start something for, Box? You know Dicey ain't going to get on Big Sweet. Not unlessen she's braver than I figure her out to be.

ELLA: Dicey don't have to act scared. She got somebody to back her up.

BIG SWEET: I ain't looking for no trouble, but if anybody pay their way on me, God knows I'll pay it off.

*(A yell of expectant excitement.)*

BOX CAR: Of course, now, Dicey is going to back her crap.

DICEY: *(Afraid)* Us come in here for pleasure. Us didn't come here to fight. *(With a knowing leer)* And then again, I don't have to be fighting and carrying on. Some folks that's around here thinking they got the world by the tail ain't going to be here long. Then everything will be nice. *(She looks venomously from Big Sweet to Leafy.)*

LEAFY: If you're talking about me, I'm in the *be* class—be here while you're here, and be here when you're gone.

LAURA B: *(Proudly)* Listen at little crowing!

LEAFY: Yeah, I'm getting married to My Honey, and it won't be long, either, and it ain't no help for it. I got more right here than you have. *(Beams up proudly at My Honey)* I got a *husband* on this job.

*(Dicey, full of hate and frustration, instantly puts her hand in her pocket. Everybody sees the gesture and grows tense.)*

BIG SWEET: Don't you pull no knife in here. I dare you to even take it out! And Ella Wall, you don't belong on this place at all. The Bossman said *particular* he didn't want no stragglers on the premises. Git on out here and take your yard dog along with you. Git!

ELLA: *(Shows hot resentment in her face, but looking around she sees nothing friendly in any of the faces. No possible help.)* I'm going, but I'll be back. Your time now, but it will be mine after while. Come on, Dicey.

DICEY: *(As they retrace their steps)* Hanh! Big Sweet won't be here long. *(Laughs gloatingly)* Nobody didn't tell me, but I heard. Then other folks *(Pointedly at Leafy)* can be straightened out.

LONNIE: Big Sweet can stay here just as long as she please, and go when she gits ready.

DICEY: *(At door)* That ain't what the Quarters Boss say.

*(She and Ella exit laughing triumphantly. A profound silence settles over the place.)*

LONNIE: Now, what you reckon that Dicey mean by that? *(He looks at Big Sweet, questioning)*

STEW BEEF: I sure don't know.

BIG SWEET: *(Sighs)* Oh, you all leave me be. *(She drags over to the table, left, and drops down in a chair. She sits a moment gloomily.)* It's another song I got to teach you, Leafy. It ain't got no laughing in it, but I reckon you got to learn it. Help me out on it, My Honey, much as you can. *(Begins to sing to herself, gradually swells.)*[36]

Ever been down, know just how I feel
Ever been down, know just how I feel
Been down so long till down don't worry me

I wonder will he answer if I write
I wonder will he answer if I write
I wonder will he answer if I write

Well you may leave and go to Hali-muh-fack
But my slow-drag will bring you back
Well, you may go, but this will bring you back.

*(She gets an ovation as she ends first chorus. As she begins second verse Lonnie moves in closer as My Honey moves closer in his enthusiasm of playing.)*

LONNIE: *(Crosses and puts his arm about Big Sweet's shoulders)* It's something wrong. Why you don't tell me what it is?

BIG SWEET: *(Breaks down)* You so nice. I didn't want to hurt your feelings.

LONNIE: *(Commanding)* Tell me what it is.

BIG SWEET: Well, the Quarters Boss come to me last night right after you left and said I had to leave. *(This stuns everybody.)*

LONNIE: *You* leave? What he mean by that?

BIG SWEET: Said somebody been coming to him saying I makes all the trouble around here. Said I had to leave—no later than pay day. *(A deep gloom settles over the place.)* And that's how come I tell Leafy to do the best she can whilst I'm here, so her and My Honey can git gone. Somebody is liable to hurt her when I'm gone.

MY HONEY: I begs to differ with you—not to give you no short answer—but Leafy got me behind her.

BIG SWEET: I know, and I don't doubt you one bit. But you have to be on the job all day long, and a whole heap could happen in that time. Folks can steal her.

LAURA B: Some lowdown jig been toting lies to the white folks on Big Sweet. That's what's the matter.

LONNIE: Wish I was sure who it was. I sure would hang for 'em.

STEW BEEF: Me too. *(General chorus of agreement.)*

BIG SWEET: *(Idea)* Maybe it was the same one that wrote Lonnie that lying letter on me. You still got it, Lonnie?

LONNIE: *(Fooling in his pockets)* Maybe I is. Done most forgot I had it. *(Pulls out a crumpled letter written in pencil and hands it to Big Sweet.)* I always thought I didn't have no sense, and every time I thinks about the fuss I had with you, I know it.

BIG SWEET: *(Unfolding letter and scanning it)* This letter say it's from Three-Card Charlie, turning me some humble thanks for the spending-money I sent him. *(Looks all around amazed.)* He must be crazy! I ain't never sent him dime one.

BOX CAR: When was it wrote?

BIG SWEET: Oh, little better than a month back.

BOX CAR: Then, Charlie sure never wrote it.

LONNIE: How come he didn't? It would be just like the dirty mink to try to git my baby away from me.

BOX CAR: Because Charlie been dead to my knowing for more than over a year. Woman killed him in Savannah.

LONNIE: Sure enough?

BOX CAR: I know it for a fact. I was there. Remember I quit here and was off a couple of months. Seen her when she stabbed him. He sure did die.

LONNIE: *(Hugs Big Sweet impulsively.)* Well, well!

BOX CAR: So if Charlie wrote you that letter, things must be different down in hell from what it used to be. They didn't used to send out no mail from there.

LONNIE: This don't say hell. It say, Mulberry, Florida.

BOX CAR: Maybe they done took in Mulberry for a new addition, but I ain't heard nothing about it. I knows the place well.

SOP-THE-BOTTOM: Hush your lying, Box Car! How you know anything about hell?

BOX CAR: Don't tell me, man. I don't stay in one place like the rest of you all. I gets around.

LONNIE: So now, us know that Charlie ain't wrote no letter back. Wonder who?

BIG SWEET: And went and lied on me to the Quarters Boss?

LAURA B: Aw, you know nobody done it but Dicey. Nobody else on the job would want to hurt you.

MY HONEY: Sure. She's trying to hit a straight lick with a crooked stick. She figger she can git to Leafy if you is out the way. And she don't love me to all of that, neither. She just hate to be outdone.

LONNIE: Well, I reckon she will move off with Ella now, so—

LAURA B: But you heard both of 'em put out they brags that they will be back with help.

BIG SWEET: *(Resigned)* I reckon they will have they swing. Everything will be back like it used to be.

LONNIE: But you can't go.

BOX CAR: Nobody here want you to go no where, do us? *(A general protest against her leaving.)*

BIG SWEET: But the man done told me that the company would rather have my room than my company. *(Sighs heavily. General desperation and gloom.)*

LEAFY: *(Almost in tears)* I'm the cause of it all.

BIG SWEET: In a way you is, and then again you ain't. All you done was come here and put words to the feeling I already had. I ever wanted things to be nicer than what they was. Ever since I been with Lonnie, more especial.

STEW BEEF: But My Honey and Leafy is gitting married. We going to cut Big Jim by the acre when that come off. Big woods picnic and everything. Who is going to general our business for us if you ain't here?

BUNCH: Nobody can't do nothing right on this place without you. What *will* us do if you ain't here?

BIG SWEET: Do like the folks over the creek, I reckon. Do without.

LONNIE: *(Pulls out a chair and drops down in it backwards and sits in gloomy thought.)* I reckon you all know that if Big Sweet has to go, I don't aim to be here another minute. 'Tain't nothing bad about Big Sweet at all. She got plenty good friending in her if you let her be.

BUNCH: We all knows that.

LONNIE: *(Face hard)* Something is wrong 'round here if somebody like Big Sweet can be told to go. Somebody trying to drive her.

SOP-THE-BOTTOM: And it sure ain't clean.

MY HONEY: *(Most dejected)* Everything was going along so good. Big Sweet doing the best she could to make everything nice—

LONNIE: What is we? We ain't nothing. We didn't come from nothing. We ain't got nothing but the little wages we makes. Look like then us ought not to be bothered with trouble. That's for big, rich folks that got their many pleasures. Why we got to have troubles too? *(A harmonic, vocal chant whispers under him and gets a little stronger as he talks.)* Where is these quarters nohow? Wild woods all around and the mill in the middle. *(As if [in] sudden discovery)* We'se in a cage! Like a mule-lot down in a swamp.

BIG SWEET: *(Takes lead in chant and puts softly sung words to chant and the others follow her. Humming)*

I got my hands in my Jesus hands

ALL:

I got my hands in my Jesus hands.

LONNIE:

Panthers in the swamp. Moccasins 'round your feet all day. Standing in water.

*(Chant grows intense but not loud. More fervent)*

Trees falling on men and killing 'em. Saw liable to cut you in two. Sundown, nothing but these quarters to come to and keep on like that until you die.

*(Chant dominates the pause with repetition of "Jesus, Jesus, Jesus, Jesus, Jesus.")*

It's something wrong. But what can we do? You don't know and I don't know, so I can't tell you. Just moving around in the cage.

*(The chant comes out in the open, while Lonnie sits and looks off into space.)*

BIG SWEET: Sawdust, even if it do shine sometime.

*(The faint whisper of distant drums comes and Lonnie begins to smile. More and more. The others, watching Lonnie's face, begin to smile too, as the drums become more audible.)*

LONNIE: *(Smiling and chuckling)* What make me talk so disencouraged like? Old John de Conquer would know how to beat the thing. *(Chuckles broadly)* Shucks! High John could git out of things don't care how bad they was, and finish it off with a laugh.

*(The drums are very pronounced now, and some pat their feet, and in other ways accent the rhythm of the drums.)*

Big Sweet ain't going nowhere. That Quarters Boss ain't got no stuff for me. If he got to listen to everything that old Dicey say—

LAURA B: Every lie she make up and tell.

LONNIE: I'm going to make my left-here now.

*(Chorus of "and we're going when you go!")*

STEW BEEF: One day after you leave, there won't be a soul in the quarters.

LONNIE: And I'm going to be the one to tell the Big Boss my ownself. The man can wait till he git the straight of things, or else we all can go. If the Boss ruther for him listen to lies than for us to do his work, then we still can go.

*(A great cheer goes up.)*

Tomorrow will tell the tale.

*(The prayer-chant for victory takes up again. Getting to his feet dramatically.)*

Something ought to be like we want it. We ain't got nothing. We ain't never had nothing. Our folks ain't left us nothing.

*(Chant dominates for a moment.)*

Six feet of earth when the deal goes down.

*(Chant)*

And we ain't never asked for much.

*(Chant over drums is repeated and variated till curtain.)*

## ACT THREE
### Scene 1

*Scene: The following Saturday night. Interior of Dicey's shack. At the rise, the shack is empty. It is of the same crude construction as Big Sweet's house, but little has been done here to relieve the raw unpainted lumber and careless structure. The bed is lumpy and covered by a worn, faded quilt. There is a small iron heater in the corner, downstage right. It needs polish. The bed is across the center of the wall upstage. Two or three shoddy dresses hang against the door, which is left. A cheap suitcase is under the edge of the bed. The thin curtains are only half, and hung on strings that sag. Two unpainted kitchen chairs and a goods box covered with newspaper complete the furnishings of the room, except for a chipped slop-jar in the corner behind the door.*

*There is no one in the room at the rise. One hears a key thrust hurriedly and nervously in the door, then Dicey opens the door and fairly leaps inside, looking back over her shoulder as she enters.*

DICEY: *(Shutting the door quickly and locking it)* I don't reckon nobody seen me come in. *(She turns on the light above her head and looks all around the room furtively.)* Better git all ready before Nunkie git here for me. *(Pulls suitcase from under bed and puts it on the bed and opens it.)* Don't want to forgit a thing! When I leave here this time, this place won't never see me no more. *(She takes down the clothes from the door and hurriedly folds them into the bag. Picks up a cheap comb with some of the teeth missing, a box of talcum, and puts them in. Keeps looking about to miss nothing.)* They can have this little old furniture. I can't tote it nohow. Crip owed the man for it anyhow. Let 'em git it. *(She suddenly remembers the package that she brought in and eagerly grabs it and packs it.)* Lord, I sure don't want to forgit my regalia! Got to have that with me tonight. *(Rushes to head of bed and lifts the corner of the mattress and takes out a "hand,"*[37] *a small bundle about three inches long sewed up in red flannel and regards it fondly.)* Wouldn't that be awful if I was to go off and forget my mojo? *(Regards it gloating.)* It was fixed for me to conquer and overcome. Big Sweet don't need to think she got no stuff for me—not with the help *I* got. *(Thrusts it deep into her bosom and smiles.)* The voodoo-man and Ella Wall say it will sure do the work. *(Sees the small, cheap mirror on the improvised dresser and takes it and carries it to the bed. Starts to pack it, then sits down on the bed and studies her features in the glass. Feels her hair first, then passes her fingers over her face in concentration in the mirror.)* How come I got to look like I do? Why couldn't I have that long straight hair like—like—Big Sweet got, and that Leafy? They own looks like horse's mane, and mine looks like drops of rain. *(Feels disgust, self-pity, then resentment.)* And these mens is so crazy! They ain't got no sense. Always pulling after hair and looks. And these womens that got it is so grasping, and griping, and mean. They wants EVERYTHING—and they gits it too. Look like they would be satisfied with *some!* Naw, they wants it all. Takes pleasure in making other folks feel bad. *(Hurls mirror into bag face down and slams it shut.)* How come I got to be a swill barrel to take they leavings? *(In utter revolt)* Things ought not to be that way. What do they do more'n me? I wish they all was dead! Wish I could cut 'em and mark 'em in they faces, till they all looks worser than me! They acts like they thinks the world is made just for them to strut around and brag on they selves in.

*(She leans against the bed post and thinks aloud on life and what it has done to her and comes to her conclusions. Because they are unsuitable, she laments.*[38] *During the lament, a dance group interprets Dicey's despair.)*

Pretty women! How I hate their guts!
This talk about equality is nuts.
Have *I* got an equal chance
With anything that's wearing pants?
I'll tell the world, and Georgia too, 'tain't so.

(*Examines herself in mirror.*[39])

My looks is just a heavy load
That sends me down a lonesome road
And *no one* cares the way I have to go.

(*Looks again in glass and sighs.*)

I ain't a woman in a way
Where men have anything to say
Of love, and tenderness, and such.
I'm just another kind of mule—
A bad exception to a rule
So what I feel don't seem to matter much.

(*Conversational outburst of outrage at inequality*) What did the white folks do to Big Sweet for shooting them men? Nothing! Naw, with that hair and them looks, she could kill a thousand and they wouldn't care.

Yeah, a pretty gal can *kill* a man
And never sleep a night in [the] can
They'll give *her* back her gun and let her go.
But let an ugly gal like *me*
So much as cripple up a flea
And they will build a new and better jail.
The judge and jury'll sit in state
And ponder grimly on my fate
And give me *time,* I've never seen it fail.
They won't try me by no law books
They'll see the crime right in my looks
And sentence me according to my shape.
There'll be no mercy on the bench
I'll get a look that's meant to lynch
Good riddance for a trashy, ugly ape.
If Leafy Lee would shoot me dead
And weigh me down with red hot lead
It will be only a regrettable mistake.
But if I scratch her yellow skin
It is a deathly, mortal sin
They'll put me in the chair and let me bake.
No, it ain't right, and it ain't fair

'Cause I ain't got that skin and hair
I wasn't born the way I ought to be.
I'm on the outside looking in
So don't expect to see me grin
And laugh the way that pretty women do.
I have to scramble for a kiss
When they get all this married bliss
The men, the world, and Heaven too.
So I feels mean, and I get sad
I tries to laugh, but I ain't glad.
I often curse the day that I was born.
I build some lovely dreams at night
Then see them killed in broad daylight
And all my tender feelings laughed to scorn.
I sure can't help the way I'm made
And so, when all is done and said
I'm just a victim of relentless fate.
I got big love, that I can't give.
I got a life, still, I can't live.
Just all dammed[40] up and turning into hate.
I hate the women through and through
Who get the things that I want, too.
I wouldn't like 'em, even if I could!
And women thwarted, just like me
Thought up those fires in hell, in *glee*
So come on, Evil! Be thou now my good![41]

(*Takes her knife out of her pocket, feels the edge carefully, and begins to whet it grimly on the edge of the stove. Stops and tests it on her thumb, and whets again vigorously. Sings briefly.*)

Get your razor 'cause I got mine
Feel mistreated and I don't mind dying—

(*There comes a swift, but stealthy, insistent knocking at the door. Dicey halts whetting abruptly, looks scared, but on guard, wonders whether to open door or not, but as the knocking begins again, she hears the voice of Nunkie frightened outside.*)

NUNKIE: (*Offstage*) Dicey! Dicey! Let me in here!

(*Dicey, relieved, hurries to door, turns key and opens it partly. Nunkie burst[s] past her into the room.*)

What you keep me out there knocking for? Somebody could have cut my throat.

DICEY: I didn't know if it was you or not. Somebody could have seen me coming in.

NUNKIE: Oh, they don't know—

DICEY: I bet they does, too. Lonnie—'course I don't expect no more out of him. Big Sweet must got him fixed. He believe what she say all the time. It's a hidden mystery how she got him so tied up. And that Quarters Boss, he ain't nothing. Made out he was going to run Big Sweet off, but you see she's here right on.

NUNKIE: *(Outdone and depressed)* Oh, you didn't tell him like I told you! If you had of made it bad enough—

DICEY: *(Hotly)* Yes I did too! I made it real distressing. But look like it don't do no good at all, no matter what you say about her.

NUNKIE: *(Glum)* I sure hopes we git her good tonight. Ella Wall say it will. She say they don't last when she hold that kind of dance on 'em. *(Animated)* Lord, if it work like she say! We dance on 'em and they all stand there in they tracks and can't move. Just like statues!⁴² *(Happy anticipation)* And whilst they standing there and can't move at all, we go in on 'em with our knives and ruin 'em! I takes Big Sweet first one.

DICEY: And I takes that Leafy Lee. My Honey too. I hates him now just as bad as I used to love him. All I want to do is to git them two good. Then I'm long gone, like a turkey through the corn.

NUNKIE: We better be fast. Just in case, you know. Big Sweet might be able to move some, and if she do—

DICEY: Didn't Ella say they won't be able to move atall? Just like they made out of wood till we git through, and be out and gone.

NUNKIE: *(Not too assured)* Yeah, but voodoo don't take on some folks. Specially if they got this straight hair. It ain't got nothing to tangle in. Us better dash in and do what we got to do, and light out. After me and Ella gits Big Sweet, hack all of 'em a lick or two and git for Mulberry. *(Imagines he hears a sound outside and is frightened)* What's that? *(They both listen for a while.)*

DICEY: I reckon it wasn't nobody. They all down in the woods not far from where we going. *(Face goes grim)* My Honey and that Leafy thinks they going to git married.

NUNKIE: *(Restless)* You ready? Come on let's git out of here. I don't want to git hemmed up in here.

DICEY: Me neither, as far as that is concerned. But they all off down there carrying on over My Honey and Leafy.

NUNKIE: (*Very nervous*) Ella and them is waiting on us. Come on. Where your things?

DICEY: (*Indicates suitcase on bed*) There everything is. You tote it while I put out the light and lock the door.

NUNKIE: (*Grabs up the bag and hurries to the door*) Hurry up.

DICEY: (*Takes a few more whets with her knife*) In just a minute.

NUNKIE: (*Hand on door knob*) Aw, make haste!

DICEY: (*Tests knife edge and is satisfied. Smiles and puts it in her pocket, and moves to the light.*) Don't crack that door till I outen the light. Then wait for me. It's more better for both of us to step out at the same time. (*She turns off light and goes softly towards the door.*) I don't see to my rest what My Honey want with that Leafy nohow.

NUNKIE: 'Tain't nothing wrong with her. She sure is pretty, now.

DICEY: I can't see where at. She's too poor. She ain't got no meat on her bones at all. And My Honey, he's kind of rawbony, too. I bet you when they gits in the bed together they bones sound like a dishpan full of crockery.

NUNKIE: (*Outside*) Aw, come on!

(*The door closes softly, and the key is turned in the lock. Curtain.*)

## Scene 2

*Scene: An hour later, the same night. A clearing deep in the woods. The clearing is small, and freshly cleared. Brush hurriedly cut away. Wall of tropical growth around. Big trees, hung with Spanish moss. Glistening leaves and trailing vines, and bright flowers. Lush. Upstage center is a rude seat covered with a symbolic cloth like a throne. Before it is a short length of log for a footstool. The drums are against the shrubbery, right. In the center is a miniature coffin with a circle of candles about it.*

*At the rise, Ella Wall in full ceremonials is seated on the throne. Two men, naked to the waist, stand on either side of her with a gourd rattle, highly decorated, in each hand. A red candle is fixed to Ella's headdress and is alight. There is a small white candle fixed to the back of each of her hands.[43] All of the others wear lighted candles also. The dancers are ranged around the clearing in a circle. Two women downstage right and left have no candles on their hands. They have cymbals poised to play. The men with the rattles have their arms uplifted tensely, waiting for the downstroke. The drums are playing the introduction. All the dancers have their hands extended toward the throne. The right hand is drawn back stiffly, while the left is extended full length, palms down, with knees flexed. They hold this pose rigidly while the drums mount and Ella begins to make rhythmic motions as she sits. The gourd-rattles take up and the "rattling men" beating a counter time on the back of the drums take up, and Ella steps down to the drums and begins to dance.*

ELLA: *(Chanting)* Ah, minni wa oh! Ah, minni wa oh!

DANCERS: *(Beginning to dance)* Say kay ah, brah aye!

ELLA: *(Dances to coffin, makes some liquid movement of her upper body.)* Yekko tekko! Yekko tekko! Yahm pahn sah ay!

MEN: Ah yah yee-ay! Ah, yah yee-ay! Ah say oh!

ELLA: *(A vigorous solo about the coffin. Comes to dramatic pause.)* Yekko tekko! Ah pah sah ay!

*(Up to now, the dance has been mostly movements of the upper body. Posture dancing. Now it mounts. Ella is dancing solo against the Congo[44] of the group. They circle the coffin in a wide circle as they dance with hands stiff at the wrist, palms down. Ella begins to sing and they fall in behind her.)*

Hand a-bowl, knife a-throat
Rope a-tie me, hand a-bowl

*(Drums and rattles have mounted to furious pitch.)*

Hand a-bowl knife a-throat
Wang ingwalla, knife a-throat
Hand a-bowl, knife a-throat
Wango doe-doe, fum dee ah!

*(The dance reaches a frenzy. Some leap over the coffin. Others do other steps. Ella dances furiously in the[ir] midst. Now their movements blend with hers. Now the others are more background for her. At the climax, suddenly every candle is blown out and in the dim light, the dancers depart silently to the throb of the diminished drum tones. Curtain.)*

## Scene 3

*Scene: Immediately after scene 2. Woods, picnic grounds. This clearing differs from the other only in that it is larger and shows signs of long use. A rude table has been contrived by laying long boards on saw-horses. An old tree stump is downstage center. A few wooden boxes are scattered around the edges for seats. A quilt or two have been brought along to sit on. These, too, are along the edges, so that the main clearing is left for movement. Just beyond the clearing, upstage left, a crude dressing booth has been erected of palm fronds. Several large market baskets covered with colored table cloths and towels are under the table. They have the refreshments in them.*

*At the rise, Bunch, Laura B and Maudella are fussing around the table unpacking baskets and setting out the pans and dishes of foods, and tasting things here and there as they work. My Honey is seated on the stump, with Few Clothes squatting on the ground beside him. Both have their instruments and are playing. All the men are grouped around the musicians harmonizing "Georgia Buck."*

LONNIE: *(Singing)*

> Oh, Georgia Buck is dead!
> Last word he said
> I don't want no shortening in my bread.

CHORUS:

> Is that you, Reuben?
> Is that you, Reuben?
> And they laid poor Reuben's body down.

MY HONEY:

> Oh, rabbit on the log, ain't got no dog
> How am I going git him?
> Lord knows!

CHORUS:

> Is that you, Reuben?
> Is that you, Reuben?
> And they laid poor Reuben's body down.

STEW BEEF:

> Oh, Reuben had a wife
> Swapped her for a Barlow knife
> And they laid poor Reuben's body down.

CHORUS:

> Is that you, Reuben?
> Is that you, Reuben?
> And they laid poor Reuben's body down.

LAURA B: *(Admiringly)* Now, listen at Stew! *(Beaming at his cleverness)* That's the biggest fool!

STEW BEEF: *(Acknowledging the compliment)* Being a fool never kilt nobody. All it do is make you sweat.

LAURA B: *(Even prouder)* Didn't I tell you he was crazy?

STEW BEEF: Did you cook that stew beef and bring it with you like I told you? I'm gitting peckish. *(Rubs his stomach.)*

LONNIE: Me too.

FEW CLOTHES: *(Starting to get up hurriedly)* Let's eat!

LONNIE: Big Sweet and Leafy say you ain't supposed to eat before a marriage. After the couple stands up is when you eats.

STEW BEEF: My Honey, go ahead and git your marrying done so we can eat. My biggest gut feel like it done dwindled down to a fiddle-string.

*(They all get up and look towards the table.)*

LAURA B: Naw. Big Sweet said not to touch a thing till after the marriage.

BUNCH: *(Heaping up a pan of fried chicken)* These mens! They sure favors they stomachs. If Judgment Day was to come, Few would expect me to fix him a bucket to carry along.

LAURA B: Stew Beef is just the same. He ever love beef stew. Look like I can't never fill him up. Just like Eating-Flukus—eat up camp meeting, back off of Association and drink Jordan dry.

LONNIE: Look like the thing to do is to git the marrying done. You ready, ain't you, My Honey?

MY HONEY: *(Nervous, but trying to be casual)* Just as ready as a meat axe.

SOP-THE-BOTTOM: Turn 'round here let's see how you look in your new suit. *(They all scatter back in a rough circle around My Honey and look him over from head to foot.)* You looks fine, man. Any gal ought to be glad to git you, looking like that.

STEW BEEF: That suit is ready! Believe I'll git me one like that. Laura B, you want me in a double-breaster like My Honey got on when we jump over the broomstick?

LAURA B: *(Bridling)* Yeah. You would look good in it, all right.

LONNIE: 'Course My Honey look good. I picked out that suit for him to stand up in. *(Looks to table)* Maudella, run back there and see if Big Sweet done got Leafy dressed.

MAUDELLA: *(Hurrying towards booth)* Yessir.

LAURA B: Oh, don't worry the gal. It takes time for dressing for gitting married.

LONNIE: You women and your dressing! *(Sighs)* But I reckon us men just have to put up with you. We can't git along without you. But you sure got funny ways.

*(The women protest this but the men laugh in agreement.)*

STEW BEEF: Lonnie, you acts slow and everything, but you sure knows a heap. Always saying something deep.

*(Big Sweet enters with Leafy all dressed in white with a veil. Big Sweet is holding the veil up from the grass with one hand, Maudella is walking behind and admiring Leafy with open mouthed wonder. Leafy advances slowly with a nervous smile and downcast eyes. All the men gaze at her with awe and admiration. My Honey stares in awe, then takes a step or two towards her and stops as if approaching an altar. Box Car, more brazen, walks nearer and stands and admires.)*

BOX CAR: Lord! I could lick icing off of that all day long.

LONNIE: Leafy, you looks like a glance from God.

*(My Honey advances slowly as Big Sweet looks at her handiwork and beams.)*

MY HONEY: Baby. *(Swallows hard)* Baby, you looks too good to walk on the ground.

LEAFY: Much obliged for your compliments. *(They start to hold hands.)*

LONNIE: *(Looking around)* Now, where is that preacher? He was here just a while ago.

SOP-THE-BOTTOM: *(Indicates the woods)* Oh, he stepped off a piece. Be back after while.

BIG SWEET: *(Fussing with the wreath)* Hold on a minute. I needs another hairpin right here. *(Turns to hurry off)* Be back in just a second. Want to catch that up a little more.

*(She darts off and disappears into the booth. My Honey takes Leafy's hand and they stand there smiling and swinging hands without speaking.)*

DO-DIRTY: This marrying business is nice. Us could have been having fun like this all the time, but we didn't have no sense. If Big Sweet and Lonnie hadn't of told us, we wouldn't know.

STEW BEEF: That's a fact. You just wait till next month when me and Laura B stand up. We going to have—

FEW CLOTHES: Man, but me and Bunch is going to really break it up. She's going to have a dress like that and I'm going to be togged down in a suit and white shoes and everything. Lonnie, you sure done started something.

(*Preacher enters upstage left on a run, with his eyes wild and popping. He stumbles to center stage with his mouth working, but no words come out. They look at him for a moment in astonishment. But Maudella cries out and points upstage left as Dicey leaps out into the clearing with her knife drawn. Her entrance is like the spring of a lioness. She is only a few yards off and behind My Honey and Leafy who are looking at each other. Dicey, after her initial spring, stops dramatically, with her knife in hand and takes in the situation gloating. She has all the manner of a lioness ready to charge.*)

DICEY: Well, I told you I would be back, didn't I?

(*My Honey whirls, leaps in front of Leafy instinctively and holds his guitar like a shield. The group is struck dumb for an instant. Everyone is frozen in their tracks. Leafy gives a little cry of helplessness. Dicey laughs, wringing herself from her hips.*)

You can't do nothing. Youse planted in your tracks. I'm going to cut you all in your face. (*Venomously as she crouches*) Slice you too thin to fry. (*Gestures to the woods behind her*) I got plenty help to do it with.

(*She advances slowly, knife poised and laughing. Suddenly, Ella and Nunkie run on to the edge of the clearing behind Dicey. Big Sweet enters hurriedly. Is brought up short by the tableau and gets set to spring, at the same time yelling.*)

BIG SWEET: Lonnie! Stew!

(*Her cry and movement bring everybody alive, and they rush to the charge. It also affects Dicey profoundly and she leaps back in fright.*)

DICEY: (*Backing up in betrayed horror of her situation*) They ain't 'sleep! They can move! (*It is a bitter accusation of Ella who is also retreating.*)

ELLA: (*Dazed and terrified by the danger, and astonished by the failure of her magic, leaps back and looks at the onrush in unbelief.*) Make it to the hard road! Dicey!

(*They all turn and flee pell mell through the woods. The men start to pursue, but Lonnie halts them.*)

LONNIE: Stop! Box! Stew! My Honey! All you all! Stop!

BOX CAR: (*Unwilling*) They will make they git-away!

LONNIE: Naw, they won't. Listen to me, now.

MY HONEY: We got to make it so they can't come back, Lonnie.

*(There is a shot offstage right and a loud voice cries "Halt!" Another shot.)*

QUARTER BOSS: *(Offstage)* I said "halt!" I'm shooting to kill next time.

BIG SWEET: The Quarters Boss!

LONNIE: That's what I'm trying to tell you all. He knowed we was going to have this picnic down here, and you know he's always hanging around close enough to hear what go on.

LAURA B: That sure is so. Soon as you make the least noise, here he come.

LONNIE: That's what I knowed. Its better for him to handle 'em than for us. You know they ain't coming back now—Not for years to come.

BIG SWEET: Won't that be nice and fine?

LONNIE: And another thing, when I got to talking to Pringle and the Big Boss about Big Sweet going off, I took and told 'em not to listen to everything they hear. Just be around and see for theyselves who was stirring up trouble and who wasn't.

LAURA B: *(Laughs)* Dicey was so glad to git to Pringle to talk, she got plenty chance to talk with him all she want to tonight. *(All laugh.)*

STEW BEEF: Yeah, but she don't much no talk with him tonight.[45]

LONNIE: Oh, poor Dicey was all right as far as she could see.

BIG SWEET: But she couldn't see no further than from the handle of a tea cup 'round the rim.

LONNIE: Maybe she done the best she knowed how. It wasn't her fault.

BIG SWEET: Well whose fault was it then?

LONNIE: Nobody's exactly. Her mama's womb just played a dirty trick on her when she borned Dicey. That's all. *(They laugh, but lightly.)*

PREACHER: *(Mopping his face from fright, but getting control)* I seen them folks a-coming while I was out there.

LONNIE: I could tell you had seen something, but I couldn't know what. You ready to go to work?

PREACHER: *(Assuming his official manner)* If the bride and groom will take [the] floor.

*(He advances toward them pompously as Big Sweet arranges the couple center but a little upstage.)*

LONNIE: This is more like my dream. *(Musing)* Things is going to be better now. Folks everywhere will look upon us more. Us can make things more better all around. *(Unconsciously begins to hum, and the others drift in.)*

Troubles will be over, Amen
Troubles will be over, Amen
Troubles will be over, when I see Jesus
Troubles will be over, Amen.

*(Preacher takes his stand before My Honey and Leafy, opens his book dramatically, and begins to perform the ceremony in pantomime. The singing goes on and the audience only sees the motions of the marriage and the movements of lips.)*

I see the light-house, Amen
I see the light-house, Amen
I see the light-house, when I see Jesus
Troubles will be over, Amen.

PREACHER: *(Triumphantly)* I now pronounce you man and wife. Salute the bride.

*(A shout of joy breaks out and everybody rushes up to kiss Leafy and congratulate My Honey. Box Car, Sop-The-Bottom and Do-Dirty kiss enthusiastically. My Honey pulls Do-Dirty away.)*

MY HONEY: That's enough, Do. You only supposed to kiss a bride in a manner of speaking. You ain't supposed to taste it at all.

DO-DIRTY: Aw, man, don't be so selfish! You can git your little old kiss back when I gits me a wife. *(Starts to kiss Leafy again, but My Honey grabs him.)* Man, I likes this thing. 'Tain't going to be no time at all before I'm going to be asking a gal to gimme some hand.

SOP-THE-BOTTOM: Give Lonnie credit. He sure do think up some nice things.

LONNIE: I got another notion right now.

SOP-THE-BOTTOM: What is it?

LONNIE: *(Getting a head start towards the table)* Let's eat!!

*(The men all break for the table except My Honey, who leads Leafy over tenderly and self-consciously.)*

BIG-SWEET: *(Presiding at distribution of plates)* One at a time! One at at time! Like gamblers going to heaven. It's plenty for everybody.

LONNIE: *(Stepping back from the table with his plate.)* Ummmmm! This is nice! Chicken purleau![46]

*(Strolls over to the stump with his plate and sits down and eats a few mouthfuls. As the others get their plates they scatter from the table and sit about laughing and talking happily. My Honey and Leafy go sit on a a quilt with their plates and she feeds him with her fork.)*

MY HONEY: This is love, baby, with the sun and the moon thrown in.

LEAFY: That's right. EVERYTHING! With the sun and the moon thrown in.

BIG SWEET: *(With her plate in her hand)* Everybody got what you want?

ALL: Yes, indeed!

BIG SWEET: Well, all right now. I'm going and set down by Lonnie. Come on Bunch and Laura B. Let's sit down by our men folks.

*(They cross to their places and sit down contentedly and all begin to eat.)*

LONNIE: Just like I keep telling you all. You can git what you want if you go about things the right way. *(Pets Big Sweet on the ground beside him.)* Now, I can fly. Everything is going to be just fine.

*(There comes the sound of the mystic drums. They all listen. Lonnie smiles in his peculiar way as the drums grow in volume. They smile, they laugh, then begin to sway to the drums.)*

I ride the rainbow, Amen
I ride the rainbow, Amen

*(A huge rainbow descends. They all scramble on board, plates in hand, and take seats. Lonnie in the very center with Big Sweet on one side—My Honey and Leafy on the other, keep singing.)*

[ALL:]

I ride the rainbow, when I see Jesus
Troubles will be over, Amen.

*(The rainbow begins to rise as the verse is repeated. The rainbow rises slowly and the curtain begins to descend at the same time slowly.)*

CURTAIN

# Appendix
## Programs from *The Great Day* (1932), *From Sun to Sun* (1932), and *All de Live Long Day* (1934)

SUNDAY EVENING, JANUARY 10, 1932
ZORA HURSTON

Presents

"THE GREAT DAY"

A PROGRAM OF ORIGINAL NEGRO FOLKLORE
With a
CHORAL AND DRAMATIC CAST

Ensembles and Vocal effects under the direction of "Wen" Talbert
Musical Arrangements by Porter G[r]ainger

FIRST PART

1. LEIGH WHIPPER
2. IN THE QUARTERS. WAKING THE CAMP
   Shack Rouser ............................ Percy Punter
   Joe Brown................................. Male Chorus
3. LEIGH WHIPPER
4. WORKING ON THE RAILROAD
   a. Captain Keep a-Hollerin'.
   b. Oh, Lulu!
   c. Can't You Line It?
   d. Mule on de Mount.
   e. East Coast Blues.
   f. Black Gal.
   g. John Henry ............................ lead [sic] by Percy Punter
5. LEIGH WHIPPER

6. BACK IN THE QUARTERS. DUSK DARK
    a. Children's Games.
    b. Chick–ma–chick.
    c. Mistah Frog ............................ sung by Sadie McGill
7. ITINERANT PREACHER AT THE QUARTERS
    a. Death Comes a-Creepin'.
    b. Sermon ................................….. Leigh Whipper
    c. All You People Got To Go.
    d. You Can't Hide.

<u>INTERMISSION</u>

<u>SECOND PART</u>

8. LEIGH WHIPPER
9. IN THE "JOOK." BLACK DARK
    a. Cold Rainy Day.
    b. Frankie and Albert.
    c. Halimuh Fack.
    d. Palm Beach.
    e. Let de Deal Go Down.
    f. Alabama Bound.
10. LEIGH WHIPPER
11. CONJURE CEREMONY
    Pea-vine Candle Dance.
    9 Hairs in the Graveyard.
12. LEIGH WHIPPER
13 IN THE PALM WOODS
    Fire Dance.
    a. Bellamina.
    b. Wasp Bite Noby.
    c. Evalina.
    d. 1. Jumping Dance.
       2. Ring Play.
    e. Crow Dance ............................ by Joseph Neeley
14. LEIGH WHIPPER
15 GROUP FINALE
    Deep River.

Piano Accompaniment ....... "WEN" TALBERT

NOTE—From Stephen Foster to contemporary Broadway the folkways and folk-arts of the American Negro have been presented in tinctured and adulterated approximations. That they have seemed characteristic and have been so movingly effective is, in view of this fact, all the greater testimony to their power and originality in the pure undiluted folk-forms that for generations have been in the shrewd and disarming custody of the common people. These folk have always had two arts, —one for themselves and one for the amusement and beguilement of their masters. And seldom, if ever, can the white man or even the sophisticated Negro break through to that inner circle so well-guarded by the instinctive make-believe and "possum-play" of the Negro peasant.

"Great Day" is a stage arrangement of part of a cycle of Negro folk-song, dance and pantomime collected and recorded by Miss Zora Hurston over three years of intimate living among the common folk in the primitive privacy of their own Negro way of life. It is thus a rare sample of the pure and unvarnished materials from which the stage and concert tradition has been derived; and ought to show how much more unique and powerful and spirit-compelling the genuine Negro folk-things really are. That this legacy has not been irrevocably lost or completely overlaid is good news of the highest spiritual and practical importance for all who wish to know and understand the true elements of the Negro heart and soul.                    —Alain Locke.

ACKNOWLEDGMENT—The complete cycle of which this concert material is a part was collected by Miss Zora Hurston during four years' travel (1927–31) in the far South.

Throughout these years, this work of salvaging some of the supriving [sic] portions of the original primitive life of the Negro has had spiritual and material support from Mrs. R. Osgood Mason of New York.

## THE CAST

| | | |
|---|---|---|
| ALFRED STROCHAN | ROSINA LEFROY | JAMES DAVIS |
| LEONARD STURRUP | MURIEL AMBRISTER | JAMES ARNOLD |
| JOHN DAMSON | ZORA HURSTON | VAN JACKSON |
| JOSEPH NEELEY | OLLIE HOPKINS | HAROLD SMITH |
| EDWARD WILSON | HATTIE KING REAVES | JOHN ROBINSON |
| JAMES WHITE | MABEL HOWARD | WILLIAM SANDRIDGE |
| JAMES BETHEL | DORA THOMPSON | PERCY PUNTER |
| NEHEMIAH CASH | HELEN DOWDY | DORA BACOTE |
| CAROLYNE RICH | RED DAVIES | VIOLA ANDERSON |
| LUCILLE SMITH | GEORGE SIMMONS | ROSETTA CRAWFORD |
| MARY SANDS | JAMES LORING | SADIE MCGILL |
| BELLE FERGUSON | WILLIAM WINTER | SARA EVANS |
| CLEMENTINE WILLS | JAMES PARKER | JOHN MOBLEY |
| ANNA WASHINGTON | LEIGH WHIPPER | WILLIAM POHLAMUS |

THE NEW SCHOOL PRESENTS

## "FROM SUN TO SUN"
### A Program of Original Negro Folklore

PRODUCED BY ZORA HURSTON
WITH A CHORAL AND DRAMATIC CAST

ENSEMBLE AND VOCAL EFFECTS UNDER
THE DIRECTION OF GEORGETTE HARVEY
MUSICAL ARRANGEMENTS BY PORTER GRAINGER

TUESDAY EVENING
MARCH 29 AT 8:30
RESERVED SEATS NOW
ON SALE $1.50–$1.00

### NEW SCHOOL AUDITORIUM
### 66 WEST 12TH STREET NEW YORK

PROGRAM

1. IN THE QUARTERS—WAKING THE CAMP
   a. Shack Rouser . . . . . . . . . . . . . . . . . Percy Punter
   b. Joe Brown . . . . . . . . . . . . . . . . . Male Chorus

2. WORKING ON THE RAILROAD
   a. Captain Keel a-Hollerin' . . . . . . . led by James Davis
   b. Oh, Lulu! . . . . . . . . . . . . . . . . . led by William Winters
   c. Can't You Line It? . . . . . . . . . . . . led by James Davis
   d. Mule on de Mount . . . . . . . . . . . led by William Winters
   e. East Coast Blues . . . . . . . . . . . . . sung by Georgia Burke
   f. Black Gal . . . . . . . . . . . . . . . . . led by William Winters
   g. John Henry . . . . . . . . . . . . . . . . sung by William Davis

3. BACK IN THE QUARTERS—DUSK DARK
   a. Children's Games
   b. Chick–mah–chick
   c. Mistah Frog . . . . . . . . . . . . . . . . sung by Rosetta Crawford

4. ITINERANT PREACHER AT THE QUARTERS
   a. Death Comes a-Creepin'
   b. Sermon . . . . . . . . . . . . . . . . . . . Richard Huey
   c. All You People Got To Go
   d. You Can't Hide

INTERMISSION—TEN MINUTES

5. IN THE "JOOK"—BLACK DARK
   a. Cold Rainy Day . . . . . . . . . . . . . led by Rosetta Crawford
   b. Frankie and Albert . . . . . . . . . . sung by Rosetta Crawford,
   Oline Hopkins and Viola Anderson
   c. Halimuh Fack . . . . . . . . . . . . . . sung by Georgia Burke
   d. Palm Beach . . . . . . . . . . . . . . . sung by Rosetta Crawford,
   Oline Hopkins and Viola Anderson
   e. Let de Deal Go Down . . . . . . . . led by Joseph Neely
   f. Alabama Bound . . . . . . . . . . . . led by William Davis
   g. Guitar Solo . . . . . . . . . . . . . . . by John Dawson

6. THE FIERY CHARIOT
   Original Negro Folk Tale . . . . . . . Georgette Harvey, Joseph
   Neely and William Davis

7. IN THE PALM WOODS—FIRE DANCE
   a. Bellamina . . . . . . . . . . . . . . . . . led by Joseph Neely
   b. Mama Don't Want No Peas . . . . . sung by Leonard Sturrup
   c. Evalina . . . . . . . . . . . . . . . . . . . led by Joseph Neely
   d. 1. Jumping Dance . . . . . . . . . . . . led by Joseph Neely
   2. Ring Play . . . . . . . . . . . . . . . . led by Joseph Neely
   e. Crow Dance . . . . . . . . . . . . . . . led by Joseph Neely
   (Cutamacah—Thomas Lee)

PIANO ACCOMPANIMENT—ELINOR BOXWILL
GUITAR ACCOMPANIMENT—JOHN DAWSON
AND ALFRED STROCHAN

## THE CAST

| | | |
|---|---|---|
| REGINALD ALDAY | JOHN DAWSON | JOSEPH NEELY |
| VIOLA ANDERSON | SARAH EVANS | INEZ PERSAND |
| DORA BASCOTE | GEORGETTE HARVEY | PERCY PUNTER |
| JAMES BETHEL | OLINE HOPKINS | CAROL RICH |
| BERLEANA BLANKS | BRUCE HOWARD | ALFRED STROCHAN |
| GEORGIA BURKE | RICHARD HUEY | LEONARD STURRUP |
| NEHEMIAH CASH | ZORA HURSTON | JAMES WHITE |
| ROSETTA CRAWFORD | VAN JACKSON | CLEMENTINE WILLS |
| JAMES DAVIS | THOMAS FLETCHER LEE | WILLIAM WINTERS |
| WILLIAM DAVIS | ESTELLE MILLER | |

## NOTES ON THE PROGRAM

MISS ZORA HURSTON spent four years (1927–1931) in the far South collecting the material used in this production, in an effort to assemble an authentic Negro folk-cycle of representative songs, dances, tales and rituals. Throughout these years, this work of salvaging some of the surviving portions of the original primitive life of the Negro has been actively supported by Mrs. R. Osgood Mason of New York.

THE WORK SONGS in the second number on the program are representative of the songs sung to the rhythm of the work as the men labor on the railroads, in the saw mills, in the phosphate mines. The words often merely add body to the tunes, but all the songs fit some definite rhythm—the swinging of a pick . . . the driving of a nail . . . the sawing of a log.

THE SERMON BY AN ITINERANT PREACHER is a study of Negro religious expression, shown by a scene in a village church, with the congregation working itself to fever pitch, exhorting, and finally breaking into several original and moving spirituals.

THE JOOK SONGS are commonly known as "blues," but many of them tell stories and belong in the ballad class. They originate in the places of entertainment, or jooks, of the South and travel by word of mouth from one jook to another. Few of them are ever heard by a person literate enough to preserve them in writing.

THE CROW DANCE is a primitive and exciting folk dance performed by a group from the Bahama Islands.

ROLLINS COLLEGE
## Dramatic Art Department

PRESENTS

## ZORA HURSTON

IN HER ALL-NEGRO PRODUCTION
OF AFRO-AMERICAN FOLKLORE

## "ALL DE LIVE LONG DAY"

An Unique and Authentic Representation of
Real Negro Folk Life by Talented
Native Artists

A RETURN ENGAGEMENT WITH
A NEW PROGRAM AND A NEW CAST

All Students (College and Public School)... $ .35
Reserved Seats ... $ .75 and $ .50
(Reservations may be made by mail,
or through The Bookery, Winter Park.)

RECREATION HALL, ROLLINS COLLEGE
FRIDAY EVENING AT 8:15
JANUARY 5, 1934

PROGRAM

1. MAKING THIS TIME—DAYBREAK
   a. "Baby Chile"
      Pauline Foster and Female Ensemble
   b. "I'm Goin' to Make a Graveyard of My Own"
      Gabriel Brown, guitarist, and Male Chorus

2. WORKING ON THE ROAD
   a. "Cuttin' Timber"
   b. "You Won't Do"
      Buddy Brown and Ensemble

   c. "John Henry"
      A. B. Hicks, tenor-baritone
   d. "Please Don't Drive Me"
      Buddy Brown and Ensemble
   e. "Halimuhfack"
      Bernice Knight, soprano
   f. "Fat Gal"
      Mellard Strickland, A. B. Hicks, and Oscar Anderson
   g. "Water Boy"
      A. B. Hicks, tenor-baritone

3. "DE POSSUM'S TAIL HAIRS"—A ONE-ACT FOLK PLAY
     De Possum  . . . . . . . . . . . . . . . . . Maggie Mae Fredericks
     Brer Noah . . . . . . . . . . . . . . . . . . . . . . . . . . Lewey Wright
     Ham . . . . . . . . . . . . . . . . . . . . . . . . . . . . . Gabriel Brown

4. SPIRITUALS
   a. "O Lord"
   b. "I'm Going Home"
      Ensemble
   c. "Sit Down"
      Buddy Brown and Ensemble
   d. "Swing Low"
      A. B. Hicks, tenor-baritone
   e. "All My Sins"
      Ensemble
   f. "Go Down Moses"
      A. B. Hicks, tenor-baritone
   g. "I'm Your Child"
      Ensemble

INTERMISSION

5. "FUNNIN' AROUND"
   a. "Ever Been Down?"
      Female Quartet—Bernice Knight, Willaouise Dorsey,
      Maggie Mae Fredericks, Billy Hurston
   b. Harmonica Solo
   c. "Let the Deal Go Down"
   d. Guitar Solo
      Gabriel Brown
   e. Buck and Wing Specialties
      Curtis Bacott, Willie Matthews, Alphonso Johnson
   f. "St. Louis Blues"
      Bernice Knight, soprano

    g. Piano Solo
       Curtis Bacott
    h. "Break Away"—Folk Dancing
       Ensemble. John Love, fiddler

## 6. STRING BAND IN THE NEGRO MANNER

Banjo . . . . . . . . . . . . . . . . . . . . . . . . . . . . . . . . . . S. E. Boyd
Fiddle . . . . . . . . . . . . . . . . . . . . . . . . . . . . . . . . John Love
Guitar . . . . . . . . . . . . . . . . . . . . . . . . . . . . Bubble Mimms

## 7. ON THE NIGER

    a. Ahaco
    b. Bellamina
    c. Mamma Don't Want No Peas
    d. Courtship—"Jumping Dance"
       George Nichols, Maggie Mae Fredericks, Lewey Wright
    e. Crow Dance
       ZORA HURSTON
    f. Fire Dance
       Ensemble. George Nichols, African drummer, and Oscar Anderson,
       "Kuta-Mah-Kah" (beating the off rhythm on the rear end of the
       drum).

Rollins College is delighted again to extend its hospitality to Miss Zora Hurston and her company for a return engagement at Recreation Hall. Last year's performance was so creditable to the negro race, which composed, produced, and acted the various features of the evening's entertainment, that I hope Miss Hurston will be able to extend her performances to other audiences throughout the State.

HAMILTON HOLT.

"From Sun to Sun" was a remarkable revelation of the negro heart and mind. In its primitive spontaneity, its exaggerated rhythms, its intermingled melodies and its vivid coloring it produced a riotous spectacle that thrilled the audience. Zora Hurston and her group of Negro Chanters reveal, as has never been done before, the native instinct of the negro for art expression.

EDWIN OSGOOD GROVER.

The folk lore concert given by Zora Hurston and her company of negroes at Rollins College last year was one of the outstanding events of the season for me both from the artistic and entertainment standpoint. Anyone wishing to get a real glimpse into negro life in Florida should not miss the performance to be given in Recreation Hall on the evening of Jan. 5th. It is a real event.

R. W. FRANCE,<br>Professor of Economics.

# EXPLANATORY NOTES

## Meet the Mamma

1. "Cashier" has been replaced with "Essie" throughout to minimize confusion.
2. "Boss" or "the boss" has been replaced throughout to read "Pete" where appropriate.
3. Famed thoroughbred who dominated racing in 1919–1920, when he won twenty of twenty-one races and set three world records.
4. At this point, the manuscript reads, "Song: 'Now why did he kill Ananias.'" The song, appended to the end of the manuscript, has been inserted.
5. "Mother-in-law," "the mother-in-law," and "mother" have been replaced throughout to read "Edna" where appropriate.
6. "Wife" and "the wife" have been replaced throughout to read "Carrie" where appropriate.
7. Here the manuscript reads, "Song: 'Everybody's man is better to me than my own.'" The song, appended to the end of the manuscript, has been inserted.
8. Original reads "Hors de heuvof."
9. Original reads "of."
10. Carrie's reentrance (necessary for her lines later in the scene) is not indicated in the original. We have emended the text so that she reenters when Pete sings "Oh, Fireman, Save My Bustle!"
11. Original reads "Jim."
12. Here the manuscript reads, "Song: 'Belly Rub Rag.'" A song appended to the end of the manuscript, originally titled "Belly Rub Rag" (the title has been crossed out and emended to read "Granny Blues"), has been inserted here.
13. This word may have been intended to read "who."
14. The Florida East Coast railroad line, known as "The Railroad to Cuba" because it ran as far south as Key West. From there, passengers could take a ferry to Cuba.
15. The Illinois Central rail line connected the Midwestern city of Chicago to New Orleans and Birmingham, Alabama.
16. Original reads "Any."
17. Original reads "FINAL CURTAIN."
18. Davy Jones' locker, or chest, was a metaphor for the bottom of the sea.
19. Stands for the Society for the Prevention of Cruelty to Animals, founded in New York City in 1866 and modeled on England's Royal Society for the Prevention of Cruelty to Animals, founded in 1840.
20. Original reads "Enter one of crew and place a steamer chair."
21. No scene division is marked on the manuscript here or at the beginning of scene 3. However, "scene 4" is handwritten on the manuscript; we have thus extrapolated the placement of scenes 2 and 3 based on curtain directions.
22. "Galli Cursey" is a misspelled reference to the Italian coloratura soprano Amelita Galli-Curci (1882–1963), who sang with the Chicago Opera Company from 1916 to 1924 and at the New York Metropolitan Opera regularly from 1926 to 1930, when she retired due

to throat problems. John Philip Sousa (1854–1932) was known not only for his military marches, but also for writing music and libretti for a number of operettas. "Rosa Raza" probably refers to Rosa Raisa (1893–1963), a star with the Chicago Civic Opera in the 1910s and 1920s. Born Rosa Burchstein, the Polish American soprano sang the title role of *Aida* in the inaugural production of the Chicago Opera House in 1929. In the following line, Pete refers to renowned Italian tenor Enrico Caruso (1873–1921).

23. Manuscript indicates "Sea Song." Song appended to end of manuscript inserted here.

24. The manuscript includes a cast list for each of the following three sketches. They have been incorporated into the stage directions.

25. An untitled song appended to end of manuscript, containing appropriate lyrics, is inserted here.

26. The boundary from shore (in actuality, an hour's cruising distance) within which alcoholic beverages could be seized by U.S. authorities during Prohibition. Alcoholic beverages were not allowed within a twelve-mile distance from American shores.

27. Emile Coué (1857–1926) popularized the psychotherapy technique of optimistic auto-suggestion in his work *La maîtrise de soi-même par l'autosuggestion consciente* (1922). The best-known example of the "Coué method" was to repeat the phrase "Every day, in every way, I'm getting better and better" (*Tous les jours à tous points de vue je vais de mieux en mieux*) at regular intervals every day, to condition the mind for self-improvement and achievement.

28. Negro spiritual with the following chorus:

> Hark, the downward road is crowded, crowded, crowded,
>
> Yes, the downward road is crowded with unbelieving souls.

29. The word *shall* may have been mistyped on the typescript. Clearly, however, Lord Suds here is cut or stabbed by the Count.

30. Pluto Water, "America's physick," was first bottled from the French Lick, Indiana mineral springs in the 1850s; the company did not go out of business until the 1930s. The Carbona company, still in operation today, has made spot removers, home dry cleaning products, and other cleaning supplies since the 1870s.

31. The Black Bottom dance originated in New Orleans in the late 1910s and achieved widespread popularity during the mid-1920s, being most notably featured in *George White's Scandals* in 1926. Perhaps because of its popularity, the song is not included in the typescript. If one were to produce the play, Jelly Roll Morton's rendition of "The Black Bottom Stomp" (1919) would be appropriate.

32. A constellation near Centaurus (the Centaur), only visible in the southern hemisphere. Because its crucifix form points to the South Pole, it was used by navigators—for example, those sailing from Europe to Africa or South America. It is the constellation depicted on the Australian national flag.

33. Indications of the solo dancer or "the princess" have been replaced to read "Zido" where appropriate.

34. *September Morn* (1912), a painting by Frenchman Paul Chabas, won the Medal of Honor at the Paris Salon of 1912, but became infamous in the United States a year later when it was shown in a Manhattan art gallery. Showing a nude young woman standing in the middle of a stream, the New York Society for the Suppression of Vice considered it too

risque for public display and ordered it to be removed. The gallery owner refused. The ensuing controversy assured its indelible imprint in the American mind's eye. Over the next decade, the image appeared on postcards, figurines, calendars, and even clothing. And, as we see here, the "September Morn pose" became a common sight gag in popular drama of the 1910s and 1920s. The painting currently hangs in the Metropolitan Museum of Art.

35. "King" or "the king" has been replaced with "Uncle Cliff" where appropriate.

36. Hurston may be referring to the town of Hushpuckena, Mississippi, sixty miles south of Memphis.

37. Original reads "warrior."

38. In the manuscript, "and Edna" has been crossed out; Edna's entrance is indicated several lines later. However, because the two women's appearances are described together, we have let the original stage direction stand.

39. Manuscript indicates "Song: 'Over the Bridge.'" Song appended to end of manuscript inserted here.

## Color Struck

1. Emmaline's last name is spelled various ways throughout the original text: Beazely, Beazeley, Beasely, and Beazby.

2. I.e., a train car reserved for blacks only.

3. Original reads "They."

4. This word is spelled "lake" several times in the first half of the play, but is consistently spelled "lak" in the second half of the play as well as in the bulk of Hurston's published work. It has been changed to reflect Hurston's general usage.

5. I.e., with the protruding upper lip of a shad fish. Derogatory term applied to blacks.

6. Like the cake-walk, a dance with ties to plantation life.

7. A sexually suggestive dance, popular in vaudeville shows from the 1890s through the early twentieth century and the precursor to burlesque and table dancing.

8. I.e., a hall whose siding has been left to "weather" naturally.

9. Original reads "and."

10. Original reads "wook." A fascinator—now thought of as a dressy headpiece or hat—originally referred to a light shawl or scarf, worn on the head and shoulders, often made of lightweight wool.

11. Original reads "it."

12. These two paragraphs appear in reverse order in the original. The editing reflects Hurston's customary organization of scene and action descriptions.

13. I.e., conté crayon, pastel, or chalk—not children's wax crayons.

14. Slang term for a less than luxurious automobile.

## Spears

1. Original reads "Luallaba." The text contains the following additional variations: Lualaha, Lualbaba, Lualaba. All have been changed to "Lualaba," by far the most prevalent. Note that

Hurston uses a similarly named imaginary location, Luababa, in *Meet the Mamma,* written the year before.

2. Spelled "Zaida" here, but "Zaidi" throughout the play.

3. Original reads "out."

4. The foregoing sentences appear to have been garbled during the course of transcription and typesetting.

5. This word, perhaps, is *flourish* inaccurately transcribed, or perhaps a word is missing before *south.*

## The First One

1. Eve is referred to as "Mrs. Ham" in the original. The name has been replaced throughout where appropriate.

2. The word *tent* would make more sense here.

## Cold Keener

1. McKay qtd. in Monique M. Taylor, *Harlem Between Heaven and Hell* (Minneapolis: University of Minnesota Press, 2002), 129; Hughes qtd. in Jim Haskins, *The Cotton Club* (New York: Random House, 1977), 6.

2. Vulcanization is a process by which rubber (especially that used for tires) is made harder and more elastic.

3. According to Carla Kaplan, "a plantation slave-dance imitating a buzzard in flight" (*Every Tongue Got to Confess: Negro Folk-tales of the Gulf States*, 105).

4. Reference to the Florida state road numbering system, retired in 1945. Old State Road 4, running north-south from north of Hilliard, Florida, to Miami, became State Highway 1; Old State Road 2 (mentioned several lines later) ran parallel to Old State Road 4, but from Jennings, on the Florida-Georgia state line, to Fort Myers.

5. Parody of the spiritual "All God's Chillun Got Wings," in particular, the lines:

    I got wings, you got wings,
    All o' God's chillun got wings.

6. A term for idle boasting. See the play titled *Woofing* included as part of *Fast and Furious,* also in this volume.

7. I.e., a "haint," or ghost. The term comes from the word *haunt.*

8. Alfred P. Sloan was elected president of General Motors in 1923, and eventually served as chairman of the company from 1937 to 1956.

9. In her field notes, Hurston describes "Diddy-Wah-Diddy" as a heavenly "place of no work and no worry for man and beast," full of good food and amusement (Bordelon, ed., *Go Gator and Muddy the Water*, 107).

10. Refers to a deep level in a coal mine (i.e., eight levels, or "rocks," down). Also a term for a black man—indicating he is as black as coal.

11. Examples of diner slang that would be yelled from the waiter or waitress to the cook—for example, "Adam and Eve on a raft—wreck 'em!" would be an order for two scrambled eggs on toast.

12. Original reads "The Bull"; the change makes sense not just given the plot, but because Sparrow is also referred to as "Bull Sparrow" in the typescript.

13. The names that follow satirize the fanciful names and officer titles of African American fraternal organizations that flourished from the Reconstruction through the mid-twentieth century—for example, the Ground Fountain of the United Order of the True Reformers, which had branches in twenty states by the mid-1890s, or the Improved Benevolent and Protective Order of Elks of the World (later simplified to the "Black Elks") founded in Cincinnati in 1899.

14. The Palmer House, a luxury hotel in Chicago, was noted for having an all-black staff. Stavin' Chain (the name is misspelled in the typescript) was the sobriquet of Wilson Jones, a boogie woogie and blues musician from Louisiana, who was active throughout the first few decades of the twentieth century and subsequently immortalized in such songs as "The Stavin' Chain Blues" (Big Joe Williams) and "Winin' Boy Blues" (Jelly Roll Morton, later sung by Janis Joplin, among others). The line is probably an allusion to "Winin' Boy Blues" ("Pick it up and shake it like Stavin' Chain").

15. Front Street was the center of the cotton trade in Memphis, Tennessee; the region surrounding it and Beale Street, which runs perpendicular to it, was home to a large African American community beginning in the Civil War. Beale Street is well known today as an entertainment district and the "birthplace of the blues."

16. This play clearly comes out of Hurston's fieldwork. See the "story about the man who went to Heaven from Johnstown" in chapter 1 of *Mules and Men* (11–13) and three tales in *Every Tongue Got to Confess: Negro Folk-tales of the Gulf States* (76–78).

17. See Revelation 4:10: "The four and twenty elders fall down before him that sat on the throne, and worship him that liveth for ever and ever, and cast their crowns before the throne." The fact that the crowns are being retrieved is a sardonic indication that the elders are playing a game of heavenly craps.

18. See *Every Tongue Got to Confess: Negro Folk-Tales from the Gulf States,* ed. Carla Kaplan (New York: HarperCollins, 2001), 78, for another version of this exchange.

19. See "De Flying Negro," in *Every Tongue Got to Confess,* 76–77, for another version of this scene.

20. Jack o' Lantern was also a term for *ignis fatuus* (foolish light or fatuous fire, also known as will-o'-the-wisp), the phosphorescent light emitted by marsh gas.

21. The original has only one "unh hunh" in this line.

22. A rotating backdrop used to suggest motion.

23. Hurston perhaps intended to have children playing a game here, along the lines of the game "Chick Ma Chick Ma Craney Crow" played at the beginning of *De Turkey and De Law* and in act 1, scene 2, of *Polk County*.

24. Original reads "some done."

25. *Polk County* also contains a version of the song that follows, in act 2, scene 3.

26. Original reads "ever morn."

27. The typescript is marked out with light pencil scribbles up to the "seaman's chorus."

28. Original reads "biddy."

29. I.e., "copasetic," excellent, fine.

30. Original reads "tipping."

31. Hurston published a transcription of this song, described as a "Seaman chantey," in "Dance Songs and Tales from the Bahamas" (*The Journal of American Folklore* 43, no. 169 [July–September 1930]: 297). The article also includes transcriptions (including musical notation) of several of the songs used in the fire dance staged later in the play: "Down De Road, Baby," "Bimini Gal," "Mama I Saw a Sailboat," "Odessa," and "Wheel Miss Curry."

32. In the margin at the beginning of this line are the following notes, written in pencil:
    Rise
    1. John Canoe
    2. Crawing [? possibly "Crowing"]

33. Hurston includes discussion of this song and other Bahaman music in chapter 10 of *Dust Tracks on a Road* ("Research"), of which she writes, "The music of the Bahaman Negroes was more original, dynamic, and African, than American Negro songs" (140). She would go on to make Bahaman music the centerpiece of *From Sun to Sun*. Of "Bellamina," she writes, "it was a song about a rum-running boat that had been gleaming white, but after it had been captured by the United States Coast Guard and released, it was painted black for obvious reasons" (141). The Library of Congress Florida Folklife collection has two recordings of this song (title spelled "Bellamena").

34. The song "Don't You Hurry, Worry with Me" is not included in the typescript. A song with the same title recorded by Alan Lomax is included in *Deep River of Song: Bahamas 1935,* vol. 2: *Ring Games and Round Dances* (Rounder Records, 2002). The reference to "pee vee voo" is unknown.

35. This line and the following one from the Emperor are struck out in pencil on the typescript.

36. A West Indian festival where an appointed king leads a parade accompanied by drums, rattles, and other percussion instruments.

37. In "Dance Songs and Tales from the Bahamas" (*Journal of American Folk-Lore,* 1930), Hurston described the fire-dance as an "exceedingly African" social folk dance. She continues:
    > There are two kinds of the dance, the jumping dance, and the ring play, which is merely a more elaborate form of the jumping dance . . . In either form of this dancing, the players form a ring, with the bonfire to one side. The drummer usually takes his place near the fire. The drum is held over the blaze until the skin tightens to the right tone. There is a flourish signifying that the drummer is all set. The players begin to clap with their hands. The drummer cried, "Gimbay" (a corruption of the African word *gumbay*, a large drum) and begins the song . . . One player is inside the ring. He or she does his preliminary flourish, which comes on the first line of the song, does his dance on the second line, and chooses his successor on the third line and takes his place in the circle. The chosen dancer takes his place and the dance goes on until the drum gets cold. (294)

38. See tapes transcribed in *Go Gator and Muddy the Water* for a more detailed description of railroad camp songs.

39. See the appendix to *Mules and Men* for two different versions of this song, one with musical arrangement (264–265).

40. Refers to trains run by Southern Railway and Louisville and Nashville Railroad.

41. An early Cadillac dating from the 1910s.
42. In the appendix to *Mules and Men*, Hurston writes that this song, titled "Mule on de Mount," is "the most widely distributed and best known of all Negro work songs . . . This has every-thing in folk life in it. Several stories to say nothing of just lyric matter. It is something like the Odyssey, or the Iliad." Also see the musical accompaniment she provides (269–270).
43. Original reads "biddy."
44. In the appendix to *Mules and Men,* the lines "Oh Lulu, oh gal" and "Gointer see my long-haired babe" come from the same song. Also see the musical arrangement provided (261–263).
45. James Presley is an important source for Hurston's folk material. He appears frequently in *Mules and Men* and *Every Tongue Got to Confess: Negro Folk-Tales of the Gulf States.*
46. Note the characters named Ella Wall in *Polk County* as well as the Ella Wall depicted in chapter 9 of *Mules and Men.*
47. Blue Front and Muttsy also figure in Hurston's story "Muttsy" (1926).
48. Typescript indicates that "John Barton" is to be sung here. Lyrics included at the end of the typescript corresponding to "John Barton" have been inserted.
49. Lyrics from the end of the typescript have been inserted here. The original stage directions indicate how the verses are to be interspersed between the spoken lines; these directions have been replaced with lyrics as indicated. See the appendix of *Mules and Men* for addi-tional information about this song and a musical arrangement (271–272). This song is also used in *Polk County*, act 2, scene 1.
50. To cheat by arranging to get a winning card.
51. The typescript indicates "See you when your troubles git like mine" to be sung here. Cor-responding lyrics included at the end of the typescript have been inserted.
52. The typescript indicates an additional line or lines to be sung here. Given the structure of the song, we have included a line from the published version of the song in the appendix of *Mules and Men.* See this source (258–260) for a musical arrangement.
53. See the appendix of *Mules and Men* (252–255) for a musical arrangement of this song. It is also sung in *Polk County,* act 1, scene 4.
54. This verse is not included in the version published in *Mules and Men.*

## De Turkey and De Law

1. The Library of Congress has in its holdings both the October 1930 script titled *De Turkey and De Law* (reproduced here), listing Hurston as the sole author, and *The Mule-Bone,* which Hughes sent to be copyrighted on January 19, 1931, listing both writers on the title page.
2. Character descriptions were originally included for Jim Weston, Dave Carter, Daisy Blunt, Joe Clarke, Walter, Hambo, Lindsay, Lige, Lum, Lucy Taylor, Della Lewis, and the two preach-ers. The other descriptions have been added, following the style of the originals. A number of characters in this play recur in Hurston's short fiction and novels. Joe and Mattie Clarke, Lige (Elijah) Moseley, Joe Lindsay, Mrs. McDuffy, and Daisy, for example, all appear in "The Eaton Anthology" (1926); some of these as well as others figure in "Spunk" (1925)—though not in the play *Spunk* included here—and *Their Eyes Were Watching God* (1937).

3. "Boger" in the original, reflecting the character's origins in "The Eatonville Anthology" and "The Bone of Contention." Within the text of the play, "Boger" has been struck out and replaced by "Bailey," perhaps to more clearly reflect Lum's role as bailiff of the court in the courtroom scene of act 2, scene 2.

4. See *Go Gator and Muddy the Water,* "Children's Games," for Hurston's explanation of this game and its significance. This game is also played in act 1, scene 2, of *Polk County.*

5. Original reads "Tillie."

6. This word may have been intended to be *bitch* or *bunch.*

7. Original reads "same."

8. This song appears in slightly different versions in a number of Hurston's works, including *Jook* in *Cold Keener.* See the appendix of *Mules and Men* for additional information about this song and a musical arrangement (271–272).

9. Herbert Hoover was president from 1928 to 1932.

10. I.e., he takes his gun and makes to exit quickly.

11. Original reads "Jenny."

12. "Singleton" in the original.

13. Places in church reserved for those leading congregational responses.

14. Original reads "you and soap and soap and water."

15. Original reads "sit."

16. Original reads "want."

17. Original reads "Now."

18. A kind of revolver.

19. *Diddy-Wah-Diddy* (spelled "Diddy war Diddy" in the original): see *Filling Station* in *Cold Keener,* n. 9. *Ginny-Gall*: slang term for a suburb of hell.

20. I.e., his arm (see "The Eatonville Anthology," 70).

21. Original reads "you done done off."

22. Original reads "I have studied jury and I know."

23. "Halimuhfack" is also used in *Spunk, Woofing,* and *Polk County* (*Woofing* and *Polk County* cite lyrics). The Library of Congress has a 1939 recording of Hurston singing this song in their "Florida Folklife from the WPA" collection.

24. A page break occurs here in the typescript. On the next page, part of Jim's speech is re-typed, with minor variations in dialect and punctuation.

25. Original reads "that."

26. This courtship scene is similar to that depicted between John Pearson and Lucy Potts (also the name of Hurston's mother) in *Jonah's Gourd Vine* (1934), as well as the scene between Box Car and Leafy Lee at the end of act 2, scene 1 of *Polk County.* For more on this reference, see Robert Hemenway's "Are You a Flying Lark or a Setting Dove," 122–152, in *Afro-American Literature: The Reconstruction of Instruction,* edited by Dexter Fisher and Robert B. Stepto (New York: Modern Language Association, 1979).

27. Nickname for Noah Webster's *American Spelling Book,* popular from the late eighteenth century through the early twentieth century and recognizable by its blue covers.

28. At this point, the typescript has the stage direction, "(She turns to Dave finally.)," which is also included at the beginning of her line farther down the page. Since she is clearly still speaking to Jim at this point, we have deleted the stage direction.

29. Original reads "bought."

## The Sermon in the Valley

1. Johnson's work also may have influenced Rowena Jelliffe. Her addition of Caroline's "preliminary prayer" parallels, in many ways, the first poem in *God's Trombones*, "Listen, Lord—A Prayer," which announces to the Lord the readiness of the congregation to hear the sermon and introduces the preacher. Johnson writes in his preface to *God's Trombones* that these preliminary prayers "were often products hardly less remarkable than the sermons" (*James Weldon Johnson: Complete Poems* [New York: Penguin, 2000], 12).

2. Hurston's original text begins with the next line.

3. The following passage was included in an earlier version of the text, but marked out during revision:

> I have seen gamblers wounded, I have seen desperadoes wounded, thieves
> and robbers and every other kinds of character, lawbreakers and all of them
> had a reason for their wounds. Some of em was unthoughtful, some of em
> was overbearin some of em was with the doctors knife. But all wounds dis-
> figures a person. Jesus was not unthoughtful, He was never careless, He
> was never overbearing, He was never sick, He was never a criminal before
> the law and yet he was wounded. A man usually gets wounded in the midst
> of his enemies but the text says He was wounded in the midst of his friends.
> It's not yo enemies that harms you all the time oh no—watch that close
> friend. Every believer in Christ is considered his friend and every sin we
> commit is a wound to Jesus. The blues we play in our homes aint nothin
> but a club to beat up Jesus and these social card parties . . .
>
> Jesus have always loved us.

   This text appears, with slight alterations, in "The Sermon," published in Nancy Cunard's *Negro* anthology (1934) and as John Pearson's prelude to his sermon in *Jonah's Gourd Vine* (174–175).

4. The plow-shaped "fender" on the front of a locomotive that helped push cattle and other obstructions off railroad tracks.

## Fast and Furious

1. Cited in Bernard L. Peterson Jr., *A Century of Musicals in Black and White: An Encyclopedia of Musical Stage Works By, About, or Involving African Americans* (Westwood, CT: Greenwood Press, 1993), 128.

2. See the appendix of *Mules and Men* (255–256) for lyrics and a musical arrangement of this song.

3. References to the Seaboard Airline and Atlantic Coast Line railways.

4. See *The Turkey and the Law,* act 3, scene 1, for information on this song.

5. Original reads "hells." In a recording of "Halimuhfack" held at the Library of Congress, she clearly sings "heels."

6. Possibly "Jimpson" mistyped.

7. Original reads "in, in a chair."

8. Typescript reads "two or three," but later specifies three.

9. This song is also used in *Jook* in *Cold Keener*. See appendix of *Mules and Men* (258–260) for lyrics and a musical arrangement.

10. Short for "Lindy Hop," a popular dance that originated in Harlem in the mid-1920s.

11. Corner of typescript has been torn off. The original reads "everythin' [missing text] playin' checkers"; the word *but* has been inserted here for sense.

12. The first self-service grocery store, begun in Memphis, Tennessee, in 1916 and still in existence today, primarily serving the southeastern United States.

13. This song is also used in *Jook* in *Cold Keener*. See the appendix of *Mules and Men* (252–255) for lyrics and a musical arrangement.

14. Reference to an African American fraternal organization.

15. A cowardly man who beats his wife to prove his masculinity. See *Jonah's Gourd Vine*, where Hurston writes, "He's a woman-jessie. Beat up women and run from mens" (56).

16. Note that for the purposes of the pun in the next line, *fracas* should be pronounced "FRACK-as."

17. These lines here are rendered in prose in the original. They have been reconfigured to show more clearly the divisions between rhymed and unrhymed speech.

18. The line refers to other historically black colleges.

19. The typescript includes the following lines after the curtain:

> Lincoln's Prayer:
> Ah, ah, they shall not ah pass us
> Lord, Lord, Lord, Lord
> They shall not pass us, Ah-h-h-h.

These lines may have been intended to be sung here.

20. The name is listed as "Peckerwood" in the cast list, but "Beckerwood" is used throughout the play itself. We have followed the spelling in the cast list, which was also used in the playbill for *Fast and Furious*.

21. Following this line is a handwritten note: "(Get your feet offa my chair etc.)"

## Spunk

1. Hurston describes the role of the "singing-liner" in an interview with Herb Halpert of the Federal Writers' Project as the member of the railroad crew who sets the rhythm of the work through the song he leads. The interview is available through the Library of Congress American Memory Web site, and is also transcribed in *Go Gator and Muddy the Water*.

2. See the appendix of *Mules and Men* for additional lyrics and a musical arrangement of this song (264–266).

3. Lyrics for this song are not included in the typescript. Hurston could be referring to one of two railroad work songs, "This Old Hammer" or "This Old Hammer Killed John Henry." The latter can be sung to the tune of "The Mule on the Mount," and may make a more appropriate choice since Spunk sings the second verse of that song at the end of the scene. See the appendix of *Mules and Men* for complete lyrics and a musical arrangement (269–270).

4. See *Polk County,* act 1, scene 2, for more on this song.

5. See *Railroad Camp* in *Cold Keener* for information on this song.

6. A blank space was left in the typescript, indicating that a word would be inserted later. The word *mess* has been inserted, following Hurston's general image.

7. Original reads "Now."

8. Since Blue Trout has not exited earlier in the scene, dialogue and/or stage directions will need to be added in order to preserve continuity.

9. The ring play is related to the fire-dance (see *Bahamas,* in *Cold Keener*); these dance/games originated in the Caribbean. Hurston included a "ring play" in both *The Great Day* and *From Sun to Sun* (both 1932); see the programs included in the Appendix.

10. The typescript names this girl Palmetto. No character with that name appears anywhere else in the play; we have thus edited the text to make the reference generic.

11. This song is not included in the typescript.

12. See *The Turkey and the Law,* act 3, scene 1, for information on this song.

13. See *Filling Station,* in *Cold Keener,* for information about "Diddy-Wah-Diddy." Ginny-Gall is a slang term for a suburb of hell.

14. I.e., the joker.

15. Original reads "stone."

16. Original reads "I would have been done stopped you."

17. Original reads "might."

18. Original reads "He's."

19. Title of song is inserted here: "Oh Lulu, Oh Gal." A song that begins with this line is included in the appendix of *Mules and Men* (under the title "Going to See My Long-Haired Babe") but does not match the lyrics included here.

20. Title of song is inserted here: "Whip-poor-will."

21. The script indicates the song to be sung here is titled "Gethsemane."

22. Original reads "I'be be."

23. The Library of Congress has a recording of Hurston singing this song as part of their "Florida Folklife from the WPA" collection. The lyrics are as follows:

> Evalina, Evalina you know the baby don't favor me
>
> Eh, you know the baby don't favor me.
>
> Evalina, Evalina don't you tell your mama you belong to me
>
> Eh, you know the baby don't favor me.

In response to an interviewer, Hurston claims that the song originated with Bahamanians and is sung from Key West to Miami and the Everglades.

24. A version of this ceremony is described in *Mules and Men* (197); another is described in "De Witch Woman," in *Every Tongue Got to Confess: Negro Folk-Tales from the Gulf States,* ed. Carla Kaplan (New York: HarperCollins, 2001), 63–64.

25. A dish made with black-eyed peas.

26. Original reads "kiering."

27. Original reads "tips."


## Polk County

1. Jayne M. Blanchard, "Rousing Visit to "Polk County," *Washington Times,* April 13, 2002, D02; Holly Bass, "Better Late Than Never: After 60 Years, Zora Neale Hurston's Flavorful

*Polk County* Comes to Life," *American Theatre* (July–August 2002): 50–52; and Bruce Weber, "Joy and Blues In Florida's Piney Woods," *New York Times*, April 25, 2002, E1.

2. This game is described at some length in the "Glossary" section of *Mules and Men* (249). The game is played here in act 2, scene 1.

3. Workers on a turpentine camp slash the bark of trees to collect gum.

4. Original reads "poor white would would be a misfit."

5. See chapter 9 of *Mules and Men*.

6. Hurston's note: "A southern community is clannish. Both white and black will get together on an outsider of either race. Hence the reaction of the Quarters Boss to Nunkie."
A song list is included after this page in the typescript but has been omitted here.

7. The Library of Congress has a 1939 recording of Hurston singing a version of the "Wake Up, Jacob" chant in their "Florida Folklife from the WPA" collection. In introductory remarks, Hurston claims that she heard the song at a sawmill camp in Polk County, Florida.

8. The following animal sequence is a stylistic anomaly in what is otherwise a solid piece of realism. It is hard to imagine that this scene would have survived if the New York production had gone forward.

9. To cheat by arranging to get a winning card.

10. See Hurston's article, "High John de Conquer," published in *The American Mercury* in November 1943 and included in *Folklore, Memoirs, and Other Writings* (Library of America, 1995: 922–931). Most stories cast High John as a popular folk hero, a slave from Africa who outwits characters such as Ole Massa, God, or the Devil with great joviality.

11. Original reads "Awe, and can it be possible? in their faces."

12. Sweetheart Soap was the brand name for a common perfumed soap. Octogon Soap was a harsh lye soap used for laundry. In *Dust Tracks on a Road,* Hurston writes that her family customarily used Octagon Soap, reserving the "sweet soap" for company (16–17, 39).

13. A word is possibly missing between "old" and "free."

14. Though the word meant here is clearly "double-teamed," Hurston uses the same malapropism in *Dust Tracks on a Road* (31).

15. See *Mules and Men* (258–260) for lyrics and a musical arrangement of this song, which is also included in *Cold Keener (Jook)*.

16. See *Go Gator and Muddy the Water*, "Children's Games," for Hurston's explanation of this game and its significance. This game is also played in *De Turkey and de Law*.

17. See "Zora Neale Hurston Out of Obscurity" by Marian Smith Holmes (*Smithsonian* 31, no. 10 [January 2001]: 96–108) for a photograph of Hurston playing a children's game in Eatonville in 1935.

18. Slang term for a promiscuous woman. It comes from the nickname of a species of gecko that was believed to have venomous toes.

19. *Dust Tracks on a Road* contains a few more snippets of lyrics from the song:

> Polk County! Ah!
> Where the water tastes like cherry wine.
> Where they fell great trees with axe and muscle. (131)
> . . . . . . . .
> I got up this morning, and I knowed I didn't want it,
> Yea! Polk County!

> You don't know Polk County like I do
>
> Anybody been there, tell you the same thing, too.
>
> Eh, rider, rider!
>
> Polk County, where the water tastes like cherry wine. (132)

"Polk County Blues" apparently existed in several versions in the 1930s, when Hurston collected the song during her fieldwork in Florida with Alan Lomax. The recording of Philip Anderson of Belle Glade, Florida, made in 1935 (Library of Congress Archive of Folk Song 373-B) includes the following verses pertinent to both *Spunk* and *Polk County* (though it does not include the lines sung either by Big Sweet or included by Hurston in *Dust Tracks on a Road*):

> Had a little old woman, about four feet from the ground
>
> When I carried her out of Polk County, Lord, that woman could not be found
>
> Oh boys, if you go to Polk County, it's a lesson I give to you
>
> Oh boys, if you go to Polk County, it's a lesson I give to you
>
> Don't take your woman, or she will be lost before you do.
>
> Polk County, Polk County blues, boys, I don't know what you going to do
>
> When you go to Polk County, [Lord knows you lost Sunday (? line unintelligible)]
>
> . . . . . . . . .
>
> Baby when I got that letter, I throwed it in your backyard
>
> Baby when I got that letter, I throwed it in your back yard
>
> [line unintelligible]
>
> Baby you don't know Polk County like I do
>
> Oh the reason I know it
>
> I done roamed it through and through.

20. Ethel Waters (1896–1977), renowned blues singer, first sang in Harlem in 1919 and made her first recording with Columbia Records in 1925. Hurston commemorates her in *Dust Tracks on a Road,* where she describes Waters and Fannie Hurst as "two women, among the number whom I have known intimately, [who] force me to keep them well in mind . . . both of them have meant a great deal to me in friendship and inward experience" (173).

21. Original reads "being."

22. A blues standard, recorded by the likes of Janis Joplin and Ray Charles.

23. Original reads "a many."

24. Original reads "Sebastopol."

25. See the appendix of *Mules and Men* (252–255) for a musical arrangement of this song. It is also sung in *Jook* in *Cold Keener.*

26. Hurston expounds on this phrase in *Dust Tracks on a Road* (1942), where she writes, "Now, the well-mannered Negro is embarrassed by the crude behavior of the others. . . . he is dismayed at the sight of other Negroes tearing down what he is trying to build up. It is said

every day, 'And that good-for-nothing, trashy Negro is the one the white people judge us all by. They think we're all just alike. My people! My people!" (157–158, HarperPerennial). Obviously, Box Car is using the phrase ironically in this case.

27. Probably a reference to Peetie Wheatstraw, a blues recording artist of the 1930s, who called himself "the High Sheriff from Hell" and "the Devil's Son-in-Law."

28. A type of design used on the backs of the cards.

29. See the appendix of *Mules and Men* for additional information about this song and a musical arrangement (271–272). This song is also used in *Cold Keener (Jook)* and *Poker!*

30. I.e., causes a sensation in the room.

31. See act 3 of *De Turkey and De Law* for another version of this courtship scene.

32. Description of Big Sweet's house, repeated from act 1, scene 3, has been omitted here.

33. Original reads "ear-laps."

34. A worker who drives a heavy tractor.

35. An early form of rummy.

36. See *The Turkey and the Law,* act 3, scene 1, for information on this song.

37. A "luck charm" (*Mules and Men,* 240).

38. Original reads "comes to her conclusions, because they are unsuitable, as she laments."

39. Since the mirror has already been packed, stage business will need to be adapted.

40. Original reads "damned."

41. An allusion to Satan's famous statement in Book IV of Milton's *Paradise Lost* ("Evil, be thou my good").

42. Original reads "statutes."

43. Hurston writes in *Mules and Men* that red candles are burned in voodoo "for victory" and white candles "for peace and to uncross and for weddings" (280). Given the context, the burning of the white candles either indicates Hurston's choice to privilege dramatic effect over anthropological accuracy—or a faulty memory.

44. Referring to the type of loa or spiritual ancestor that is conjured in a voodoo ceremony or, in this case, a man possessed by a loa.

45. This line appears to have been garbled by the typist.

46. A chicken-and-rice dish. "Purleau" is probably a creolization of either *poulet* (French) or *pollo* (Spanish). Hurston also mentions "chicken purlo" in "The Eatonville Anthology" (66).

# BIBLIOGRAPHY

Boas, Franz. "Some Philological Aspects of Anthropological Research" (1905). In *A Franz Boas Reader: The Shaping of American Anthropology, 1883–1911*, edited by George W. Stocking Jr. Chicago: University of Chicago Press, 1974.

Bordelon, Pamela, ed. *Go Gator and Muddy the Water: Writings by Zora Neale Hurston from the Federal Writers Project.* New York: W. W. Norton, 1999.

Bower, Martha Gilman. *"Color Struck" Under the Gaze: Ethnicity and the Pathology of Being in the Plays of Johnson, Hurston, Childress, Hansberry, and Kennedy.* Westport, Conn.: Praeger, 2003.

Boyd, Valerie. *Wrapped in Rainbows: The Life of Zora Neale Hurston.* New York: Scribner, 2003.

Brown-Guillory, Elizabeth. *Their Place on the Stage: Black Women Playwrights in America.* Westport, Conn.: Praeger, 1988.

Burton, Jennifer. Introduction. In *Zora Neale Hurston, Eulalie Spence, Marita Bonner, and Others: The Prize Plays and Other One-Acts Published in Periodicals,* edited by Henry Louis Gates Jr. and Jennifer Burton. New York: G. K. Hall, 1996.

Gates, Henry Louis, Jr. "A Tragedy of Negro Life." In *Mule Bone: A Comedy of Negro Life by Langston Hughes and Zora Neale Hurston,* edited by George Houston Bass and Henry Louis Gates Jr., 5–24. New York: Harper Perennial, 1991.

———. "Why the *Mule Bone* Debate Goes On." *New York Times,* February 10, 1991, H5.

Gates, Henry Louis, Jr., and Sieglinde Lemke, eds. *Zora Neale Hurston: The Complete Stories.* New York: HarperPerennial, 1995.

Glassman, Steve, and Kathryn Lee Seidel, eds. *Zora in Florida.* Orlando: University of Central Florida Press, 1991.

Gray, Christine, and Willis Richardson. Introductions to *Plays and Pageants from the Life of the Negro.* Jackson: University Press of Mississippi (orig. published by Associated Publishers, Inc., in 1930).

Hatch, James V., and Leo Hamalian, eds. *Lost Plays of the Harlem Renaissance, 1920–1940.* Detroit: Wayne State University Press, 1996.

Hemenway, Robert. *Zora Neale Hurston: A Literary Biography.* Urbana: University of Illinois Press, 1977.

Hill, Lynda Marion. *Social Rituals and the Verbal Art of Zora Neale Hurston.* Washington: Howard University Press, 1996.

Holloway, Karla F. *The Character of the Word: The Texts of Zora Neale Hurston.* New York: Greenwood Press, 1987.

Houseman, John. *Run-Through: A Memoir by John Houseman.* New York: Simon and Schuster, 1972.

Hughes, Langston. "The Negro Artist and the Racial Mountain." In *Double-Take: A Revisionist Harlem Renaissance Anthology,* edited by. Venetria Patton and Maureen Honey. New Brunswick, N.J.: Rutgers University Press, 2001.

Hurston, Zora Neale. *Negro Folk-Tales from the Gulf States*. In *Every Tongue Got to Confess: Negro Folk-Tales from the Gulf States,* edited by Carla Kaplan. New York: Harper Collins, 2001.

————. "Characteristics of Negro Expression" (1934) and other essays. In *Zora Neale Hurston: Folklore, Memoirs, and Other Writings,* edited by Cheryl Wall. New York: Library of America, 1995.

————. *Dust Tracks on a Road: An Autobiography*. New York: J. B. Lippincott, 1942; reissued by University of Illinois Press, 1984, and HarperPerennial, 1991.

————. *Moses, Man of the Mountain*. New York: J. B. Lippincott, 1939; reissued by HarperPerennial, 1991.

————. *Seraph on the Suwanee*. New York: J. B. Lippincott, 1948; reissued by HarperPerennial, 1991.

————. *Jonah's Gourd Vine*. New York: J. B. Lippincott, 1934; reissued by HarperPerennial, 1990.

————. *Mules and Men*. New York: J. B. Lippincott, 1935; reissued by HarperPerennial, 1990.

————. *Tell My Horse: Voodoo and Life in Haiti and Jamaica*. New York: J. B. Lippincott, 1938; reissued by HarperPerennial, 1990.

————. *Their Eyes Were Watching God*. New York: J. B. Lippincott, 1937; reissued by University of Illinois Press, 1978, and HarperPerennial, 1990.

————. "How It Feels to Be Colored Me." In *I Love Myself When I Am Laughing . . . and Then Again When I Am Looking Mean and Impressive: A Zora Neale Hurston Reader,* edited by Alice Walker. New York: The Feminist Press at The City University of New York, 1979.

————. *The Sanctified Church: The Folklore Writings of Zora Neale Hurston*. Turtle Island Foundation, 1981.

Kaplan, Carla, ed. *Every Tongue Got to Confess: Negro Folk-tales from the Gulf States*. New York: HarperPerennial, 2002.

————. *Zora Neale Hurston: A Life in Letters*. New York: Doubleday, 2002.

Kornweibel, Theodore, Jr. "Theophilus Lewis and the Theater of the Harlem Renaissance." In *The Harlem Renaissance Remembered,* edited by Arna Bontemps. New York: Dodd, Mead and Co., 1972.

Krasner, David. *A Beautiful Pageant: African American Theatre, Drama, and Performance in the Harlem Renaissance, 1910–1927*. New York: Palgrave Macmillan, 2002.

————. "Migration, Fragmentation, and Identity: Zora Neale Hurston's *Color Struck* and the Geography of the Harlem Renaissance." *Theatre Journal* 53, no. 4 (December 2001): 533–550.

Locke, Alain. *The New Negro: An Interpretation*. New York: Albert and Charles Boni, 1925.

Lowe, John. "'Let the People Sing!': Zora Neale Hurston and the Dream of a Negro Theater." In *Southern Women Playwrights: New Essays in Literary History and Criticism,* edited by Robert L. McDonald and Linda Rohrer Paige, 11–26. Tuscaloosa: University of Alabama Press, 2002.

————. "From Mule Bones to Funny Bones: The Plays of Zora Neale Hurston." *Southern Quarterly* 33, nos. 2–3 (Winter–Spring 1995): 65–78.

————. *Jump at the Sun: Zora Neale Hurston's Cosmic Comedy*. Urbana: University of Illinois Press, 1994.

Meisenhelder, Susan. "Conflict and Resistance in Zora Neale Hurston's *Mules and Men*. *The Journal of American Folklore* 109, no. 433 (Summer 1996): 267–288.

Plant, Deborah G. *Every Tub Must Sit on its Own Bottom: The Politics and Philosophy of Zora Neale Hurston.* Urbana: University of Illinois Press, 1995.

Richards, Sandra L. "Writing the Absent Potential: Drama, Performance and the Canon of African-American Literature." In *Performativity and Performance,* edited by Andrew Parker and Eve Kosofsky Sedgwick, 64–88. New York: Routledge, 1995.

Robeson, Paul. "Reflections on Eugene O'Neill's Plays." *Opportunity* (December 1924). Reprinted in *The Portable Harlem Renaissance Reader*, edited by David L. Lewis, 58–60. New York: Penguin Books, 1994.

Speisman, Barbara, "From 'Spears' to The Great Day: Zora Neale Hurston's Vision of a Real Negro Theater." *The Southern Quarterly* 36, no. 3 (Spring 1998): 34–46.

Thurman, Wallace. *The Collected Writings of Wallace Thurman: A Harlem Renaissance Reader.* Ed. Daniel M. Scott III, Amritjit Singh, and Daniel Scott. New Brunswick, N.J.: Rutgers University Press, 2003.

Walker, Alice, ed. *I Love Myself When I Am Laughing . . . and Then Again When I am Looking Mean and Impressive: A Zora Neale Hurston Reader.* New York: Feminist Press, 1979.

## ABOUT THE EDITORS

Jean Lee Cole is an associate professor of English at Loyola College in Maryland. She is the author of *The Literary Voices of Winnifred Eaton: Redefining Ethnicity and Authenticity* and the coeditor, with Maureen Honey, of *Madame Butterfly by John Luther Long and A Japanese Nightingale by Winnifred Eaton: Two Orientalist Texts.*

Charles Mitchell is an assistant professor of theater at Loyola College. He is the author of *Shakespeare and Public Execution* as well as a playwright and theatrical director.